Jonathan Swift, Walter Scott

Works, Containing additional Letters, Tracts, and Poems

Vol. 9

Jonathan Swift, Walter Scott

Works, Containing additional Letters, Tracts, and Poems
Vol. 9

ISBN/EAN: 9783744718721

Printed in Europe, USA, Canada, Australia, Japan

Cover: Foto ©ninafisch / pixelio.de

More available books at **www.hansebooks.com**

Only 750 *copies of this Edition have been printed for sale,* 250 *of which are reserved for America. Each copy is numbered.*

This copy is No.

Bickers & Son

THE
WORKS OF JONATHAN SWIFT

THE WORKS OF
Jonathan Swift

DEAN OF ST. PATRICK'S, DUBLIN

CONTAINING

ADDITIONAL LETTERS, TRACTS, AND POEMS

NOT HITHERTO PUBLISHED

WITH NOTES AND A LIFE OF THE AUTHOR

BY

SIR WALTER SCOTT

Second Edition

IN NINETEEN VOLUMES

VOL. IX.

LONDON
BICKERS & SON, LEICESTER SQUARE
1883

CONTENTS OF VOLUME NINTH.

MISCELLANEOUS ESSAYS.

	PAGE
REMARKS BY THE EDITOR,	3
TATLERS—	
THE TATLER, No. XXXII.	4
No. XXXV.	10
No. LIX.	11
No. LXIII.	14
No. LXVI.	17
No. LXVII.	21
No. LXVIII.	23
No. LXX.	26
No. LXXI.	28
No. LXXIV.	29
No. LXXXI.	31
No. CCXXX.	40
No. CCLVIII.	47
No. I.	48
No. II.	52
No. V.	56
No. XX.	62
No. XXIV.	67
No. XXVIII.	69
THE SPECTATOR, No. L.	74
THE GUARDIAN, No. XCVI.	79
THE INTELLIGENCER, No. I.	84
No. III.	86
No. XIX.	93
Preface to Temple's Works,	103
Preface to the Third Part of Sir William Temple's Miscellanea,	108
Preface to the Third Volume of Sir William Temple's Letters,	110

CONTENTS.

	PAGE
Preface to the Third Part of Sir William Temple's Memoirs; from the Peace concluded 1679 to the Time of the Author's Retirement from Public Business,	112
A Meditation upon a Broomstick,	118
A Tritical Essay upon the Faculties of the Mind,	123
A Proposal for Correcting, Improving, and Ascertaining the English Tongue, in a Letter to the most Honourable Robert, Earl of Oxford and Mortimer, Lord High Treasurer of Great Britain,	133
An Essay on Modern Education,	156
Hints toward an Essay on Conversation,	167
A Letter of Advice to a Young Poet. Together with a Proposal for the Encouragement of Poetry in Ireland,	178
A Letter to a very young Lady, on her Marriage,	202
Resolutions when I come to be Old,	215
Thoughts on Various Subjects, Moral and Diverting,	217
A Treatise on Good Manners and Good Breeding,	237
Hints on Good Manners,	246
Of Mean and Great Figures, made by several Persons,	249
Of Public Absurdities in England,	255
Of the Education of Ladies,	260
Character of Aristotle,	265
Character of Herodotus,	266
Character of Primate Marsh,	267
Character of Mrs. Howard,	270
On the Death of Mrs. Johnson, [Stella,]	274
Bon Mots De Stella,	286
Three Prayers used by the Dean for Mrs. Johnson, in her last Sickness,	289
An Evening Prayer, by Dean Swift, from the Original Manuscript found amongst Dr. Lyon's Papers,	294
Letter to Mr. —— Archi-Rabbi Sophi Diotrephes, &c.	299
Character of Dr. Sheridan,	302
The History of the Second Solomon,	306
A serious and useful Scheme to make an Hospital for Incurables,	314
A complete Collection of General and Ingenious Conversation, according to the most Polite Mode and Method, now used at Court, and in the best Companies of England,	339
Remarks by the Editor,	340
Introduction,	341
Dialogue I.	379
Dialogue II.	428
Dialogue III.	459

MISCELLANEOUS ESSAYS.

TATLERS.

TATLERS.

IN projecting the *Tatler*, the first of those excellent periodical publications which are almost peculiar to our nation, and have had no small effect in fixing and refining its character, Steele, to whom the merit of the invention is due, rested chiefly upon the assistance of Swift in carrying it into execution. The public was already familiar with the name of Isaac Bickerstaff, and, as Steele himself expresses it, "It happened very luckily, that, a little before I had resolved upon this design, a gentleman had written Predictions, and two or three other pieces in my name, which rendered it famous through all parts of Europe, and, by an inimitable spirit and humour, raised it to as high a pitch of reputation as it could possibly arrive at.

"By this good fortune the name of Isaac Bickerstaff gained an audience of all who had any taste of wit; and the addition of the ordinary occurrences of common journals of news brought in a multitude of other readers. I could not, I confess, long keep up the opinion of the town, that these lucubrations were written by the same hand with the first works which were published under my name; but, before I lost the participation of that author's fame, I had already found the advantage of his authority, to which I owe the sudden acceptance which my labours met with in the world."

Swift accordingly for some time fulfilled the expectations and hopes of the editor of the *Tatler*, and the following numbers are usually ascribed to him. But the ardour of party politics speedily deprived Steele of any assistance from that valuable quarter.

THE TATLER, No. XXXII.

THURSDAY, JUNE 23, 1709.

"To ISAAC BICKERSTAFF, Esquire.*

"SIR,   *June* 18, 1709.

" I KNOW not whether you ought to pity or laugh at me; for I am fallen desperately in love with a professed Platonne, the most unaccountable creature

---

* This paper is written in ridicule of some affected ladies of the period, who pretended, with rather too much ostentation, to embrace the doctrines of Platonic Love. Mrs. Mary Astell, a learned and worthy woman, had embraced this fantastic notion so deeply, that, in an essay upon the female sex, in 1696, she proposed a sort of female college, in which the young might be instructed, and "ladies nauseating the parade of the world," might find a happy retirement. The plan was disconcerted by Bishop Burnet, who, understanding that the Queen intended to give £10,000 towards the establishment, dissuaded her, by an assurance, that it would lead to the introduction of Popish orders, and be called a nunnery. This lady is the Madonella of the Tatler. The Rake is supposed to be Mr. Repinton, a fashionable gallant. This paper has been censured as a gross reflection on Mrs. Astell's character, but on no very just foundation. Swift only prophesies the probable issue of such a scheme, as that of the Protestant nunnery; and it is a violent interpretation of his words to suppose him to insinuate, that the conclusion had taken place without the premises. Indeed, the scourge of ridicule is seldom better employed than on that species of *Precieuse*, who is anxious to confound the boundaries which nature has fixed for the employments and studies of the two sexes. No man was more zealous than Swift for informing the female mind, in those points most becoming and useful to their sex. His Letter to a Young Married Lady, and Thoughts on Education, point out the extent of those studies, which embraced a general knowledge of history, some taste for poetry, and a general acquaintance with

of her sex. To hear her talk seraphics, and run over Norris,* and More,† and Milton, and the whole set of Intellectual Triflers, torments me heartily; for, to a lover who understands metaphors, all this pretty prattle of ideas gives very fine views of pleasure, which only the dear declaimer prevents, by understanding them literally: why should she wish to be a cherubim, when it is flesh and blood that makes her adorable? If I speak to her, that is a high breach of the idea of intuition. If I offer at her hand or lip, she shrinks from the touch like a sensitive plant, and would contract herself into mere spirit. She calls her chariot, vehicle; her furbelowed scarf, pinions; her blue manteau and petticoat is her azure dress; and her footman goes by the name of Oberon. It is my misfortune to be six feet and a half high, two full spans between the shoulders, thirteen inches diameter in the calves; and, before I was in love, I had a noble stomach, and usually went to bed sober with two bottles. I am not quite six-and-twenty, and my nose is marked truly aquiline. For these reasons, I am in a very particular manner her aversion. What shall I do? Impudence itself cannot reclaim her. If I write

---

books of travels, and moral and entertaining discourses:—it seems very doubtful, whether most ladies, who advance into abstruser branches of knowledge, do not lose more than they can possibly gain.

* John Norris, author of "The Theory and Regulation of Love." His correspondence with Mrs. Astell was published under the following title:—"Letters concerning the Love of God, between the Author of the Proposal to the Ladies and Mr. John Norris, wherein his late Discourse, shewing it ought to be entire and exclusive of all other Loves, is cleared and justified. Published by J. Norris, M.A., Rector of Bamerton, near Sarum. London, 1695."

† Dr. Henry More, well known as a fanciful Platonist and Divine.

miserably, she reckons me among the children of perdition, and discards me her region: if I assume the gross and substantial, she plays the real ghost with me, and vanishes in a moment. I had hopes in the hypocrisy of her sex; but perseverance makes it as bad as fixed aversion. I desire your opinion, whether I may not lawfully play the inquisition upon her, make use of a little force, and put her to the rack and torture, only to convince her, she has really fine limbs, without spoiling or distorting them. I expect your directions, before I proceed to dwindle and fall away with despair; which at present I do not think advisable, because, if she should recant, she may then hate me, perhaps in the other extreme, for my tenuity. I am (with impatience) your most humble servant,

"CHARLES STURDY."

My patient has put his case with very much warmth, and represented it in so lively a manner, that I see both his torment and tormentor with great perspicuity. This order of Platonic ladies are to be dealt with in a manner peculiar from all the rest of the sex. Flattery is the general way, and the way in this case; but it is not to be done grossly. Every man that has wit, and humour, and raillery, can make a good flatterer for women in general; but a Platonne is not to be touched with panegyric: she will tell you, it is a sensuality in the soul to be delighted that way. You are not therefore to commend, but silently consent to all she does and says. You are to consider, in her the scorn of you is not humour, but opinion.

There were, some years since, a set of these ladies who were of quality, and gave out, that virginity was to be their state of life during this mortal condition, and therefore resolved to join their fortunes and erect a nunnery. The place of residence was pitched upon; and a pretty situation, full of natural falls and risings of waters, with shady coverts, and flowery arbours, was approved by seven of the founders. There were as many of our sex who took the liberty to visit their mansions of intended severity; among others, a famous rake of that time, who had the grave way to an excellence. He came in first; but, upon seeing a servant coming towards him, with a design to tell him this was no place for him or his companions, up goes my grave impudence to the maid; "Young woman," said he, "if any of the ladies are in the way on this side of the house, pray carry us on the other side towards the gardens: we are, you must know, gentlemen that are travelling England; after which we shall go into foreign parts, where some of us have already been." Here he bows in the most humble manner, and kissed the girl, who knew not how to behave to such a sort of carriage. He goes on: "Now you must know we have an ambition to have it to say, that we have a Protestant nunnery in England: but pray, Mrs. Betty——"—"Sir," she replied, "my name is Susan, at your service."—"Then I heartily beg your pardon——"—"No offence in the least," said she, "for I have a cousin-german, whose name is Betty."—"Indeed," said he, "I protest to you, that was more than I knew; I spoke at random: but since it happens that I was near in the right, give me leave to present this gentleman to the favour of a civil salute." His friend advances, and so on, until they had all saluted her. By this means the poor girl was in the middle of the crowd of these fellows, at a loss what to do, without courage to pass through them; and the Platonics, at several peepholes, pale, trembling, and fretting. Rake perceived they were observed, and therefore took care to keep Sukey in chat with questions concerning their way of life; when appeared at last Madonella, a lady who had writ a fine book concerning the recluse life, and was the projectrix of the foundation. She approaches into the hall; and Rake, knowing the dignity of his own mien and aspect, goes deputy from his company. She begins, "Sir, I am obliged to follow the servant, who was sent out to know what affair could make strangers press upon a solitude which we, who are to inhabit this place, have devoted to heaven and our own thoughts?"—"Madam," replies Rake, with an air of great distance, mixed with a certain indifference, by which he could dissemble dissimulation, "your great intention has made more noise in the world than you design it should; and we travellers, who have seen many foreign institutions of this kind, have a curiosity to see, in its first rudiments, the seat of primitive piety; for such it must be called by future ages, to the eternal honour of the founders: I have read Madonella's excellent and seraphic discourse on this subject." The lady immediately answered, "If what I have said could have contributed to raise any thoughts in you that may make for the advancement of intellectual and divine conversation, I should think myself extremely happy." He immediately fell back with the profoundest veneration; then advancing, "Are you then that admired lady? If I may approach lips which have uttered things so sacred—" He salutes her. His friends followed his example. The devoted within stood in amazement where this would end, to see Madonella receive their address and their company. But Rake goes on.—"We would not transgress rules; but if we may take the liberty to see the place you have thought fit to choose for ever, we would go into such parts of the gardens, as is consistent with the severities you have imposed on yourselves."

To be short, Madonella permitted Rake to lead

her into the assembly of nuns, followed by his friends, and each took his fair one by the hand, after due explanation, to walk round the gardens. The conversation turned upon the lilies, the flowers, the arbours, and the growing vegetables; and Rake had the solemn impudence, when the whole company stood round him, to say, that "he sincerely wished men might rise out of the earth like plants; and that our minds were not of necessity to be sullied with carnivorous appetites for the generation, as well as support, of our species." This was spoken with so easy and fixed an assurance, that Madonella answered, "Sir, under the notion of a pious thought, you deceive yourself in wishing an institution foreign to that of Providence. These desires were implanted in us for reverend purposes, in preserving the race of men, and giving opportunites for making our chastity more heroic." The conference was continued in this celestial strain, and carried on so well by the managers on both sides, that it created a second and a third interview; and, without entering into farther particulars, there was hardly one of them but was a mother or father that day twelvemonth.

Any unnatural part is long taking up, and as long laying aside; therefore Mr. Sturdy may assure himself, Platonica will fly for ever from a forward behaviour; but if he approaches her according to this model, she will fall in with the necessities of mortal life, and condescend to look with pity upon an unhappy man, imprisoned in so much body, and urged by such violent desires.

THE TATLER, No. XXXV.

THURSDAY, JUNE 30, 1709.

"To ISAAC BICKERSTAFF, Esq.

"SIR,

"NOT long since, you were pleased to give us a chimerical account of the famous family of the *Staffs*, from whence I suppose you would insinuate, that it is the most ancient and numerous house in all Europe. But, I positively deny that it is either, and wonder much at your audacious proceedings in this manner, since it is well known, that our most illustrious, most renowned, and most celebrated, Roman family of *Ix*, has enjoyed the precedency to all others from the reign of good old Saturn. I could say much to the defamation and disgrace of your family; as, that your relations *Distaff* and *Broomstaff* were both inconsiderable, mean persons, one spinning, the other sweeping the streets, for their daily bread. But I forbear to vent my spleen on objects so much beneath my indignation. I shall only give the world a catalogue of my ancestors, and leave them to determine which hath hitherto had, and which for the future ought to have, the preference.

"First then comes the most famous and popular lady *Meretrix*, parent of the fertile family of *Bellatrix, Lotrix, Netrix, Nutrix, Obstetrix, Famulatrix, Coctrix, Ornatrix, Sarcinatrix, Fextrix, Balneatrix, Portatrix, Saltatrix, Divinatrix, Conjectrix, Comtrix, Debitrix, Creditrix, Donatrix, Ambulatrix, Mercatrix, Adsectrix, Assectatrix, Palpatrix, Præceptrix, Pistrix.*

"I am yours,

"ELIZ. POTATRIX."

THE TATLER, No. LIX.

THURSDAY, AUGUST 25, 1709.

Will's Coffeehouse, August 24.

THE author of the ensuing letter, by his name and the quotations he makes from the ancients, seems a sort of spy from the old world, whom we moderns ought to be careful of offending; therefore I must be free, and own it a fair hit where he takes me, rather than disoblige him.*

"Sir, having a peculiar humour of desiring to be somewhat the better or wiser for what I read, I am always uneasy when, in any profound writer, for I read no others, I happen to meet with what I cannot understand. When this falls out, it is a great grievance to me that I am not able to consult the author himself about his meaning, for commentators are a sect that has little share in my esteem: your elaborate writings have, among many others, this advantage, that their author is still alive, and ready, as his extensive charity makes us expect, to explain whatever may be found in them too sublime for vulgar understandings. This, sir, makes me presume to ask you, how the Hampstead hero's character could be perfectly new when the last letters came away, and yet Sir John Suckling so well

---

* Swift, under the character of Obadiah Greenhat, ridicules Steele for a seeming inconsistency in a former paper. Steele in return gives an excellent account of Swift's talents for irony,

Which he was born to introduce,
Refined it first, and shew'd its use.

acquainted with it sixty years ago?* I hope, sir, you will not take this amiss: I can assure you, I have a profound respect for you, which makes me write this, with the same disposition with which Longinus bids us read Homer and Plato. When in reading, says he, any of those celebrated authors, we meet with a passage to which we cannot well reconcile our reasons, we ought firmly to believe, that were those great wits present to answer for themselves, we should to our wonder be convinced, that we only are guilty of the mistakes we before attributed to them. If you think fit to remove the scruple that now torments me, it will be an encouragement to me to settle a frequent correspondence with you; several things falling in my way which would not, perhaps, be altogether foreign to your purpose, and whereon your thoughts would be very acceptable to your most humble servant,

"OBADIAH GREENHAT."

I own this is clean, and Mr. Greenhat has convinced me that I have writ nonsense, yet am I not at all offended at him.

---

* "Letters from Hampstead say, there is a coxcomb arrived there, of a kind which is utterly new. The fellow has courage, which he takes himself to be obliged to give proofs of every hour he lives. He is ever fighting with the men, and contradicting the women. A lady, who sent to me, superscribed him with this description out of Suckling:—

> I am a man of war and might,
> And know this much, that I can fight,
> Whether I am i'th' wrong or right,
>   Devoutly.
>
> No man under heaven I fear,
> New oaths I can exactly swear;
> And forty healths my brain will bear
>   Most Stoutly."

Scimus, et hanc veniam petimusque damusque vicissim.*
                                HOR. Ars Poet. ver. 11.

    This is the true art of raillery, when a man turns another into ridicule, and shews at the same time he is in good humour, and not urged on by malice against the person he rallies. Obadiah Greenhat has hit this very well: for to make an apology to Isaac Bickerstaff, an unknown student and horary historian, as well as astrologer, and with a grave face to say, he speaks of him by the same rules with which he would treat Homer or Plato, is to place him in company where he cannot expect to make a figure; and makes him flatter himself, that it is only being named with them that renders him most ridiculous.

    I have not known, and I am now past my grand climacteric, being sixty-four years of age, according to my way of life; or rather, if you will allow punning in an old gentleman, according to my way of *pastime;* I say, as old as I am, I have not been acquainted with many of the Greenhats. There is indeed one Zedekiah Greenhat, who is lucky also in this way. He has a very agreeable manner; for when he has a mind thoroughly to correct a man, he never takes from him anything, but he allows him something for it; or else he blames him for things wherein he is not defective, as well as for matters wherein he is. This makes a weak man believe he is in jest in the whole. The other day he told Beau Brim, who is thought impotent, that his mistress had declared she would not have him, because he was a sloven, and had committed a rape. The beau bit at the banter, and said very gravely, "he thought to be clean was as much as was necessary; and that

---

    * "I own th' indulgence——Such I give and take."
                                                    FRANCIS.

as to the rape, he wondered by what witchcraft that should come to her ears; but it had indeed cost him an hundred pounds, to hush the affair."

The Greenhats are a family with small voices and short arms, therefore they have power with none but their friends: they never call after those who run away from them, or pretend to take hold of you if you resist. But it has been remarkable, that all who have shunned their company, or not listened to them, have fallen into the hands of such as have knocked out their brains, or broken their bones. I have looked over our pedigree upon the receipt of this epistle, and find the Greenhats are akin to the Staffs. They descend from Maudlin, the left-handed wife of Nehemiah Bickerstaff, in the reign of Harry the Second. And it is remarkable, that they are all left-handed, and have always been very expert at single rapier. A man must be much used to their play to know how to defend himself, for their posture is so different from that of the right-handed, that you run upon their swords if you push forward; and they are in with you, if you offer to fall back without keeping your guard.—*Tatler*, *No.* 59.

THE TATLER, No. LXIII.

SATURDAY, SEPT. 10, 1709.

"To ISAAC BICKERSTAFF, Esq.

"Sir,

"It must be allowed, that Esquire Bickerstaff is of all others the most ingenuous. There are few, very few, that will own themselves in a mistake, though all the world see them to be in downright nonsense. You will be pleased, sir, to pardon this expression, for the same reason for which you once desired us to excuse you, when you seemed anything dull. Most writers, like the generality of Paul Lorraine's * saints, seem to place a peculiar vanity in dying hard. But you, sir, to shew a good example to your brethren, have not only confessed, but of your own accord mended the indictment. Nay, you have been so good-natured as to discover beauties in it, which, I will assure you, he that drew it never dreamed of. And, to make your civility the more accomplished, you have honoured him with the title of your kinsman, which, though derived by the left hand, he is not a little proud of. My brother, for such Obadiah is, being at present very busy about nothing, has ordered me to return you his sincere thanks for all these favours; and as a small token of his gratitude, to communicate to you the following piece of intelligence, which, he thinks, belongs more properly to you, than to any others of our modern historians.

"*Madonella*,† who, as it was thought, had long since taken her flight towards the ethereal mansions, still walks, it seems, in the regions of mortality; where she has found, by deep reflections on the revolution mentioned in yours of June the twenty-third, that where early instructions have been wanting to imprint true ideas of things on the tender souls of those of her sex, they are never after able to arrive at such a pitch of perfection, as to be above the laws of matter and motion; laws which are considerably enforced by the principles usually imbibed

---

* Paul Lorraine was the ordinary of Newgate.
† The subsequent passage alludes to Mrs. Astell's proposal for establishing a seminary for the education of young ladies.

in nurseries and boarding-schools. To remedy this evil she has laid the scheme of a college for young damsels: where (instead of scissars, needles, and samplers) pens, compasses, quadrants, books, manuscripts, Greek, Latin, and Hebrew, are to take up their whole time. Only on holidays the students will, for moderate exercise, be allowed to divert themselves with the use of some of the lightest and most voluble weapons; and proper care will be taken to give them as least a superficial tincture of the ancient and modern Amazonian tactics. Of these military performances, the direction is undertaken by Epicene,* the writer of "Memoirs from the Mediterranean," who, by the help of some artificial poisons conveyed by smells, has within these few weeks brought many persons of both sexes to an untimely fate; and, what is more surprising, has, contrary to her profession, with the same odours, revived others who had long since been drowned in the whirlpools of Lethe. Another of the professors is said to be a certain lady, who is now publishing two of the choicest Saxon novels,† which are said to have been in as great repute with the ladies of Queen Emma's Court, as the "Memoirs from the New Atalantis" are with those of ours. I shall make it my business to inquire into the progress of this learned institution, and give you the first notice of their "Philosophical Transactions, and Searches after Nature."

"Yours, &c.

"TOBIAH GREENHAT."

---

* Mrs. Manley, author of the Memoirs of the New Atalantis.
† Mrs. Elizabeth Elstob, eminent for her knowledge of the Anglo-Saxon language and antiquities. See an account of her in Ballard's Memoirs of Learned Ladies.

TLER, No. LXVI.

Y, SEPT. 10, 1709.

Will's Coffeehouse, Sept. 9.

discourse this evening was elo-
ction. Lysander, who is some-
way of thinking and speaking,
not be eloquent without action;
the body, the turn of the eye,
every word that is uttered,
make an accomplished speaker.
speaks in public, is the same
in ordinary life. Thus, as a
the countenance recommends
and jest, so it must be a very
hat gives grace to great senti-
s to be a thing unexpected;
signing manner is a beauty in
; but when you are to talk on
re you are moved yourself, the
others.
he, "a remarkable example of
s, a famous orator of antiquity,
ns in a great cause against De-
ing lost it, retired to Rhodes.
the quality most admired among
ates of that place, having heard
speech of Demosthenes, desired
their pleadings. After his own,
ration of his antagonist. The
ir admiration of both, but more
es. 'If you are,' said he, 'thus
g only what that great orator

B

in nurseries and boarding-school
evil she has laid the scheme of
damsels: where (instead of sc
samplers) pens, compasses, quad
scripts, Greek, Latin, and Hebr
their whole time. Only on ho
will, for moderate exercise, be
themselves with the use of some
most voluble weapons; and prop
to give them as least a superfi
ancient and modern Amazonian
military performances, the direc
by Epicene,* the writer of "
Mediterranean," who, by the hel
poisons conveyed by smells, ha
weeks brought many persons of
untimely fate; and, what is mo
contrary to her profession, with t
vived others who had long sinc
the whirlpools of Lethe. Anothe
is said to be a certain lady, who
two of the choicest Saxon novels,
have been in as great repute v
Queen Emma's Court, as the "
New Atalantis" are with those
make it my business to inquire ir
this learned institution, and give
of their "Philosophical Transacti
after Nature."

"Yours, &c.

"Tof

---

* Mrs. Manley, author of the Memoirs
† Mrs. Elizabeth Elstob, eminent for
Anglo-Saxon language and antiquities. S
Ballard's Memoirs of Learned Ladies.

THE TATLER, No. LXVI.

SATURDAY, SEPT. 10, 1709.

Will's Coffeehouse, Sept. 9.

THE subject of the discourse this evening was eloquence and graceful action. Lysander, who is something particular in his way of thinking and speaking, told us, "a man could not be eloquent without action; for the deportment of the body, the turn of the eye, and an apt sound to every word that is uttered, must all conspire to make an accomplished speaker. Action in one that speaks in public, is the same thing as a good mien in ordinary life. Thus, as a certain insensibility in the countenance recommends a sentence of humour and jest, so it must be a very lively consciousness that gives grace to great sentiments. The jest is to be a thing unexpected; therefore your undesigning manner is a beauty in expressions of mirth; but when you are to talk on a set subject, the more you are moved yourself, the more you will move others.

"There is," said he, "a remarkable example of that kind. Æschines, a famous orator of antiquity, had pleaded at Athens in a great cause against Demosthenes; but having lost it, retired to Rhodes. Eloquence was then the quality most admired among men, and the magistrates of that place, having heard he had a copy of the speech of Demosthenes, desired him to repeat both their pleadings. After his own, he recited also the oration of his antagonist. The people expressed their admiration of both, but more of that of Demosthenes. 'If you are,' said he, 'thus touched with hearing only what that great orator said, how would you have been affected had you seen him speak? for he who hears Demosthenes only, loses much the better part of the oration.' Certain it is, that they who speak gracefully, are very lamely represented in having their speeches read or repeated by unskilful people; for there is something native to each man, so inherent to his thoughts and sentiments, which it is hardly possible for another to give a true idea of. You may observe in common talk, when a sentence of any man's is repeated, an acquaintance of his shall immediately observe, 'That is so like him, methinks I see how he looked when he said it.'

"But of all the people on the earth, there are none who puzzle me so much as the clergy of Great Britain, who are, I believe, the most learned body of men now in the world: and yet this art of speaking, with the proper ornaments of voice and gesture, is wholly neglected among them; and I will engage, were a deaf man to behold the greater part of them preach, he would rather think they were reading the contents only of some discourse they intended to make, than actually in the body of an oration, even when they were upon matters of such a nature, as one would believe it were impossible to think of without emotion.

"I own there are exceptions to this general observation, and that the Dean we heard the other day together is an orator.* He has so much regard to his congregation, that he commits to his memory what he is to say to them; and has so soft and graceful a behaviour, that it must attract your atten-

---

* This fine character is drawn for Bishop Atterbury, then Dean of Carlisle, one of the Queen's chaplains. It seems as if it cost Steele some effort to permit insertion of a passage so favourable to a Tory divine, for he appeals to it more than once as a decisive proof of his impartiality.

tion. His person, it is to be confessed, is no small recommendation; but he is to be highly commended for not losing that advantage; and adding to the propriety of speech, which might pass the criticism of Longinus, an action which would have been approved by Demosthenes. He has a peculiar force in his way, and has charmed many of his audience, who could not be intelligent hearers of his discourse, were there not explanation as well as grace in his action. This art of his is useful with the most exact and honest skill: he never attempts your passions, until he has convinced your reason. All the objections which he can form, are laid open and dispersed, before he uses the least vehemence in his sermon; but when he thinks he has your head, he very soon wins your heart; and never pretends to shew the beauty of holiness, until he has convinced you of the truth of it.

"Would every one of our clergymen be thus careful to recommend truth and virtue in their proper figures, and shew so much concern for them as to give them all the additional force they were able, it is not possible that nonsense should have so many hearers as you find it has in dissenting congregations, for no reason in the world, but because it is spoken extempore; for ordinary minds are wholly governed by their eyes and ears; and there is no way to come at their hearts but by power over their imaginations.

"There is my friend and merry companion Daniel;[*] he knows a great deal better than he speaks, and can form a proper discourse as well as any orthodox neighbour. But he knows very well, that to bawl

---

[*] The celebrated Daniel Burgess, of whose pulpit buffoonery many examples are still preserved. His meeting-house near Lincoln's Inn was destroyed by the high-church mob upon occasion of Sacheverell's trial.

out, 'My beloved!' and the words 'grace! regeneration! sanctification! a new light! the day! the day! ay, my beloved, the day! or rather the night! the night is coming!' and 'judgment will come when we least think of it!' and so forth—He knows, to be vehement is the only way to come at his audience. Daniel, when he sees my friend Greenhat come in, can give a good hint, and cry out, 'This is only for the saints! the regenerated!' By this force of action, though mixed with all the incoherence and ribaldry imaginable, Daniel can laugh at his diocesan, and grow fat by voluntary subscription, while the parson of the parish goes to law for half his dues. Daniel will tell you, it is not the shepherd, but the sheep with the bell, which the flock follows.

"Another thing, very wonderful this learned body should omit, is, learning to read; which is a most necessary part of eloquence in one who is to serve at the altar; for there is no man but must be sensible, that the lazy tone, and inarticulate sound of our common readers, depreciates the most proper form of words that were ever extant in any nation or language, to speak their own wants, or his power from whom we ask relief.

"There cannot be a greater instance of the power of action than in little parson Dapper,[*] who is the common relief to all the lazy pulpits in town. This smart youth has a very good memory, a quick eye, and a clean handkerchief. Thus equipped, he opens his text, shuts his book fairly, shews he has no notes in his bible, opens both palms, and shews all is fair there too. Thus, with a decisive air, my young man goes on without hesitation; and though from the beginning to the end of his pretty discourse, he has

---

[*] Supposed to be Dr. Joseph Trapp, of whom Swift speaks with contempt in his Journal.

not used one proper gesture, yet, at the conclusion, the churchwarden pulls his gloves from off his hands; 'Pray, who is this extraordinary young man?' Thus the force of action is such, that it is more prevalent, even when improper, than all the reason and argument in the world without it." This gentleman concluded his discourse by saying, "I do not doubt but if our preachers would learn to speak, and our readers to read, within six months' time we should not have a dissenter within a mile of a church in Great Britain."

THE TATLER, No. LXVII.

TUESDAY, SEPT. 13, 1709.

From my own Apartments, Sept. 12.

My province is much larger than at first sight men would imagine, and I shall lose no part of my jurisdiction, which extends not only to futurity, but also is retrospect to things past; and the behaviour of persons, who have long ago acted their parts, is as much liable to my examination as that of my own contemporaries.

In order to put the whole race of mankind in their proper distinctions, according to the opinion their cohabitants conceived of them, I have with very much care, and depth of meditation, thought fit to erect a chamber of Fame; and established certain rules, which are to be observed in admitting members into this illustrious society.

In this chamber of Fame there are to be three tables, but of different lengths; the first is to contain exactly twelve persons; the second, twenty;

and the third, a hundred. This is reckoned to be the full number of those who have any competent share of fame. At the first of these tables are to be placed, in their order, the twelve most famous persons in the world; not with regard to the things they are famous for, but according to the degree of their fame, whether in valour, wit, or learning. Thus, if a scholar be more famous than a soldier, he is to sit above him. Neither must any preference be given to virtue, if the person be not equally famous.

When the first table is filled, the next in renown must be seated at the second, and so on in like manner to the number of twenty; as also in the same order at the third, which is to hold a hundred. At these tables no regard is to be had to seniority; for if Julius Cæsar shall be judged more famous than Romulus and Scipio, he must have the precedence. No person who has not been dead a hundred years, must be offered to a place at any of these tables; and because this is altogether a lay society, and that sacred persons move upon greater motives than that of fame, no persons celebrated in holy writ, or any ecclesiastical man whatsoever, are to be introduced here.

At the lower end of the room is to be a sidetable for persons of great fame, but dubious existence; such as Hercules, Theseus, Æneas, Achilles, Hector, and others. But because it is apprehended, that there may be great contention about precedence, the proposer humbly desires the opinion of the learned, toward his assistance, in placing every person according to his rank, that none may have just occasion of offence. The merits of the cause shall be judged by plurality of voices.

For the more impartial execution of this important affair, it is desired, that no man will offer his favourite hero, scholar, or poet; and that the learned will be pleased to send to Mr. Bickerstaff, at Mr. Morphew's, near Stationers' Hall, their several lists for the first table only, and in the order they would have them placed; after which, the proposer will compare the several lists, and make another for the public, wherein every name shall be ranked according to the voices it has had. Under this chamber is to be a dark vault, for the same number of persons of evil fame.

It is humbly submitted to consideration, whether the project would not be better, if the persons of true fame meet in a middle room, those of dubious existence in an upper room, and those of evil fame in a lower dark room.

It is to be noted, that no historians are to be admitted at any of these tables; because they are appointed to conduct the several persons to their seats, and are to be made use of as ushers to the assemblies.

I call upon the learned world to send me their assistance toward this design, it being matter of too great moment for any one person to determine. But I do assure them, their lists shall be examined with great fidelity, and those that are exposed to the public, made with all the caution imaginable.

THE TATLER, No. LXVIII.

THURSDAY, SEPT. 15, 1709.

THE progress of our endeavours will, of necessity, be very much interrupted, except the learned world will please to send their lists to the chamber of

Fame with all expedition. There is nothing can so much contribute to create a noble emulation in our youth, as the honourable mention of such whose actions have outlived the injuries of time, and recommended themselves so far to the world, that it is become learning to know the least circumstance of their affairs. It is a great incentive to see that some men have raised themselves so highly above their fellow-creatures, that the lives of ordinary men are spent in inquiries after the particular actions of the most illustrious. True it is, that without this impulse to fame and reputation, our industry would stagnate, and that lively desire of pleasing each other die away. This opinion was so established in the heathen world, that their sense of living appeared insipid, except their being was enlivened with a consciousness that they were esteemed by the rest of the world.

Upon examining the proportion of men's fame for my table of twelve, I thought it no ill way, (since I had laid it down for a rule, that they were to be ranked simply as they were famous, without regard to their virtue,) to ask my sister Jenny's advice; and particularly mentioned to her the name of Aristotle. She immediately told me he was a very great scholar, and that she had read him at the boarding-school. She certainly means a trifle, sold by the hawkers, called "Aristotle's Problems." * But this raised a great scruple in me, whether a fame increased by imposition of others is to be added to his account, or that these excrescences, which grow out of his real reputation, and give encouragement to others to pass things under the covert of his name, should be considered in giving him his seat in the chamber? This punctilio is

---

* An indecent pamphlet bearing that name.

referred to the learned. In the meantime, so ill-natured are mankind, that I believe I have names already sent me sufficient to fill up my lists for the dark room, and every one is apt enough to send in their accounts of ill deservers. This malevolence does not proceed from a real dislike of virtue, but a diabolical prejudice against it, which makes men willing to destroy what they care not to imitate. Thus you see the greatest characters among your acquaintance, and those you live with, are traduced by all below them in virtue, who never mention them but with an exception. However, I believe I shall not give the world much trouble about filling my tables for those of evil fame; for I have some thoughts of clapping up the sharpers there as fast as I can lay hold of them.

At present I am employed in looking over the several notices which I have received of their manner of dexterity, and the way at dice of making all *rugg*, as the cant is. The whole art of securing a die has lately been sent me, by a person who was of the fraternity, but is disabled by the loss of a finger; by which means he cannot practise that trick as he used to do. But I am very much at a loss how to call some of the fair sex, who are accomplices with the Knights of Industry;* for my metaphorical dogs are easily enough understood; but the feminine gender of dogs has so harsh a sound, that we know not how to name it. But I am credibly informed, that there are female dogs as voracious as the males, and make advances to young fellows, without any other design

---

* Steele, to his great honour, under the allegory of dogs of different kinds, described and held up to disgrace the principal gamblers in London. One of the fraternity was denouncing personal vengeance in a coffeehouse, when the spirited Lord Forbes silenced him with these words: "You will find it safer, sir, in this country, to cut a purse than to cut a throat."

but coming to a familiarity with their purses. I have also long lists of persons of condition, who are certainly of the same regimen with these banditti, and instrumental to their cheats upon undiscerning men of their own rank. These add their good reputation to carry on the impostures of others, whose very names would else be defence enough against falling into their hands. But, for the honour of our nation, these shall be unmentioned; provided we hear no more of such practices, and that they shall not from henceforward suffer the society of such as they know to be the common enemies of order, discipline, and virtue. If it appear that they go on in encouraging them, they must be proceeded against according to the severest rules of history, where all is to be laid before the world with impartiality, and without respect to persons,

"So let the stricken deer go weep."

THE TATLER, No. LXX.

TUESDAY, SEPT. 20, 1709.

"To ISAAC BICKERSTAFF, Esq.

" SIR,

" I READ with great pleasure, in the Tatler of Saturday last, the conversation upon eloquence; permit me to hint to you one thing the great Roman orator observes upon this subject: *Caput enim arbitrabatur oratoris*, (he quotes Menedemus, an Athenian,) *ut ipsis apud quos ageret talis qualem ipse optaret videretur; id fieri vitæ dignitate.* (Tull. de

Oratore.) It is the first rule in oratory, that a man must appear such as he would persuade others to be; and that can be accomplished only by the force of his life. I believe it might be of great service to let our public orators know, that an unnatural gravity, or an unbecoming levity, in their behaviour out of the pulpit, will take very much from the force of their eloquence in it. Excuse another scrap of Latin; it is from one of the fathers; I think it will appear a just observation to all, and it may have authority with some: *Qui autem docent tantum, nec faciunt, ipsi præceptis suis detrahunt pondus; quis enim obtemperet, cum ipsi præceptores doceant non obtemperare?* Those who teach, but do not act agreeably to the instructions they give to others, take away all weight from their doctrine; for who will obey the precepts they inculcate, if they themselves teach us by their practice to disobey them?

"I am, Sir,

"Your most humble servant,

"Jonathan Rosehat.

"P.S.—You were complaining in that paper, that the clergy of Great Britain had not yet learned to speak: a very great defect indeed: and, therefore, I shall think myself a well-deserver of the church, in recommending all the dumb clergy to the famous speaking doctor at Kensington.* This ingenious gentleman, out of compassion to those of a bad utterance, has placed his whole study in the newmodelling the organs of voice; which art, he has so far advanced, as to be able even to make a good orator of a pair of bellows. He lately exhibited a

---

* Dr. James Ford, who professed to remove impediments in speech.

specimen of his skill in this way, of which I was informed by the worthy gentlemen then present; who were at once delighted and amazed to hear an instrument of so simple an organization, use an exact articulation of words, a just cadency in its sentences, and a wonderful pathos in its pronunciation: not that he designs to expatiate in this practice; because he cannot, as he says, apprehend what use it may be of to mankind, whose benefit he aims at in a more particular manner: and for the same reason, he will never more instruct the feathered kind, the parrot having been his last scholar in that way. He has a wonderful faculty in making and mending echoes; and this he will perform at any time for the use of the solitary in the country; being a man born for universal good, and for that reason recommended to your patronage by,

"Sir, yours," &c.

---o---

THE TATLER, No. LXXI.

THURSDAY, SEPT. 22, 1709.

"Esquire Bickerstaff,

" Finding your advice and censure to have a good effect, I desire your admonition to our vicar and schoolmaster, who, in his preaching to his auditors, stretches his jaws so wide, that, instead of instructing youth, it rather frightens them: likewise in reading prayers, he has such a careless loll, that people are justly offended at his irreverent posture; besides the extraordinary charge they are put to in sending their children to dance, to bring them off of those ill gestures. Another evil faculty he has, in making the bowling-green his daily residence, instead of his church, where his curate reads prayers every day. If the weather is fair, his time is spent in visiting; if cold or wet, in bed, or at least at home, though within a hundred yards of the church. These, out of many such irregular practices, I write for his reclamation: but two or three things more before I conclude; to wit, that generally when his curate preaches in the afternoon, he sleeps sotting in the desk on a hassock. With all this, he is so extremely proud, that he will go but once to the sick, except they return his visit."

THE TATLER, No. LXXIV.

THURSDAY, SEPT. 29, 1709.

Grecian Coffeehouse, Sept. 29.

THIS evening I thought fit to notify to the literati of this house, and by that means to all the world, that on Saturday, the fifteenth of October next ensuing I design to fix my first Table of Fame; and desire that such as are acquainted with the characters of the twelve most famous men that have ever appeared in the world, would send in their lists, or name any one man for that table, assigning also his place at it, before that time, upon pain of having such his man of fame postponed, or placed too high, for ever. I shall not, upon any application whatever, alter the place which upon that day I shall give to any of these worthies. But whereas there are many who take upon them to admire this hero, or that author, upon second-hand, I expect each subscriber should underwrite his reason for the place he allots his candidate.

The thing is of the last consequence; for we are about settling the greatest point that ever has been debated in any age; and I shall take precautions accordingly. Let every man who votes, consider that he is now going to give away that, for which the soldier gave up his rest, his pleasure, and his life; the scholar resigned his whole series of thought, his midnight repose, and his morning slumbers. In a word, he is, as I may say, to be judge of that afterlife, which noble spirits prefer to their very real beings. I hope I shall be forgiven, therefore, if I make some objections against their jury, as they shall occur to me. The whole of the number by whom they are to be tried, are to be scholars. I am persuaded, also, that Aristotle will be put up by all of that class of men. However, in behalf of others, such as wear the livery of Aristotle, the two famous universities are called upon on this occasion: but I except the men of Queen's, Exeter, and Jesus Colleges, in Oxford, who are not to be electors,* because he shall not be crowned from an implicit faith in his writings, but receive his honour from such judges as shall allow him to be censured. Upon this election, as I was just now going to say, I banish all who think and speak after others, to concern themseves in it. For which reason, all illiterate distant admirers are forbidden to corrupt the voices by sending, according to the new mode, any poor students coals and candles † for their votes

---

* The members of these three colleges were obliged, by their statutes, to keep to Aristotle for their texts.
† This mode of bribery had been recently practised, in the election of Sir Benjamin Green as alderman of the ward of Queenhithe.

in behalf of such worthies as they pretend to esteem. All new-writers are also excluded, because they consider fame as it is a report which gives foundation to the filling up their rhapsodies, and not as it is the emanation or consequence of good and evil actions. These are excepted against as justly as butchers in case of life and death: their familiarity with the greatest names takes off the delicacy of their regard, as dealing in blood makes the lanii less tender of spilling it.

THE TATLER,* No. LXXXI.

SATURDAY, OCT. 15, 1709.

Hic manus ob patriam pugnando vulnera passi,——
Quique pii vates, et Phœbo digna locuti,
Inventas aut qui vitam excoluêre per artes,
Quique sui memores alios fecêre merendo.
        VIRG. Æn. vi. 660.

Here Patriots live, who, for their country's good,
In fighting fields were prodigal of blood;—
Here Poets, worthy their inspiring god,
And of unblemished life make their abode,
And searching Wits, of more mechanic parts,
Who graced their age with new-invented arts:
Those who to worth their bounty did extend;
And those who knew that bounty to commend.
        DRYDEN.

From my own Apartments, Oct. 14.

THERE are two kinds of immortality; that which the soul really enjoys after this life, and that imaginary

---

* This essay has been retained in all editions of Swift's works, though, in the edition of the Tatler, 1786, it is ascribed, for reasons there alleged, to Steele and Addison exclusively.

existence, by which men live in their fame and reputation. The best and greatest actions have proceeded from the prospect of the one or the other of these; but my design is to treat only of those who have chiefly proposed to themselves the latter, as the principal reward of their labours. It was for this reason that I excluded from my Tables of Fame, all the great founders and votaries of religion; and it is for this reason also, that I am more than ordinarily anxious to do justice to the persons of whom I am now going to speak; for, since fame was the only end of all their enterprises and studies, a man cannot be to scrupulous in alloting them their due proportion of it. It was this consideration which made me call the whole body of the learned to my assistance; to many of whom I must own my obligations for the catalogues of illustrious persons which they have sent me in upon this occasion. I yesterday employed the whole afternoon in comparing them with each other; which made so strong an impression upon my imagination, that they broke my sleep for the first part of the following night, and at length threw me into a very agreeable vision, which I shall beg leave to describe in all its particulars.

I dreamed that I was conveyed into a wide and boundless plain, that was covered with prodigious multitudes of people, which no man could number. In the midst of it there stood a mountain, with its head above the clouds. The sides were extremely steep, and of such a particular structure, that no creature which was not made in human figure, could possibly ascend it. On a sudden, there was heard from the top of it a sound like that of a trumpet; but so exceedingly sweet and harmonious, that it filled the hearts of those who heard it with raptures, and gave such high and delightful sensations, as seemed to animate and raise human nature above itself. This made me very much amazed to find so very few in that innumerable multitude, who had ears fine enough to hear or relish this music with pleasure: but my wonder abated, when, upon looking round me, I saw most of them attentive to three sirens, clothed like goddesses, and distinguished by the names of Sloth, Ignorance, and Pleasure. They were seated on three rocks, amid a beautiful variety of groves, meadows, and rivulets, that lay on the borders of the mountain. While the base and grovelling multitude of different nations, ranks, and ages, were listening to these delusive deities, those of a more erect aspect, and exalted spirit, separated themselves from the rest, and marched in great bodies toward the mountain, from whence they heard the sound, which still grew sweeter the more they listened to it.

On a sudden methought this select band sprang forward, with a resolution to climb the ascent, and follow the call of that heavenly music. Every one took something with him, that he thought might be of assistance to him in his march. Several had their swords drawn, some carried rolls of paper in their hands, some had compasses, others quadrants, others telescopes, and others pencils; some had laurels on their heads, and others buskins on their legs: in short, there was scarce any instrument of a mechanic art, or liberal science, which was not made use of on this occasion. My good demon, who stood at my right hand during the course of this whole vision, observing in me a burning desire to join that glorious company, told me, "He highly approved that generous ardour with which I seemed transported; but, at the same time, advised me to cover my face with a mask all the while I was to labour on the ascent." I took his counsel, without inquiring into his reasons. The whole body now broke into different parties, and began to climb the precipice by ten thousand different paths. Several got into little alleys, which did not reach far up the hill, before they ended and led no farther; and I observed, that most of the artisans, which considerably diminished our number, fell into these paths.

We left another considerable body of adventurers behind us, who thought they had discovered by-ways up the hill, which proved so very intricate and perplexed, that, after having advanced in them a little, they were quite lost among the several turns and windings; and though they were as active as any in their motions, they made but little progress in the ascent. These, as my guide informed me, were "men of subtle tempers, and puzzled politics, who would supply the place of real wisdom, with cunning and artifice." Among those who were far advanced in their way, there were some, that by one false step fell backward, and lost more ground in a moment than they had gained for many hours, or could be ever able to recover. We were now advanced very high, and observed that all the different paths, which ran about the sides of the mountain, began to meet in two great roads: which insensibly gathered the whole multitude of travellers into two great bodies. At a little distance from the entrance of each road, there stood a hideous phantom, that opposed our farther passage. One of these apparitions had his right hand filled with darts, which he brandished in the face of all who came up that way: crowds ran back at the appearance of it, and cried out Death! The spectre that guarded the other road was Envy: she was not armed with weapons of destruction like the former; but by dreadful hissings, noises of reproach, and a horrid distracted laughter, she appeared more frightful than Death itself; insomuch, that abundance of our company were discouraged from passing any farther, and some appeared ashamed of having come so far. As for myself, I must confess my heart shrunk within me at the sight of these ghastly appearances: but on a sudden, the voice of the trumpet came more full upon us, so that we felt a new resolution reviving in us; and in proportion as this resolution grew, the terrors before us seemed to vanish. Most of the company, who had swords in their hands, marched on with great spirit, and an air of defiance, up the road that was commanded by Death; while others, who had thought and contemplation in their looks, went forward, in a more composed manner, up the road possessed by Envy. The way above these apparitions grew smooth and uniform, and was so delightful, that the travellers went on with pleasure, and in a little time arrived at the top of the mountain. They here began to breathe a delicious kind of ether, and saw all the fields about them covered with a kind of purple light, that made them reflect with satisfaction on their past toils; and diffused a secret joy through the whole assembly, which shewed itself in every look and feature. In the midst of these happy fields, there stood a palace of a very glorious structure: it had four great folding doors, that faced the four several quarters of the world. On the top of it was enthroned the Goddess of the Mountain, who smiled upon her votaries, and sounded the silver trumpet which had called them up, and cheered them in their passage to her palace. They had now formed themselves into several divisions; a band of historians taking their stations at each door, according to the persons whom they were to introduce.

On a sudden the trumpet, which had hitherto sounded only a march, or point of war, now swelled all its notes into triumph and exultation: the whole fabric shook, and the doors flew open. The first that stepped forward was a beautiful and blooming hero, and, as I heard by the murmurs round me, Alexander the Great. He was conducted by a crowd of historians. The person who immediately walked before him, was remarkable for an embroidered garment, who, not being well acquainted with the place, was conducting him to an apartment appointed for the reception of fabulous heroes. The name of this false guide was Quintus Curtius. But Arrian and Plutarch, who knew better the avenues of this palace, conducted him into the great hall, and placed him at the upper end of the first table. My good demon, that I might see the whole ceremony, conveyed me to a corner of this room, where I might perceive all that passed, without being seen myself. The next who entered was a charming virgin, leading in a venerable old man that was blind. Under her left arm she bore a harp, and on her head a garland. Alexander, who was very well acquainted with Homer, stood up at his entrance, and placed him on his right hand. The virgin, who it seems was one of the nine sisters that attended on the goddess of Fame, smiled with an ineffable grace at their meeting, and retired.

Julius Cæsar was now coming forward; and though most of the historians offered their service to introduce him, he left them at the door, and would have no conductor but himself.

The next who advanced, was a man of a homely but cheerful aspect, and attended by persons of greater figure than any that appeared on this occasion. Plato was on his right hand, and Xenophon on his left. He bowed to Homer, and sat down by him. It was expected that Plato would himself have taken a place next to his master Socrates; but on a sudden there was heard a great clamour of disputants at the door, who appeared with Aristotle at the head of them. That philosopher, with some rudeness, but great strength of reason, convinced the whole table, that a title to the fifth place was his due, and took it accordingly.

He had scarce sat down, when the same beautiful virgin that had introduced Homer, brought in another, who hung back at the entrance, and would have excused himself, had not his modesty been overcome by the invitation of all who sat at the table. His guide and behaviour made me easily conclude it was Virgil. Cicero next appeared, and took his place. He had inquired at the door for one Lucceius to introduce him; but not finding him there, he contented himself with the attendance of many other writers, who all, except Sallust, appeared highly pleased with the office.

We waited some time in expectation of the next worthy, who came in with a great retinue of historians, whose names I could not learn, most of them being natives of Carthage. The person thus conducted, who was Hannibal, seemed much disturbed, and could not forbear complaining to the board, of the affronts he had met with among the Roman historians, "who attempted," says he, "to carry me into the subterraneous apartment; and perhaps would have done it, had it not been for the impartiality of this gentleman," pointing to Polybius, "who was the only person, except my own countrymen, that was willing to conduct me hither."

The Carthaginian took his seat, and Pompey entered with great dignity in his own person, and preceded by several historians. Lucan the poet was at the head of them, who, observing Homer and Virgil at the table, was going to sit down himself, had not the latter whispered him, that whatever pretence he might otherwise have had, he forfeited his claim to it, by coming in as one of the historians.

Lucan was so exasperated with the repulse, that he muttered something to himself; and was heard to say, that since he could not have a seat among them himself, he would bring in one who alone had more merit than their whole assembly; upon which he went to the door, and brought in Cato of Utica. That great man approached the company with such an air, that shewed he contemned the honour which he laid a claim to. Observing the seat opposite to Cæsar was vacant, he took possession of it, and spoke two or three smart sentences upon the nature of precedency, which, according to him, "consisted not in place, but in intrinsic merit;" to which he added, "that the most virtuous man, wherever he was seated, was always at the upper end of the table." Socrates, who had a great spirit of raillery with his wisdom, could not forbear smiling at a virtue which took so little pains to make itself agreeable. Cicero took the occasion to make a long discourse in praise of Cato, which he uttered with much vehemence. Cæsar answered him with a great deal of seeming temper; but, as I stood at a great distance from them, I was not able to hear one word of what they said. But I could not forbear taking notice, that in all the discourse which passed at the table, a word or nod from Homer decided the controversy.

After a short pause Augustus appeared, looking round him, with a serene and affable countenance, upon all the writers of his age, who strove among themselves which of them should shew him the greatest marks of gratitude and respect. Virgil rose from the table to meet him; and though he was an acceptable guest to all, he appeared more such to the learned, than the military worthies. The next man astonished the whole table with his appearance: he was slow, solemn, and silent, in his behaviour, and wore a raiment curiously wrought with hieroglyphics. As he came into the middle of the room, he threw up the skirts of it, and discovered a golden thigh. Socrates, at the sight of it, declared "against keeping company with any who were not made of flesh and blood:" and therefore desired Diogenes the Laertian "to lead him to the apartment allotted for fabulous heroes and worthies of dubious existence." At his going out, he told them, "that they did not know whom they dismissed: that he was now Pythagoras, the first of philosophers, and that formerly he had been a very brave man at the siege of Troy."—"That may be very true," said Socrates; "but you forget that you have likewise been a very great harlot in your time." This exclusion made way for Archimedes, who came forward with a scheme of mathematical figures in his hand; among which I observed a cone and a cylinder.

Seeing this table full, I desired my guide, for variety, to lead me to the fabulous apartment, the roof of which was painted with gorgons, chimeras, and centaurs, with many other emblematical figures, which I wanted both time and skill to unriddle. The first table was almost full: at the upper end sat Hercules, leaning an arm upon his club; on his right hand were Achilles and Ulysses, and between them Æneas; on his left were Hector, Theseus, and Jason: the lower end had Orpheus, Æsop, Phalaris, and Musæus. The ushers seemed at a loss for a twelfth man, when, methought, to my great joy and surprise, I heard some at the lower end of the table mention Isaac Bickerstaff: but those of the upper end received it with disdain; and said, "If they must have a British worthy, they would have Robin Hood."

While I was transported with the honour that was done me, and burning with envy against my competitor, I was awakened by the noise of the cannon which were then fired for the taking of Mons. I should have been very much troubled at being thrown out of so pleasing a vision on any other occasion; but thought it an agreeable change, to have my thoughts diverted from the greatest among the dead and fabulous heroes, to the most famous among the real and the living.*

THE TATLER, No. CCXXX.

THURSDAY, SEPT. 28, 1710.

From my own Apartments, September 27.

THE following letter has laid before me many great and manifest evils in the world of letters, which I had overlooked; but it opens to me a very busy scene, and it will require no small care and application to amend errors, which are become so universal. The affectation of politeness is exposed in this epistle with a great deal of wit and discernment; so that, whatever discourses I may fall into hereafter, upon the subject the writer treats of, I shall at present lay the matter before the world without the least alteration from the words of my correspondent.†

---

* This number of the Tatler, with the omission of the final paragraph, relating to the taking of Mons, is printed in Addison's Works, vol. II. p. 182, 4to; with a note, saying, "This last paragraph was written by Sir R. Steele."

† "I have sent a long letter to Bickerstaff. Let the Bishop of Clogher *smoak* it if he can." Journal to Stella, Sept. 23, 1710.— "I made a Tatler since I came; guess which it is, and whether

"To Isaac Bickerstaff, Esq.

"Sir,

"There are some abuses among us of great consequence, the reformation of which is properly your province; although, as far as I have been conversant in your papers, you have not yet considered them. These are, the deplorable ignorance that for some years hath reigned among our English writers, the great depravity of our taste, and the continual corruption of our style. I say nothing here of those who handle particular sciences, divinity, law, physic, and the like; I mean the traders in history, and politics, and the *belles lettres*, together with those by whom books are not translated, but (as the common expressions are) done' out of French, Latin, or other languages, and made English. I cannot but observe to you, that, until of late years, a Grub Street book was always bound in sheepskin, with suitable print and paper, the price never above a shilling, and taken off wholly by common tradesmen or country pedlars; but now they appear in all sizes and shapes, and in all places: they are handed about from lapfuls in every coffeehouse to persons of quality; are shewn in Westminster Hall and the Court of Requests; you may see them gilt, and in royal paper, of five or six hundred pages, and rated accordingly. I would engage to furnish you with a catalogue of English books, published within the compass of seven years past, which at the first hand would cost you a hundred pounds, wherein you shall not be able to find ten lines together of common grammar, or common sense.

---

the Bishop of Clogher *smoaks* it." Ibid. Sept. 29.—" Have you *smoak'd* the Tatler that I writ? It is much liked here, and I think it is a fine one." Ibid. Oct. 1.

"These two evils, ignorance and want of taste, have produced a third, I mean the continual corruption of our English tongue,* which, without some timely remedy, will suffer more by the false refinements of twenty years past, than it has been improved in the foregoing hundred. And this is what I design chiefly to enlarge upon, leaving the former evils to your animadversion.

"But, instead of giving you a list of the late refinements crept into our language, I here send you a copy of a letter I received some time ago from a most accomplished person in this way of writing, upon which I shall make some remarks. It is in these terms:—

"'SIR,

"'I COU'DN'T *get the things you sent for all* about town.—*I* tho't *to* ha' *come down myself, and then* I'd ha' bro't um; *but* ha'nt don't, *and I believe I* can't do't, *that's* pozz.—Tom† *begins to* g'imself *airs, because* he's *going with the* plenipos.—'*Tis said the French King will* bamboozl us agen, *which* causes many speculations. *The* Jacks, *and others of that* kidney, *are very* uppish *and* alert upon't, *as you may see by their* phizz's.—Will Hazard *has got the* hipps, *having lost* to the tune of *five hundr'd pound*, tho' *he understands play very well*, nobody better. *He has promis't me upon* rep *to leave off play; but you know 'tis a weakness* he's *too apt to* give into, tho' *he has as much wit as any man*, nobody more: *he has lain* incog *ever since.—The* mobb's *very quiet with us now.—I believe you* tho't *I* banter'd *you in my last*

---

* It is very remakable, that, notwithstanding the ridicule so justly thrown by our author on barbarous contractions, he constantly fell into that error in his private letters to Stella.
† Mr. Thomas Harley is here alluded to.

like a country put.—I shan't *leave town this month*,' &c.

"This letter is, in every point, an admirable pattern of the present polite way of writing; nor is it of less authority for being an epistle: you may gather every flower of it, with a thousand more of equal sweetness from the books, pamphlets, and single papers, offered us every day in the coffee-houses. And these are the beauties introduced to supply the want of wit, sense, humour, and learning, which formerly were looked upon as qualifications for a writer. If a man of wit, who died forty years ago, were to rise from the grave on purpose, how would he be able to read this letter? and, after he had gone through that difficulty, how would he be able to understand it? The first thing that strikes your eye, is the breaks at the end of almost every sentence; of which I know not the use, only that it is a refinement, and very frequently practised. Then you will observe the abbreviations and elisions, by which consonants of most obdurate sounds are joined together, without one softening vowel to intervene: and all this only to make one syllable of two, directly contrary to the example of the Greeks and Romans, altogether of the Gothic strain, and of a natural tendency towards relapsing into barbarity, which delights in monosyllables, and uniting of mute consonants, as it is observable in all the northern languages. And this is still more visible in the next refinement, which consists in pronouncing the first syllable in a word that has many, and dismissing the rest; such as *phizz, hipps, mobb, pozz, rep*, and many more; when we are already overloaded with monosyllables, which are the disgrace of our language. Thus we cram one syllable, and cut off the rest, as the owl fattened her mice after she had bit off their legs, to prevent them from running away; and if ours be the same reason for maiming words, it will certainly answer the end; for I am sure no other nation will desire to borrow them. Some words are hitherto but fairly split, and therefore only in their way to perfection, as incog and plenipo; but in a short time, it is to be hoped, they will be farther docked to inc and plen. This reflection has made me of late years very impatient for a peace, which I believe would save the lives of many brave words as well as men. The war has introduced abundance of polysyllables, which will never be able to live many more campaigns. *Speculations, operations, preliminaries, ambassadors, palisadoes, communications, circumvallations, battalions,* as numerous as they are, if they attack us too frequently in our coffeehouses, we shall certainly put them to flight, and cut off the rear.

"The third refinement observable in the letter I send you, consists in the choice of certain words invented by some pretty fellows, such as *banter, bamboozle, country put,* and *kidney,* as it is there applied; some of which are now struggling for the vogue, and others are in possession of it. I have done my utmost, for some years past, to stop the progress of *mobb* and *banter*, but have been plainly borne down by numbers, and betrayed by those who promised to assist me.*

"In the last place, you are to take notice of certain choice phrases scattered through the letter;

---

* The Dean carried on the war against the word *mob* to the very last. A lady, who died in 1788, and was well known to Swift, used to say, that the greatest scrape into which she got with him was by using the word *mob.* "Why do you say that?" said he, in a passion: "never let me hear you say that word again." "Why, sir," said she, "what am I to say?" "The rabble, to be sure," answered he.

some of them tolerable enough, till they were worn to rags by servile imitators. You might easily find them, although they were not in a different print, and therefore I need not disturb them.

"These are the false refinements in our style, which you ought to correct: first, by arguments and fair means; but if those fail, I think you are to make use of your authority as censor, and, by an annual *index expurgatorius*, expunge all words and phrases that are offensive to good sense, and condemn those barbarous mutilations of vowels and syllables. In this last point, the usual pretence is, that they spell as they speak: a noble standard for language! to depend upon the caprice of every coxcomb, who, because words are the clothing of our thoughts, cuts them out, and shapes them as he pleases, and changes them oftener than his dress. I believe all reasonable people would be content that such refiners were more sparing of their words, and liberal in their syllables. On this head I should be glad you would bestow some advice upon several young readers in our churches, who, coming up from the university full fraught with admiration of our town politeness, will needs correct the style of our prayer-books. In reading the absolution, they are very careful to say "*Pardons and absolves;*" and in the prayer for the royal family it must be *endue'um, enrich'um, prosper'um,* and *bring'um;* then, in their sermons, they use all the modern terms of art, *sham, banter, mobb, bubble, bully, 'cutting, shuffling,* and *palming;* all which, and many more of the 'like stamp, as I have heard them often in the pulpit from some young sophisters, so I have read them in some of those sermons that have made a great noise of late. The design, it seems, is to avoid the dreadful imputation of pedantry; to shew us that they know the town, understand men and manners, and have not been poring upon old unfashionable books in the university.

"I should be glad to see you the instrument of introducing into our style that simplicity, which is the best and truest ornament of most things in human life; which the politer ages always aimed at in their building and dress, (*simplex munditiis,*) as well as their productions of wit. It is manifest that all new affected modes of speech, whether borrowed from the court, the town, or the theatre, are the first perishing parts in any language; and, as I could prove by many hundred instances, have been so in ours. The writings of Hooker, who was a country clergyman, and of Parsons the Jesuit, both in the reign of Queen Elizabeth, are in a style, that, with very few allowances, would not offend any present reader; much more clear and intelligible than those of Sir Henry Wotton, Sir Robert Naunton, Osborn, Daniel the Historian, and several others who writ later; but, being men of the court, and affecting the phrases then in fashion, they are often either not to be understood, or appear perfectly ridiculous.

"What remedies are to be applied to these evils I have not room to consider, having, I fear, already taken up most of your paper: besides, I think it is our office only to represent abuses, and yours to redress them.

"I am, with great respect,

"Sir,

"Yours," &c.

THE TATLER, No. CCLVIII.

SATURDAY, DEC. 2, 1710.*

SIR,   *Nov.* 22, 1710.

DINING yesterday with Mr. *South-British* and Mr. *William North-Briton*, two gentlemen, who, before you ordered it otherwise, were known by the names of Mr. *English* and Mr. *William Scot:* among other things, the maid of the house, who in her time, I believe, may have been a *North-British* warming-pan, brought us up a dish of *North-British* collops. We liked our entertainment very well; only we observed the table-cloth, being not so fine as we could have wished, was *North-British* cloth. But the worst of it was, we were disturbed all dinner-time by the noise of the children, who were playing in the paved court at *North-British* hoppers; so we paid our *North-Briton* sooner than we designed, and took coach to *North-Britain* yard, about which place most of us live. We had indeed gone a-foot; only we were under some apprehensions lest a *North British* mist should wet a *South-British* man to the skin.—We think this matter properly ex-

---

* "Steele, the rogue, has done the impudentest thing in the world: he said something in a Tatler, that we ought to use the word Great Britain, and not England, in common conversation, as, 'the finest lady in Great Britain,' &c. Upon this, Rowe, Prior, and I, sent him a letter, turning this into ridicule. He has to-day printed the letter, and signed it J. S., M. P., and N. R., the first letters of all our names." Journal to Stella, Dec. 2, 1710.—"The modern phrase, 'Great Britain,' is only to distinguish it from Little Britain, where old clothes and old books are to be bought and sold." Letter to Alderman Barber, Aug. 8, 1738.

pressed, according to the accuracy of the new style, settled by you in one of your late papers. You will please to give your opinion upon it to,

   Sir,

  Your most humble servants,

     J. S., M. P., N. R.

---o---

THE TATLER, No. I.

Quis ergo sum saltem, si non sum Sosia? Te interrogo.
     PLAUT. AMPHYTRUO.

SATURDAY, JANUARY 13, 1710–11.*

IT is impossible, perhaps, for the best and wisest among us to keep so constant a guard upon our temper, but that we may at one time or other lie

---

* Jan. 2, 1710–11, Dr. Swift tells Stella, "Steele's last Tatler came out to-day. You will see it before this comes to you, and how he takes leave of the world. He never told so much as Mr. Addison of it, who was surprised as much as I; but, to say truth, it was time, for he grew cruel dull, and dry. To my knowledge, he had several good hints to go upon; but he was so lazy, and weary of the work, that he would not improve them."—Jan. 11, he adds, " I am setting up a new Tatler: little Harrison, whom I have mentioned to you. Others have put him on it, and I encourage him; and he was with me this morning and evening, shewing me his first, which comes out on Saturday. I doubt he will not succeed, for I do not much approve his manner; but the scheme is Mr. Secretary St. John's and mine, and would have done well enough in good hands. I recommended him to a printer, whom I sent for, and settled the matter between them this evening. Harrison has just left me; and I am tired with correcting his trash."

open to the strokes of fortune, and such incidents as we cannot foresee. With sentiments of this kind I came home to my lodgings last night, much fatigued with a long and sudden journey from the country, and full of the ungrateful occasion of it. It was natural for me to have immediate recourse to my pen and ink; but before I would offer to make use of them, I resolved deliberately to tell over a hundred, and when I came to the end of that sum, I found it more advisable to defer drawing up my intended remonstrance, till I had slept soundly on my resentments. Without any other preface than this, I shall give the world a fair account of the treatment I have lately met with, and leave them to judge whether the uneasiness I have suffered be inconsistent with the character I have generally pretended to. About three weeks since, I received an invitation from a kinsman in Staffordshire, to spend my Christmas in those parts. Upon taking leave of Mr. Morphew, I put as many papers into his hands as would serve till my return, and charged him, at parting, to be very punctual with the town. In what manner he and Mr. Lillie have been tampered with since, I cannot say; they have given me my revenge, if I desired any, by allowing their names to an idle paper, that, in all human probability, cannot live a fortnight to an end.

Myself, and the family I was with, were in the midst of gaiety, and a plentiful entertainment, when I received a letter from my sister Jenny, who, after mentioning some little affairs I had entrusted to her, goes on thus:—"The enclosed, I believe, will give you some surprise, as it has already astonished everybody here: who Mr. Steele is, that subscribes it, I do not know, any more than I can comprehend what could induce him to it. Morphew and Lillie, I am told, are both in the secret. I shall not presume to instruct you, but hope you will use some means to disappoint the ill nature of those who are taking pains to deprive the world of one of its most reasonable entertainments. I am," &c.

I am to thank my sister for her compliment; but be that as it will, I shall not easily be discouraged from my former undertaking. In pursuance of it, I was obliged upon this notice to take places in the coach for myself and my maid with the utmost expedition, lest I should, in a short time, be rallied out of my existence, as some people will needs fancy Mr. Partridge has been, and the real Isaac Bickerstaff have passed for a creature of Mr. Steele's imagination. This illusion might have hoped for some tolerable success, if I had not more than once produced my person in a crowded theatre; and such a person as Mr. Steele, if I am not misinformed in the gentleman, would hardly think it an advantage to own, though I should throw him in all the little honour I have gained by my Lucubrations. I may be allowed, perhaps, to understand pleasantry as well as other men, and can (in the usual phrase) take a jest without being angry; but I appeal to the world, whether the gentleman has not carried it too far, and whether he ought not to make a public recantation, if the credulity of some unthinking people should force me to insist upon it. The following letter is just come to hand, and I think it not improper to be inserted in this paper.

"To Isaac Bickerstaff, Esq.

"Sir, I am extremely glad to hear you are come to town; for in your absence we were all mightily surprised with an unaccountable paper, signed Richard Steele, who is esteemed by those that know him, to be a man of wit and honour; and therefore we took it either to be a counterfeit, or perfect Christmas frolic of that ingenious gentleman. But then your paper ceasing immediately after, we were at a loss what to think : if you were weary of the work you had so long carried on, and had given this Mr. Steele orders to signify so to the public, he should have said it in plain terms; but as that paper is worded, one would be apt to judge, that he had a mind to persuade the town that there was some analogy between Isaac Bickerstaff and him. Possibly there may be a secret in this which I can. not enter into : but I flatter myself that you never had any thoughts of giving over your labours for the benefit of mankind, when you cannot but know how many subjects are yet unexhausted, and how many others, as being less obvious, are wholly untouched. I dare promise, not only for myself, but many other abler friends, that we shall still continue to furnish you with hints on all proper occasions, which is all your genius requires. I think, by the way, you cannot in honour have any more to do with Morphew and Lillie, who have gone beyond the ordinary pitch of assurance, and transgressed the very letter of the proverb, by endeavouring to cheat you of your christian and surname too. Wishing you, sir, long to live for our instruction and diversion, and to the defeating of all impostors, I remain,

"Your most obedient humble servant,

"and affectionate kinsman,

"Humphry Wagstaff." *

---

* "To-day little Harrison's new Tatler came out; there is not much in it, but I hope he will mend. You must understand that, upon Steele's leaving off, there were two or three scrub Tatlers came out, and one of them holds on still, and to-day it

THE TATLER, No. II.*

Alios viri reverentia, vultusque ad continendum populum mire formatus: alios etiam, quibus ipse interesse non potuit, vis scribendi tamen, &c., magni nominis autoritas pervicere.—TULL. EPIST.

TUESDAY, JANUARY 16, 1710–11.

I REMEMBER Menage tells a story of Monsieur Racan, who had appointed a day and hour to meet a certain lady of great wit whom he had never seen, in order to make an acquaintance between them. " Two of Racan's friends, who had heard of the appointment, resolved to play him a trick. The first went to the lady two hours before the time, said his name was Racan, and talked with her an hour; they were both mightily pleased, began a great friendship, and parted with much satisfaction. A few minutes after comes the second, and sends up the same name; the lady wonders at the meaning, and tells him Mr. Racan had just left her. The gentleman says it was some rascally impostor, and that he had been frequently used in that manner. The lady is convinced, and they laugh at the oddness of the adventure. She now calls to mind several passages which confirm her that the former was a cheat. He appoints a second meeting, and takes his leave. He was no sooner gone, but the true Racan comes to the door, and

---

advertised against Harrison's; and so there must be disputes which are genuine, like the straps for razors."—Journal to Stella, Jan. 13, 1710–11.

* " I have given Harrison hints for another Tatler to-morrow.' —Journal to Stella, Jan. 15, 1710–11.

desires, under that name, to see the lady. She was out of all patience, sends for him up, rates him for an impostor, and after a thousand injuries, flings a slipper at his head. ' It was impossible to pacify or disabuse her; he was forced to retire; and it was not without some time, and the intervention of friends, that they could come to an eclaircissement." This, as I take it, is exactly the case with Mr. Steele, the pretended TATLER from Morphew, and myself, only (I presume) the world will be sooner undeceived than the lady in Menage. The very day my last paper came out, my printer brought me another of the same date, called the Tatler, by Isaac Bickerstaff, Esq., and, which was still more pleasant, with an advertisement at the end, calling me the Female TATLER: it is not enough to rob me of my name, but now they must impose a sex on me, when my years have long since determined me to be of none at all. There is only one thing wanting in the operation, that they would renew my age, and then I will heartily forgive them all the rest. In the meantime, whatever uneasiness I have suffered from the little malice of these men, and my retirement in the country, the pleasures I have received from the same occasion will fairly balance the account. On the one hand I have been highly delighted to see my name and character assumed by the scribblers of the age, in order to recommend themselves to it; and on the other, to observe the good taste of the town, in distinguishing and exploding them through every disguise, and sacrificing their trifles to the supposed names of Isaac Bickerstaff, Esq. But the greatest merit of my journey into Staffordshire is, that it has opened to me a new fund of unimproved follies and errors, that have hitherto lain out of my view, and by their situation, escaped my censure: for, as I have lived generally in town, the images I had of the country were such only as my senses received very early, and my memory has since preserved with all the advantages they first appeared in.

Hence it was that I thought our parish church the noblest structure in England, and the Esquire's place house, as we called it, a most magnificent palace. I had the same opinion of the alms-house in the churchyard, and of a bridge over the brook that parts our parish from the next. It was the common vogue of our school, that the master was the best scholar in Europe, and the usher the second. Not happening to correct these notions by comparing them with what I saw when I came into the world; upon returning back, I began to resume my former imaginations, and expected all things should appear in the same view as I left them when I was a boy; but, to my utter disappointment, I found them wonderfully shrunk, and lessened almost out of my knowledge, I looked with contempt on the tribes painted on the church walls, which I once so much admired, and on the carved chimneypiece in the esquire's hall. I found my old master to be a poor ignorant pedant; and, in short, the whole scene to be extremely changed for the worse. This I could not help mentioning, because though it be of no consequence in itself, yet it is certain, that most prejudices are contracted and retained by this narrow way of thinking, which, in matters of the greatest moment, are hardly shook off; and which we only think true, because we were made to believe so before we were capable to distinguish between truth and falsehood. But there was one prepossession, which I confess to have parted with, much to my regret: I mean the opinion of that native honesty and simplicity of manners, which I had always imagined to be inherent in country people.

I soon observed it was with them and us, as they say of animals; that every species at land has one to resemble it at sea; for it was easy to discover the seeds and principles of every vice and folly that one meets with in the more known world, though shooting up in different forms. I took a fancy, out of the several inhabitants round, to furnish the camp, the bar, and the Exchange, and some certain chocolate and coffeehouses, with exact parallels to what, in many instances, they already produce. There was a drunken quarrelsome smith, whom I have a hundred times fancied at the head of a troop of dragoons. A weaver, within two doors of my kinsman, was perpetually setting neighbours together by the ears. I lamented to see how his talents were misplaced, and imagined what a figure he might make in Westminster-hall. Goodman Crop, of Compton farm, wants nothing but a plum and a gold chain, to qualify him for the government of the city. My kinsman's stable-boy was a gibing companion, that would always have his jest. He would often put cow-itch in the maid's bed, pull stools from under folks, and lay a coal upon their shoes when they were asleep. He was at last turned off for some notable piece of roguery; and, when I came away, was loitering among the ale-houses. Bless me, thought I, what a prodigious wit would this have been with us! I could have matched all the sharpers between St. James's and Covent Garden, with a notable fellow in the same neighbourhood, (since hanged for picking pockets at fairs,) could he have had the advantages of their education. So nearly are the corruptions of the country allied to those of the town, with no farther difference than what is made by another turn of thought and method of living!

THE TATLER, No. V.

——Laceratque, trahitque
Molle pecus. VIRG.

SATURDAY, JANUARY 27, 1710–11.

AMONG other services I have met with from some critics, the cruellest for an old man is, that they will not let me be at quiet in my bed, but pursue me to my very dreams. I must not dream but when they please, nor upon long-continued subjects, however visionary in their own natures, because there is a manifest moral quite through them, which to produce as a dream is improbable and unnatural. The pain I might have had from this objection, is prevented, by considering they have missed another, against which I should have been at a loss to defend myself. They might have asked me whether the dreams I publish can properly be called lucubrations, which is the name I have given to all my papers, whether in volumes or half sheets: so manifest a contradiction *in terminis*, that I wonder no sophister ever thought of it. But the other is a cavil. I remember, when I was a boy at school, I have often dreamed out the whole passages of a day; that I rode a journey, baited, supped, went to bed, and rose next morning: and I have known young ladies, who could dream a whole texture of adventures in one night, large enough to make a novel. In youth the imagination is strong, not mixed with cares, nor tinged with those passions that most disturb and confound it: such as avarice, ambition, and many others. Now, as old men are said to grow children again, so, in this article of dreaming, I am returned to my childhood. My imagination is at full ease, without care, avarice, or ambition, to clog it; by which, among many others, I have this advantage, of doubling the small remainder of my time, and living four-and-twenty hours in the day. However, the dream I am now going to relate, is as wild as can well be imagined, and adapted to please these refiners upon sleep, without any moral that I can discover.

"It happened, that my maid left on the table in my bedchamber one of her story books, (as she calls them,) which I took up, and found full of strange impertinence, fitted to her taste and condition; of poor servants who came to be ladies, and serving men, of low degree, who married king's daughters. Among other things, I met this sage observation, 'That a lion would never hurt a true virgin.' With this medley of nonsense in my fancy, I went to bed, and dreamed that a friend waked me in the morning, and proposed, for pastime, to spend a few hours in seeing the parish lions, which he had not done since he came to town; and because they shewed but once a-week, he would not miss the opportunity. I said I would humour him: although, to speak the truth, I was not fond of those cruel spectacles; and, if it were not so ancient a custom, founded (as I had heard) upon the wisest maxims, I should be apt to censure the inhumanity of those who introduced it."

All this will be a riddle to the waking reader, until I discover the scene my imagination had formed upon this maxim, "That a lion would never hurt a true virgin." "I dreamed, that by a law of immemorial time, a he lion was kept in every parish at the common charge, and in a place provided, adjoining to the churchyard; that before any one of the fair sex was married, if she affirmed herself to be a virgin, she must on her wedding day, and in her wedding clothes, perform the ceremony of going alone into the den, and stay an hour with the lion, let loose, and kept fasting four-and-twenty hours on purpose. At a proper height above the den were convenient galleries for the relations and friends of the young couple, and open to all spectators. No maiden was forced to offer herself to the lion; but, if she refused it was a disgrace to marry her, and every one might have liberty of calling her a whore. And methought it was as usual a diversion to see the parish lions, as with us to go to a play or an opera. And it was reckoned convenient to be near the church, either for marrying the virgin, if she escaped the trial, or for burying her bones, when the lion had devoured the rest, as he constantly did."

To go on therefore with the dream: "We called first (as I remember) to see St. Dunstan's lion: but we were told they did not shew to-day. From thence we went to that of Covent Garden, which, to my great surprise, we found as lean as a skeleton, when I expected quite the contrary; but the keeper said it was no wonder at all, because the poor beast had not got an ounce of woman's flesh since he came into the parish. This amazed me more than the other, and I was forming to myself a mighty veneration for the ladies in that quarter of the town, when the keeper went on, and said he wondered the parish would be at the charge of maintaining a lion for nothing. Friend, (said I,) do you call it nothing to justify the virtue of so many ladies; or has your lion lost his distinguishing faculty? Can there be anything more for the honour of your parish than that all the ladies married in your church were pure virgins?—That is true, (said he,) and the doctor knows it to his sorrow; for there has not been a couple married in our church since his worship came among us. The virgins hereabouts are too wise to venture the claws of the lion; and, because nobody will marry them, have all entered into a vow of virginity; so that in proportion we have much the largest nunnery in the whole town. This manner of ladies entering into a vow of virginity, because they were not virgins, I easily conceived; and my dream told me, that the whole kingdom was full of nunneries, plentifully stocked from the same reason.

"We went to see another lion, where we found much company met in the gallery. The keeper told us we should see sport enough, as he called it; and in a little time we saw a young beautiful lady put into the den, who walked up toward the lion with all imaginable security in her countenance, and looked smiling upon her lover and friends in the gallery; which I thought nothing extraordinary, because it was never known that any lion had been mistaken. But, however, we were all disappointed, for the lion lifted up his right paw, which was the fatal sign, and advancing forward, seized her by the arm, and began to tear it. The poor lady gave a terrible shriek, and cried out, 'The lion is just, I am no virgin! Oh! Sappho! Sappho!' She could say no more, for the lion gave her the *coup de grace* by a squeeze in the throat, and she expired at his feet. The keeper dragged away her body, to feed the animal after the company should be gone: for the parish lion never used to eat in public. After a little pause, another lady came on toward the lion in the same manner as the former. We observed the beast smell her with diligence. He scratched both her hands with lifting them to his nose, and laying one of his claws on her bosom drew blood; however, he let her go, and at the same time turned from her with a sort of contempt, at which she was not a little mortified, and retired with some confusion to her friends in the gallery. Methought the whole company immediately understood the meaning of this; that the easiness of the lady had suffered her to admit certain imprudent and dangerous familiarities, bordering too much upon what is criminal; neither was it sure whether the lover then present had not some sharers with him in those freedoms, of which a lady can never be too sparing.

"This happened to be an extraordinary day; for a third lady came into the den laughing loud, playing with her fan, tossing her head, and smiling round on the young fellows in the gallery. However, the lion leaped on her with great fury, and we gave her for gone; but on a sudden he let go his hold, and turned from her as if he was nauseated; then gave her a lash with his tail; after which she returned to the gallery; not the least out of countenance: and this, it seems, was the usual treatment of coquettes.

"I thought we had seen enough; but my friend would needs have us go and visit one or two lions in the city. We called at two or three dens where they happened not to shew; but we generally found half a score young girls, between eight and eleven years old, playing with each lion, sitting on his back, and putting their hands into his mouth; some of them would now and then get a scratch, but we always discovered, upon examining, that they had been hoidening with the young apprentices. One of them was calling to a pretty girl, about twelve years old, who stood by us in the gallery, to come down to the lion, and, upon her refusal, said, 'Ah! Miss Betty, we could never get you to come near the lion, since you played at hoop and hide with my brother in the garret.'

"We followed a couple, with the wedding-folks, going to the church of St. Mary-Axe. The lady, though well stricken in years, extremely crooked and deformed, was dressed out beyond the gaiety of fifteen; having jumbled together, as I imagined, all the tawdry remains of aunts, godmothers, and grandmothers, for some generations past. One of the neighbours whispered me, that she was an old maid, and had the clearest reputation of any in the parish. There is nothing strange in that, thought I; but was much surprised when I observed afterward, that she went toward the lion with distrust and concern. The beast was lying down; but, upon sight of her, snuffed up his nose two or three times, and then, giving the sign of death, proceeded instantly to execution. In the midst of her agonies, she was heard to name the words Italy and artifices with the utmost horror, and several repeated execrations, and at last concluded, 'Fool that I was, to put so much confidence in the toughness of my skin!'

"The keeper immediately set all in order again for another customer, which happened to be a famous prude, whom her parents, after long threatenings and much persuasion, had, with the extremest difficulty, prevailed on to accept a young handsome goldsmith, who might have pretended to five times her fortune. The fathers and mothers in the neighbourhood used to quote her for an example to their daughters; her elbows were riveted to her sides, and her whole person so ordered, as to inform everybody that she was afraid they should touch her. She only dreaded to approach the lion, because it was a he one, and abhorred to think a male animal should presume to breathe on her. The sight of a man at twenty yards' distance, made her draw back her head. She always sat upon the farther corner of the chair, although there were six chairs between her and her lover, and with the door wide open, and her little sister in the room. She was never saluted but at the tip of the ear; and her father had much ado to make her dine without her gloves, when there was a man at table. She entered the den with some fear, which we took to proceed from the height of her modesty, offended at the sight of so many men in the gallery. The lion, beholding her at a distance, immediately gave the deadly sign, at which the poor creature (methinks I see her still!) miscarried in a fright before us all. The lion seemed to be as much surprised as we, and gave her time to make her confession; 'That she was five months gone by the foreman of her father's shop; and that this was her third big belly:' and when her friends asked, why she would venture the trial? she said, Her nurse told her, that a lion would never hurt a woman with child." Upon this I immediately awaked, and could not help wishing, that the deputy censors of my late institution, were endued with the same instinct as these parish lions.

THE TATLER, No. XX.*

Ingenuas didicisse fideliter artes
Emollit mores.   OVID.

TUESDAY, MARCH 6, 1710–11.

From my own Apartment in Channel-row, March 5.

THOSE inferior duties of life, which the French call *les petites morales*, or the smaller morals, are, with us,

---

* Several of the maxims so humorously exemplified in this Tatler, occur in Swift's Treatise of Good Breeding.

distinguished by the name of good manners, or breeding. This I look upon, in the general notion of it, to be a sort of artificial good sense, adapted to the meanest capacities, and introduced to make mankind easy in their commerce with each other. Low and little understandings, without some rules of this kind, would be perpetually wandering into a thousand indecencies and irregularities in behaviour; and in their ordinary conversation, fall into the same boisterous familiarities, that one observes among them when a debauch has quite taken away the use of their reason. In other instances it is odd to consider, that, for want of common discretion, the very end of good breeding is wholly perverted; and civility, intended to make us easy, is employed in laying chains and fetters upon us, in debarring us of our wishes, and in crossing our most reasonable desires and inclinations. This abuse reigns chiefly in the country, as I found, to my vexation, when I was last there, in a visit I made to a neighbour about two miles from my cousin. As soon as I entered the parlour, they put me into the great chair that stood close by a huge fire, and kept me there by force, until I was almost stifled. Then a boy came in a great hurry to pull off my boots, which I in vain opposed, urging that I must return soon after dinner. In the meantime, the good lady whispered her eldest daughter, and slipped a key into her hand; the girl returned instantly with a beer glass half full of *aqua mirabilis* and syrup of gilly-flowers. I took as much as I had a mind for, but madam avowed that I should drink it off; for she was sure it would do me good after coming out of the cold air; and I was forced to obey, which absolutely took away my stomach. When dinner came in, I had a mind to sit at a distance from the fire; but they told me it was as much as my life was worth, and set me with my back against it. Although my appetite was quite gone, I was resolved to force down as much as I could, and desired the leg of a pullet. "Indeed, Mr. Bickerstaff, (says the lady,) you must eat a wing, to oblige me;" and so put a couple upon my plate. I was persecuted at this rate during the whole meal; as often as I called for small-beer, the master tipped the wink, and the servant brought me a brimmer of October. Some time after dinner, I ordered my cousin's man, who came with me, to get ready the horses; but it was resolved I should not stir that night; and when I seemed pretty much bent upon going, they ordered the stable door to be locked, and the children hid my cloak and boots. The next question was, What would I have for supper? I said, I never eat anything at night: but was at last, in my own defence, obliged to name the first thing that came into my head. After three hours spent chiefly in apologies for my entertainment, insinuating to me, "That this was the worst time of the year for provisions; that they were at a great distance from any market; that they were afraid I should be starved; and that they knew they kept me to my loss;" the lady went, and left me to her husband; for they took special care I should never be alone. As soon as her back was turned, the little misses ran backward and forward every moment, and constantly as they came in, or went out, made a curtsey directly at me, which, in good manners, I was forced to return with a bow, and "Your humble servant, pretty miss." Exactly at eight the mother came up, and discovered, by the redness of her face, that supper was not far off. It was twice as large as the dinner, and my persecution doubled in proportion. I desired, at my usual hour, to go to my repose, and was conducted to my chamber, by the gentleman, his lady, and the whole train of children. They importuned me to drink something before I went to bed; and, upon my refusing, left at last a bottle of stingo, as they called it, for fear I should wake, and be thirsty in the night. I was forced in the morning to rise and dress myself in the dark, because they would not suffer my kinsman's servant to disturb me at the hour I desired to be called. I was now resolved to break through all measures to get away; and, after sitting down to a monstrous breakfast of cold beef, mutton, neat's tongues, venison-pasty, and stale beer, took leave of the family. But the gentleman would needs see me part of the way, and carry me a short cut through his own ground, which he told me would save half a mile's riding. This last piece of civility had like to have cost me dear, being once or twice in danger of my neck, by leaping over his ditches, and at last forced to alight in the dirt, when my horse, having slipped his bridle, ran away, and took us up more than an hour to recover him again.

It is evident, that none of the absurdities I met with in this visit proceeded from an ill intention, but from a wrong judgment of complaisance, and a misapplication in the rules of it. I cannot so easily excuse the more refined critics upon behaviour, who having professed no other study, are yet infinitely defective in the most material parts of it. Ned Fashion has been bred all his life about court, and understands to a tittle all the punctilios of a drawing-room. He visits most of the fine women near St. James's, and, upon every occasion, says the civillest and softest things to them of any breathing. To Mr. Le Sack * he owes an easy slide in his bow, and a graceful manner of coming into a room: but, in some other cases, he is very far from being a

---

* A famous dancing-master in those days.

well-bred person. He laughs at men of far superior understanding to his own for not being as well dressed as himself; despises all his acquaintance who are not of quality, and in public places has, on that account, often avoided taking notice of some among the best speakers of the House of Commons. He rails strenuously at both universities before the members of either; and is never heard to swear an oath, and break in upon religion and morality, except in the company of divines. On the other hand, a man of right sense has all the essentials of good breeding, although he may be wanting in the forms of it. Horatio has spent most of his time at Oxford: he has a great deal of learning, an agreeable wit, and as much modesty as may serve to adorn, without concealing, his other good qualities. In that retired way of living, he seems to have formed a notion of human nature, as he has found it described in the writings of the greatest men, not as he is likely to meet with it in the common course of life. Hence it is that he gives no offence, but converses with great deference, candour, and humanity. His bow, I must confess, is somewhat awkward; but then he has an extensive, universal, and unaffected knowledge, which may perhaps a little excuse him. He would make no extraordinary figure at a ball; but I can assure the ladies, in his behalf, and for their own consolation, that he has writ better verses on the sex than any man now living, and is preparing such a poem for the press, as will transmit their praises, and his own, to many generations.

THE TATLER, No. XXIV.*

*O Lycida, vivi pervenimus, advena nostri
(Quod nunquam veriti sumus) ut possessor agelli
Diceret, Hæc mea sunt, veteres migrate coloni.*
                                              VIRG.

THURSDAY, MARCH 15, 1710–11.

From my own Apartment in Channel-row, March 14.

THE dignity and distinction of men of wit is seldom enough considered, either by themselves or others; their own behaviour, and the usage they meet with, being generally very much of a piece. I have at this time in my hands an alphabetical list of the *beaux esprits* about this town, four or five of whom have made the proper use of their genius, by gaining the esteem of the best and greatest men, and by turning it to their own advantage in some establishment of their fortunes, however unequal to their merit; others, satisfying themselves with the honour of having access to great tables, and of being subject to the call of every man of quality, who, upon occasion, wants one to say witty things for the diversion of the company. This treatment never moves my indignation so much as when it is practised by a person who, though he owes his own rise purely to the reputation of his parts, yet appears to be as much ashamed of it, as a rich city knight to be denominated from the trade he was first apprenticed to; and affects the air of a man born to his titles, and consequently above the character of a wit or a scholar. If those who possess great endowments of the mind would set

---

* "Little Harrison came to me, and begged me to dictate a paper to him, which I was forced in charity to do."—Journal to Stella, March 14, 1710–11.

a just value upon themselves, they would think no man's acquaintance whatsoever a condescension, nor accept it from the greatest upon unworthy or ignominious terms. I know a certain lord, that has often invited a set of people, and proposed for their diversion a buffoon player, and an eminent poet, to be of the party; and, which was yet worse, thought them both sufficiently recompensed by the dinner and the honour of his company. This kind of insolence is risen to such a height, that I myself was the other day sent to by a man with a title, whom I had never seen, desiring the favour that I should dine with him and half a dozen of his select friends. I found afterward, the footman had told my maid below stairs, that my lord, having a mind to be merry, had resolved, right or wrong, to send for honest Isaac. I was sufficiently provoked with the message; however, I gave the fellow no other answer than that " I believed he had mistaken the person; for I did not remember that his lord had ever been introduced to me." I have reason to apprehend that this abuse has been owing rather to a meanness of spirit in men of parts, than to the natural pride or ignorance of their patrons. Young students, coming up to town from the places of their education, are dazzled with the grandeur they everywhere meet; and, making too much haste to distinguish their parts, instead of waiting to be desired and caressed, are ready to pay their court at any rate to a great man, whose name they have seen in a public paper, or the frontispiece of a dedication. It has not always been thus; wit in polite ages has ever begot either esteem or fear: the hopes of being celebrated, or the dread of being stigmatized, procured a universal respect and awe for the persons of such as were allowed to have the power of distributing fame or infamy where they pleased. Aretine had all the princes of Europe his tributaries :* and when any of them had committed a folly that laid them open to his censure, they were forced, by some present extraordinary, to compound for his silence; of which there is a famous instance on record. When Charles the Fifth had miscarried in his African expedition, which was looked upon as the weakest undertaking of that great Emperor, he sent Aretine a gold chain, who made some difficulty of accepting it, saying, "It was too small a present, in all reason, for so great a folly." For my own part, in this point I differ from him; and never could be prevailed upon, by any valuable consideration, to conceal a fault or a folly, since I first took the censorship upon me.

THE TATLER, No. XXVIII.†

Morte carent animæ; semperque, priore relicta
Sede, novis domibus vivunt habitantque receptæ.
Ipse ego (nam memini) Trojani tempore belli
Panthoides Euphorbus eram———   OVID. Met.

SATURDAY, MARCH 24, 1710-11.

From my own Apartment, March 22.

MY other correspondents will excuse me if I give the precedency to a lady, whose letter, among many more, is just come to hand.

---

* There is a letter of his extant, in which he makes his boast that he had laid the Sophi of Persia under contribution.—Spectator, No. 23.

† From some particulars in this paper, it would seem to be the production of Harrison, with some hints from Swift.

"Dear Isaac,

"I burn with impatience to know what and who you are. The curiosity of my whole sex is fallen upon me, and has kept me waking these three nights. I have dreamed often of you within this fortnight, and every time you appeared in a different form. As you value my repose, tell me in which of them I am to be

"Sylvia,

"Your admirer."

It is natural for a man who receives a favour of this kind from an unknown fair, to frame immediately some idea of her person, which, being suited to the opinion we have of our own merit, is commonly as beautiful and perfect as the most lavish imagination can furnish out. Strongly possessed with these notions, I have read over Sylvia's billet; and notwithstanding the reserve I have had upon this matter, am resolved to go a much greater length than I yet ever did, in making myself known to the world, and in particular to my charming correspondent. In order to it I must premise, that the person produced as mine in the play-house last winter did in nowise appertain to me. It was such a one, however, as agreed well with the impression my writings had made, and served the purpose I intended it for; which was to continue the awe and reverence due to the character I was vested with, and, at the same time, to let my enemies see how much I was the delight and favourite of this town. This innocent imposture, which I have all along taken care to carry on, as it then was of some use, has since been of regular service to me, and, by being mentioned in one of my papers, effectually recovered my egoity out of the hands of some gentlemen who endeavoured to wrest it from me. This is saying, in short, what I am not: what I am, and have been for many years, is next to be explained. Here it will not be improper to remind Sylvia, that there was formerly such a philosopher as Pythagoras, who, among other doctrines, taught the transmigration of souls; which if she sincerely believes, she will not be much startled at the following relation.

I will not trouble her, nor my other readers, with the particulars of all the lives I have successively passed through since my first entrance into mortal being, which is now many centuries ago. It is enough that I have in every one of them opposed myself with the utmost resolution to the follies and vices of the several ages I have been acquainted with; that I have often rallied the world into good manners, and kept the greatest princes in awe of my satire. There is one circumstance which I shall not omit, though it may seem to reflect on my character; I mean, that infinite love of change which has ever appeared in the disposal of my existence. Since the days of the Emperor Trajan, I have not been confined to the same person for twenty years together; but have passed from one abode to another much quicker than the Pythagorean system generally allows. By this means I have seldom had a body to myself, but have lodged up and down wherever I found a genius suitable to my own. In this manner I continued some time with the top wit of France; at another with that of Italy, who had a statue erected to his memory in Rome. Toward the end of the seventeenth century I set out for England; but the gentleman I came over in dying as soon as he got to shore, I was obliged to look out again for a new habitation. It was not long before I met with one to my mind; for, having mixed myself invisibly with the literati of this kingdom, I found it was unanimously agreed among them, That nobody was endued with greater talents than Hiereus;* or, consequently, would be better pleased with my company. I slipped down his throat one night as he was fast asleep; and the next morning, as soon as he awaked, he fell to writing a treatise that was received with great applause, though he had the modesty not to set his name to that nor to any other of our productions. Some time after, he published a paper of predictions, which were translated into several languages, and alarmed some of the greatest princes in Europe. To these he prefixed the name of Isaac Bickerstaff, Esq., which I have been extremely fond of ever since, and have taken care that most of the writings I have been concerned in should be distinguished by it; though I must observe, that there have been many counterfeits imposed upon the public by this means. This extraordinary man being called out of the kingdom by affairs of his own, I resolved, however, to continue somewhat longer in a country where my works had been so well received, and accordingly bestowed myself with Hilario.† His natural wit, his lively turn of humour, and great penetration into human nature, easily determined me to this choice, the effects of which were soon after produced in this paper, called the Tatler. I know not how it happened, but in less than two years' time Hilario grew weary of my company, and gave me warning to be gone. In the height of my resentment, I cast my eyes on a young fellow, of no extraordinary qualifications,‡ whom for that very reason I had the more pride in taking under my direction, and enabling him by some means or other to carry on the work I was before engaged in. Lest he should grow too

---

* Swift. † Mr. Steele. ‡ Mr. Harrison.

vain upon this encouragement, I to this day keep him under due mortification. I seldom reside with him when any of his friends are at leisure to receive me, by whose hands, however, he is duly supplied. As I have passed through many scenes of life, and a long series of years, I choose to be considered in the character of an old fellow, and take care that those under my influence should speak consonantly to it. This account, I presume, will give no small consolation to Sylvia, who may rest assured that Isaac Bickerstaff is to be seen in more forms than she dreamt of; out of which variety she may choose what is most agreeable to her fancy. On Tuesdays, he is sometimes a black proper young gentleman, with a mole on his left cheek.* On Thursdays, a decent well-looking man, of a middle stature, long flaxen hair, and a florid complexion.† On Saturdays, he is somewhat of the shortest, and may be known from others of that size by talking in a low voice, and passing through the streets without much precipitation.‡

---

* Swift.   † Perhaps Mr. Henley.   ‡ Harrison himself.

THE SPECTATOR, No. L.*

FRIDAY, APRIL 27, 1711.

Nunquam aliud natura, aliud sapientia dixit.
                                    JUV. Sat. xiv. 321.
Good sense and nature always speak the same.

WHEN the four Indian kings were in this country about a twelvemonth ago, I often mixed with the rabble, and followed them a whole day together, being wonderfully struck with the sight of everything that is new or uncommon. I have, since their departure, employed a friend to make many inquiries of their landlord the upholsterer, relating to their manners and conversation, as also concerning the remarks which they made in this country; for, next to forming a right notion of such strangers, I should be desirous of learning what ideas they have conceived of us.

The upholsterer, finding my friend very inquisitive about these his lodgers, brought him some time since a little bundle of papers, which he assured him were written by King Sa Ga Yean Qua Rash Tow, and, as he supposes, left behind him by some mistake. These papers are now translated, and contain abundance of very odd observations, which I find this little fraternity of kings made during their stay in the isle of Great Britain. I shall present my

---

* "The Spectator is written by Steele, with Addison's help; it is often very pretty. Yesterday it was made of a noble hint I gave him long ago for his Tatlers, about an Indian supposed to write his Travels into England. I repent he ever had it. I intended to have written a book on that subject. I believe he has spent it all in one paper; and all the under hints there are mine too; but I never see him or Addison."—Journal to Stella, April 28, 1711.

reader with a short specimen of them in this paper, and may perhaps communicate more to him hereafter. In the article of London are the following words, which, without doubt, are meant of the church of St. Paul :—

"On the most rising part of the town there stands a huge house, big enough to contain the whole nation of which I am king. Our good brother E Tow O Koam, king of the Rivers, is of opinion it was made by the hands of that great God to whom it is consecrated. The kings of Granajah and of the Six Nations believe that it was created with the earth, and produced on the same day with the sun and moon. But for my own part, by the best information that I could get of this matter, I am apt to think that this prodigious pile was fashioned into the shape it now bears by several tools and instruments, of which they have a wonderful variety in this country. It was probably at first a huge misshapen rock that grew upon the top of the hill, which the natives of the country, (after having cut it into a kind of regular figure,) bored and hollowed with incredible pains and industry, till they had wrought it into all those beautiful vaults and caverns into which it is divided at this day. As soon as this rock was thus curiously scooped to their liking, a prodigious number of hands must have been employed in chipping the outside of it, which is now as smooth as the surface of a pebble; and is in several places hewn out into pillars, that stand like the trunks of so many trees bound about the top with garlands of leaves. It is probable that when this great work was begun, which must have been many hundred years ago, there was some religion among this people; for they give it the name of a temple, and have a tradition that it was designed for men to pay their devotion in. And indeed there are several reasons which make us think that the natives of this country had formerly among them some sort of worship; for they set apart every seventh day as sacred; but, upon my going into one of these holy houses on that day, I could not observe any circumstances of devotion in their behaviour. There was indeed a man in black, who was mounted above the rest, and seemed to utter something with a great deal of vehemence; but as for those underneath him, instead of paying their worship to the deity of the place, they were most of them bowing and curtseying to one another, and a considerable number of them fast asleep.

"The queen of the country appointed two men to attend us, that had enough of our language to make themselves understood in some few particulars. But we soon perceived these two were great enemies to one another, and did not always agree in the same story. We could make shift to gather out of one of them, that this island was very much infested with a monstrous kind of animals, in the shape of men, called Whigs; and he often told us that he hoped we should meet with none of them in our way, for that, if we did, they would be apt to knock us down for being kings.

"Our other interpreter used to talk very much of a kind of animal called a Tory, that was as great a monster as the Whig, and would treat us ill for being foreigners. These two creatures, it seems, are born with a secret antipathy to one another, and engage when they meet as naturally as the elephant and the rhinoceros. But as we saw none of either of these species, we are apt to think that our guides deceived us with misrepresentations and fictions, and amused us with an account of such monsters as are not really in their country. These particulars we made a shift to pick out from the discourse of our interpreters; which we put together as well as we could, being able to understand but here and there a word of what they said, and afterwards making up the meaning of it among ourselves. The men of the country are very cunning and ingenious in handicraft works, but withal so very idle, that we often saw young lusty raw-boned fellows carried up and down the streets in little covered rooms by a couple of porters, who are hired for that service. Their dress is likewise very barbarous; for they almost strangle themselves about the neck, and bind their bodies with many ligatures, that we are apt to think are the occasion of several distempers among them, which our country is entirely free from. Instead of those beautiful feathers with which we adorn our heads, they often buy up a monstrous bush of hair, which covers their heads, and falls down in a large fleece below the middle of their backs; with which they walk up and down the streets, and are as proud of it as if it was of their own growth.

"We were invited to one of their public diversions, where we hoped to have seen the great men of their country running down a stag, or pitching a bar, that we might have discovered who were the persons of the greatest abilities among them ; but, instead of that, they conveyed us into a huge room lighted up with abundance of candles, where this lazy people sat still above three hours, to see several feats of ingenuity performed by others, who it seems were paid for it.

"As for the women of the country, not being able to talk with them, we could only make our remarks upon them at a distance. They let the hair of their heads grow to a great length ; but as the men make a great show with heads of hair that are none of their own, the women, who they say have very fine heads of hair, tie it up in a knot and cover it from being seen. The women look like angels; and would be more beautiful than the sun, were it not for little black spots that are apt to break out in their faces, and sometimes rise in very odd figures. I have observed that those little blemishes wear off very soon; but when they disappear in one part of the face, they are very apt to break out in another, insomuch, that I have seen a spot upon the forehead in the afternoon, which was upon the chin in the morning."

The author then proceeds to shew the absurdity of breeches and petticoats; with many other curious observations, which I shall reserve for another occasion. I cannot, however, conclude this paper without taking notice, that amidst these wild remarks there now and then appears something very reasonable. I cannot likewise forbear observing, that we are all guilty, in some measure, of the same narrow way of thinking which we meet with in this abstract of the Indian journal, when we fancy the customs, dresses, and manners of other countries are ridiculous and extravagant, if they do not resemble those of our own.

In the Spectator, No. 575, August 2, 1714, the following article was proposed by Dr. Swift:—

"The following question is started by one of the schoolmen: Supposing the body of the earth were a great ball or mass of the finest sand, and that a single grain or particle of this sand should be annihilated every thousand years. Supposing, then, that you had it in your choice to be happy all the while this prodigious mass of sand was consuming by this slow method, until there was not a grain of it left, on condition you were to be miserable for ever after;

or supposing that you might be happy for ever after, on condition you would be miserable until the whole mass of sand were thus annihilated at the rate of one sand in a thousand years; which of these two cases would you make your choice?"

---o---

THE GUARDIAN, No. XCVI.

AN ESSAY ON NATIONAL REWARDS;

BEING A PROPOSAL FOR BESTOWING THEM ON A PLAN MORE DURABLE AND RESPECTABLE.*

Cuncti adsint, meritæque expectent præmia palmæ.
VIRG.

THERE is no maxim in politics more indisputable, than that a nation should have many honours to reserve for those who do national services. This raises emulation, cherishes public merit, and inspires every one with an ambition which promotes the good of his country. The less expensive these honours are to the public, the more still do they turn to its advantage.

The Romans abounded with these little honorary rewards, that, without conferring wealth and riches, gave only place and distinction to the person who

---

* This paper is usually attributed to Swift, but has been retained by the editor of the 4to edition of Addison's works. Addison's Dissertation on Medals seems to justify this resumption, as well as the allusion in the paper to a recent communication with the Lord Treasurer Godolphin.

received them. An oaken garland, to be worn on festivals and public ceremonies, was the glorious recompense of one who had covered a citizen in battle. A soldier would not only venture his life for a mural crown, but think the most hazardous enterprise sufficiently repaid by so noble a donation.

But, among all honorary rewards which are neither dangerous nor detrimental to the donor, I remember none so remarkable as the titles which are bestowed by the Emperor of China. "These are never given to any subject," says Monsieur Le Comte, "till the subject is dead. If he has pleased his emperor to the last, he is called in all public memorials by the title which the emperor confers on him after his death, and his children take their ranks accordingly." This keeps the ambitious subject in a perpetual dependence, making him always vigilant and active, and in everything conformable to the will of his sovereign.

There are no honorary rewards among us which are more esteemed by the persons who receive them, and are cheaper to the prince, than the giving of medals. But there is something in the modern manner of celebrating a great action in medals, which makes such a reward much less valuable than it was among the Romans. There is generally but one coin stamped upon the occasion, which is made a present to the person who is celebrated on it. By this means the whole fame is in his own custody. The applause that is bestowed upon him is too much limited and confined. He is in possession of an honour which the world perhaps knows nothing of. He may be a great man in his own family; his wife and children may see the monument of an exploit, which the public in a little time is a stranger to. The Romans took a quite different method in this particular. Their medals were their current money.

When an action deserved to be recorded on a coin, it was stamped perhaps upon a hundred thousand pieces of money, like our shillings or halfpence, which were issued out of the mint, and became current. This method published every noble action to advantage, and, in a short space of time, spread through the whole Roman empire. The Romans were so careful to preserve the memory of great events upon their coins, that when any particular piece of money grew very scarce, it was often re-coined by a succeeding emperor, many years after the death of the emperor to whose honour it was first struck.

A friend of mine drew up a project of this kind during the late ministry, which would then have been put in execution, had it not been too busy a time for thoughts of that nature. As this project has been very much talked of by the gentleman abovementioned to men of the greatest genius as well as quality, I am informed there is now a design on foot for executing the proposal which was then made, and that we shall have several farthings and halfpence charged on the reverse with many of the glorious particulars of her Majesty's reign. This is one of those arts of peace which may very well deserve to be cultivated, and which may be of great use to posterity.

As I have in my possession the copy of the paper abovementioned, which was delivered to the late Lord Treasurer,* I shall here give the public a sight of it; for I do not question but that the curious part of my readers will be very well pleased to see so much matter, and so many useful hints upon this subject, laid together in so clear and concise a manner.—

---

* Earl of Godolphin.

"The English have not been so careful as other polite nations to preserve the memory of their great actions and events on medals. Their subjects are few, their mottoes and devices mean, and the coins themselves not numerous enough to spread among the people, or descend to posterity.

"The French have outdone us in these particulars, and, by the establishment of a society for the invention of proper inscriptions and designs, have the whole history of their present King in a regular series of medals.

"They have failed, as well as the English, in coining so small a number of each kind, and those of such costly metals, that each species may be lost in a few ages, and is at present nowhere to be met with but in the cabinets of the curious.

"The ancient Romans took the only effectual method to disperse and preserve their medals, by making them their current money.

"Everything glorious or useful, as well in peace as war, gave occasion to a different coin. Not only an expedition, victory, or triumph, but the exercise of a solemn devotion, the remission of a duty or tax, a new temple, sea-port, or highway, were transmitted to posterity after this manner.

"The greatest variety of devices are on their copper money, which have most of the designs that are to be met with on the gold and silver, and several peculiar to that metal only. By this means they were dispersed into the remotest corners of the empire, came into the possession of the poor as well as the rich, and were in no danger of perishing in the hands of those that might have melted down coins of a more valuable metal.

"Add to all this, that the designs were invented by men of genius, and executed by a decree of the senate.

"It is therefore proposed:

"1. That the English farthings and halfpence be recoined upon the Union of the two nations.

"2. That they bear devices and inscriptions alluding to all the most remarkable parts of her Majesty's reign.

"3. That there be a society established for the finding out of proper subjects, inscriptions, and devices.

"That no subject, inscription, or device, be stamped without the approbation of this society; nor, if it be thought proper, without the authority of the Privy-council.

"By this means, medals, that are at present only a dead treasure, or mere curiosities, will be of use in the ordinary commerce of life, and at the same time perpetuate the glories of her Majesty's reign, reward the labours of her greatest subjects, keep alive in the people a gratitude for public services, and excite the emulation of posterity. To these generous purposes nothing can so much contribute as medals of this kind, which are of undoubted authority, of necessary use and observation, not perishable by time, nor confined to any certain place; properties not to be found in books, statues, pictures, buildings, or any other monuments of illustrious actions."

THE INTELLIGENCER, No. I.*

It may be said, without offence to other cities of much greater consequence to the world, that our town of Dublin does not want its due proportion of folly and vice, both native and imported; and as to those imported, we have the advantage to receive them last, and consequently, after our happy manner, to improve and refine upon them.

But because there are many effects of folly and vice among us, whereof some are general, others confined to smaller numbers, and others again perhaps to a few individuals, there is a society lately established, who, at great expense, have erected an office of intelligence, from which they are to receive weekly information of all important events and singularities which this famous metropolis can furnish. Strict injunctions are given to have the truest information; in order to which, certain qualified persons are employed to attend upon duty in their several posts; some at the play-house, others in churches; some at balls, assemblies, coffeehouses, and meetings for quadrille; some at the several courts of justice, both spiritual and temporal; some at the college, some upon my lord mayor and aldermen in their public affairs; lastly, some to converse with favourite chambermaids, and to frequent those alehouses and brandy-shops where the footmen of great families meet in a morning; only the barracks and parliament-house are excepted; because we have yet found no *enfans perdus* bold enough to venture

---

* These Numbers are extracted from a periodical paper, published at Dublin, by Sheridan, with the occasional assistance of his illustrious friend.

their persons at either. Out of these and some other storehouses, we hope to gather materials enough to inform, or divert, or correct, or vex the town.

But as facts, passages, and adventures of all kinds, are likely to have the greatest share in our paper, whereof we cannot always answer for the truth; due care shall be taken to have them applied to feigned names, whereby all just offence will be removed; for if none be guilty, none will have cause to blush or be angry; if otherwise, then the guilty person is safe for the future upon his present amendment, and safe for the present from all but his own conscience.

There is another resolution taken among us, which I fear will give a greater and more general discontent, and is of so singular a nature that I have hardly confidence enough to mention it, although it be absolutely necessary by way of apology for so bold and unpopular an attempt. But so it is, that we have taken a desperate counsel, to produce into the world every distinguished action either of justice, prudence, generosity, charity, friendship, or public spirit, which comes well attested to us. And although we shall neither here be so daring as to assign names, yet we shall hardly forbear to give some hints, that perhaps, to the great displeasure of such deserving persons, may endanger a discovery. For we think that even virtue itself should submit to such a mortification, as by its visibility and example will render it more useful to the world. But, however, the readers of these papers need not be in pain of being overcharged with so dull and ungrateful a subject. And yet who knows, but such an occasion may be offered to us once in a year or two, after we have settled a correspondence round the kingdom.

But, after all our boast of materials sent us by

our several emissaries, we may probably soon fall short, if the town will not be pleased to lend us farther assistance toward entertaining itself. The world best knows its own faults and virtues, and whatever is sent shall be faithfully returned back, only a little embellished according to the custom of authors. We do therefore demand and expect continual advertisements in great numbers to be sent to the printer of this paper, who has employed a judicious secretary to collect such as may be most useful for the public.

And although we do not intend to expose our own persons by mentioning names, yet we are so far from requiring the same caution in our correspondents, that, on the contrary, we expressly charge and command them, in all facts they send us, to set down the names, titles, and places of abode, at length; together with a very particular description of the persons, dresses, dispositions, of the several lords, ladies, 'squires, madams, lawyers, gamesters, toupees, sots, wits, rakes, and informers, whom they shall have occasion to mention; otherwise it will not be possible for us to adjust our style to the different qualities and capacities of the persons concerned, and treat them with the respect or familiarity that may be due to their stations and characters, which we are determined to observe with the utmost strictness, that none may have cause to complain.

THE INTELLIGENCER, No. III.

————Ipse per omnes
Ibit personas, et turbam reddet in unam.

THE players having now almost done with the comedy called the Beggars' Opera for the season;

it may be no unpleasant speculation, to reflect a little upon this dramatic piece, so singular in the subject and manner, so much an original, and which has frequently given so very agreeable an entertainment.

Although an evil taste be very apt to prevail, both here and in London; yet there is a point, which whoever can rightly touch, will never fail of pleasing a very great majority; so great, that the dislikers out of dulness or affectation will be silent, and forced to fall in with the herd: the point I mean is, what we call humour; which, in its perfection, is allowed to be much preferable to wit; if it be not rather the most useful and agreeable species of it.

I agree with Sir William Temple, that the word is peculiar to our English tongue; but I differ from him in the opinion, that the thing itself is peculiar to the English nation, because the contrary may be found in many Spanish, Italian, and French productions; and particularly, whoever has a taste for true humour, will find a hundred instances of it in those volumes printed in France under the name of Le Theatre Italien; to say nothing of Rabelais, Cervantes, and many others.

Now I take the comedy, or farce, (or whatever name the critics will allow it,) called the Beggars' Opera, to excel in this article of humour; and upon that merit to have met with such prodigious success both here and in England.

As to poetry, eloquence, and music, which are said to have most power over the minds of men; it is certain that very few have a taste or judgment of the excellencies of the two former; and if a man succeed in either, it is upon the authority of those few judges, that lend their taste to the bulk of readers, who have none of their own. I am told there are as few good judges in music; and that among those who crowd the operas, nine in ten go thither merely out of curiosity, fashion, or affectation.

But a taste for humour is in some manner fixed to the very nature of man, and generally obvious to the vulgar; except upon subjects too refined, and superior to their understanding.

And as this taste of humour is purely natural, so is humour itself; neither is it a talent confined to men of wit or learning; for we observe it sometimes among common servants, and the meanest of the people, while the very owners are often ignorant of the gift they possess.

I know very well that this happy talent is contemptibly treated by critics, under the name of low humour or low comedy; but I know likewise that the Spaniards and Italians, who are allowed to have the most wit of any nations in Europe, do most excel in it, and do most esteem it.

By what disposition of the mind, what influence of the stars, or what situation of the climate, this endowment is bestowed upon mankind, may be a question fit for philosophers to discuss. It is certainly the best ingredient toward that kind of satire which is most useful, and gives the least offence; which, instead of lashing, laughs men out of their follies and vices; and is the character that gives Horace the preference to Juvenal.

And, although some things are too serious, solemn, or sacred, to be turned into ridicule, yet the abuses of them are certainly not; since it is allowed that corruptions in religion, politics, and law, may be proper topics for this kind of satire.

There are two ends that men propose in writing satire; one of them less noble than the other, as regarding nothing farther than the private satisfaction and pleasure of the writer; but without any view toward personal malice; the other is a public spirit, prompting men of genius and virtue to mend the world as far as they are able. And as both these ends are innocent, so the latter is highly commendable. With regard to the former, I demand, whether I have not as good a title to laugh as men have to be ridiculous; and to expose vice, as another has to be vicious. If I ridicule the follies and corruptions of a court, a ministry, or a senate, are they not amply paid by pensions, titles, and power, while I expect and desire no other reward, than that of laughing with a few friends in a corner? yet, if those who take offence think me in the wrong, I am ready to change the scene with them whenever they please.

But, if my design be to make mankind better, then I think it is my duty; at least, I am sure it is the interest of those very courts, and ministers, whose follies or vices I ridicule, to reward me for my good intention; for if it be reckoned a high point of wisdom to get the laughers on our side, it is much more easy, as well as wise, to get those on our side who can make millions laugh when they please.

My reason for mentioning courts and ministers, (whom I never think on but with the most profound veneration,) is, because an opinion obtains, that in the Beggars' Opera there appears to be some reflection upon courtiers and statesmen, whereof I am by no means a judge.*

It is true, indeed, that Mr. Gay, the author of

---

* Besides the general reflections on courts and courtiers, it is well known that the quarrelling scene between Peachum and Lockit was written in express ridicule of certain disputes among the ministers of the day, and accordingly excited the most ungovernable mirth among the audience.

this piece, has been somewhat singular in the course of his fortunes; for it has happened, that after fourteen years attending the court, with a large stock of real merit, a modest and agreeable conversation, a hundred promises, and five hundred friends, he has failed of preferment; and upon a very weighty reason. He lay under the suspicion of having written a libel, or lampoon, against a great minister.* It is true, that great minister was demonstratively convinced, and publicly owned his conviction, that Mr. Gay was not the author; but having lain under the suspicion, it seemed very just that he should suffer the punishment; because in this most reformed age, the virtues of a prime minister are no more to be suspected than the chastity of Cæsar's wife.

It must be allowed that the Beggars' Opera is not the first of Mr. Gay's works wherein he has been faulty with regard to courtiers and statesmen. For, to omit his other pieces, even in his fables, published within two years past, and dedicated to the Duke of Cumberland, for which he was promised a reward, he has been thought somewhat too bold upon the courtiers. And although it be highly probable he meant only the courtiers of former times, yet he acted unwarily, by not considering that the malignity of some people might misinterpret what he said to the disadvantage of present persons and affairs.

But I have now done with Mr. Gay as a politician; and shall consider him henceforward only as author of the Beggars' Opera, wherein he has, by a turn of humour entirely new, placed vices of all kinds in the strongest and most odious light; and thereby done eminent service both to religion and

---

* Sir Robert Walpole.

morality. This appears from the unparalleled success he has met with. All ranks, parties, and denominations of men, either crowding to see his opera, or reading it with delight in their closets; even ministers of state, whom he is thought to have most offended, (next to those whom the actors represent,) appearing frequently at the theatre, from a consciousness of their own innocence, and to convince the world how unjust a parallel malice, envy, and disaffection to the government, have made.

I am assured that several worthy clergymen in this city went privately to see the Beggars' Opera represented: and that the fleering coxcombs in the pit amused themselves with making discoveries, and spreading the names of those gentlemen round the audience.

I shall not pretend to vindicate a clergyman who would appear openly in his habit at the theatre, with such a vicious crew as might probably stand round him, at such comedies and profane tragedies as are often represented. Besides, I know very well, that persons of their function are bound to avoid the appearance of evil, or of giving cause of offence. But when the lords chancellors, who are keepers of the king's conscience; when the judges of the land, whose title is reverend; when ladies, who are bound by the rules of their sex to the strictest decency, appear in the theatre without censure; I cannot understand why a young clergyman, who comes concealed out of curiosity to see an innocent and moral play, should be so highly condemned; nor do I much approve the rigour of a great prelate, who said, "he hoped none of his clergy were there." I am glad to hear there are no weightier objections against that reverend body, planted in this city, and I wish there never may. But I should be very sorry that any of them should be so weak as to imitate a court chaplain* in England, who preached against the Beggars' Opera, which will probably do more good than a thousand sermons of so stupid, so injudicious, and so prostitute a divine.

In this happy performance of Mr. Gay's, all the characters are just, and none of them carried beyond nature, or hardly beyond practice. It discovers the whole system of that commonwealth, or that *imperium in imperio* of iniquity established among us, by which neither our lives nor our properties are secure, either in the highways, or in public assemblies, or even in our own houses. It shews the miserable lives, and the constant fate, of those abandoned wretches; for how little they sell their lives and souls; betrayed by their whores, their comrades, and the receivers and purchasers of those thefts and robberies. This comedy contains likewise a satire, which, without inquiring whether it affects the present age, may possibly be useful in times to come; I mean, where the author takes the occasion of comparing the common robbers of the public, and their several stratagems of betraying, undermining, and hanging each other, to the several arts of the politicians in times of corruption.

This comedy likewise exposes, with great justice, that unnatural taste for Italian music among us, which is wholly unsuitable to our northern climate, and the genius of the people, whereby we are overrun with Italian effeminacy and Italian nonsense. An old gentleman said to me, that many years ago, when the practice of an unnatural vice grew frequent in London, and many were prosecuted for it, he was sure it would be the forerunner of Italian operas and

---

* Dr. Thomas Herring, afterwards primate, then preacher at Lincoln's Inn.

singers; and then we should want nothing but stabbing, or poisoning, to make us perfect Italians.

Upon the whole, I deliver my judgment, that nothing but servile attachment to a party, affectation of singularity, lamentable dulness, mistaken zeal, or studied hypocrisy, can have the least reasonable objection against this excellent moral performance of the celebrated Mr. Gay.

THE INTELLIGENCER, No. XIX.

Sic vos non vobis vellera fertis, oves.

Not for yourselves, ye sheep, your fleeces grow.

Having, on the 12th of October last, received a letter signed ANDREW DEALER, *and* PATRICK PENNYLESS, *I believe the following* PAPER, *just come to my hands, will be a sufficient answer to it.*

SIR,   *County of Down, Dec.* 2, 1728.

I AM a country gentleman, and a member of Parliament, with an estate of about £1400 a-year; which, as a northern landlord, I receive from above two hundred tenants; and my lands having been let near twenty years ago, the rents, until very lately, were esteemed to be not above half value; yet, by the intolerable scarcity of silver, I lie under the greatest difficulties in receiving them, as well as paying my labourers, or buying anything necessary for my family, from tradesmen who are not able to be long out of their money. But the sufferings of me, and those of my rank, are trifles in comparison of what the meaner sort undergo: such as the buyers and sellers at fairs and markets; the shopkeepers in every town; and farmers in general; all those who travel with fish, poultry, pedlary-ware, and other conveniences to sell: but more especially handicraftsmen, who work for us by the day; and common labourers, whom I have already mentioned. Both these kinds of people I am forced to employ, until their wages amount to a double pistole, or a moidore, (for we hardly have any gold of lower value left us,) to divide it among themselves as they can: and this is generally done at an alehouse, or brandy shop: where, besides the cost of getting drunk, (which is usually the case,) they must pay tenpence, or a shilling, for changing their piece into silver, to some huckstering fellow, who follows that trade. But, what is infinitely worse, those poor men, for want of due payment, are forced to take up their oatmeal, and other necessaries of life, at almost double value; and consequently are not able to discharge half their score, especially under the scarceness of corn for two years past, and the melancholy disappointment of the present crop.

The causes of this, and a thousand other evils, are clear and manifest to you and all thinking men, although hidden from the vulgar: these indeed complain of hard times, the dearth of corn, the want of money, the badness of seasons; that their goods bear no price, and the poor cannot find work; but their weak reasonings never carry them to the hatred and contempt borne us by our neighbours and brethren, without the least grounds of provocation; who rejoice at our sufferings, although sometimes to their own disadvantage. They consider not the dead weight upon every beneficial branch of our trade; that half our revenues are annually sent to England; with many other grievances peculiar to this unhappy kingdom, which keeps us from enjoying the common benefits of mankind; as you and some other lovers of their country have so often observed, with such good inclinations, and so little effect.

It is true indeed, that under our circumstances in general, this complaint for the want of silver may appear as ridiculous, as for a man to be impatient about a cut finger, when he is struck with the plague: and yet a poor fellow going to the gallows may be allowed to feel the smart of wasps while he is upon Tyburn road. This misfortune is so urging and vexatious in every kind of small traffic, and so hourly pressing upon all persons in the country whatsoever, that a hundred inconveniences, of perhaps greater moment in themselves, have been tamely submitted to, with far less disquietude and murmur. And the case seems yet the harder, if it be true, what many skilful men assert, that nothing is more easy than a remedy; and, that the want of silver, in proportion to the little gold remaining among us, is altogether as unnecessary as it is inconvenient. A person of distinction assured me very lately, that, in discoursing with the lord-lieutenant* before his last return to England, his excellency said, "He had pressed the matter often, in proper time and place, and to proper persons; and could not see any difficulty of the least moment, that could prevent us from being made easy upon this article."

Whoever carries to England twenty-seven English shillings, and brings back one moidore of full weight, is a gainer of ninepence Irish: in a guinea, the advantage is threepence; and twopence in a pistole. The BANKERS, who are generally masters of all our gold and silver, with this advantage, have sent over as much of the latter as came into their hands. The

---

* The Lord Carteret.

value of one thousand moidores in silver would thus amount in clear profit to £37, 10s. The shopkeepers, and other traders, who go to London to buy goods, followed the same practice; by which we have been driven to this insupportable distress.

To a common thinker, it would seem, that nothing would be more easy than for the government to redress this evil, at any time they shall please. When the value of guineas was lowered in England from 21s. and 6d. to only 21s., the consequences to this kingdom were obvious and manifest to us all: and a sober man may be allowed at least to wonder, although he dare not complain, why a new regulation of coin among us was not then made; much more, why it has never been since. It would surely require no very profound skill in algebra to reduce the difference of ninepence in thirty shillings, or threepence in a guinea, to less than a farthing; and so small a fraction could be no temptation either to bankers, to hazard their silver at sea, or tradesmen to load themselves with it in their journeys to England. In my humble opinion, it would be no unseasonable condescension, if the government would graciously please to signify to the poor loyal Protestant subjects of Ireland, either that this miserable want of silver is not possibly to be remedied in any degree by the nicest skill in arithmetic: or else that it does not stand with the good pleasure of England to suffer any silver at all among us. In the former case, it would be madness to expect impossibilities; and, in the other, we must submit: for lives and fortunes are always at the mercy of the CONQUEROR.

The question has been often put in printed papers, by the DRAPIER and others, or perhaps by the same WRITER under different styles, why this kingdom should not be permitted to have a mint of its own, for the coinage of gold, silver, and copper; which is a power exercised by many bishops, and every petty prince in Germany? But this question has never been answered; nor the least application, that I have heard of, made to the Crown from hence for the grant of a public mint; although it stands upon record, that several cities and corporations here had the liberty of coining silver. I can see no reasons, why we alone, of all nations, are thus restrained, but such as I dare not mention: only thus far I may venture, that Ireland is the first imperial kingdom since Nimrod, which ever wanted power to coin their own money.

I know very well, that in England it is lawful for any subject to petition either the prince or the Parliament, provided it be done in a dutiful and regular manner: but what is lawful for a subject of Ireland, I profess I cannot determine: nor will I undertake that the printer shall not be prosecuted in a court of justice for publishing my wishes, that a poor shopkeeper might be able to change a guinea or a moidore when a customer comes for a crown's worth of goods. I have known less crimes punished with the utmost severity, under the title of disaffection. And I cannot but approve the wisdom of the ancients, who, after Astrea had fled from the earth, at least took care to provide three upright judges for hell. Men's ears among us are indeed grown so nice, that whoever happens to think out of fashion, in what relates to the welfare of this kingdom, dare not so much as complain of the toothache, lest our weak and busy dabblers in politics should be ready to swear against him for disaffection.

There was a method practised by Sir Ambrose Crawley, the great dealer in iron works, which I wonder the gentlemen of our country, under this great exigence, have not thought fit to imitate. In the several towns and villages where he dealt, and many miles round, he gave notes instead of money, (from twopence to twenty shillings,) which passed current in all shops and markets, as well as in houses where meat or drink was sold. I see no reason, why the like practice may not be introduced among us with some degree of success; or, at least, may not serve as a poor expedient in this our blessed age of paper; which, as it discharges all our greatest payments, may be equally useful in the smaller, and may just keep us alive, until an English act of Parliament shall forbid it.

I have been told, that among some of our poorest American colonies upon the continent, the people enjoy the liberty of cutting the little money among them into halves and quarters, for the conveniences of small traffic. How happy should we be in comparison of our present condition, if the like privilege were granted to us of employing the shears for want of a mint, upon our foreign gold, by clipping it into half-crowns, and shillings, and even lower denominations: for beggars must be content to live upon scraps; and it would be our felicity, that these scraps could never be exported to other countries while anything better was left.

If neither of these projects will avail, I see nothing left us but to truck and barter our goods, like the wild Indians, with each other, or with our too powerful neighbours; only with this disadvantage on our side, that the Indians enjoy the product of their own land; whereas the better half of ours is sent away, without so much as a recompense in bugles or glass in return.

It must needs be a very comfortable circumstance in the present juncture, that some thousand families are gone, are going, or preparing to go from hence, and settle themselves in America: the poorer sort for want of work; the farmer, whose beneficial bargains are now become a rack-rent too hard to be borne, and those who have any ready money, or can purchase any by the sale of their goods or leases, because they find their fortunes hourly decaying, that their goods will bear no price, and that few or none have any money to buy the very necessaries of life, are hastening to follow their departed neighbours. It is true, corn among us carries a very high price; but it is for the same reason, that rats and cats, and dead horses, have been often bought for gold in a town besieged.

There is a person of quality in my neighbourhood, who, twenty years ago, when he was just come to age, being unexperienced, and of a generous temper, let his lands, even as times went then, at a low rate to able tenants; and, consequently, by the rise of lands since that time, looked upon his estate to be set at half value; but numbers of these tenants, or their descendants, are now offering to sell their leases by cant,* even those which were for lives, some of them renewable for ever, and some fee-farms, which the landlord himself has bought in at half the price. they would have yielded seven years ago. And some leases let at the same time for lives, have been given up to him without any consideration at all.

This is the most favourable face of all things at present among us; I say, among us of the north, who were esteemed the only thriving people of the kingdom. And how far, and how soon, this misery and desolation may spread, it is easy to foresee.

The vast sums of money daily carried off by our

---

* Or auction.

numerous adventurers to America, have deprived us of our gold in these parts, almost as much as of our silver. And the good wives who come to our houses, offer us their pieces of linen, upon which their whole dependence lies, for so little profit, that it can neither half pay their rents, nor half support their families.

It is remarkable, that this enthusiasm spread among our northern people, of sheltering themselves in the continent of America, has no other foundation than their present insupportable condition at home. I have made all possible inquiries to learn what encouragement our people have met with, by any intelligence from those plantations, sufficient to make them undertake so tedious and hazardous a voyage in all seasons of the year, and so ill accommodated in their ships, that many of them have died miserably in their passage, but could never get one satisfactory answer. Somebody, they knew not who, had written letters to his friend or cousin from thence, inviting him by all means to come over; that it was a fine fruitful country, and to be held for ever at a penny an acre. But the truth of the fact is this: the English established in those colonies are in great want of men to inhabit that tract of ground which lies between them and the wild Indians, who are not reduced under their dominion. We read of some barbarous people, whom the Romans placed in their army for no other service than to blunt their enemies' swords, and afterward to fill up trenches with their dead bodies. And thus our people, who transport themselves, are settled into those interjacent tracts, as a screen against the insults of the savages; and many have as much land as they can clear from the woods, at a very reasonable rate, if they can afford to pay about a hundred years' purchase by their labour.

Now, beside the fox's reason,* which inclines all those who have already ventured thither to represent everything in a false light, as well for justifying their own conduct, as for getting companions in their misery, the governing people in those plantations have also wisely provided, that no letters shall be suffered to pass from thence hither, without being first viewed by the council; by which our people here are wholly deceived in the opinions they have of the happy condition of their friends gone before them. This was accidentally discovered some months ago by an honest man, who, having transported himself and family thither, and finding all things directly contrary to his hope, had the luck to convey a private note by a faithful hand to his relation here, entreating him not to think of such a voyage, and to discourage all his friends from attempting it. Yet this, although it be a truth well known, has produced very little effect; which is no manner of wonder; for, as it is natural to a man in a fever to turn often, although without any hope of ease; or, when he is pursued, to leap down a precipice, to avoid an enemy just at his back; so, men in the extremest degree of misery and want, will naturally fly to the first appearance of relief, let it be ever so vain or visionary.

You may observe, that I have very superficially touched the subject I began with, and with the utmost caution; for I know how criminal the least complaint has been thought, however seasonable or just or honestly intended, which has forced me to offer up my daily prayers, that it may never, at least in my time, be interpreted by inuendoes as a false, scandalous, seditious, and disaffected action, for a

---

* The fox, who, having lost his tail, would have persuaded the rest to cut off theirs.

man to roar under an acute fit of the gout; which, beside the loss and the danger, would be very inconvenient to one of my age, so severely afflicted with that distemper.

I wish you good success, but I can promise you little, in an ungrateful office you have taken up without the least view either to reputation or profit. Perhaps your comfort is, that none but villains and betrayers of their country can be your enemies. Upon which I have little to say, having not the honour to be acquainted with many of that sort; and therefore, as you may easily believe, am compelled to lead a very retired life.

I am, Sir,
Your most obedient humble servant,
A. NORTH.

PREFACE TO TEMPLE'S WORKS.

Sir William Temple having bequeathed to Swift the care and property of his Posthumous Works, he published, in 1700, "Letters written by Sir William Temple, Bart., and other Ministers of State, both at home and abroad; containing an Account of the most important Transactions that passed in Christendom, from 1665 to 1672: Reviewed by Sir William Temple some time before his death, and published by Jonathan Swift, Domestic Chaplain to his Excellency the Earl of Berkeley, one of the Lords Justices of Ireland." The publication was accompanied by the following Dedication and Preface.

---o---

DEDICATION*

TO THE TWO FIRST VOLUMES OF

SIR WILLIAM TEMPLE'S LETTERS.

To his most sacred Majesty, William the Third, King of England, Scotland, France, and Ireland, &c. These letters of Sir William Temple having been left to my care, they are most humbly presented to your Majesty, by

      Your Majesty's
        Most dutiful
          And obedient Subject,
              Jonathan Swift.

---

* "Neither this Dedication, nor tenderness for the man whom once he had loaded with confidence and fondness, revived in King William the remembrance of his promise. Swift awhile attended the Court, but soon found his solicitations hopeless."—Johnson.

PREFACE.

THE collection of the following letters is owing to the diligence of Mr. Thomas Downton, who was one of the secretaries during the whole time wherein they bear date; and it has succeeded very fortunately for the public, that there is contained in them an account of all the chief transactions and negotiations which passed in Christendom during the seven years wherein they are dated; as the war from Holland, which began in 1665; the treaty between his Majesty and the Bishop of Munster, with the issue of it; the French invasion of Flanders in the year 1667; the peace concluded between Spain and Portugal by the King's mediation; the treaty at Breda; the triple alliance; the peace at Aix-la-Chapelle, in the first part; and in the second part, the negotiations in Holland in consequence of those alliances, with the steps and degrees by which they came to decay; the journey and death of Madam; the seizure of Lorrain and his excellency's recalling; with the first unkindness between England and Holland, upon the yacht's transporting his lady and family; and the beginning of the second Dutch war in 1672. With these are intermixed several letters, familiar and pleasant.

I found the book among Sir William Temple's papers, with many others, wherewith I had the opportunity of being long conversant, having passed several years in his family.

I pretend no other part than the care that Mr. Downton's book should be correctly transcribed, and the letters placed in the order they were writ. I have also made some literal amendments, especially in the Latin, French, and Spanish; these I took care should be translated and printed in another column, for the use of such readers as may be unacquainted with the originals. Whatever fault there may be in the translation, I doubt I must answer for the greater part, and must leave the rest to those friends who were pleased to assist me. I speak only of the French and Latin; for the few Spanish translations I believe need no apology.

It is generally believed that this author has advanced our English tongue to as great a perfection as it can well bear; and yet how great a master he was of it, as I think, never appeared so much as it will in the following letters, wherein the style appears so very different, according to the difference of the persons to whom they were addressed; either men of business or idle, of pleasure or serious, of great or of less parts or abilities, in their several stations; so that one may discover the characters of most of those persons he writes to, from the style of his letters.

At the end of each volume is added a collection, copied by the same hand, of several letters to this ambassador, from the chief persons employed, either at home or abroad, in these transactions, and during six years' course of his negotiations; among which are many from the pensionary John de Witt, and all the writings of this kind that I know of, which remain of that minister, so renowned in his time.

It has been justly complained of as a defect among us, that the English tongue has produced no letters of any value; to supply which it has been the vein of late years, to translate several out of other languages, though I think with little success; yet among many advantages, which might recommend this sort of writing, it is certain that nothing is so capable of giving a true account of stories, as letters are; which describe actions while they are breathing, whereas all other relations are of actions past and dead; so as it has been observed, that the epistles of Cicero to Atticus give a better account of those times than is to be found in any other writer.

In the following letters the reader will everywhere discover the force and spirit of this author; but that which will most value them to the public, both at home and abroad, is, first, that the matters contained in them were the ground and foundation, whereon all the wars and invasions, as well as all the negotiations and treaties of peace in Christendom, have since been raised. And next, that they are written by a person who had so great a share in all those transactions and negotiations.

By residing in his family, I know the author has had frequent instances from several great persons, both at home and abroad, to publish some memoirs of those affairs and transactions, which are the subject of the following papers; and particularly of the treaties of the triple alliance, and those of Aix-la-Chapelle; but his usual answer was, that whatever memoirs he had written of those times and negotiations were burnt; however, that perhaps after his death some papers might come out, wherein there would be some account of them. By which, as he often told me, he meant these letters.

I had begun to fit them for the press during the author's life, but never could prevail for leave to publish them; though he was pleased to be at the pains of reviewing, and to give me his directions for digesting them in order. It has since pleased God to take this great and good person to himself; and he having done me the honour to leave and recommend to me the care of his writings, I thought I could not at present do a greater service to my country, or to the author's memory, than by making these papers public.

By way of introduction, I need only take notice, that after the peace of the Pyrenees, and his Majesty's happy restoration in 1660, there was a general peace in Christendom, (except only the remainder of a war between Spain and Portugal,) until the year 1665; when that between England and Holland began, which produced a treaty between his Majesty and the Bishop of Munster. And this commences the following letters.

PREFACE

TO

THE THIRD PART

OF

SIR WILLIAM TEMPLE'S MISCELLANEA, 1701.*

HE two following essays, "Of Popular Discontents," and "Of Health and Long Life," were written many years before the author's death. They were revised and corrected by himself; and were designed to have been part of a Third Miscellanea, to which some others were to have been added, if the latter part of his life had been attended with any sufficient degree of health.

For the third paper, relating to the controversy about "Ancient and Modern Learning," I cannot well inform the reader upon what occasion it was writ,

---

* These Miscellanies form an additional volume to two of the same description, which Sir William Temple had published during his own life.

having been at that time in another kingdom; but it appears never to have been finished by the author.*

The two next papers contain the heads of two essays intended to have been written upon the "Different Conditions of Life and Fortune," and upon "Conversation." I have directed they should be printed among the rest, because I believe there are few who will not be content to see even the first draught of anything from the author's hand.

At the end I have added a few translations from Virgil, Horace, and Tibullus, or rather imitations, done by the author above thirty years ago; whereof the first was printed among other Eclogues of Virgil, in the year 1679, but without any mention of the author. They were indeed not intended to have been made public, till I was informed of several copies, that were got abroad, and those very imperfect and corrupt. Therefore the reader finds them here, only to prevent him from finding them in other places very faulty, and perhaps accompanied with many spurious additions.

JONATHAN SWIFT.

---

* It seems very improbable that Dr. Swift should be altogether ignorant of the famous dispute about "Ancient and Modern Learning." If he had not made his public declaration, he would highly, and with justice, have resented the being taxed by any other with being ignorant of a passage which made so great a noise in the commonwealth of learning. At this time, however, the doctor, (being generally suspected of being the author of "The Tale of a Tub," which came abroad some time before, and which he did not think fit to own,) might fancy, that by his disclaiming the knowledge of the occasion on which Sir William wrote the above Essay, he should weaken the suspicion of his having written "The Tale of a Tub," which last is a subsidiary defence of Sir William Temple.—D. S.

PREFACE

TO

THE THIRD VOLUME

OF

SIR WILLIAM TEMPLE'S LETTERS,

1703.*

---o---

THE following papers are the last of this, or indeed of any kind, about which the author ever gave me his particular commands. They were corrected by himself, and fairly transcribed in his lifetime. I have in all things followed his directions as strictly as I could; but accidents unforeseen having since intervened, I have thought convenient to lessen the bulk of this volume. To which end, I have omitted several letters addressed to persons with whom this author corresponded without any particular confidence, farther than upon account of their posts: because great numbers of such letters, procured out of the office, or by other means, (how justifiable I

---

* This was a separate publication, intended to complete the series of Temple's political correspondence.

shall not examine,) have been already printed: but, running wholly upon long dry subjects of business, have met no other reception than merely what the reputation of the author would give them. If I could have foreseen an end of this trade, I should, upon some considerations, have longer forborn sending these into the world. But I daily hear, that new discoveries of *original* letters are hasting to the press: to stop the current of which, I am forced to an earlier publication than I designed. And therefore I take this occasion to inform the reader, that these letters, ending with the author's revocation from his employments, abroad, (which in less than two years was followed by his retirement from all public business,) are the last he ever intended for the press: having been selected by himself from great numbers yet lying among his papers.

If I could have been prevailed with by the rhetoric of booksellers, or any other little regards I might easily, instead of retrenching, have made very considerable additions: and by that means have perhaps taken the surest course to prevent the interloping of others. But if the press must needs be loaded, I would rather it should not be by my means. And therefore I may hope to be allowed one word in the style of a publisher, (an office liable to much censure without the least pretension to merit or to praise,) that if I have not been much deceived in others and myself, the reader will hardly find one Letter in this collection unworthy of the author, or which does not contain something either of entertainment or of use.

PREFACE

TO

THE THIRD PART

OF

SIR WILLIAM TEMPLE'S MEMOIRS;*

FROM THE PEACE CONCLUDED 1679 TO THE TIME OF THE AUTHOR'S RETIREMENT FROM PUBLIC BUSINESS.

[FIRST PUBLISHED IN 1709.]

Et ille quidem plenus annis obiit, plenus honoribus, illis etiam quos recusavit —PLIN. Epist. ii. 1.

———o———

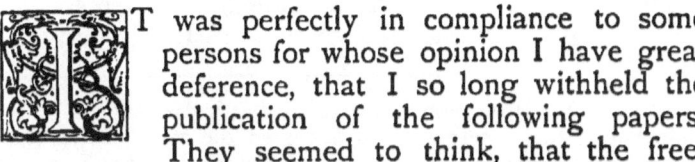T was perfectly in compliance to some persons for whose opinion I have great deference, that I so long withheld the publication of the following papers. They seemed to think, that the freedom of some passages in these Memoirs might give

---

* The *Third* Part of Sir William Temple's Memoirs, he himself declared to be "written for the satisfaction of my friends hereafter, upon the grounds of my retirement, and resolution never to meddle again with any public affairs, from this present February 1680–1." As they embraced the latter part of the reign

offence to several who were still alive; and whose part in those affairs which are here related, could not be transmitted to posterity with any advantage to their reputation. But whether this objection be in itself of much weight, may perhaps be disputed; at least it should have little with me, who am under no restraint in that particular; since I am not of an age to remember those transactions, nor had any acquaintance with those persons whose counsels or proceedings are condemned, and who are all of them now dead.

But as this author is very free in exposing the weakness and corruptions of ill ministers, so he is as ready to commend the abilities and virtue of others, as may be observed from several passages of these Memoirs; particularly of the late Earl of Sunderland, with whom the author continued in the most intimate friendship to his death; and who was father of that most learned and excellent lord, now secretary of state: as likewise, of the present Earl of Rochester; and the Earl of Godolphin, now lord treasurer, represented by this impartial author as a person at that time deservedly entrusted with so great a part in the prime ministry; an office he now executes again with such universal applause, so much to the Queen's honour and his own, and to the advan-

---

of Charles II., they contained many particulars affecting the character of the statesmen who occupied the stage during that bustling and intriguing period. Several of Sir William Temple's friends, and in particular his sister Lady Gifford, judged the Memoirs on this account unfit for publication. But, although Swift deferred his intention at their request, he afterwards resumed it, and printed the work with the following preface; at which Lady Gifford was so much incensed, as to publish an advertisement against him; nor does there at any time afterwards appear to have been a reconciliation. The price received by Swift for the Memoirs, appears from a document published by Mr. Nichols, to have been forty pounds.

tage of his country, as well as of the whole confederacy.

There are two objections I have sometimes heard to have been offered against those Memoirs that were printed in the author's lifetime, and which these now published may perhaps be equally liable to. First, as to the matter; that the author speaks too much of himself: next, as to the style; that he affects the use of French words, as well as some turns of expression peculiar to that language.

I believe, those who make the former criticism do not well consider the nature of memoirs : it is to the French (if I mistake not) we chiefly owe that manner of writing : and Sir William Temple is not only the first, but I think the only Englishman, (at least of any consequence,) who ever attempted it. The best French memoirs are writ by such persons as were the principal actors in those transactions they pretend to relate, whether of wars or negotiations. Those of Sir William Temple are of the same nature : and therefore, in my judgment, the publisher* (who sent them into the world without the author's privity) gave them a wrong title, when he called them "Memoirs of what passed in Christendom," &c., whereas it should rather have been "Memoirs of the Treaty at Nimeguen," which was plainly the sense of the author, who in the epistle tells his son, that "in compliance with his desire, he will leave him some memoirs of what passed in his public employments abroad;" and in the book itself, when he deduces an account of the state of war in Christendom, he says, it is only to prepare the reader for a relation of that famous treaty ; where he and Sir Lionel Jenkins were the only mediators

---

* They were first published in 1689, by R. Chiswell, whose advertisement is preserved in Temple's Works, vol. II. p. 242.

that continued any considerable time; and as the author was first in commission, so in point of abilities or credit, either abroad or at home, there was no sort of comparison between the two persons. Those memoirs, therefore, are properly a relation of a general treaty of peace, wherein the author had the principal as well as the most honourable part in quality of mediator; so that the frequent mention of himself seems not only excusable but necessary. The same may be offered in defence of the following papers; because, during the greatest part of the period they treat of, the author was in chief confidence with the king his master. To which may be added, that, in the few preliminary lines at the head of the first page, the author professes he writ those papers " for the satisfaction of his friends hereafter, upon the grounds of his retirement, and his resolution never to meddle again with public affairs." As to the objection against the style of the former Memoirs, that it abounds in French words and turns of expression; it is to be considered, that at the treaty of Nimeguen, all business, either by writing or discourse, passed in the French tongue; and the author having lived so many years abroad, in that and foreign embassies, where all business, as well as conversation, ran in that language, it was hardly possible for him to write upon public affairs without some tincture of it in his style, though in his other writings there be little or nothing of it to be observed; and as he has often assured me, it was a thing he never affected; so, upon the objections made to his former Memoirs, he blotted out some French words in these, and placed English in their stead, though perhaps not so significant.

There is one thing proper to inform the reader, why these Memoirs are called the Third Part, there having never been published but one part before, where, in the beginning, the author mentions a former part, and in the conclusion promises a third. The subject of the first part was chiefly the triple alliance, during the negotiation of which my Lord Arlington was secretary of state and chief minister. Sir William Temple often assured me, he had burnt those Memoirs ; and for that reason was content his letters during his embassies at the Hague and Aix-la-Chapelle, should be printed after his death, in some manner to supply that loss.

What it was that moved Sir William Temple to burn those first Memoirs, may perhaps be conjectured from some passages in the second part, formerly printed. In one place, the author has these words ; " My Lord Arlington, who made so great a figure in the former part of these Memoirs, was now grown out of all credit," &c. In other parts he tells us, " That lord was of the ministry which broke the triple league ; advised the Dutch war and French alliance ; and, in short, was the bottom of all those ruinous measures which the court of England was then taking ; " so that, as I have been told from a good hand, and as it seems very probable, he could not think that lord a person fit to be celebrated for his part in forwarding that famous league while he was secretary of state, who had made such counter-paces to destroy it. At the end I have subjoined an Appendix, containing, besides one or two other particulars, a Speech of Sir William Temple's in the House of Commons ; and an Answer of the King's to an Address of that House, relating to the Bill of Exclusion ; both which are mentioned in these Memoirs.

I have only farther to inform the reader, that, although these papers were corrected by the author, yet he had once intended to insert some additions in several places, as appeared by certain hints or memorandums in the margin; but whether they were omitted out of forgetfulness, neglect, or want of health, I cannot determine; one passage relating to Sir William Jones he was pleased to tell me, and I have added it in the Appendix.* The rest I know nothing of; but the thread of the story is entire without them.

---

* Sir William Jones was reputed one of the best speakers in the House, and was very zealous in his endeavours for promoting the bill of exclusion [in 1679]. He was a person of great piety and virtue; and having taken an affection to Sir William Temple, was sorry to see him employed in the delivery of so unacceptable a message to the House. The substance of what he said to the author upon it was, that, "for himself, he was old and infirm, and expected to die soon: but you," said he, "will, in all probability, live to see the whole kingdom lament the consequences of this message you have now brought us from the King."—SWIFT, Appendix to Temple's Memoirs, 8vo, vol. II. p. 565.

A MEDITATION UPON A BROOMSTICK.

ACCORDING TO THE STYLE AND MANNER OF THE HONOURABLE ROBERT BOYLE'S MEDITATIONS.

THIS celebrated parody is said by Mr. Sheridan to have been composed upon the following occasion:
"In the yearly visits which Swift made to London, during his stay there he passed much of his time at Lord Berkeley's, officiating as chaplain to the family, and attending Lady Berkeley in her private devotions; after which the doctor, by her desire, used to read to her some moral or religious discourse. The Countess had at this time taken a great liking to Mr. Boyle's Meditations, and was determined to go through them in that manner: but as Swift had by no means the same relish for that kind of writing which her ladyship had, he soon grew weary of the task; and a whim coming into his head, resolved to get rid of it in a way which might occasion some sport in the family; for which they had as high a relish as himself. The next time he was employed in reading one of these Meditations, he took an opportunity of conveying away the book, and dexterously inserted a leaf, on which he had written his own Meditation on a Broomstick; after which he took care to have the book restored to its proper place, and in his next attendance on my lady, when he was desired to proceed to the next Meditation, Swift opened upon the place where the leaf had been inserted, and with great composure read

the title, 'A Meditation on a Broomstick.' Lady Berkeley, a little surprised at the oddity of the title, stopped him, repeating the words, 'A Meditation on a Broomstick! What a strange subject! But there is no knowing what useful lessons of instruction this wonderful man may draw from things apparently the most trivial. Pray let us hear what he says upon it.' Swift then, with an inflexible gravity of countenance, proceeded to read the Meditation, in the same solemn tone which he had used in delivering the former. Lady Berkeley, not at all suspecting a trick, in the fulness of her prepossession, was every now and then, during the reading of it, expressing her admiration of this extraordinary man, who could draw such fine moral reflections from so contemptible a subject; with which, though Swift must have been inwardly not a little tickled, yet he preserved a most perfect composure of features, so that she had not the least room to suspect any deceit. Soon after, some company coming in, Swift pretended business, and withdrew, foreseeing what was to follow. Lady Berkeley, full of the subject, soon entered upon the praises of those heavenly Meditations of Mr. Boyle. 'But,' said she, 'the doctor has been just reading one to me, which has surprised me more than all the rest.' One of the company asked which of the Meditations she meant? She answered directly, in the simplicity of her heart, 'I mean, that excellent Meditation upon the Broomstick.' The company looked at each other with some surprise, and could scarce refrain from laughing. But they all agreed that they had never heard of such a Meditation before. 'Upon my word,' said my lady, 'there it is, look into that book, and convince yourselves.' One of them opened the book, and found it there indeed, but in Swift's handwriting; upon which a general burst of laughter ensued; and my lady, when the first surprise was over, enjoyed the joke as much as any of them; saying, 'What a vile trick has that rogue played me! But it is his way, he never baulks his humour in anything.' The affair ended in a great deal of harmless mirth, and Swift, you may be sure, was not asked to proceed any further into the Meditations."

Whoever has read the vapid and metaphorical flourishes of this once celebrated moralist, (only equalled in the flowery pages of Harvey's Meditations,) will find, in the pretended violation of Mr. Boyle's dignity, a pedantic and affected style, justly exposed to the ridicule of the world.

A MEDITATION UPON A BROOMSTICK.

THIS single stick, which you now behold ingloriously lying in that neglected corner, I once knew in a flourishing state in a forest: it was full of sap, full of leaves, and full of boughs: but now, in vain does the busy art of man pretend to vie with nature, by tying that withered bundle of twigs to its sapless trunk; it is now, at best, but the reverse of what it was, a tree turned upside down, the branches on the earth, and the root in the air; it is now handled by every dirty wench, condemned to do her drudgery, and, by a capricious kind of fate, destined to make other things clean, and be nasty itself: at length, worn to the stumps in the service of the maids, it is either thrown out of doors, or condemned to the last use, of kindling a fire. When I beheld this I sighed, and said within myself, **Surely man is a Broomstick!** Nature sent him into the world strong and lusty, in a thriving condition, wearing his own hair on his head, the proper branches of this reasoning vegetable, until the axe of intemperance has lopped off his green boughs, and left him a withered trunk: he then flies to art, and puts on a periwig, valuing himself upon an unnatural bundle of hairs, (all covered with powder,) that never grew on his head; but now, should this our broomstick pretend to enter the scene, proud of those birchen spoils it never bore, and all covered with dust, though the sweepings of the finest lady's chamber, we should be apt to ridicule and despise its vanity. Partial judges that we are of our own excellencies, and other men's defaults!

But a broomstick, perhaps, you will say, is an emblem of a tree standing on its head; and pray what is man, but a topsyturvy creature, his animal faculties perpetually mounted on his rational, his head where his heels should be, grovelling on the earth! and yet, with all his faults, he sets up to be a universal reformer and corrector of abuses, a remover of grievances, rakes into every slut's corner of nature, bringing hidden corruption to the light, and raises a mighty dust where there was none before; sharing deeply all the while in the very same pollutions he pretends to sweep away: his last days are spent in slavery to women, and generally the least deserving; till, worn out to the stumps, like his brother besom, he is either kicked out of doors, or made use of to kindle flames for others to warm themselves by.

A TRITICAL ESSAY

UPON THE

FACULTIES OF THE MIND.

TO ———

SIR,

BEING so great a lover of antiquities, it was reasonable to suppose, you would be very much obliged with anything that was new. I have been of late offended with many writers of essays and moral discourses, for running into stale topics and thread-bare quotations, and not handling their subject fully and closely: all which errors I have carefully avoided in the following essay, which I have proposed as a pattern for young writers to imitate. The thoughts and observations being entirely new, the quotations untouched by others, the subject of mighty importance, and treated with much order and perspicuity, it has cost me a great deal of time; and I desire you will accept and consider it as the utmost effort of my genius.

A TRITICAL ESSAY

UPON THE

FACULTIES OF THE MIND.*

HILOSOPHERS say, that man is a microcosm, or little world, resembling in miniature every part of the great; and, in my opinion, the body natural may be compared to the body politic; and if this be so, how can the Epicurean's opinion be true, that the universe was formed by a fortuitous concourse of atoms: which I will no more believe, than that the accidental jumbling of the letters of the alphabet, could fall by chance into a most ingenious and learned treatise of philosophy. *Risum teneatis amici?* This false opinion must needs create many more: it is like an error in the first concoction, which cannot be corrected in the second; the foundation is weak, and whatever superstructure you raise upon it, must, of necessity, fall to the ground. Thus, men are led from one error to another, until, with Ixion, they embrace a cloud instead of Juno; or, like the dog in the fable, lose

---

* The object and irony of this piece are obvious.

the substance in gaping at the shadow. For such opinions cannot cohere; but, like the iron and clay in the toes of Nebuchadnezzar's image, must separate and break in pieces. I have read in a certain author, that Alexander wept because he had no more worlds to conquer; which he needed not have done, if the fortuitous concourse of atoms could create one: but this is an opinion, fitter for that many-headed beast, the vulgar, to entertain, than for so wise a man as Epicurus; the corrupt part of his sect only borrowed his name, as the monkey did the cat's claw to draw the chestnut out of the fire.

However, the first step to the cure is to know the disease; and though truth may be difficult to find, because, as the philosopher observes, she lives in the bottom of a well, yet we need not, like blind men, grope in open daylight. I hope I may be allowed, among so many far more learned men, to offer my mite, since a stander-by may sometimes, perhaps, see more of the game than he that plays it. But I do not think a philosopher obliged to account for every phenomenon in nature, or drown himself with Aristotle, for not being able to solve the ebbing and flowing of the tide, in that fatal sentence he passed upon himself, *Quia te non capio, tu capies me.* Wherein he was at once the judge and the criminal, the accuser and executioner. Socrates, on the other hand, who said he knew nothing, was pronounced by the oracle to be the wisest man in the world.

But to return from this digression: I think it as clear as any demonstration of Euclid, that nature does nothing in vain; if we were able to dive into her secret recesses, we should find that the smallest blade of grass, or most contemptible weed, has its particular use: but she is chiefly admirable in her minutest compositions; the least and most contemptible insect most discovers the art of nature, if I may so call it, though nature, which delights in variety, will always triumph over art: and as the poet observes,

> *Naturam expellas furcâ licet, usque recurret.**
> HOR. Lib. I. Epist. X. 24.

But the various opinions of philosophers have scattered through the world as many plagues of the mind, as Pandora's box did those of the body; only with this difference, that they have not left hope at the bottom. And if Truth be not fled with Astrea, she is certainly as hidden as the source of Nile, and can be found only in Utopia. Not that I would reflect on those wise sages, which would be a sort of ingratitude; and he that calls a man ungrateful, sums up all the evil that a man can be guilty of,

> *Ingratum si dixeris, omnia dicis.*

But, what I blame the philosophers for, (though some may think it a paradox,) is chiefly their pride; nothing less than an *ipse dixit*, and you must pin your faith on their sleeve. And though Diogenes lived in a tub, there might be for aught I know, as much pride under his rags as in the fine-spun garments of the divine Plato. It is reported of this Diogenes, that when Alexander came to see him, and promised to give him whatever he would ask, the cynic only answered, "Take not from me what thou canst not give me, but stand from between me and the light;" which was almost as extravagant as the philosopher, that flung his money into the sea, with this remarkable saying——

---

* For Nature driven out, with proud disdain,
All-powerful goddess, will return again.
FRANCIS.

How different was this man from the usurer, who, being told his son would spend all he had got, replied, " He cannot take more pleasure in spending, that I did in getting it." These men could see the faults of each other, but not their own; those they flung into the bag behind; *non videmus id manticæ quod in tergo est.* I may perhaps be censured for my free opinions by those carping Momuses whom authors worship, as the Indians do the devil, for fear. They will endeavour to give my reputation as many wounds, as the man in the almanack: but I value it not; and perhaps like flies, they may buzz so often about the candle, till they burn their wings. They must pardon me, if I venture to give them this advice, not to rail at what they cannot understand; it does but discover that self-tormenting passion of envy, than which the greatest tyrant never invented a more cruel torment:

Invidiâ Siculi non invenere Tyranni
Tormentum majus—
Hor. Lib. I. Epist. II. 58.

I must be so bold to tell my critics and witlings, that they can no more judge of this, than a man that is born blind can have any true idea of colours. I have always observed, that your empty vessels sound loudest: I value their lashes as little as the sea did those of Xerxes, when he whipped it. The utmost favour a man can expect from them is, that which Polyphemus promised Ulysses, that he would devour him the last: they think to subdue a writer, as Cæsar did his enemy, with a *Veni, vidi, vici.* I confess I value the opinion of the judicious few, a Rymer, a Dennis, or a W——k; but for the rest, to give my judgment at once, I think the long dispute among the philosophers about a *vacuum,* may be determined in the affirmative, that it is to be found in a critic's head. They are at best but the drones of the learned world, who devour the honey, and will not work themselves: and a writer need no more regard them, than the moon does the barking of a little senseless cur. For, in spite of their terrible roaring, you may, with half an eye, discover the ass under the lion's skin.

But to return to our discourse: Demosthenes being asked what was the first part of an orator, replied, action: what was the second, action: what was the third, action: and so on, *ad infinitum*. This may be true in oratory; but contemplation in other things, exceeds action. And therefore, a wise man is never less alone, than when he is alone: *Nunquam minus solus, quam cum solus.*

And Archimedes, the famous mathematician, was so intent upon his problems, that he never minded the soldiers who came to kill him. Therefore, not to detract from the just praise which belongs to orators, they ought to consider, that nature, which gave us two eyes to see, and two ears to hear, has given us but one tongue to speak; wherein, however, some do so abound, that the virtuosi, who have been so long in search for the perpetual motion, may infallibly find it there.

Some men admire republics, because orators flourish there most, and are the greatest enemies of tyranny; but my opinion is, that one tyrant is better than a hundred. Besides these orators inflame the people, whose anger is really but a short fit of madness.

Ira furor breves est.
Hor. Lib. I. Epist. II. 62.

After which, laws are like cobwebs, which may

catch small flies, but let wasps and hornets break through. But in oratory the greatest art is to hide art. *Artis est celare artem.*

But this must be the work of time, we must lay hold on all opportunities, and let slip no occasion; else we shall be forced to weave Penelope's web, unravel in the night what we spun in the day. And therefore I have observed, that Time is painted with a lock before, and bald behind, signifying thereby, that we must take time (as we say) by the forelock, for when it is once past, there is no recalling it.

The mind of man is at first (if you will pardon the expression) like a *tabula rasa*, or like wax, which, while it is soft, is capable of any impression, till time has hardened it. And at length death, that grim tyrant, stops us in the midst of our career. The greatest conquerors have at last been conquered by death, which spares none, from the sceptre to the spade: *Mors omnibus communis.*

All rivers go to the sea, but none return from it. Xerxes wept when he beheld his army, to consider that in less than an hundred years they would be all dead. Anacreon was choked with a grape-stone; and violent joy kills as well as violent grief. There is nothing in this world constant, but inconstancy; yet Plato thought, that if virtue would appear to the world in her own native dress, all men would be enamoured with her. But now, since interest governs the world, and men neglect the golden mean, Jupiter himself, if he came to the earth, would be despised, unless it were, as he did to Danae, in a golden shower: for men now-a-days worship the rising sun, and not the setting:

Donec eris felix multos numerabis amicos.

Thus have I, in obedience to your commands,

ventured to expose myself to censure, in this critical age. Whether I have done right to my subject, must be left to the judgment of my learned reader: however, I cannot but hope, that my attempting of it may be encouragement for some able pen to perform it with more success.

A PROPOSAL

FOR

CORRECTING, IMPROVING, AND ASCERTAINING

THE

ENGLISH TONGUE,*

IN

A LETTER TO THE MOST HONOURABLE ROBERT, EARL OF OXFORD AND MORTIMER, LORD HIGH TREASURER OF GREAT BRITAIN.

FIRST PRINTED IN MAY, 1712.

---

* This Essay, which led to no consequences, is the only trace of the literary labours of the celebrated Society of Brothers, so often mentioned in the Journal to Stella. Johnson, than whom none could judge more accurately of the value of the Proposal, has recorded his sentiments in the following words:—"Early in the next year he published a 'Proposal for Correcting, Improving, and Ascertaining the English Tongue,' in a letter to the Earl of Oxford; written without much knowledge of the general nature of language, and without any accurate inquiry into the history of other tongues. The certainty and stability which, contrary to all experience, Swift thinks attainable, he proposes to secure by instituting an academy; the decrees of which every man would have been willing, and many would have been proud, to disobey, and which, being renewed by successive elections, would, in a short time, have differed from itself."

Various answers were published upon the appearance of this Letter.

"I HAVE been six hours to-day morning writing nineteen pages of a letter to Lord-treasurer, about forming a society, or academy, to correct and fix the English language. It will not be above five or six more. I will send it him to-morrow; and will print it, if he desires me." Journal to Stella, Feb. 21, 1711–12.

"I finished the rest of my letter to Lord-treasurer to-day, and sent it to him." Ibid. Feb. 22.

"Lord-treasurer has lent the long letter I writ him to Prior; and I can't get Prior to return it. I want to have it printed; and to make up this academy for the improvement of our language." Ibid. March 11.

"My letter to the Lord-treasurer about the English tongue is now printing; and I suffer my name to be put at the end of it, which I never did before in my life." Ibid. May 10, 1712.

"Have you seen my letter to the Lord-treasurer? There are two answers come out to it already, though it is no politics, but a harmless proposal about the improvement of the English tongue. I believe, if I writ an essay upon a straw, some fool would answer it." Ibid. May 31.

"You never told me, how my letter to Lord-treasurer passes in Ireland." Ibid. July 1.

"What care I, whether my letter to Lord-treasurer be commended there or not? Why does not somebody among you answer it, as three or four have done here." Ibid. July 17.

A PROPOSAL

FOR

CORRECTING, IMPROVING, AND ASCERTAINING

THE

ENGLISH TONGUE.

My Lord,   *London, Feb. 22, 1711–12.*

WHAT I had the honour of mentioning to your lordship some time ago in conversation, was not a new thought, just then started by accident or occasion, but the result of long reflection; and I have been confirmed in my sentiments, by the opinion of some very judicious persons, with whom I consulted. They all agreed, that nothing would be of greater use towards the improvement of knowledge and politeness, than some effectual method for correcting, enlarging, and ascertaining our language; and they think it a work very possible to be compassed under the protection of a prince, the countenance and encouragement of a ministry, and the care of proper persons chosen for such an undertaking.* I was

---

* " Dr. Swift proposed a plan of this nature, (the forming a society to fix a standard to the English language,) to his friend, as he thought him, the Lord-Treasurer Oxford, but without

glad to find your lordship's answer in so different a style from what has been commonly made use of on the like occasions, for some years past, That all such thoughts must be deferred to a time of peace: a topic which some have carried so far, that they would not have us by any means think of preserving our civil or religious constitution, because we are engaged in a war abroad. It will be among the distinguishing marks of your ministry, my lord, that you have a genius above all such regards, and that no reasonable proposal for the honour, the advantage, or the ornament of your country, however foreign to your more immediate office, was ever neglected by you. I confess the merit of this candour and condescension is very much lessened, because your lordship hardly leaves us room to offer our good wishes; removing all our difficulties, and supplying our wants, faster than the most visionary projector can adjust his schemes. And, therefore, my lord, the design of this paper is not so much to offer you ways and means, as to complain of a grievance, the redressing of which is to be your own work, as much as that of paying the nation's debts, or opening a trade into the South-Sea; and though not of such immediate benefit as either of these, or any other of your glorious actions, yet perhaps, in future ages, not less to your honour.

My lord, I do here, in the name of all the learned and polite persons of the nation, complain to your lordship, as first minister, that our language is extremely imperfect; that its daily improvements are by no means in proportion to its daily corruptions; that the pretenders to polish and refine it,

---

success; precision and perspicuity not being in general the favourite objects of ministers, and perhaps still less so of *that* minister than any other."—CHESTERFIELD.

have chiefly multiplied abuses and absurdities; and that in many instances it offends against every part of grammar. But lest your lordship should think my censure too severe, I shall take leave to be more particular.

I believe your lordship will agree with me in the reason, why our language is less refined than those of Italy, Spain, or France. 'Tis plain, that the Latin tongue in its purity was never in this island, towards the conquest of which, few or no attempts were made till the time of Claudius; neither was that language ever so vulgar in Britain, as it is known to have been in Gaul and Spain. Farther, we find that the Roman legions here were at length all recalled to help their country against the Goths, and other barbarous invaders. Meantime, the Britons, left to shift for themselves, and daily harassed by cruel inroads from the Picts, were forced to call in the Saxons for their defence; who, consequently, reduced the greatest part of the island to their own power, drove the Britons into the most remote and mountainous parts, and the rest of the country, in customs, religion, and language, became wholly Saxon. This I take to be the reason, why there are more Latin words * remaining in the

---

* "As for our *English* tongue; the great alterations it has undergone in the two last centuries are principally owing to that vast stock of *Latin* words which we have transplanted into our own soil; which being now in a manner exhausted, one may easily presage that it will not have such changes in the two next centuries. Nay, it were no difficult contrivance, if the public had any regard to it, to make the *English* tongue immutable; unless hereafter some foreign nation shall invade and over-run us."—BENTLEY.

How very far Bentley was mistaken in his prophecy is evident, from the great number of words naturalized from the Latin during the last century, especially since the style of Johnson was adopted as a model. Many of the words quoted by Swift as the offspring of affectation and pedantry, are now in common and every-day use.

British tongue, than in the old Saxon, which, excepting some few variations in the orthography, is the same in most original words with our present English, as well as with German and other Northern dialects.

Edward the Confessor having lived long in France, appears to be the first who introduced any mixture of the French tongue with the Saxon; the court affecting what the prince was fond of, and others taking it up for a fashion, as it is now with us. William the Conqueror proceeded much farther; bringing over with him vast numbers of that nation, scattering them in every monastery, giving them great quantities of land, directing all pleadings to be in that language, and endeavouring to make it universal in the kingdom. This at least is the opinion generally received; but your lordship has fully convinced me, that the French tongue made yet a greater progress here under Harry the Second, who had large territories on that continent both from his father and his wife, made frequent journeys and expeditions thither, and was always attended with a number of his countrymen, retainers at his court.*

---

* In this passage Swift mistakes the History of the English language, which later philological researches have more accurately ascertained. After the Norman conquest, French, the language of the conquerors, was universally spoken by the court, the barons, and all who pretended to rank above the vulgar. The Anglo-Saxon was only used by the common people. But in order to maintain the necessary intercourse between the higher and lower classes, a composite language was introduced, grounded indeed upon the Anglo-Saxon vocabulary, but with the extinction of its ancient grammatical inflexions, and the addition of a strong infusion of the Norman French, for the convenience and accommodation of the victors. It is this *lingua franca*, which gradually superseded the use of both the languages, of which it was composed. Edward III. was the first monarch who adopted an English motto; and Chaucer, while he complains of the uncer-

For some centuries after, there was a constant intercourse between France and England, by the dominions we possessed there, and the conquests we made; so that our language, between two and three hundred years ago, seems to have had a greater mixture with French, than at present; many words having been afterward rejected, and some since the time of Spenser; although we have still retained not a few, which have been long antiquated in France. I could produce several instances of both kinds, if it were of any use or entertainment.

To examine into the several circumstances by which the language of a country may be altered, would force me to enter into a wide field. I shall only observe, that the Latin, the French, and the English, seem to have undergone the same fortune. The first, from the days of Romulus to those of Julius Cæsar, suffered perpetual changes; and by what we meet in those authors who occasionally speak on that subject, as well as from certain fragments of old laws, it is manifest that the Latin, three hundred years before Tully, was as unintelligible in his time, as the English and French of the same period are now; and these two have changed as much since William the Conqueror, (which is but little less than seven hundred years) as the Latin appears to have done in the like term. Whether our language, or the French, will decline as fast as

---

tainty and diversity of the English language, in his own time, had probably no small share in refining and fixing it. In the reign of Henry II., when Lord Oxford seems to have persuaded Swift that the French tongue was more intermixed than formerly with the English, it would appear, that both languages subsisted in a state unmixed and unincorporated; as the reader may see from the account of Layamon's Translation of Wace's Brut, in Ellis's Specimens of Early English Poets. Vol. I. p. 60.

the Roman did, is a question that would perhaps admit more debate than it is worth. There were many reasons for the corruptions of the last; as, the change of their government to a tyranny, which ruined the study of eloquence, there being no farther use or encouragement for popular orators; their giving not only the freedom of the city, but capacity for employments to several towns in Gaul, Spain, and Germany, and other distant parts, as far as Asia; which brought a great number of foreign pretenders into Rome; the slavish disposition of the senate and people, by which the wit and eloquence of the age were wholly turned into panegyric, the most barren of all subjects; the great corruption of manners, and introduction of foreign luxury, with foreign terms to express it, with several others that might be assigned; not to mention those invasions from the Goths and Vandals, which are too obvious to insist on.

The Roman language arrived at great perfection, before it began to decay; and the French, for these last fifty years, has been polishing as much as it will bear, and appears to be declining by the natural inconstancy of that people, and the affectation of some late authors to introduce and multiply cant words, which is the most ruinous corruption in any language. La Bruyère, a late celebrated writer among them, makes use of many new terms, which are not to be found in any of the common dictionaries before his time. But the English tongue is not arrived to such a degree of perfection, as to make us apprehend any thoughts of its decay; and if it were once refined to a certain standard, perhaps there might be ways found out to fix it for ever, or at least till we are invaded and made a conquest by some other state; and even then our best writings might probably be preserved with care, and grow into esteem, and the authors have a chance for immortality.

But without such great revolutions as these (to which we are, I think, less subject than kingdoms upon the continent) I see no absolute necessity why any language should be perpetually changing; for we find many examples to the contrary. From Homer to Plutarch are above a thousand years; so long at least the purity of the Greek tongue may be allowed to last, and we know not how far before. The Grecians spread their colonies round all the coast of Asia Minor, even to the northern parts lying toward the Euxine, in every island of the Ægean sea, and several others in the Mediterranean; where the language was preserved entire for many ages, after they themselves became colonies to Rome, and till they were overrun by the barbarous nations upon the fall of that empire. The Chinese have books in their language above two thousand years old, neither have the frequent conquests of the Tartars been able to alter it. The German, Spanish, and Italian, have admitted few or no changes for some ages past. The other languages of Europe I know nothing of; neither is there any occasion to consider them.

Having taken this compass, I return to those considerations upon our own language, which I would humbly offer your lordship. The period, wherein the English tongue received most improvement, I take to commence with the beginning of Queen Elizabeth's reign, and to conclude with the great rebellion in forty-two. It is true, there was a very ill taste both of style and wit, which prevailed under King James the First; but that seems to have been corrected in the first years of his successor, who, among many other qualifications of an excellent prince, was a great patron of learning.

From the civil war to this present time, I am apt to doubt, whether the corruptions in our language have not at least equalled the refinements of it; and these corruptions very few of the best authors in our age have wholly escaped. During the usurpation, such an infusion of enthusiastic jargon prevailed in every writing, as was not shaken off in many years after. To this succeeded that licentiousness which entered with the Restoration, and from infecting our religion and morals, fell to corrupt our language; which last was not likely to be much improved by those, who at that time made up the court of King Charles the Second; either such who had followed him in his banishment, or who had been altogether conversant in the dialect of those fanatic times; or young men, who had been educated in the same country: so that the court, which used to be the standard of propriety and correctness of speech, was then, and, I think, has ever since continued, the worst school in England for that accomplishment; and so will remain, till better care be taken in the education of our young nobility, that they may set out into the world with some foundation of literature, in order to qualify them for patterns of politeness. The consequence of this defect upon our language, may appear from the plays, and other compositions written for entertainment within fifty years past; filled with a succession of affected phrases, and new conceited words, either borrowed from the current style of the court, or from those who, under the character of men of wit and pleasure, pretended to give the law. Many of these refinements have already been long antiquated, and are now hardly intelligible; which is no wonder, when they were the product only of ignorance and caprice.

I have never known this great town without one

or more dunces of figure, who had credit enough to give rise to some new word, and propagate it in most conversations, though it had neither humour nor significancy. If it struck the present taste, it was soon transferred into the plays and current scribbles of the week, and became an addition to our language; while the men of wit and learning, instead of early obviating such corruptions, were too often seduced to imitate and comply with them.

There is another set of men, who have contributed very much to the spoiling of the English tongue; I mean the poets from the time of the Restoration. These gentlemen, although they could not be insensible how much our language was already overstocked with monosyllables, yet, to save time and pains, introduced that barbarous custom of abbreviating words, to fit them to the measure of their verses; and this they have frequently done so very injudiciously, as to form such harsh unharmonious sounds, that none but a northern ear could endure. They have joined the most obdurate consonants with one intervening vowel, only to shorten a syllable; and their taste in time became so depraved, that what was at first a poetical licence, not to be justified, they made their choice, alleging, that the words pronounced at length sounded faint and languid. This was a pretence to take up the same custom in prose; so that most of the books we see now-a-days are full of those manglings and abbreviations. Instances of this abuse are innumerable: What does your lordship think of the words, drudg'd, disturb'd, rebuk'd, fledg'd, and a thousand others everywhere to be met with in prose as well as verse? where, by leaving out a vowel to save a syllable, we form so jarring a sound, and so difficult to utter, that I have often wondered how it could ever obtain.

Another cause (and perhaps borrowed from the former) which has contributed not a little to the maiming of our language, is a foolish opinion, advanced of late years, that we ought to spell exactly as we speak; which, beside the obvious inconvenience of utterly destroying our etymology, would be a thing we should never see an end of. Not only the several towns and counties of England have a different way of pronouncing, but even here in London they clip their words after one manner about the court, another in the city, and a third in the suburbs; and in a few years, it is probable, will all differ from themselves, as fancy or fashion shall direct; all which reduced to writing, would entirely confound orthography. Yet many people are so fond of this conceit, that it is sometimes a difficult matter to read modern books and pamphlets; where the words are so curtailed, and varied from their original spelling, that whoever has been used to plain English, will hardly know them by sight.

Several young men at the universities, terribly possessed with the fear of pedantry, run into a worse extreme, and think all politeness to consist in reading the daily trash sent down to them from hence; this they call knowing the world, and reading men and manners. Thus furnished, they come up to town, reckon all their errors for accomplishments, borrow the newest set of phrases; and if they take a pen into their hands, all the odd words they have picked up in a coffeehouse, or a gaming ordinary, are produced as flowers of style; and the orthography refined to the utmost. To this we owe those monstrous productions, which, under the name of Trips, Spies, Amusements, and other conceited appellations, have overrun us for some years past. To this we owe that strange race of wits, who tell us, they write to the humour of the age. And I wish I could say, these quaint fopperies were wholly absent from graver subjects. In short, I would undertake to shew your lordship several pieces, where the beauties of this kind are so predominant, that, with all your skill in languages, you could never be able to read or understand them.

But I am very much mistaken, if many of these false refinements among us do not arise from a principle, which would quite destroy their credit, if it were well understood and considered. For I am afraid, my lord, that with all the real good qualities of our country, we are naturally not very polite. This perpetual disposition to shorten our words by retrenching the vowels, is nothing else but a tendency to lapse into the barbarity of those northern nations, from whom we are descended, and whose languages labour all under the same defect. For it is worthy our observation, that the Spaniards, the French, and the Italians, although derived from the same northern ancestors with ourselves, are with the utmost difficulty taught to pronounce our words, which the Swedes and Danes, as well as the Germans and the Dutch, attain to with ease, because our syllables resemble theirs in the roughness and frequency of consonants. Now, as we struggle with an ill climate to improve the nobler kinds of fruits, are at the expense of walls to receive and reverberate the faint rays of the sun, and fence against the northern blast, we sometimes, by the help of a good soil, equal the production of warmer countries, who have no need to be at so much cost and care. It is the same thing with respect to the politer arts among us; and the same defect of heat which gives a fierceness to our natures, may contribute to that roughness of our language, which bears some analogy to the harsh fruit of colder countries. For I do not reckon that we want a genius more than the rest of our neighbours: but your lordship will be of my opinion, that we ought to struggle with these natural disadvantages as much as we can, and be careful whom we employ, whenever we design to correct them, which is a work that has hitherto been assumed by the least qualified hands. So that if the choice had been left to me, I would rather have trusted the refinement of our language, as far as it relates to sound, to the judgment of the women, than of illiterate court fops, half-witted poets, and university boys. For it is plain, that women, in their manner of corrupting words, do naturally discard the consonants, as we do the vowels. What I am going to tell your lordship appears very trifling: that more than once, where some of both sexes were in company, I have persuaded two or three of each to take a pen, and write down a number of letters joined together, just as it came into their heads; and upon reading this gibberish, we have found that which the men had wrote, by the frequent encountering of rough consonants, to sound like High Dutch; and the other, by the women, like Italian, abounding in vowels and liquids. Now, though I would by no means give ladies the trouble of advising us in the reformation of our language, yet I cannot help thinking, that since they have been left out of all meetings, except parties at play, or where worse designs are carried on, our conversation has very much degenerated.

In order to reform our language, I conceive, my lord, that a free judicious choice should be made of such persons, as are generally allowed to be best qualified for such a work, without any regard to quality, party, or profession. These, to a certain number at least, should assemble at some appointed time and place, and fix on rules, by which they design to proceed. What methods they will take, is not for me to prescribe. Your lordship, and other persons in great employments, might please to be of the number: and I am afraid such a society would want your instruction and example, as much as your protection; for I have, not without a little envy, observed of late the style of some great ministers very much to exceed that of any other productions.

The persons who are to undertake this work, will have the example of the French before them, to imitate where these have proceeded right, and to avoid their mistakes. Beside the grammar part, wherein we are allowed to be very defective, they will observe many gross improprieties, which, however authorised by practice, and grown familiar, ought to be discarded. They will find many words that deserve to be utterly thrown out of our language, many more to be corrected, and perhaps not a few long since antiquated, which ought to be restored on account of their energy and sound.

But what I have most at heart, is, that some method should be thought on for ascertaining and fixing our language for ever, after such alterations are made in it as shall be thought requisite. For I am of opinion, it is better a language should not be wholly perfect, than that it should be perpetually changing; and we must give over at one time, or at length infallibly change for the worse; as the Romans did, when they began to quit their simplicity of style, for affected refinements, such as we meet in Tacitus and other authors; which ended by degrees in many barbarities, even before the Goths had invaded Italy.

The fame of our writers is usually confined to these two islands, and it is hard it should be limited in time, as much as place, by the perpetual variations of our speech. It is your lordship's observation, that if it were not for the Bible and Common Prayer Book in the vulgar tongue, we should hardly be able to understand anything that was written among us a hundred years ago; which is certainly true: for those books being perpetually read in churches, have proved a kind of standard for language, especially to the common people. And I doubt, whether the alterations since introduced have added much to the beauty or strength of the English tongue, though they have taken off a great deal from that simplicity, which is one of the greatest perfections in any language. You, my lord, who are so conversant in the sacred writings, and so great a judge of them in their originals, will agree, that no translation our country ever yet produced, has come up to that of the Old and New Testament: and by the many beautiful passages, which I have often had the honour to hear your lordship cite from thence, I am persuaded, that the translators of the Bible were masters of an English style much fitter for that work, than any we see in our present writings; which I take to be owing to the simplicity that runs through the whole. Then, as to the greatest part of our liturgy, compiled long before the translation of the Bible now in use, and little altered since; there seem to be in it as great strains of true sublime eloquence, as are anywhere to be found in our language; which every man of good taste will observe in the communion service, that of burial, and other parts.

But when I say, that I would have our language, after it is duly correct, always to last, I do not mean that it should never be enlarged. Provided that no word, which a society shall give a sanction to, be afterward antiquated and exploded, they may have liberty to receive whatever new ones they shall find occasion for; because then the old books will yet be always valuable according to their intrinsic worth, and not thrown aside on account of unintelligible words and phrases, which appear harsh and uncouth, only because they are out of fashion. Had the Roman tongue continued vulgar in that city till this time, it would have been absolutely necessary, from the mighty changes that have been made in law and religion, from the many terms of art required in trade and in war, from the new inventions that have happened in the world, from the vast spreading of navigation and commerce, with many other obvious circumstances, to have made great additions to that language; yet the ancients would still have been read and understood with pleasure and ease. The Greek tongue received many enlargements between the time of Homer and that of Plutarch, yet the former author was probably as well understood in Trajan's time, as the latter. What Horace says of words going off and perishing like leaves, and new ones coming in their place, is a misfortune he laments, rather than a thing he approves; but I cannot see why this should be absolutely necessary, or if it were, what would have become of his *monumentum ære perennius?*

Writing by memory only, as I do at present, I would gladly keep within my depth; and therefore shall not enter into farther particulars. Neither do I pretend more than to shew the usefulness of this design, and to make some general observations, leaving the rest to that society, which I hope will owe its institution and patronage to your lordship. Besides, I would willingly avoid repetition, having, about a year ago, communicated to the public much of what I had to offer upon this subject, by the hands of an ingenious gentleman, who, for a long time, did thrice a-week divert or instruct the kingdom by his papers; and is supposed to pursue the same design at present, under the title of Spectator. This author, who has tried the force and compass of our language with so much success, agrees entirely with me in most of my sentiments relating to it; so do the greatest part of the men of wit and learning whom I have had the happiness to converse with; and therefore I imagine that such a society would be pretty unanimous in the main points.

Your lordship must allow, that such a work as this, brought to perfection, would very much contribute to the glory of her Majesty's reign; which ought to be recorded in words more durable than brass, and such as our posterity may read a thousand years hence, with pleasure as well as admiration. I always disapproved that false compliment to princes, that the most lasting monument they can have is the hearts of their subjects. It is indeed their greatest present felicity to reign in their subjects' hearts; but these are too perishable to preserve their memories, which can only be done by the pens of able and faithful historians. And I take it to be your lordship's duty, as prime minister, to give order for inspecting our language, and rendering it fit to record the history of so great and good a princess. Besides, my lord, as disinterested as you appear to the world, I am convinced that no man is more in the power of a prevailing favourite passion than yourself; I mean, that desire of true and lasting honour, which you have borne along with you through every stage of your life. To this you have often sacrificed your interest, your ease, and your health; for preserving and increasing this, you have exposed your person to secret treachery, and open violence. There is not, perhaps, an example in history of any minister, who, in so short a time, has performed so many great things, and overcome so many difficulties. Now, though I am fully convinced that you fear God, honour your Queen, and love your country, as much as any of your fellow-subjects, yet I must believe that the desire of fame has been no inconsiderable motive to quicken you in the pursuit of those actions which will best deserve it. But, at the same time, I must be so plain as to tell your lordship, that if you will not take some care to settle our language, and put it into a state of continuance, I cannot promise that your memory shall be preserved above a hundred years, farther than by imperfect tradition.

As barbarous and ignorant as we were in former centuries, there was more effectual care taken by our ancestors to preserve the memory of times and persons, than we find in this age of learning and politeness, as we are pleased to call it. The rude Latin of the monks is still very intelligible; whereas, had their records been delivered down only in the vulgar tongue, so barren and so barbarous, so subject to continual succeeding changes, they could not now be understood, unless by antiquaries who make it their study to expound them. And we must, at this day, have been content with such poor abstracts of our English story, as laborious men of low genius would think fit to give us; and even these, in the next age, would be likewise swallowed up in succeeding collections. If things go on at this rate, all I can promise your lordship is, that, about two hundred years hence, some painful compiler, who will be at the trouble of studying old language, may inform the world, that in the reign of Queen Anne, Robert, Earl of Oxford, a very wise and excellent man, was made high treasurer, and saved his country, which in those days was almost ruined by a foreign war, and a domestic faction. Thus much he may be able to pick out, and willing to transfer into his new history; but the rest of your character, which I, or any other writer, may now value ourselves by drawing, and the particular account of the great things done under your ministry, for which you are already so celebrated in most parts of Europe, will probably be dropped, on account of the antiquated style and manner they are delivered in.

How then shall any man, who has a genius for history equal to the best of the ancients, be able to undertake such a work with spirit and cheerfulness, when he considers that he will be read with pleasure but a very few years, and, in an age or two, shall hardly be understood without an interpreter? This is like employing an excellent statuary to work upon mouldering stone. Those who apply their studies to preserve the memory of others, will always have some concern for their own; and I believe it is for this reason that so few writers among us, of any distinction, have turned their thoughts to such a discouraging employment; for the best English historian must lie under this mortification, that when his style grows antiquated, he will be only considered as a tedious relater of facts, and perhaps consulted in his turn, among other neglected authors, to furnish materials for some future collector.

I doubt your lordship is but ill entertained with a few scattered thoughts upon a subject that deserves to be treated with ability and care. However, I must beg leave to add a few words more, perhaps not altogether foreign to the same matter. I know not whether that which I am going to say may pass for caution, advice, or reproach, any of which will be justly thought very improper from one in my station to one in yours. However, I must venture to affirm, that if genius and learning be not encouraged under your lordship's administration, you are the most inexcusable person alive. All your other virtues, my lord, will be defective without this; your affability, candour, and good-nature; that perpetual agreeableness of conversation, so disengaged in the midst of such a weight of business and opposition; even your justice, prudence, and magnanimity, will shine less bright without it. Your lordship is universally allowed to possess a very large portion in most parts of literature; and to this you owe the cultivating of those many virtues, which otherwise would have been less adorned, or in lower perfection. Neither can you acquit yourself of these obligations, without letting the arts, in their turn, share your influence and protection: besides, who knows but some true genius may happen to arise under your ministry, *exortus ut æthereus sol.* Every age might perhaps produce one or two of these to adorn it, if they were not sunk under the censure and obloquy of plodding, servile, imitating pedants. I do not mean, by a true genius, any bold writer, who breaks through the rules of decency to distinguish himself by the singularity of his opinions; but one who, upon a deserving subject, is able to open new scenes, and discover a vein of true and noble thinking, which never entered into any imagination before; every stroke of whose pen is worth all the paper blotted by hundreds of others in the compass of their lives. I know, my lord, your friends will offer in your defence, that, in your private capacity, you never refused your purse and credit to the service and support of learned or ingenious men; and that, ever since you have been in public employment, you have constantly bestowed your favours to the most deserving persons. But I desire your lordship not to be deceived; we never will admit of these excuses, nor will allow your private liberality, as great as it is, to atone for your excessive public thrift. But here again I am afraid most good subjects will interpose in your defence, by alleging the desperate condition you found the nation in, and the necessity there was for so able and faithful a steward to retrieve it, if possible, by the utmost frugality. We grant all this, my lord; but then it ought likewise to be considered, that you have already saved several millions to the public, and that what we ask is too inconsiderable to break into any rules of the strictest good husbandry. The French King bestows about half a dozen pensions to learned men in several parts of Europe, and perhaps a dozen in his own kingdom; which, in the whole, do probably not amount to half the income of many a private commoner in England, yet have more contributed to the glory of that prince than any million he has otherwise employed. For learning, like all true merit, is easily satisfied; while the false and counterfeit is perpetually craving, and never thinks it has enough. The smallest favour given by a great prince, as a mark of esteem, to reward the endowments of the mind, never fails to be returned with praise and gratitude, and loudly celebrated to the world. I have known, some years ago, several pensions given to particular persons, (how deservedly I shall not inquire,) any one of which, if divided into several parcels, and distributed by the Crown to those who might, upon occasion, distinguish themselves by some extraordinary production of wit or learning, would be amply sufficient to answer the end. Or, if any such persons were above money, (as every great genius certainly is, with very moderate conveniencies of life,) a medal, or some mark of distinction, would do full as well.

But I forget my province, and find myself turning projector before I am aware; although it be one of the last characters under which I should desire to appear before your lordship, especially when I have the ambition of aspiring to that of being, with the greatest respect and truth,

My Lord,

Your Lordship's most obedient,

most obliged,

and most humble servant,

J. Swift.

AN ESSAY

ON

MODERN EDUCATION.

---o---

THE following treatise is excellent on all points, excepting, perhaps, the tone of bitterness with which Swift reprobates persons and professions of a different turn from his own. The zeal with which he maintains the cause of sound classic learning is worthy of his genius. And it is a matter of important remark, that since the continent has been shut against wanderers of rank and wealth, we have seen symptoms of the revival of ancient discipline among our nobility and youths of fortune.

---o---

FROM frequently reflecting upon the course and method of educating youth in this and a neighbouring kingdom, with the general success and consequence thereof, I am come to this determination,—that education is always the worse, in proportion to the wealth and grandeur of the parents; nor do I doubt in the least, that if the whole world were now under the dominion of one monarch, (provided I might be allowed to choose where he should fix the seat of his empire,) the only son and heir of that monarch would be the worst educated mortal that ever was born since the creation; and I doubt the same proportion will hold through all degrees and titles, from an emperor downward to the common gentry.

I do not say that this has been always the case; for, in better times, it was directly otherwise, and a scholar may fill half his Greek and Roman shelves with authors of the noblest birth, as well as highest virtue: nor do I tax all nations at present with this defect, for I know there are some to be excepted, and particularly Scotland, under all the disadvantages of its climate and soil, if that happiness be not rather owing even to those very disadvantages. What is then to be done, if this reflection must fix on two countries, which will be most ready to take offence, and which, of all others, it will be least prudent or safe to offend?

But there is one circumstance yet more dangerous and lamentable: for if, according to the *postulatum* already laid down, the higher quality any youth is of, he is in greater likelihood to be worse educated, it behoves me to dread and keep far from the verge of *scandalum magnatum*.

Retracting, therefore, that hazardous *postulatum*, I shall venture no farther at present than to say, that perhaps some additional care in educating the sons of nobility, and principal gentry, might not be ill employed. If this be not delivered with softness enough, I must for the future be silent.

In the meantime, let me ask only two questions, which relate to England. I ask, first, how it comes about that, for above sixty years past, the chief conduct of affairs has been generally placed in the hands of new men, with very few exceptions? The noblest blood of England having been shed in the grand rebellion, many great families became extinct, or were supported only by minors. When the King was restored, very few of those lords remained who began, or at least had improved, their education under the reigns of King James or King Charles I., of which lords the two principal were the Marquis of Ormond, and the Earl of Southampton. The minors had, during the rebellion and usurpation, either received too much tincture of bad principles from those fanatic times, or, coming to age at the Restoration, fell into the vices of that dissolute reign.

I date from this era the corrupt method of education among us, and, in consequence thereof, the necessity the Crown lay under of introducing new men into the chief conduct of public affairs, or to the office of what we now call prime ministers; men of art, knowledge, application and insinuation, merely for want of a supply among the nobility. They were generally (though not always) of good birth; sometimes younger brothers, at other times such, who, although inheriting good estates, yet happened to be well educated, and provided with learning. Such, under that king, were Hyde, Bridgeman, Clifford, Osborn, Godolphin, Ashley Cooper: few or none under the short reign of King James II.: under King William, Somers, Montague, Churchill, Vernon, Boyle, and many others: under the Queen, Harley, St. John, Harcourt, Trevor: who, indeed, were persons of the best private families, but unadorned with titles. So in the following reign, Mr. Robert Walpole was for many years prime minister, in which post he still happily continues: his brother Horace is ambassador extraordinary to France. Mr. Addison and Mr. Craggs, without the least alliance to support them, have been secretaries of state.

If the facts have been thus for above sixty years past, (whereof I could, with a little farther recollection, produce many more instances,) I would ask again, how it has happened, that in a nation plentifully abounding with nobility, so great share in the most competent parts of public management has been for so long a period chiefly entrusted to commoners; unless some omissions or defects of the highest import may be charged upon those, to whom the care of educating our noble youth had been committed? For, if there be any difference between human creatures in the point of natural parts, as we usually call them, it should seem, that the advantage lies on the side of children born from noble and wealthy parents; the same traditional sloth and luxury, which render their body weak and effeminate, perhaps refining and giving a freer motion to the spirits, beyond what can be expected from the gross, robust issue of meaner mortals. Add to this the peculiar advantages, which all young noblemen possess by the privileges of their birth. Such as a free access to courts, and a universal deference paid to their persons.

But, as my Lord Bacon charges it for a fault on princes, that they are impatient to compass ends, without giving themselves the trouble of consulting or executing the means; so, perhaps, it may be the disposition of young nobles, either from the indulgence of parents, tutors, and governors, or their own inactivity, that they expect the accomplishments of a good education, without the least expense of time or study to acquire them.

What I said last, I am ready to retract, for the case is infinitely worse; and the very maxims set up to direct modern education are enough to destroy all the seeds of knowledge, honour, wisdom, and virtue, among us. The current opinion prevails, that the study of Greek and Latin is loss of time; that public schools, by mingling the sons of noblemen with those of the vulgar, engage the former in bad company;

that whipping breaks the spirits of lads well born; that universities make young men pedants; that to dance, fence, speak French, and know how to behave yourself among great persons of both sexes, comprehends the whole duty of a gentleman.

I cannot but think, this wise system of education has been much cultivated among us, by those worthies of the army, who during the last war returned from Flanders at the close of each campaign, became the dictators of behaviour, dress, and politeness, to all those youngsters, who frequent chocolate-coffee-gaminghouses, drawing-rooms, operas, levees, and assemblies: where a colonel, by his pay, perquisites, and plunder, was qualified to outshine many peers of the realm; and by the influence of an exotic habit and demeanour, added to other foreign accomplishments, gave the law to the whole town, and was copied as the standard pattern of whatever was refined in dress, equipage, conversation, or diversions.

I remember, in those times, an admired original of that vocation sitting in a coffeehouse near two gentlemen, whereof one was of the clergy, who were engaged in some discourse, that savoured of learning. This officer thought fit to interpose, and professing to deliver the sentiments of his fraternity, as well as his own, (and probably he did so of too many among them,) turned to the clergyman, and spoke in the following manner: " D——n me, doctor, say what you will, the army is the only school for gentlemen. Do you think my Lord Marlborough beat the French with Greek and Latin? D——n me, a scholar when he comes into good company, what is he but an ass? D——n me, I would be glad by G——d to see any of your scholars with his nouns and his verbs, and his philosophy, and trigonometry, what a figure he would make at a siege, or blockade, or rencountering——

D—n me," &c.* After which he proceeded with a volley of military terms, less significant, sounding worse, and harder to be understood, than any that were ever coined by the commentators upon Aristotle. I would not here be thought to charge the soldiery with ignorance and contempt of learning, without allowing exceptions, of which I have known many; but, however, the worst example, especially in a great majority, will certainly prevail.

I have heard, that the late Earl of Oxford, in the time of his ministry, never passed by White's chocolatehouse (the common rendezvous of infamous sharpers and noble cullies) without bestowing a curse upon that famous academy, as the bane of half the English nobility. I have likewise been told another passage concerning that great minister, which, because it gives a humorous idea of one principal ingredient in modern education, take as follows. Le Sack, the famous French dancing master, in great admiration, asked a friend, whether it were true that Mr. Harley was made an earl and lord treasurer? and finding it confirmed, said, "Well; I wonder what the devil the Queen could see in him; for I attended him two years, and he was the greatest dunce that ever I taught."†

Another hindrance to good education, and I think the greatest of any, is that pernicious custom in rich and noble families, of entertaining French tutors in their houses. These wretched pedagogues are enjoined by the father, to take special care that the boy shall be perfect in his French; by the mother, that master must not walk till he is hot, nor be suffered

---

* Swift has versified very near the whole of this passage in his poem on Hamilton's Bawn, where it is put in the mouth of the Captain of Dragoons.

† The story of Le Sack many of the Dean's friends have heard him tell, as he had it from the Earl himself. See Tatler, No. xx.

to play with other boys, nor be wet in his feet, nor daub his clothes, and to see the dancing master attends constantly, and does his duty; she farther insists, that he be not kept too long poring on his book, because he is subject to sore eyes, and of a weakly constitution.

By these methods, the young gentleman is, in every article, as fully accomplished at eight years old, as at eight and twenty, age adding only to the growth of his person and his vice; so that if you should look at him in his boyhood through the magnifying end of a perspective, and in his manhood through the other, it would be impossible to spy any difference; the same airs, the same strut, the same cock of his hat, and posture of his sword, (as far as the change of fashions will allow,) the same understanding, the same compass of knowledge, with the very same absurdity, impudence, and impertinence of tongue.*

He is taught from the nursery, that he must inherit a great estate, and has no need to mind his book, which is a lesson he never forgets to the end of his life. His chief solace is to steal down and play at spanfarthing with the page or young blacka-

---

* The late Sir David Dalrymple gives this account of the state of the gay world in the reign of Queen Anne:—

"General Bland told me that every gay man about the town did not pretend to be a beau in the days of Queen Anne; it was a peculiar character, and distinguished by bold strokes, as having horses of a particular colour, or the like. In process of time this distinction was lost, and the word was applied to all *fine men*, as the lower female vulgar term them. As soon as beau became a *nomen multitudinis*, there was a necessity of ranging the fine men under different classes; and it is but justice to this age to say, that it has invented a name for almost every character that distinguishes itself by dress or behaviour, from the plain men who choose to pass unobserved in the 'crowd."—*Letter, dated Edin.*, *May* 4, 1776.

moor, or little favourite footboy, one of which is his principal confidant and bosom friend.

There is one young lord* in this town, who, by an unexampled piece of good fortune, was miraculously snatched out of the gulph of ignorance, confined to a public school for a due term of years, well whipped when he deserved it, clad no better than his comrades, and always their playfellow on the same foot, had no precedence in the school, but what was given him by his merit, and lost it whenever he was negligent. It is well known, how many mutinies were bred at this unprecedented treatment, what complaints among his relations, and other great ones of both sexes; that his stockings with silver clocks were ravished from him; that he wore his own hair; that his dress was undistinguished; that he was not fit to appear at a ball or assembly, nor suffered to go to either: and it was with the utmost difficulty he became qualified for his present removal, where he may probably be farther persecuted, and possibly with success, if the firmness of a very worthy governor and his own good dispositions will not preserve him. I confess, I cannot but wish, he may go on in the way he began; because I have a curiosity to know by so singular an experiment, whether truth, honour, justice, temperance, courage, and good sense, acquired by a school and college education, may not produce a very tolerable lad, although he should happen to fail in one or two of those accomplishments, which, in the general vogue, are held so important to the finishing of a gentleman.

It is true, I have known an academical education to have been exploded in public assemblies; and have heard more than one or two persons of high

---

* Lord Mountcashel, bred at Dr. Sheridan's school.

rank declare, they could learn nothing more at Oxford and Cambridge, than to drink ale and smoke tobacco; wherein I firmly believed them, and could have added some hundred examples from my own observation in one of those universities; but they all were of young heirs sent thither only for form; either from schools, where they were not suffered by their careful parents to stay above three months in the year; or from under the management of French family tutors, who yet often attended them to their college, to prevent all possibility of their improvement; but I never yet knew any one person of quality, who followed his studies at the university, and carried away his just proportion of learning, that was not ready upon all occasions to celebrate and defend that course of education, and to prove a patron of learned men.

There is one circumstance in a learned education, which ought to have much weight, even with those who have no learning at all. The books read at school and college are full of incitements to virtue, and discouragements from vice, drawn from the wisest reasons, the strongest motives, and the most influencing examples. Thus young minds are filled early with an inclination to good, and an abhorrence of evil, both which increase in them, according to the advances they make in literature; and although they may be, and too often are, drawn by the temptations of youth, and the opportunities of a large fortune, into some irregularities, when they come forward into the great world, yet it is ever with reluctance and compunction of mind; because their bias to virtue still continues. They may stray sometimes, out of infirmity or compliance; but they will soon return to the right road, and keep it always in view. I speak only of those excesses, which are too much the attendants of youth and warmer blood; for as to the points of honour, truth, justice, and other noble gifts of the mind, wherein the temperature of the body has no concern, they are seldom or ever known to be wild.

I have engaged myself very unwarily in too copious a subject for so short a paper. The present scope I would aim at, is, to prove that some proportion of human knowledge appears requisite to those, who by their birth or fortune are called to the making of laws, and, in a subordinate way, to the execution of them; and that such knowledge is not to be obtained, without a miracle, under the frequent, corrupt, and sottish methods of educating those who are born to wealth or titles. For I would have it remembered, that I do by no means confine these remarks to young persons of noble birth; the same errors running through all families, where there is wealth enough to afford, that their sons (at least the eldest) may be good for nothing. Why should my son be a scholar, when it is not intended that he should live by his learning? By this rule, if what is commonly said be true, that "money answers all things," why should my son be honest, temperate, just, or charitable, since he has no intention to depend upon any of these qualities for a maintenance?

When all is done, perhaps, upon the whole, the matter is not so bad as I would make it; and God, who works good out of evil, acting only by the ordinary course and rule of nature, permits this continual circulation of human things, for his own unsearchable ends. The father grows rich by avarice, injustice, oppression; he is a tyrant in the neighbourhood over slaves and beggars, whom he calls his tenants. Why should he desire to have qualities infused into his son, which himself never possessed, or knew, or found the want of, in the acquisition of his wealth? The son, bred in sloth and idleness, becomes a spendthrift, a cully, a profligate, and goes out of the world a beggar, as his father came in: thus the former is punished for his own sins, as well as for those of the latter. The dunghill, having raised a huge mushroom of short duration, is now spread to enrich other men's lands. It is indeed of worse consequence, where noble families are gone to decay: because their titles and privileges outlive their estates: and politicians tell us, that nothing is more dangerous to the public, than a numerous nobility without merit or fortune. But even here God has likewise prescribed some remedy in the order of nature; so many great families coming to an end by the sloth, luxury, and abandoned lusts, which enervated their breed through every succession, producing gradually a more effeminate race wholly unfit for propagation.

HINTS TOWARD AN ESSAY

ON

CONVERSATION.

 HAVE observed few obvious subjects to have been so seldom, or at least so slightly handled as this; and indeed I know few so difficult to be treated as it ought, nor yet, upon which there seems so much to be said.

Most things pursued by men for the happiness of public or private life, our wit or folly have so refined, that they seldom subsist but in idea; a true friend, a good marriage, a perfect form of government, with some others, require so many ingredients, so good in their several kinds, and so much niceness in mixing them, that for some thousands of years men have despaired of reducing their schemes to perfection: but, in conversation, it is, or might be otherwise; for here we are only to avoid a multitude of errors, which, although a matter of some difficulty, may be in every man's power, for want of which it remains as mere an idea as the other. Therefore it seems to me, that the truest way to understand conversation, is to know the faults and errors to which it is subject, and from thence every man to form maxims to himself whereby it may be regulated, because it requires few talents to which most men are not born, or at least may not acquire, without any great genius or study. For nature has left every man a capacity of being agreeable, though not of shining in company; and there are a hundred men sufficiently qualified for both, who, by a very few faults, that they might correct in half an hour, are not so much as tolerable.

I was prompted to write my thoughts upon this subject by mere indignation, to reflect that so useful and innocent a pleasure, so fitted for every period and condition of life, and so much in all men's power, should be so much neglected and abused.

And in this discourse it will be necessary to note those errors that are obvious, as well as others which are seldomer observed, since there are few so obvious, or acknowledged, into which most men, some time or other, are not apt to run.

For instance: nothing is more generally exploded than the folly of talking too much; yet I rarely remember to have seen five people together, where some one among them has not been predominant in that kind, to the great constraint and disgust of all the rest. But among such as deal in multitudes of words, none are comparable to the sober deliberate talker, who proceeds with much thought and caution, makes his preface, branches out into several digressions, finds a hint that puts him in mind of another story, which he promises to tell you when this is done; comes back regularly to his subject, cannot readily call to mind some person's name, holding his head, complains of his memory; the whole company all this while in suspense; at length says, it is no matter, and so goes on. And, to crown the business, it perhaps proves at last a story the company has heard fifty times before; or, at best, some insipid adventure of the relater.

Another general fault in conversation, is that of those who affect to talk of themselves; some, without any ceremony, will run over the history of their lives; will relate the annals of their diseases, with the several symptoms and circumstances of them; will enumerate the hardships and injustice they have suffered in court, in parliament, in love, or in law. Others are more dexterous, and with great art will lie on the watch to hook in their own praise: they will call a witness to remember they always foretold what would happen in such a case, but none would believe them; they advised such a man from the beginning, and told him the consequences, just as they happened; but he would have his own way. Others make a vanity of telling their faults; they are the strangest men in the world; they cannot dissemble; they own it is a folly; they have lost abundance of advantages by it; but if you would give them the world, they cannot help it; there is something in their nature that abhors insincerity and constraint; with many other insufferable topics of the same altitude.

Of such mighty importance every man is to himself, and ready to think he is so to others; without once making this easy and obvious reflection, that his affairs can have no more weight with other men than theirs have with him; and how little that is, he is sensible enough.

Where a company has met, I often have observed two persons discover, by some accident, that they were bred together at the same school or university; after which the rest are condemned to silence, and to listen while these two are refreshing each other's memory, with the arch tricks and passages of themselves and their comrades.

I know a great officer of the army, who will sit for some time with a supercilious and impatient silence, full of anger and contempt for those who are talking; at length, of a sudden, demanding audience, decide the matter in a short dogmatical way; then withdraw within himself again, and vouchsafe to talk no more, until his spirits circulate again to the same point.

There are some faults in conversation, which none are so subject to as the men of wit, nor ever so much as when they are with each other. If they have opened their mouths, without endeavouring to say a witty thing, they think it is so many words lost: it is a torment to the hearers, as much as to themselves, to see them upon the rack for invention, and in perpetual constraint, with so little success. They must do something extraordinary, in order to acquit themselves, and answer their character, else the standers-by may be disappointed, and be apt to think them only like the rest of mortals. I have known two men of wit industriously brought together, in order to entertain the company, where they have made a very ridiculous figure, and provided all the mirth at their own expense.

I know a man of wit, who is never easy but where he can be allowed to dictate and preside; he neither expects to be informed or entertained, but to display his own talents. His business is to be good company, and not good conversation; and therefore he chooses to frequent those who are content to listen, and profess themselves his admirers. And, indeed, the worst conversation I ever remember to have heard in my life, was that at Will's coffee-house, where the wits (as they were called) used formerly to assemble; that is to say, five or six men who had writ plays, or at least prologues, or had share in a miscellany, came thither, and entertained one another with their trifling composures, in so important an air, as if they had been the noblest efforts of human nature, or that the fate of kingdoms depended on them; and they were usually attended with an humble audience of young students from the inns of court, or the universities; who, at due distance, listened to these oracles, and returned home with great contempt for their law and philosophy, their heads filled with trash, under the name of politeness, criticism, and belles lettres.*

By these means, the poets, for many years past, were all overrun with pedantry. For, as I take it, the word is not properly used; because pedantry is the too frequent or unseasonable obtruding our own knowledge in common discourse, and placing too great a value upon it; by which definition, men of the court, or the army, may be as guilty of pedantry as a philosopher or a divine; and it is the same vice in women, when they are over copious upon the subject of their petticoats, or their fans, or their china. For which reason, although it be a piece of prudence, as well as good manners, to put men upon talking on subjects they are best versed in, yet that is a liberty a wise man could hardly take; because, beside the imputation of pedantry, it is what he would never improve by.

The great town is usually provided with some player, mimic, or buffoon, who has a general reception at the good tables; familiar and domestic with persons of the first quality, and usually sent for at every meeting to divert the company; against which I have no objection. You go there as to a farce or a puppetshow; your business is only to laugh in season, either out of inclination or civility, while

---

* Probably Addison's perpetual presidency increased Swift's dislike to these coffeehouse meetings.

this merry companion is acting his part. It is a business he has undertaken, and we are to suppose he is paid for his day's work. I only quarrel, when, in select and private meetings, where men of wit and learning are invited to pass an evening, this jester should be admitted to run over his circle of tricks, and make the whole company unfit for any other conversation, beside the indignity of confounding men's talents at so shameful a rate.

Raillery is the finest part of conversation; but, as it is our usual custom to counterfeit and adulterate whatever is too dear for us, so we have done with this, and turned it all into what is generally called repartee, or being smart; just as when an expensive fashion comes up, those who are not able to reach it, content themselves with some paltry imitation. It now passes for raillery to run a man down in discourse, to put him out of countenance, and make him ridiculous; sometimes to expose the defects of his person or understanding; on all which occasions, he is obliged not to be angry, to avoid the imputation of not being able to take a jest. It is admirable to observe one who is dexterous at this art, singling out a weak adversary, getting the laugh on his side, and then carrying it all before him. The French, from whence we borrow the word, have a quite different idea of the thing, and so had we in the politer age of our fathers. Raillery was to say something that at first appeared a reproach or reflection, but, by some turn of wit, unexpected and surprising, ended always in a compliment, and to the advantage of the person it was addressed to. And surely one of the best rules in conversation is, never to say a thing which any of the company can reasonably wish we had rather left unsaid: nor can there anything be well more contrary to the ends for which people meet together than to part unsatisfied with each other or themselves.

There are two faults in conversation, which appear very different, yet arise from the same root, and are equally blameable; I mean an impatience to interrupt others; and the uneasiness of being interrupted ourselves. The two chief ends of conversation are to entertain and improve those we are among, or to receive those benefits ourselves; which whoever will consider, cannot easily run into either of these two errors; because, when any man speaks in company, it is to be supposed he does it for his hearers' sake, and not his own; so that common discretion will teach us not to force their attention, if they are not willing to lend it; nor, on the other side, to interrupt him who is in possession, because that is in the grossest manner to give the preference to our own good sense.

There are some people, whose good manners will not suffer them to interrupt you, but, what is almost as bad, will discover abundance of impatience, and lie upon the watch until you have done, because they have started something in their own thoughts, which they long to be delivered of. Meantime, they are so far from regarding what passes, that their imaginations are wholly turned upon what they have in reserve, for fear it should slip out of their memory; and thus they confine their invention, which might otherwise range over a hundred things full as good, and that might be much more naturally introduced.

There is a sort of rude familiarity, which some people, by practising among their intimates, have introduced into their general conversation, and would have it pass for innocent freedom or humour; which is a dangerous experiment in our northern climate, where all the little decorum and politeness we have, are purely forced by art, and are so ready to lapse into barbarity. This, among the Romans, was the raillery of slaves, of which we have many instances in Plautus. It seems to have been introduced among us by Cromwell,* who, by preferring the scum of the people, made it a court entertainment, of which I have heard many particulars; and, considering all things were turned upside down, it was reasonable and judicious: although it was a piece of policy found out to ridicule a point of honour in the other extreme, when the smallest word misplaced among gentlemen ended in a duel.

There are some men excellent at telling a story, and provided with a plentiful stock of them, which they can draw out upon occasion in all companies; and, considering how low conversation runs now among us, it is not altogether a contemptible talent; however, it is subject to two unavoidable defects, frequent repetition, and being soon exhausted; so that, whoever values this gift in himself, has need of a good memory, and ought frequently to shift his company, that he may not discover the weakness of his fund; for those who are thus endued have seldom any other revenue, but live upon the main stock.

Great speakers in public are seldom agreeable in private conversation, whether their faculty be natural, or acquired by practice, and often venturing. Natural elocution, although it may seem a paradox, usually springs from a barrenness of invention, and of words; by which men who have only one stock of notions

---

* Cromwell's taste for buffoonery is well known. Captain Hodgson describes him as greatly diverted with the predicament of a soldier, whose head stuck fast in a butter-churn, as he attempted to drink the cream; and adds, "Oliver loved an innocent jest."—*Hodgson's Memoirs*, p. 131.

upon every subject, and one set of phrases to express them in, they swim upon the superficies, and offer themselves on every occasion; therefore, men of much learning, and who know the compass of a language, are generally the worst talkers on a sudden, until much practice has inured and emboldened them; because they are confounded with plenty of matter, variety of notions and of words, which they cannot readily choose, but are perplexed and entangled by too great a choice; which is no disadvantage in private conversation; where, on the other side, the talent of haranguing is, of all others, most unsupportable.

Nothing has spoiled men more for conversation, than the character of being wits; to support which, they never fail of encouraging a number of followers and admirers, who list themselves in their service, wherein they find their accounts on both sides by pleasing their mutual vanity. This has given the former such an air of superiority, and made the latter so pragmatical, that neither of them are well to be endured. I say nothing here of the itch of dispute and contradiction, telling of lies, or of those who are troubled with the disease called the wandering of the thoughts, so that they are never present in mind at what passes in discourse; for whoever labours under any of these possessions, is as unfit for conversation as a madman in Bedlam.

I think I have gone over most of the errors in conversation that have fallen under my notice or memory, except some that are merely personal, and others too gross to need exploding; such as lewd or profane talk; but I pretend only to treat the errors of conversation in general, and not the several subjects of discourse, which would be infinite. Thus we see how human nature is most debased, by the abuse of that faculty which is held the great distinction between men and brutes: and how little advantage we make of that, which might be the greatest, the most lasting, and the most innocent, as well as useful pleasure of life: in default of which, we are forced to take up with those poor amusements of dress and visiting, or the more pernicious ones of play, drink, and vicious amours; whereby the nobility and gentry of both sexes are entirely corrupted both in body and mind, and have lost all notions of love, honour, friendship, generosity; which, under the name of fopperies, have been for some time laughed out of doors.

This degeneracy of conversation, with the pernicious consequences thereof upon our humours and dispositions, has been owing, among other causes, to the custom arisen, for some time past, of excluding women from any share in our society, farther than in parties at play, or dancing, or in the pursuit of an amour. I take the highest period of politeness in England (and it is of the same date in France) to have been the peaceable part of King Charles the First's reign; and from what we read of those times, as well as from the accounts I have formerly met with from some who lived in that court, the methods then used for raising and cultivating conversation were altogether different from ours: several ladies, whom we find celebrated by the poets of that age, had assemblies at their houses, where persons of the best understanding, and of both sexes, met to pass the evenings in discoursing upon whatever agreeable subjects were occasionally started; and although we are apt to ridicule the sublime platonick notions they had, or personated, in love and friendship, I conceive their refinements were grounded upon reason, and that a little grain of the romance is no ill ingredient to preserve and exalt the dignity of human nature, without which it is apt to degenerate into everything that is sordid, vicious, and low. If there were no other use in the conversation of ladies, it is sufficient that it would lay a restraint upon those odious topics of immodesty and indecencies, into which the rudeness of our northern genius is so apt to fall. And, therefore, it is observable in those sprightly gentlemen about the town, who are so very dexterous at entertaining a vizard mask in the park or the playhouse, that in the company of ladies of virtue and honour, they are silent and disconcerted, and out of their element.

There are some people who think they sufficiently acquit themselves, and entertain their company, with relating facts of no consequence, nor at all out of the road of such common incidents as happen every day; and this I have observed more frequently among the Scots than any other nation, who are very careful not to omit the minutest circumstances of time or place;* which kind of discourse, if it were not a little relieved by the uncouth terms and phrases, as well as accent and gesture, peculiar to that country, would be hardly tolerable. It is not a fault in company to talk much; but to continue it long is certainly one; for, if the majority of those who are got together be naturally silent or cautious, the conversation will flag, unless it be often renewed by one among them, who can start new subjects, provided he does not dwell upon them, that leave room for answers and replies.

---

* Persons of this country are at present prone to entertain company rather by the display of their argumentative than of their narrative powers.

A LETTER OF ADVICE

TO

A YOUNG POET.

TOGETHER WITH A PROPOSAL FOR THE ENCOURAGEMENT OF POETRY IN IRELAND.

*Sic honor et nomen divinis vatibus atque
Carminibus venit.**————
HOR. DE ART. POET. 400.

————o————

SIR, *Dec.* 1, 1720.

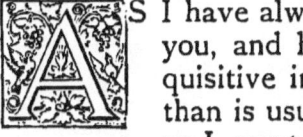S I have always professed a friendship for you, and have therefore been more inquisitive into your conduct and studies than is usually agreeable to young men; so I must own I am not a little pleased to find, by your last account, that you have entirely bent your thoughts to English poetry, with design to make it your profession and business. Two reasons incline me to encourage you in this study; one, the narrowness of your present circumstances; the other, the great use of poetry to mankind and society, and in every employment of life. Upon these views, I

---

* So verse became divine, and poets gain'd applause.
FRANCIS.

cannot but commend your wise resolution to withdraw so early from other unprofitable and severe studies, and betake yourself to that, which, if you have good luck, will advance your fortune, and make you an ornament to your friends and your country. It may be your justification, and farther encouragement, to consider, that history, ancient or modern, cannot furnish you an instance of one person, eminent in any station, who was not in some measure versed in poetry, or at least a well-wisher to the professors of it; neither would I despair to prove, if legally called thereto, that it is impossible to be a good soldier, divine, or lawyer, or even so much as an eminent bellman, or ballad-singer, without some taste of poetry, and a competent skill in versification; but I say the less of this, because the renowned Sir P. Sidney has exhausted the subject before me, in his defence of poesie, on which I shall make no other remark but this, that he argues there as if he really believed himself.

For my own part, having never made one verse since I was at school, where I suffered too much for my blunders in poetry to have any love to it ever since, I am not able, from any experience of my own, to give you those instructions you desire; neither will I declare (for I love to conceal my passions) how much I lament my neglect of poetry in those periods of my life which were properest for improvements in that ornamental part of learning; besides, my age and infirmities might well excuse me to you, as being unqualified to be your writing-master, with spectacles on, and a shaking hand. However, that I may not be altogether wanting to you in an affair of so much importance to your credit and happiness, I shall here give you some scattered thoughts upon the subject, such as I have gathered by reading and observation.

There is a certain little instrument, the first of those in use with scholars, and the meanest, considering the materials of it, whether it be a joint of wheaten straw (the old Arcadian pipe) or just three inches of slender wire, or a stripped feather, or a corking-pin. Farthermore, this same diminutive tool, for the posture of it, usually reclines its head on the thumb of the right hand, sustains the foremost finger upon its breast, and is itself supported by the second. This is commonly known by the name of a fescue; I shall here, therefore, condescend to be this little elementary guide, and point out some particulars, which may be of use to you in your hornbook of poetry.

In the first place, I am not yet convinced, that it is at all necessary for a modern poet to believe in God, or have any serious sense of religion; and in this article you must give me leave to suspect your capacity; because, religion being what your mother taught you, you will hardly find it possible, at least not easy, all at once to get over those early prejudices, so far as to think it better to be a great wit than a good Christian, though herein the general practice is against you; so that, if, upon inquiry, you find in yourself any such softnesses, owing to the nature of your education, my advice is, that you forthwith lay down your pen, as having no farther business with it in the way of poetry; unless you will be content to pass for an insipid, or will submit to be hooted at by your fraternity, or can disguise your religion, as well-bred men do their learning, in complaisance to company.

For poetry, as it has been managed for some years past, by such as make a business of it, (and of such only I speak here, for I do not call him a poet that writes for his diversion, any more than that gentleman a fiddler who amuses himself with a violin,) I say, our poetry of late has been altogether disengaged from the narrow notions of virtue and piety, because it has been found, by experience of our professors, that the smallest quantity of religion, like a single drop of malt liquor in claret, will muddy and discompose the brightest poetical genius.

Religion supposes heaven and hell, the word of God, and sacraments, and twenty other circumstances, which, taken seriously, are a wonderful check to wit and humour, and such as a true poet cannot possibly give in to, with a saving to his poetical licence; but yet it is necessary for him, that others should believe those things seriously, that his wit may be exercised on their wisdom for for so doing; for though a wit need not have religion, religion is necessary to a wit, as an instrument is to the hand that plays upon it; and for this, the moderns plead the example of their great idol Lucretius, who had not been by half so eminent a poet (as he truly was) but that he stood tiptoe on religion, *Religio pedibus subjecta*, and, by that rising ground, had the advantage of all the poets of his own or following times, who were not mounted on the same pedestal.

Besides, it is farther to be observed, that Petronius, another of their favourites, speaking of the qualifications of a good poet, insists chiefly on the *liber spiritus;* by which I have been ignorant enough heretofore, to suppose he meant, a good invention, or great compass of thought, or a sprightly imagination: but I have learned a better construction, from the opinion and practice of the moderns; and, taking it literally for a free spirit, *i.e.*, a spirit, or mind, free or disengaged from all prejudices concerning God, religion, and another world, it is to me a plain account why our present set of poets are, and hold themselves obliged to be, freethinkers.

But, although I cannot recommend religion upon the practice of some of our most eminent English poets, yet I can justly advise you, from their example, to be conversant in the Scriptures, and, if possible, to make yourself entirely master of them; in which, however, I intend nothing less than imposing upon you a task of piety. Far be it from me to desire you to believe them, or lay any great stress upon their authority; in that you may do as you think fit; but to read them as a piece of necessary furniture for a wit and a poet; which is a very different view from that of a Christian. For I have made it my observation, that the greatest wits have been the best textuaries: our modern poets are, all to a man, almost as well read in the Scriptures as some of our divines, and often abound more with the phrase. They have read them historically, critically, musically, comically, poetically, and every other way except religiously, and have found their account in doing so. For the Scriptures are undoubtedly a fund of wit, and a subject for wit. You may, according to the modern practice, be witty upon them, or out of them; and, to speak the truth, but for them, I know not what our playwrights would do for images, allusions, similitudes, examples, or even language itself. Shut up the sacred books, and I would be bound our wit would run down like an alarum, or fall as the stocks did, and ruin half the poets in these kindgoms. And if that were the case, how would most of that tribe, (all, I think, but the immortal Addison, who made a better use of his Bible, and a few more,) who dealt so freely in that fund, rejoice that they had drawn out in time, and left the present generation of poets to be the bubbles!

But here I must enter one caution, and desire you to take notice, that in this advice of reading the

Scriptures, I had not the least thought concerning your qualification that way for poetical orders; which I mention, because I find a notion of that kind advanced by one of our English poets; and is, I suppose, maintained by the rest. He says to Spenser, in a pretended vision,

> "——With hands laid on, ordain me fit
> For the great cure and ministry of wit."

Which passage is, in my opinion, a notable allusion to the Scriptures; and, making but reasonable allowances for the small circumstance of profaneness, bordering close upon blasphemy, is inimitably fine; beside some useful discoveries made in it, as, that there are bishops in poetry, that these bishops must ordain young poets, and with laying on hands; and that poetry is a cure of souls; and, consequently speaking, those who have such cures ought to be poets, and too often are so: and indeed, as of old poets and priests were one and the same function, the alliance of those ministerial offices is to this day happily maintained in the same persons; and this I take to be the only justifiable reason for that appellation which they so much affect, I mean the modest title of divine poets. However, having never been present at the ceremony of ordaining to the priesthood of poetry, I own I have no notion of the thing, and shall say the less of it here.

The Scriptures then being generally both the fountain and subject of modern wit, I could do no less than give them the preference in your reading. After a thorough acquaintance with them, I would advise you to turn your thoughts to human literature, which yet I say more in compliance with vulgar opinions, than according to my own sentiments.

For, indeed, nothing has surprised me more, than to see the prejudices of mankind as to this matter of human learning, who have generally thought it necessary to be a good scholar in order to be a good poet; than which nothing is falser in fact, or more contrary to practice and experience. Neither will I dispute the matter if any man will undertake to shew me one professed poet now in being, who is anything of what may be justly called a scholar; or is the worse poet for that, but perhaps the better, for being so little encumbered with the pedantry of learning: it is true, the contrary was the opinion of our forefathers, which we of this age have devotion enough to receive from them on their own terms, and unexamined, but not sense enough to perceive it was a gross mistake in them. So Horace has told us:

> Scribendi recte sapere est et principium et fons,
> Rem tibi Socraticæ poterunt ostendere chartæ.*
>
> HOR. *de Art. Poet.* 309.

But, to see the different casts of men's heads, some, not inferior to that poet in understanding, (if you will take their own word for it,) do see no consequence in this rule, and are not ashamed to declare themselves of a contrary opinion. Do not many men write well in common account, who have nothing of that principle? Many are too wise to be poets, and others too much poets to be wise. Must a man, forsooth, be no less than a philosopher to be a poet, when it is plain that some of the greatest idiots of the age are our prettiest performers that way? And for this, I appeal to the judgment and observation of mankind. Sir P. Sidney's notable remark upon this nation, may not be improper to mention here. He says, "In our neighbour country, Ireland, where

---

* Good sense, that fountain of the Muse's art,
Let the strong page of Socrates impart.

true learning goes very bare, yet are their poets held in devout reverence;" which shews, that learning is no way necessary either to the making of a poet, or judging of him. And farther, to see the fate of things, notwithstanding our learning here is as bare as ever, yet are our poets not held, as formerly, in devout reverence; but are, perhaps, the most contemptible race of mortals now in this kingdom, which is no less to be wondered at than lamented.

Some of the old philosophers were poets, as, according to the forementioned author, Socrates and Plato were: which, however, is what I did not know before; but that does not say that all poets are, or that any need be, philosophers, otherwise than as those are so called who are a little out at the elbows. In which sense the great Shakespeare might have been a philosopher; but was no scholar, yet was an excellent poet. Neither do I think a late most judicious critic so much mistaken, as others do, in advancing this opinion, that "Shakespeare had been a worse poet, had he been a better scholar:" and Sir W. Davenant is another instance in the same kind. Nor must it be forgotten, that Plato was an avowed enemy to poets; which is, perhaps, the reason why poets have been always at enmity with his profession; and have rejected all learning and philosophy, for the sake of that one philosopher. As I take the matter, neither philosophy, nor any part of learning, is more necessary to poetry, (which, if you will believe the same author, is "the sum of all learning,") than to know the theory of light, and the several proportions and diversifications of it in particular colours, is to a good painter.

Whereas, therefore, a certain author, called Petronius Arbiter, going upon the same mistake, has confidently declared, that one ingredient of a good poet, is "*mens ingenti literarum flumine inundata;*" I do on the contrary declare, that this his assertion, (to speak of it in the softest terms,) is no better than an invidious and unhandsome reflection on all the gentlemen poets of these times: for, with his good leave, much less than a flood, or inundation, will serve the turn; and, to my certain knowledge, some of our greatest wits in your poetical way, have not as much real learning as would cover a sixpence in the bottom of a basin; nor do I think the worse of them; for, to speak my private opinion, I am for every [man's working upon his own materials, and producing only what he can find within himself, which is commonly a better stock than the owner knows it to be. I think flowers of wit ought to spring, as those in a garden do, from their own root and stem, without foreign assistance. I would have a man's wit rather like a fountain, that feeds itself invisibly, than a river, that is supplied by several streams from abroad.

Or, if it be necessary, as the case is with some barren wits, to take in the thoughts of others in order to draw forth their own, as dry pumps will not play till water is thrown into them; in that necessity, I would recommend some of the approved standard authors of antiquity for your perusal, as a poet and a wit; because, maggots being what you look for, as monkeys do for vermin in their keepers' heads, you will find they abound in good old authors, as in rich old cheese, not in the new; and for that reason you must have the classics, especially the most worm-eaten of them, often in your hands.

But with this caution, that you are not to use those ancients as unlucky lads do their old fathers, and make no conscience of picking their pockets and pillaging them. Your business is not to steal from them, but to improve upon them, and make their sentiments your own; which is an effect of great judgment; and, though difficult, yet very possible, without the scurvy imputation of filching; for I humbly conceive, though I light my candle at my neighbour's fire, that does not alter the property, or make the wick, the wax, or the flame, or the whole candle, less my own.

Possibly you may think it a very severe task, to arrive at a competent knowledge of so many of the ancients as excel in their way; and indeed it would be really so, but for the short and easy method lately found out, of abstracts, abridgments, summaries, &c., which are admirable expedients for being very learned with little or no reading; and have the same use with burning-glasses, to collect the diffused rays of wit and learning in authors, and make them point with warmth and quickness upon the reader's imagination. And to this is nearly related that other modern device of consulting indexes, which is to read books hebraically, and begin where others usually end. And this is a compendious way of coming to an acquaintance with authors; for authors are to be used like lobsters, you must look for the best meat in the tails, and lay the bodies back again in the dish. Your cunningest thieves, (and what else are readers, who only read to borrow, *i.e.*, to steal,) use to cut off the portmanteau from behind, without staying to dive into the pockets of the owner. Lastly, you are taught thus much in the very elements of philosophy; for one of the finest rules in logic is, *Finis est primus in intentione.*

The learned world is therefore most highly indebted to a late painful and judicious editor of the classics, who has laboured in that new way with exceeding felicity. Every author, by his management, sweats under himself, being overloaded with his own index, and carries, like a north-country pedlar, all his substance and furniture upon his back, and with as great variety of trifles. To him let all young students make their compliments for so much time and pains saved in the pursuit of useful knowledge; for whoever shortens a road, is a benefactor to the public, and to every particular person who has occasion to travel that way.

But to proceed. I have lamented nothing more in my time, than the disuse of some ingenious little plays, in fashion with young folks when I was a boy, and to which the great facility of that age, above ours, in composing, was certainly owing; and if anything has brought a damp upon the versification of these times, we have no farther than this to go for the cause of it. Now, could these sports be happily revived, I am of opinion your wisest course would be to apply your thoughts to them, and never fail to make a party when you can, in those profitable diversions. For example, crambo is of extraordinary use to good rhyming, and rhyming is what I have ever accounted the very essential of a good poet; and in that notion I am not singular; for the aforesaid Sir P. Sidney has declared, "That the chief life of modern versifying consists in the like sounding of words, which we call rhyme;" which is an authority, either without exception, or above any reply. Wherefore, you are ever to try a good poem as you would sound a pipkin; and if it rings well upon the knuckle, be sure there is no flaw in it. Verse without rhyme is a body without a soul, (for the "chief life consisteth in the rhyme,") or a bell without a clapper; which, in strictness, is no bell, as being neither of use nor delight. And the same ever honoured knight, with so musical an ear, had that veneration for the tunableness and chiming of verse, that he speaks of a poet as one that has "the reverend title of a rhymer." Our celebrated Milton has done these nations great prejudice in this particular, having spoiled as many reverend rhymers, by his example, as he has made real poets.

For which reason, I am overjoyed to hear that a very ingenious youth of this town is now upon the useful design, (for which he is never enough to be commended,) of bestowing rhyme upon Milton's Paradise Lost, which will make the poem, in that only defective, more heroic and sonorous than it hitherto has been. I wish the gentleman success in the performance; and, as it is a work in which a young man could not be more happily employed, or appear in with greater advantage to his character, so I am concerned that it did not fall out to be your province.

With much the same view, I would recommend to you the witty play of pictures and mottoes, which will furnish your imagination with great store of images and suitable devices. We of these kingdoms have found our account in this diversion, as little as we consider or acknowledge it; for to this we owe our eminent felicity in posies of rings, mottoes of snuff-boxes, the humours of sign-posts, with their elegant inscriptions, &c.; in which kind of productions not any nation in the world, no not the Dutch themselves, will presume to rival us.

For much the same reason it may be proper for you to have some insight into the play called, "What is it like?" as of great use in common practice, to quicken slow capacities, and improve the quickest; but the chief end of it is, to supply the fancy with varieties of similies for all subjects. It will teach you to bring things to a likeness, which have not the least imaginable conformity in nature, which is properly creation, and the very business of a poet, as his name implies; and let me tell you, a good poet can no more be without a stock of similies by him, than a shoemaker without his lasts. He should have them sized, and ranged, and hung up in order in his shop, ready for all customers, and shaped to the feet of all sorts of verse; and here I could more fully (and I long to do it) insist upon the wonderful harmony and resemblance between a poet and a shoemaker, in many circumstances common to both; such as the binding of their temples, the stuff they work upon, and the paring-knife they use, &c., but that I would not digress, nor seem to trifle in so serious a matter.

Now, I say, if you apply yourself to these diminutive sports, (not to mention others of equal ingenuity, such as draw gloves, cross purposes, questions and commands, and the rest,) it is not to be conceived what benefit (of nature) you will find by them, and how they will open the body of your invention. To these devote your spare hours, or rather spare all your hours to them, and then you will act as becomes a wise man, and make even diversions an improvement; like the inimitable management of the bee, which does the whole business of life at once, and at the same time both feeds, and works, and diverts itself.

Your own prudence will, I doubt not, direct you to take a place every evening among the ingenious, in the corner of a certain coffeehouse in this town, where you will receive a turn equally right as to wit, religion, and politics; as likewise to be as frequent at the playhouse as you can afford, without selling your books. For, in our chaste theatre, even Cato himself might sit to the falling of the curtain; besides, you will meet sometimes with tolerable conversation among the players: they are such a kind of men as may pass, upon the same sort of capacities, for wits off the stage, as they do for fine gentlemen upon it. Besides, that I have known a factor deal in as good ware, and sell as cheap, as the merchant himself that employs him.

Add to this the expediency of furnishing out your shelves with a choice collection of modern miscellanies, in the gayest edition; and of reading all sorts of plays, especially the new, and above all, those of our own growth, printed by subscription; in which article of Irish manufacture, I readily agree to the late proposal, and am altogether for " rejecting and renouncing everything that comes from England." To what purpose should we go thither for coals or poetry, when we have a vein within ourselves equally good and more convenient? Lastly,

A common-place book is what a provident poet cannot subsist without, for this proverbial reason, that " great wits have short memories;" and whereas, on the other hand, poets, being liars by profession, ought to have good memories; to reconcile these, a book of this sort is in the nature of a supplemental memory, or a record of what occurs remarkable in every day's reading or conversation. Then you enter not only your own original thoughts, (which, a hundred to one, are few and insignificant,) but such of other men as you think fit to make your own, by entering them there. For, take this for a rule, when an author is in your books, you have the same demand upon him for his wit, as a merchant has for your money, when you are in his.

By these few and easy prescriptions, (with the help of a good genius,) it is possible you may, in a short time, arrive at the accomplishments of a poet, and shine in that character. As for your manner of composing, and choice of subjects, I cannot take upon me to be your director; but I will venture to give you some short hints, which you may enlarge upon at your leisure. Let me intreat you, then, by no means to lay aside that notion peculiar to our modern refiners in poetry, which is, that a poet must never write or discourse as the ordinary part of mankind do, but in number and verse, as an oracle; which I mention the rather, because, upon this principle, I have known heroes brought into the pulpit, and a whole sermon composed and delivered in blank verse, to the vast credit of the preacher, no less than the real entertainment and great edification of the audience; the secret of which I take to be this: when the matter of such discourses is but mere clay, or, as we usually call it, sad stuff, the preacher who can afford no better, wisely moulds, and polishes, and dries, and washes this piece of earthenware, and then bakes it with poetic fire; after which it will ring like any pancrock, and is a good dish to set before common guests, as every congregation is that comes so often for entertainment to one place.

There was a good old custom in use, which our ancestors had, of invoking the muses at the entrance of their poems; I suppose, by way of craving a blessing: this the graceless moderns have in a great measure laid aside, but are not to be followed in that poetical impiety; for, although to nice ears such invocations may sound harsh and disagreeable, (as tuning instruments is before a concert,) they are equally necessary. Again, you must not fail to dress your muse in a forehead cloth of Greek or Latin; I mean, you are always to make use of a quaint motto to all your compositions; for, beside that this artifice bespeaks the reader's opinion of the writer's learning, it is otherwise useful and commendable. A bright passage in the front of a poem is a good mark, like a star in a horse's face; and the piece will certainly go off the better for it. The *os magna sonaturum*, which, if I remember right, Horace makes one qualification of a good poet, may teach you not to gag your muse, or stint yourself in words and epithets which cost you nothing, contrary to the practice of some few out-of-the-way writers, who use a natural and concise expression, and affect a style like unto a Shrewsbury cake, short and sweet upon the palate; they will not afford you a word more than is necessary to make them intelligible, which is as poor and niggardly as it would be to set down no more meat than your company will be sure to eat up. Words are but lackeys to sense, and will dance attendance without wages or compulsion; *Verba non invita sequentur*.

Farthermore, when you set about composing, it may be necessary for your ease, and better distillation of wit, to put on your worst clothes, and the worse the better; for an author, like a limbeck, will yield the better for having a rag about him: besides, that I have observed a gardener cut the outward rind of a tree, (which is the surtout of it,) to make it bear well; and this is a natural account of the usual poverty of poets, and is an argument why wits, of all men living, ought to be ill clad. I have always a sacred veneration for any one I observe to be a little out of repair in his person, as supposing him either a poet or a philosopher; because the richest minerals are ever found under the most ragged and withered surface of the earth.

As for your choice of subjects, I have only to give you this caution: that as a handsome way of praising is certainly the most difficult point in writing or speaking, I would by no means advise any young man to make his first essay in panegyric, beside the danger of it: for a particular encomium is ever attended with more ill-will than any general invective, for which I need give no reasons; wherefore my counsel is, that you use the point of your pen, not the feather: let your first attempt be a *coup d'éclat* in the way of a libel, lampoon, or satire.

Knock down half a score reputations, and you will infallibly raise your own; and so it be with wit, no matter with how little justice; for fiction is your trade.

Every great genius seems to ride upon mankind, like Pyrrhus on his elephant; and the way to have the absolute ascendant of your resty nag, and to keep your seat, is, at your first mounting, to afford him the whip and spurs plentifully; after which, you may travel the rest of the day with great alacrity. Once kick the world, and the world and you will live together at a reasonable good understanding. You cannot but know that those of your profession have been called *genus irritabile vatum;* and you will find it necessary to qualify yourself for that waspish society, by exerting your talent of satire upon the first occasion, and to abandon good nature only to prove yourself a true poet, which you will allow to be a valuable consideration: in a word, a young robber is usually entered by a murder: a young hound is blooded when he comes first into the field: a young bully begins with killing his man: and a young poet must shew his wit, as the other his courage, by cutting, and slashing, and laying about him, and banging mankind.

Lastly, It will be your wisdom to look out betimes for a good service for your muse, according to her skill and qualifications, whether in the nature of a dairymaid, a cook, or charewoman: I mean, to hire out your pen to a party, which will afford you both pay and protection; and when you have to do with the press, (as you will long to be there,) take care to bespeak an importunate friend, to extort your productions with an agreeable violence; and which, according to the cue between you, you must surrender *digito male pertinaci:* there is a decency in this; for it no more becomes an author, in modesty, to have a hand in publishing his own works than a woman in labour to lay herself.

I would be very loth to give the least umbrage or offence by what I have here said, as I may do, if I should be thought to insinuate that these circumstances of good writing have been unknown to, or not observed by, the poets of this kingdom : I will do my countrymen the justice to say, they have written by the foregoing rules with great exactness, and so far as hardly to come behind those of their profession in England, in perfection of low writing. The sublime, indeed, is not so common with us; but ample amends is made for that want, in great abundance of the admirable and amazing, which appears in all our compositions. Our very good friend, (the knight aforesaid,) speaking of the force of poetry, mentions "rhyming to death, which (adds he) is said to be done in Ireland ;" and truly, to our honour be it spoken, that power, in a great measure continues with us to this day.

I would now offer some poor thoughts of mine for the encouragement of poetry in this kingdom, if I could hope they would be agreeable. I have had many an aching heart for the ill plight of that noble profession here ; and it has been my late and early study, how to bring it into better circumstances. And, surely, considering what monstrous wits, in the poetic way, do almost daily start up and surprise us in this town ; what prodigious geniuses we have here, (of which I could give instances without number,) and withal of what great benefit it may be to our trade to encourage that science here, for it is plain our linen manufacture is advanced by the great waste of paper made by our present set of poets ; not to mention other necessary uses of the same to shop-keepers, especially grocers, apothecaries, and pastry-cooks, and I might add, but for our writers, the nation would in a little time be utterly destitute of bumfodder, and must of necessity import the same from England and Holland, where they have it in great abundance, by the indefatigable labour of their own wits: I say, these things considered, I am humbly of opinion, it would be worth the care of our governors to cherish gentlemen of the quill, and give them all proper encouragements here. And, since I am upon the subject, I shall speak my mind very freely, and if I add saucily, it is no more than my birthright as a Briton.

Seriously then, I have many years lamented the want of a Grub Street in this our large and polite city, unless the whole may be called one. And this I have accounted an unpardonable defect in our constitution, ever since I had any opinions I could call my own. Every one knows Grub Street is a market for small ware in wit, and as necessary, considering the usual purgings of the human brain, as the nose is upon a man's face: and for the same reason, we have here a court, a college, a play-house, and beautiful ladies, and fine gentlemen, and good claret, and abundance of pens, ink, and paper, clear of taxes, and every other circumstance to provoke wit; and yet those, whose province it is, have not thought fit to appoint a place for evacuations of it, which is a very hard case, as may be judged by comparisons.

And truly this defect has been attended with unspeakable inconveniences; for, not to mention the prejudice done to the commonwealth of letters, I am of opinion we suffer in our health by it: I believe our corrupted air, and frequent thick fogs, are in a great measure owing to the common exposal of our wit; and that, with good management, our poetical vapours might be carried off in a common drain, and fall into one quarter of the town without infecting the whole, as the case is at present, to the great offence of our nobility and gentry, and others of nice noses. When writers of all sizes, like freemen of the city, are at liberty to throw out their filth and excrementitious productions, in every street as they please, what can the consequence be, but that the town must be poisoned, and become such another jakes, as, by report of great travellers, Edinburgh is at night; a thing well to be considered in these pestilential times.

I am not of the society for reformation of manners, but, without that pragmatical title, I should be glad to see some amendment in the matter before us: wherefore, I humbly bespeak the favour of the Lord Mayor, the Court of Aldermen, and Common Council, together with the whole circle of arts in this town, and do recommend this affair to their most political consideration; and I persuade myself they will not be wanting in their best endeavours, when they can serve two such good ends at once, as both to keep the town sweet, and encourage poetry in it. Neither do I make any exceptions as to satirical poets and lampoon writers in consideration of their office; for though, indeed, their business is to rake into kennels, and gather up the filth of streets and families, (in which respect they may be, for aught I know, as necessary to the town as scavengers or chimney-sweeps,) yet I have observed, they too have themselves, at the same time, very foul clothes, and, like dirty persons, leave more filth and nastiness than they sweep away.

In a word, what I would be at (for I love to be plain in matters of importance to my country) is, that some private street, or blind alley, of this town, may be fitted up, at the charge of the public, as an apartment for the muses, (like those at Rome and Amsterdam, for their female relations,) and be wholly consigned to the uses of our wits, furnished completely with all appurtenances, such as authors, supervisors, presses, printers, hawkers, shops, and warehouses, abundance of garrets, and every other implement and circumstance of wit; the benefit of which would obviously be this, viz., that we should then have a safe repository for our best productions, which at present are handed about in single sheets or manuscripts, and may be altogether lost, (which were a pity,) or, at the best, are subject, in that loose dress, like handsome women, to great abuse.

Another point that has cost me some melancholy reflections, is the present state of the playhouse; the encouragement of which has an immediate influence upon the poetry of the kingdom; as a good market improves the tillage of the neighbouring country, and enriches the ploughman; neither do we of this town seem enough to know or consider the vast benefit of a playhouse to our city and nation: that single house is the fountain of all our love, wit, dress, and gallantry. It is the school of wisdom; for there we learn to know what's what; which, however, I cannot say is always in that place sound knowledge. There our young folks drop their childish mistakes, and come first to perceive their mothers' cheat of the parsley-bed; there, too, they get rid of natural prejudices, especially those of religion and modesty, which are great restraints to a free people. The same is a remedy for the spleen, and blushing, and several distempers occasioned by the stagnation of the blood. It is likewise a school of common swearing; my young master, who at first but minced an oath, is taught there to mouth it gracefully, and to swear, as he reads French, *ore rotundo*. Profaneness was before to him in the nature of his best suit, or holiday-clothes; but, upon frequenting the playhouse, swearing, cursing, and lying, become like his every-day coat, waistcoat, and breeches. Now, I say, common swearing, a produce of this country as plentiful as our corn, thus cultivated by the playhouse, might, with management, be of wonderful advantage to the nation, as a projector of the swearer's bank has proved at large. Lastly, the stage, in great measure, supports the pulpit; for I know not what our divines could have to say there against the corruptions of the age, but for the playhouse, which is the seminary of them. From which it is plain, the public is a gainer by the playhouse, and consequently ought to countenance it; and, were I worthy to put in my word, or prescribe to my betters, I could say in what manner.

I have heard that a certain gentleman has great design to serve the public, in the way of their diversion, with due encouragement; that is, if he can obtain some concordatum-money, or yearly salary, and handsome contribution; and well he deserves the favours of the nation: for, to do him justice, he has an uncommon skill in pastimes, having altogether applied his studies that way, and travelled full many a league, by sea and land, for this his profound knowledge. With that view alone he has visited all the courts and cities in Europe, and has been at more pains than I shall speak of, to take an exact draught of the playhouse at the Hague, as a model for a new one here. But what can a private man do by himself in so public an undertaking? It is not to be doubted but, by his care and industry, vast improvements may be made, not only in our playhouse, (which is his immediate province,) but in our gaming ordinaries, groom-porters, lotteries, bowling-greens, ninepin-alleys, bear-gardens, cock-pits, prizes, puppets, and rareeshows, and whatever else concerns the elegant divertisements of this town. He is truly an original genius; and I felicitate this our capital city on his residence here, where I wish him long to live and flourish, for the good of the commonwealth.

Once more: If any farther application shall be made on the other side, to obtain a charter for a bank here, I presume to make a request, that poetry may be a sharer in that privilege, being a fund as real, and to the full as well grounded, as our stocks; but I fear our neighbours, who envy our wit as much as they do our wealth or trade, will give no encouragement to either. I believe, also, it might be proper to erect a corporation of poets in this city. I have been idle enough in my time, to make a computation of wits here, and do find we have three hundred performing poets, and upward, in and about this town, reckoning six score to the hundred, and allowing for demies, like pint bottles; including also the several denominations of imitators, translators, and familiar letter-writers, &c. One of these last has lately entertained the town with an original piece, and such a one as, I dare say, the late British Spectator, in his decline, would have called, "an excellent specimen of the true sublime;" or "a noble poem;" or "a fine copy of verses, on a subject perfectly new," the author himself; and had given it a place among his latest lucubrations.

But, as I was saying, so many poets, I am confident, are sufficient to furnish out a corporation in point of number. Then, for the several degrees of subordinate members requisite to such a body, there can be no want; for, although we have not one masterly poet, yet we abound with wardens and beadles; having a multitude of poetasters, poetitoes, parcel-poets, poet-apes, and philo-poets, and many of inferior attainments in wit, but strong inclinations to it, which are, by odds, more than all the rest. Nor shall I ever be at ease, till this project of mine (for which I am heartily thankful to myself) shall be reduced to practice. I long to see the day, when our poets will be a regular and distinct body, and wait upon the Lord Mayor on public days, like other good citizens, in gowns turned up with green, instead of laurel; and when I myself, who make the proposal, shall be free of their company.

To conclude: what if our government had a poet-laureat here, as in England? what if our university had a professor of poetry here, as in England? what if our Lord Mayor had a city bard here, as in England? and, to refine upon England, what if every corporation, parish, and ward in this town, had a poet in fee, as they have not in England? Lastly, what if every one, so qualified, were obliged to add one more than usual to the number of his domestics, and, beside a fool and a chaplain, (which are often united in one person,) would retain a poet in his family? for, perhaps, a rhymer is as necessary among servants of a house, as a Dobbin with his bells at the head of a team. But these things I leave to the wisdom of my superiors.

While I have been directing your pen, I should not forget to govern my own, which has already exceeded the bounds of a letter: I must therefore take my leave abruptly, and desire you, without farther ceremony, to believe that I am,

Sir,

Your most humble servant,

J. S.

A LETTER

TO

A VERY YOUNG LADY,

ON

HER MARRIAGE.*

MADAM,

THE hurry and impertinence of receiving and paying visits on account of your marriage being now over, you are beginning to enter into a course of life, where you will want much advice to divert you from falling into many errors, fopperies, and follies, to which your sex is subject. I have

---

* "This letter ought to be read by all new-married women, and will be read with pleasure and advantage by the most distinguished and accomplished ladies." Thus saith my Lord Orrery; but he ought to have added, that much of their pleasure may consist in the reflection, that the piece was composed for the instruction of another. There is so little reverence for the individual who is addressed, and such a serious apprehension expressed lest she may fall into the worst of the errors pointed out, that one can hardly wonder the precepts of so stern a Mentor were received by the lady to whom they were addressed with more pique than complacence. Much regard is expressed for her parents and husband; but as to herself, there is only a distant prospect held forth, that

always borne an entire friendship to your father and mother; and the person they have chosen for your husband has been, for some years past, my particular favourite. I have long wished you might come together, because I hoped that, from the goodness of your disposition, and by following the counsel of wise friends, you might in time make yourself worthy of him. Your parents were so far in the right, that they did not produce you much into the world, whereby you avoided many wrong steps which others have taken, and have fewer ill impressions to be removed; but they failed, as it is generally the case, in too much neglecting to cultivate your mind; without which, it is impossible to acquire or preserve the friendship and esteem of a wise man, who soon grows weary of acting the lover, and treating his wife like a mistress, but wants a reasonable companion, and a true friend through every stage of his life. It must be therefore your business to qualify yourself for those offices; wherein I will not fail to be your director, as long as I shall think you deserve it, by letting you know how you are to act, and what you ought to avoid.

And beware of despising or neglecting my instructions, whereon will depend not only your making a good figure in the world, but your own real happiness, as well as that of the person who ought to be the dearest to you.

I must therefore desire you, in the first place, to be very slow in changing the modest behaviour of a virgin: it is usual in young wives, before they

---

in time, and with good counsel, she might become worthy of the man of her choice. Mrs. Pilkington pretends that this letter was written on Lady Betty Moore's marriage with Mr. George Rochfort. But Mr. Faulkner, who is the more sound authority, supposes it addressed to Mrs. John Rochford, daughter of Dr. Staunton.

have been many weeks married, to assume a bold forward look and manner of talking, as if they intended to signify in all companies that they were no longer girls, and consequently that their whole demeanour, before they got a husband, was all but a countenance and constraint upon their nature: whereas, I suppose, if the votes of wise men were gathered, a very great majority would be in favour of those ladies, who, after they were entered into that state, rather chose to double their portion of modesty and reservedness.

I must likewise warn you strictly against the least degree of <u>fondness</u> to your husband before any witness whatsoever, even before your nearest relations, or the very maids of your chamber. This proceeding is so exceeding odious and disgustful to all, who have either good breeding or good sense, that they assign two very unamiable reasons for it; the one is gross hypocrisy, and the other has too bad a name to mention. If there is any difference to be made, your husband is the lowest person in company either at home or abroad, and every gentleman present has a better claim to all marks of civility and distinction from you. Conceal your esteem and love in your own breast, and reserve your kind looks and language for private hours, which are so many in the four and twenty, that they will afford time to employ a passion as exalted as any that was ever described in a French romance.

Upon this head I should likewise advise you to differ in practice from those ladies, who affect abundance of uneasiness, while their husbands are abroad; start with every knock at the door, and ring the bell incessantly for the servants to let in their master; will not eat a bit at dinner or supper, if the husband happens to stay out; and receive him at his return with such a medley of chiding and kindness, and catechizing him where he has been, that a shrew from Billingsgate would be a more easy and eligible companion.

Of the same leaven are those wives, who, when their husbands are gone a journey, must have a letter every post, upon pain of fits and hysterics; and a day must be fixed for their return home, without the least allowance for business, or sickness, or accidents, or weather: upon which I can only say, that, in my observation, those ladies, who are apt to make the greatest clutter on such occasions, would liberally have paid a messenger for bringing them news, that their husbands had broken their necks on the road.

You will perhaps be offended, when I advise you to abate a little of that violent passion for fine clothes, so predominant in your sex. It is a little hard, that ours, for whose sake you wear them, are not admitted to be of your council. I may venture to assure you, that we will make an abatement at any time of four pounds a-yard in a brocade, if the ladies will but allow a suitable addition of care in the cleanliness and sweetness of their persons. For the satirical part of mankind will needs believe, that it is not impossible to be very fine and very filthy; and that the capacities of a lady are sometimes apt to fall short, in cultivating cleanliness and finery together. I shall only add, upon so tender a subject, what a pleasant gentleman said concerning a silly woman of quality; that nothing could make her supportable but cutting off her head; for his ears were offended by her tongue, and his nose by her hair and teeth.

I am wholly at a loss how to advise you in the choice of company, which, however, is a point of as great importance as any in your life. If your general acquaintance be among the ladies, who are your equals or superiors, provided they have nothing of what is commonly called an ill reputation, you think you are safe; and this, in the style of the world, will pass for good company. Whereas, I am afraid it will be hard for you to pick out one female acquaintance in this town, from whom you will not be in manifest danger of contracting some foppery, affectation, vanity, folly, or vice. Your only safe way of conversing with them is, by a firm resolution to proceed in your practice and behaviour directly contrary to whatever they shall say or do: and this I take to be a good general rule, with very few exceptions. For instance, in the doctrines they usually deliver to young married women for managing their husbands; their several accounts of their own conduct in that particular, to recommend it to your imitation; the reflections they make upon others of their sex for acting differently; their directions how to come off with victory upon any dispute or quarrel you may have with your husband; the arts, by which you may discover and practise upon his weak side; when to work by flattery and insinuation, when to melt him with tears, and when to engage him with a high hand; in these, and a thousand other cases, it will be prudent to retain as many of their lectures in your memory as you can, and then determine to act in full opposition to them all.

I hope your husband will interpose his authority to limit you in the trade of visiting: half a dozen fools are, in all conscience, as many as you should require; and it will be sufficient for you to see them twice a-year; for I think the fashion does not exact that visits should be paid to friends.

I advise that your company at home should consist of men rather than women. To say the truth, I never yet knew a tolerable woman to be fond of her own sex. I confess, when both are mixed and well chosen, and put their best qualities forward, there may be an intercourse of civility and good will; which, with the addition of some degree of sense, can make conversation or any amusement agreeable. But a knot of ladies, got together by themselves, is a very school of impertinence and detraction, and it is well if those be the worst.

Let your men acquaintance be of your husband's choice, and not recommended to you by any she companions; because they will certainly fix a coxcomb upon you, and it will cost you some time and pains before you can arrive at the knowledge of distinguishing such a one from a man of sense.

Never take a favourite waiting-maid into your cabinet council, to entertain you with histories of those ladies whom she has formerly served, of their diversions and their dresses; to insinuate how great a fortune you brought, and how little you are allowed to squander; to appeal to her from your husband, and to be determined by her judgment, because you are sure it will be always for you; to receive and discard servants by her approbation or dislike; to engage you, by her insinuations, in misunderstandings with your best friends; to represent all things in false colours, and to be the common emissary of scandal.

But the grand affair of your life will be to gain and preserve the friendship and esteem of your husband. You are married to a man of good education and learning, of an excellent understanding, and an exact taste. It is true, and it is happy for you, that these qualities in him are adorned with great modesty, a most amiable sweetness of temper, and an unusual disposition to sobriety and virtue: but neither good nature nor virtue will suffer him to esteem you against his judgment; and although he is not capable of using you ill, yet you will in time grow a thing indifferent, and perhaps contemptible, unless you can supply the loss of youth and beauty, with more durable qualities. You have but a very few years to be young and handsome in the eyes of the world; and as few months to be so in the eyes of a husband who is not a fool; for I hope you do not still dream of charms and raptures, which marriage ever did, and ever will, put a sudden end to. Besides, yours was a match of prudence and common good liking, without any mixture of that ridiculous passion which has no being but in playbooks and romances.

You must therefore use all endeavours to attain to some degree of those accomplishments which your husband most values in other people, and for which he is most valued himself. You must improve your mind by closely pursuing such a method of study as I shall direct or approve of. You must get a collection of history and travels, which I will recommend to you, and spend some hours every day in reading them, and making extracts from them if your memory be weak. You must invite persons of knowledge and understanding to an acquaintance with you, by whose conversation you may learn to correct your taste and judgment; and when you can bring yourself to comprehend and relish the good sense of others, you will arrive in time to think rightly yourself, and to become a reasonable and agreeable companion. This must produce in your husband a true rational love and esteem for you, which old age will not diminish. He will have a regard for your judgment and opinion in matters of the greatest weight; you will be able to entertain each other without a third person to relieve you by finding discourse. The endowments of your mind will even make your person more agreeable to him;

and when you are alone, your time will not lie heavy upon your hands for want of some trifling amusement.

As little respect as I have for the generality of your sex, it has sometimes moved me with pity to see the lady of the house forced to withdraw immediately after dinner, and this in families where there is not much drinking; as if it were an established maxim, that women are incapable of all conversation. In a room where both sexes meet, if the men are discoursing upon any general subject, the ladies never think it their business to partake in what passes, but in a separate club entertain each other with the price and choice of lace and silk, and what dresses they liked or disapproved at the church or the playhouse. And when you are among yourselves, how naturally after the first compliments, do you apply your hands to each other's lappets, and ruffles, and mantuas; as if the whole business of your lives and the public concern of the world depended upon the cut or colour of your dress. As divines say, that some people take more pains to be damned, than it would cost them to be saved; so your sex employ more thought, memory, and application to be fools, than would serve to make them wise and useful. When I reflect on this I cannot conceive you to be human creatures, but a certain sort of species hardly a degree above a monkey; who has more diverting tricks than any of you, is an animal less mischievous and expensive, might in time be a tolerable critic in velvet and brocade, and, for aught I know, would equally become them.

I would have you look upon finery as a necessary folly; which all great ladies did whom I have ever known; I do not desire you to be out of the fashion, but to be the last and least in it. I expect that your dress shall be one degree lower than your fortune can afford; and in your own heart I would wish you to be an utter contemner of all distinctions, which a finer petticoat can give you; because, it will neither make you richer, handsomer, younger, better natured, more virtuous or wise, than if it hung upon a peg.

If you are in company with men of learning, though they happen to discourse of arts and sciences out of your compass, yet you will gather more advantage by listening to them, than from all the nonsense and frippery of your own sex; but if they be men of breeding, as well as learning, they will seldom engage in any conversation where you ought not to be a hearer, and in time have your part. If they talk of the manners and customs of the several kingdoms of Europe, of travels into remoter nations, of the state of your own country, or of the great men and actions of Greece and Rome; if they give their judgment upon English and French writers either in verse or prose, or of the nature and limits of virtue and vice; it is a shame for an English lady not to relish such discourses, not to improve by them, and endeavour by reading and information to have her share in those entertainments, rather than turn aside, as it is the usual custom, and consult with the woman who sits next her about a new cargo of fans.

It is a little hard, that not one gentleman's daughter in a thousand should be brought to read or understand her own natural tongue, or to be judge of the easiest books that are written in it; as any one may find, who can have the patience to hear them, when they are disposed to mangle a play or novel, where the least word out of the common road is sure to disconcert them; and it is no wonder, when they are not so much as taught to spell in their childhood, nor can ever attain to it in their whole lives. I advise you therefore to read aloud, more or less, every day to your husband, if he will permit you, or to any other friend (but not a female one) who is able to set you right; and as for spelling, you may compass it in time by making collections from the books you read.

I know very well, that those who are commonly called learned women, have lost all manner of credit by their impertinent talkativeness and conceit of themselves; but there is an easy remedy for this, if you once consider, that after all the pains you may be at, you never can arrive in point of learning to the perfection of a schoolboy. The reading I would advise you to, is only for improvement of your own good sense, which will never fail of being mended by discretion. It is a wrong method, and ill choice of books, that makes those learned ladies just so much the worse for what they have read; and therefore it shall be my care to direct you better, a task for which I take myself to be not ill-qualified; because I have spent more time, and have had more opportunities, than many others to observe and discover from what source the various follies of women are derived.

Pray observe, how insignificant things are the common race of ladies, when they have passed their youth and beauty; how contemptible they appear to the men, and yet more contemptible to the younger part of their own sex; and have no relief, but in passing their afternoons in visits, where they are never acceptable; and their evenings at cards among each other; while the former part of the day is spent in spleen and envy, or in vain endeavours to repair by art and dress the ruins of time. Whereas I have known ladies at sixty, to whom all the polite part of the court and town paid their addresses, without any farther view than that of enjoying the pleasure of their conversation.

I am ignorant of any one quality that is amiable in a man, which is not equally so in a woman : I do not except even modesty and gentleness of nature. Nor do I know one vice or folly, which is not equally detestable in both. There is indeed one infirmity which is generally allowed you, I mean that of cowardice; yet there should seem to be something very capricious, that when women profess their admiration for a colonel or a captain, on account of his valour, they should fancy it a very graceful and becoming quality in themselves, to be afraid of their own shadows; to scream in a barge when the weather is calmest, or in a coach at a ring; to run from a cow at a hundred yards' distance; to fall into fits at the sight of a spider, an earwig, or a frog. At least, if cowardice be a sign of cruelty, (as it is generally granted,) I can hardly think it an accomplishment so desirable as to be thought worth improving by affectation.

And as the same virtues equally become both sexes, so there is no quality whereby women endeavour to distinguish themselves from men, for which they are not just so much the worse, except that only of reservedness; which, however, as you generally manage it, is nothing else but affectation or hypocrisy. For, as you cannot too much discountenance those of our sex who presume to take unbecoming liberties before you; so you ought to be wholly unconstrained in the company of deserving men, when you have had sufficient experience of their discretion.

There is never wanting in this town a tribe of bold, swaggering, rattling ladies, whose talents pass among coxcombs for wit and humour; their excellency lies in rude shocking expressions, and what they call running a man down. If a gentleman in their company happens to have any blemish in his birth or person, if any misfortune has befallen his family or himself for which he is ashamed, they will be sure to give him broad hints of it without any provocation. I would recommend you to the acquaintance of a common prostitute, rather than to that of such termagants as these. I have often thought, that no man is obliged to suppose such creatures to be women, but to treat them like insolent rascals disguised in female habits, who ought to be stripped and kicked down stairs.

I will add one thing, although it be a little out of place, which is to desire, that you will learn to value and esteem your husband for those good qualities which he really possesses, and not to fancy others in him which he certainly has not. For, although this latter is generally understood to be a mark of love, yet it is indeed nothing but affectation or ill judgment. It is true, he wants so very few accomplishments, that you are in no great danger of erring on this side; but my caution is occasioned by a lady of your acquaintance, married to a very valuable person, whom yet she is so unfortunate as to be always commending for those perfections to which he can least pretend.

I can give you no advice upon the article of expense; only I think, you ought to be well informed how much your husband's revenue amounts to, and be so good a computer, as to keep within it in that part of the management which falls to your share; and not to put yourself in the number of those politic ladies, who think they gain a great point, when they have teased their husbands to buy them a new equipage, a laced head, or a fine petticoat, without once considering what long score remained unpaid to the butcher.

I desire you will keep this letter in your cabinet,

and often examine impartially your whole conduct by it: and so God bless you, and make you a fair example to your sex, and a perpetual comfort to your husband and your parent.*

I am, with great truth and affection,

MADAM,

Your most faithful friend,

And humble servant.

---

* "The reader of this letter may be allowed to doubt, whether Swift's opinion of female excellence ought implicitly to be admitted; for if his general thoughts on women were such as he exhibits, a very little sense in a lady would enrapture, and a very little virtue would astonish him. Stella's supremacy, therefore, was perhaps only local. She was great, because her associates were little."—JOHNSON.

RESOLUTIONS
WHEN I COME TO BE OLD.*

WRITTEN IN 1699.

OT to marry a young woman.
Not to keep young company, unless they desire it.
Not to be peevish, or morose, or suspicious.

Not to scorn present ways, or wits, or fashions, or men, or war, &c.

Not to be fond of children.

Not to tell the same story over and over to the same people.

Not to be covetous.

Not to neglect decency or cleanliness, for fear of falling into nastiness.

---

* These resolutions form a melancholy chapter in Swift's Works, for they led to a breach with his old and faithful friend Dr. Sheridan. He had charged his friend to remind him when he saw him about to slide into the habitual breach of any of his maxims. —Sheridan, with ill-judged fidelity, ventured under this warrant to hint to the Dean the extreme parsimony which he practised as his faculties began to decay:—"Doctor," answered Swift, with an expressive look, "do you remember the Bishop of Grenada, in Gil Blas?" Their cordiality ceased from that moment.

Not to be over severe with young people, but give allowances for their youthful follies and weaknesses.

Not to be influenced by, or give ear to, knavish tattling servants, or others.

Not to be too free of advice, or trouble any but those who desire it.

To desire some good friend to inform me which of these resolutions I break or neglect, and wherein, and reform accordingly.

Not to talk much, nor of myself.

Not to boast of my former beauty, or strength, or favour with ladies, &c.

Not to hearken to flatteries, nor conceive I can be beloved by a young woman; *et eos qui hæreditatem captant, odisse ac vitare.*

Not to be positive or opinionative.

Not to set for observing all these rules, for fear I should observe none.

THOUGHTS

ON

VARIOUS SUBJECTS,

MORAL AND DIVERTING.*

(OCTOBER, 1706.)

WE have just enough religion to make us hate, but not enough to make us love one another.

Reflect on things past, as wars, negotiations, factions, &c., we enter so little into those interests, that we wonder how men could possibly be so busy and concerned for things so transitory; look on the present times, we find the same humour, yet wonder not at all.

A wise man endeavours, by considering all circumstances, to make conjectures, and form conclusions; but the smallest accident intervening, (and in

---

* These maxims were jotted down in consequence of a resolution adopted by Swift and Pope, in conjunction, to mark down the loose thoughts which occurred to them through the day, without attending to any order or formality of expression. In those of Swift, we trace his acute and penetrating knowledge of mankind, mixed with his misanthropical contempt of the world.

the course of affairs it is impossible to foresee all,) does often produce such turns and changes, that at last he is just as much in doubt of events, as the most ignorant and unexperienced person.

Positiveness is a good quality for preachers and orators, because he that would obtrude his thoughts and reasons upon a multitude, will convince others the more, as he appears convinced himself.

How is it possible to expect that mankind will take advice, when they will not so much as take warning?

I forget whether advice be among the lost things, which Ariosto says may be found in the moon; that, and time, ought to have been there.

No preacher is listened to but Time, which gives us the same train and turn of thought that elder people have in vain tried to put into our heads before.*

When we desire or solicit anything, our minds run wholly on the good side or circumstances of it; when it is obtained, our minds run wholly on the bad ones.

In a glasshouse, the workmen often fling in a small quantity of fresh coals, which seems to disturb the fire, but very much enlivens it. This seems to allude to a gentle stirring of the passions, that the mind may not languish.

Religion seems to have grown an infant with age, and requires miracles to nurse it, as it had in its infancy.

All fits of pleasure are balanced by an equal degree

---

* Were this otherwise, that is, were it possible that each passing generation of mankind could profit to the uttermost by the experience of their parents, the state of the world would be in a few generations more materially altered, than would be perhaps consistent with our finite state of being.

of pain or languor; it is like spending this year part of the next year's revenue.

The latter part of a wise man's life is taken up in curing the follies, prejudices, and false opinions he had contracted in the former.

Would a writer know how to behave himself with relation to posterity, let him consider in old books what he finds that he is glad to know, and what omissions he most laments.

Whatever the poets pretend, it is plain they give immortality to none but themselves: it is Homer and Virgil we reverence and admire, not Achilles or Æneas. With historians it is quite the contrary; our thoughts are taken up with the actions, persons, and events we read, and we little regard the authors.

When a true genius appears in the world, you may know him by this sign, that the dunces are all in confederacy against him.

Men who possess all the advantages of life, are in a state where there are many accidents to disorder and discompose, but few to please them.

It is unwise to punish cowards with ignominy; for if they had regarded that, they would not have been cowards: death is their proper punishment, because they fear it most.*

The greatest inventions were produced in the times of ignorance; as the use of the compass, gunpowder, and printing; and by the dullest nation, as the Germans.

One argument to prove that the common relations

---

* This maxim seems doubtful. The effect of punishment is example, not vengeance. And there are many men of weak nerves yet high feelings, who struggle with and overcome constitutional timidity, from the sense of the disgrace attendant on cowardice. If the dread of capital punishment were alone in the balance, the fear of remote danger would give way to apprehensions more pressing and immediate.

of ghosts and spectres are generally false, may be drawn from the opinion held, that spirits are never seen by more than one person at a time ; that is to say, it seldom happens to above one person in a company to be possessed with any high degree of spleen or melancholy.

I am apt to think, that, in the day of judgment, there will be small allowance given to the wise for their want of morals, and to the ignorant for their want of faith, because both are without excuse. This renders the advantages equal of ignorance and knowledge. But some scruples in the wise, and some vices in the ignorant, will perhaps be forgiven, upon the strength of temptation to each.

The value of several circumstances in story, lessens very much by distance of time, though some minute circumstances are very valuable ; and it requires great judgment in a writer to distinguish.

It is grown a word of course for writers to say, This critical age, as divines say, This sinful age.

It is pleasant to observe how free the present age is in laying taxes on the next : future ages shall talk of this ; this shall be famous to all posterity : whereas their time and thoughts will be taken up about present things, as ours are now.

The chameleon, who is said to feed upon nothing but air, has of all animals the nimblest tongue.

When a man is made a spiritual peer, he loses his surname ; when a temporal, his Christian name.

It is in disputes, as in armies ; where the weaker side sets up false lights, and makes a great noise, to make the enemy believe them more numerous and strong than they really are.

Some men under the notion of weeding out prejudices, eradicate virtue, honesty, and religion.

In all well-instituted commonwealths, care has been taken to limit men's possessions ; which is done for many reasons, and, among the rest, for one which, perhaps, is not often considered, that when bounds are set to men's desires, after they have acquired as much as the laws will permit them, their private interest is at an end, and they have nothing to do but to take care of the public.

There are but three ways for a man to revenge himself of the censure of the world; to despise it, to return the like, or to endeavour to live so as to avoid it: the first of these is usually pretended, the last is almost impossible, the universal practice is for the second.

Herodotus tells us, that in cold countries beasts very seldom have horns, but in hot they have very large ones. This might bear a pleasant application.

I never heard a finer piece of satire against lawyers, than that of astrologers, when they pretend, by rules of art, to tell when a suit will end, and whether to the advantage of the plaintiff or defendant; thus making the matter depend entirely upon the influence of the stars, without the least regard to the merits of the cause.

The expression in Apocrypha about Tobit and his dog following him, I have often heard ridiculed; yet Homer has the same words of Telemachus more than once; and Virgil says something like it of Evander. And I take the book of Tobit to be partly poetical.

I have known some men possessed of good qualities which were very serviceable to others, but useless to themselves; like a sun-dial on the front of a house, to inform the neighbours and passengers, but not the owner within.

If a man would register all his opinions upon love, politics, religion, learning, &c., beginning from his youth, and so go on to old age, what a bundle of inconsistencies and contradictions would appear at last!

What they do in heaven we are ignorant of; what they do not we are told expressly, that they neither marry, nor are given in marriage.

When a man observes the choice of ladies now-a-days in the dispensing of their favours, can he forbear paying some veneration to the memory of those mares mentioned by Xenophon, who, while their manes were on, that is, while they were in their beauty, would never admit the embraces of an ass.

It is a miserable thing to live in suspense: it is the life of a spider.

> *Vive quidem, pende tamen, improba, dixit.*
> OVID. *Metam.*

The stoical scheme of supplying our wants by lopping off our desires, is like cutting off our feet, when we want shoes.

Physicians ought not to give their judgment of religion, for the same reason that butchers are not admitted to be jurors upon life and death.

The reason why so few marriages are happy, is, because young ladies spend their time in making nets, not in making cages.

If a man will observe as he walks the streets, I believe he will find the merriest countenances in mourning coaches.

Nothing more unqualifies a man to act with prudence, than a misfortune that is attended with shame and guilt.

The power of fortune is confessed only by the miserable; for the happy impute all their success to prudence and merit.

Ambition often puts men upon doing the meanest offices; so climbing is performed in the same posture with creeping.

Ill company is like a dog, who dirts those most whom he loves best.

Censure is the tax a man pays to the public for being eminent.

Although men are accused for not knowing their own weakness, yet, perhaps, as few know their own strength. It is in men as in soils, where sometimes there is a vein of gold, which the owner knows not of.

Satire is reckoned the easiest of all wit; but I take it to be otherwise in very bad times: for it is as hard to satirize well a man of distinguished vices, as to praise well a man of distinguished virtues. It is easy enough to do either to people of moderate characters.

Invention is the talent of youth, and judgment of age: so that our judgment grows harder to please, when we have fewer things to offer it: this goes through the whole commerce of life. When we are old, our friends find it difficult to please us, and are less concerned whether we be pleased or not.

No wise man ever wished to be younger,

An idle reason lessens the weight of the good ones you gave before.

The motives of the best actions will not bear too strict an inquiry. It is allowed, that the cause of most actions, good or bad, may be resolved into the love of ourselves; but the self-love of some men, inclines them to please others; and the self-love of others is wholly employed in pleasing themselves. This makes the great distinction between virtue and vice. Religion is the best motive of all actions, yet religion is allowed to be the highest instance of self-love.

When the world has once begun to use us ill, it afterwards continues the same treatment with less scruple or ceremony, as men do to a whore.

Old men view best at a distance, with the eyes of their understanding, as well as with those of nature.

Some people take more care to hide their wisdom, than their folly.

Arbitrary power is the natural object of temptation to a prince, as wine or women to a young fellow, or a bribe to a judge, or avarice to old age, or vanity to a woman.

Anthony Henley's farmer dying of an asthma, said, "Well, if I can get this breath once out, I'll take care it shall never get in again."

The humour of exploding many things under the name of trifles, fopperies, and only imaginary goods, is a very false proof either of wisdom or magnanimity, and a great check to virtuous actions. For instance, with regard to fame: there is in most people a reluctance and unwillingness to be forgotten. We observe even among the vulgar, how fond they are to have an inscription over their grave. It requires but little philosophy to discover and observe that there is no intrinsic value in all this; however, if it be founded in our nature, as an incitement to virtue, it ought not to be ridiculed.

Complaint is the largest tribute Heaven receives and the sincerest part of our devotion.

The common fluency of speech in many men, and most women, is owing to a scarcity of matter, and a scarcity of words; for whoever is a master of language, and has a mind full of ideas, will be apt, in speaking, to hesitate upon the choice of both; whereas common speakers have only one set of ideas, and one set of words to clothe them in; and these are always ready at the mouth: so people come faster out of a church when it is almost empty, than when a crowd is at the door.

Few are qualified to shine in company; but it is in most men's power to be agreeable. The reason, therefore, why conversation runs so low at present, is not the defect of understanding, but pride, vanity, ill-nature, affectation, singularity, positiveness, or some other vice, the effect of a wrong education.

To be vain, is rather a mark of humility than pride. Vain men delight in telling what honours have been done them, what great company they have kept, and the like, by which they plainly confess that these honours were more than their due, and such as their friends would not believe, if they had not been told; whereas a man truly proud, thinks the greatest honours below his merit, and consequently scorns to boast. I therefore deliver it as a maxim, that whoever desires the character of a proud man, ought to conceal his vanity.

Law, in a free country, is, or ought to be, the determination of the majority of those who have property in land.

One argument used to the disadvantage of Providence, I take to be a very strong one in its defence. It is objected, that storms and tempests, unfruitful seasons, serpents, spiders, flies, and other noxious or troublesome animals, with many other instances of the same kind, discover an imperfection in nature, because human life would be much easier without them: but the design of Providence may clearly be perceived in this proceeding. The motions of the sun and moon, in short, the whole system of the universe, as far as philosophers have been able to discover and observe, are in the utmost degree of regularity and perfection; but wherever God has left to man the power of interposing a remedy by thought or labour, there he has placed things in a state of imperfection, on purpose to stir up human industry, without which life would stagnate, or indeed rather could not subsist at all: *Curis acuuntur mortalia corda.*

Praise is the daughter of present power.

How inconsistent is man with himself!

I have known several persons of great fame for wisdom in public affairs and councils, governed by foolish servants.

I have known great ministers, distinguished for wit and learning, who preferred none but dunces:

I have known men of great valour, cowards to their wives.

I have known men of the greatest cunning, perpetually cheated.

I knew three great ministers, who could exactly compute and settle the accompts of a kingdom, but were wholly ignorant of their own economy.

The preaching of divines helps to preserve well-inclined men in the course of virtue, but seldom or never reclaims the vicious.

Princes usually make wiser choices than the servants whom they trust for the disposal of places: I have known a prince, more than once, choose an able minister: but I never observed that minister to use his credit in the disposal of an employment to a person whom he thought the fittest for it. One of the greatest in this age * owned, and excused the matter, from the violence of parties, and the unreasonableness of friends.

Small causes are sufficient to make a man uneasy, when great ones are not in the way: for want of a block he will stumble at a straw.

Dignity, high station, or great riches, are in some sort necessary to old men, in order to keep the younger at a distance, who are otherwise too apt to insult them upon the score of their age.

Every man desires to live long; but no man would be old.

---

* Harley.

Love of flattery, in most men, proceeds from the mean opinion they have of themselves; in women, from the contrary.

If books and laws continue to increase as they have done for fifty years past, I am in concern for future ages, how any man will be learned, or any man a lawyer.

Kings are commonly said to have long hands; I wish they had as long ears.

Princes in their infancy, childhood, and youth, are said to discover prodigious parts and wit, to speak things that surprise and astonish: strange, so many hopeful princes, and so many shameful kings! If they happen to die young, they would have been prodigies of wisdom and virtue: if they live, they are often prodigies indeed, but of another sort.

Politics, as the word is commonly understood, are nothing but corruptions, and consequently of no use to a good king, or a good ministry: for which reason all courts are so full of politics.

Silenus, the foster-father of Bacchus, is always carried by an ass, and has horns on his head. The moral is, that drunkards are led by fools, and have a great chance to be cuckolds.

Venus, a beautiful, good-natured lady, was the goddess of love; Juno, a terrible shrew, the goddess of marriage: and they were always mortal enemies.

Those who are against religion, must needs be fools; and therefore we read that of all animals, God refused the first-born of an ass.

A very little wit is valued in a woman, as we are pleased with a few words spoken plain by a parrot.

A nice man is a man of nasty ideas.

Apollo was held the god of physic, and sender of diseases. Both were originally the same trade, and still continue.

Old men and comets have been reverenced for

the same reason; their long beards, and pretences to foretell events.

A person was asked at court, "what he thought of an ambassador, and his train, who were all embroidery and lace, full of bows, cringes, and gestures?" He said, "it was Solomon's importation, gold and apes."

There is a story in Pausanias of a plot for betraying a city discovered by the braying of an ass; the cackling of geese saved the Capitol; and Cataline's conspiracy was discovered by a whore. These are the only three animals, as far as I remember, famous in history as evidences and informers.

Most sorts of diversion in men, children, and other animals, are in imitation of fighting.

Augustus meeting an ass with a lucky name, foretold himself good fortune. I meet many asses, but none of them have lucky names.

If a man makes me keep my distance, the comfort is, he keeps his at the same time.

Who can deny that all men are violent lovers of truth, when we see them so positive in their errors, which they will maintain out of their zeal to truth, although they contradict themselves every day of their lives?

That was excellently observed, say I, when I read a passage in an author, where his opinion agrees with mine. When we differ, there I pronounce him to be mistaken.

Very few men, properly speaking, live at present, but are providing to live another time.

As universal a practice as lying is, and as easy a one as it seems, I do not remember to have heard three good lies in all my conversation, even from those who were most celebrated in that faculty.

THOUGHTS ON VARIOUS SUBJECTS

CONTINUED. 1726.

Laws penned with the utmost care and exactness, and in the vulgar language, are often perverted to wrong meanings; then why should we wonder that the Bible is so?

Although men are accused for not knowing their weakness, yet perhaps as few know their own strength.

A man seeing a wasp creeping into a vial filled with honey, that was hung on a fruit tree, said thus: "Why, thou sottish animal, art thou mad to go into the vial, where you see many hundreds of your kind dying before you?"—"The reproach is just," answered the wasp, "but not from you men, who are so far from taking example by other people's follies, that you will not take warning by your own. If after falling several times into this vial, and escaping by chance, I should fall in again, I should then but resemble you."

An old miser kept a tame jackdaw, that used to steal pieces of money and hide them in a hole; which the cat observing, asked, "Why he would hoard up those round shining things that he could make no use of?"—"Why," said the jackdaw, "my master has a whole chest full, and makes no more use of them than I."

Men are contented to be laughed at for their wit, but not for their folly.

If the men of wit and genius would resolve never to complain in their works of critics and detractors, the next age would not know that they ever had any.

After all the maxims and systems of trade and

commerce, a stander-by would think the affairs of the world were most ridiculously contrived.

There are few countries, which, if well cultivated, would not support double the number of their inhabitants, and yet fewer where one-third part of the people are not extremely stinted even in the necessaries of life. I send out twenty barrels of corn, which would maintain a family in bread for a year, and I bring back in return a vessel of wine, which half a dozen good fellows would drink in less than a month, at the expense of their health and reason.

A motto for the Jesuits:—

Quæ regio in terris nostri non plena laboris?

A man would have but few spectators, if he offered to shew for threepence how he could thrust a redhot iron into a barrel of gunpowder, and it should not take fire.

Query, Whether churches are not dormitories of the living as well as of the dead?

Harry Killegrew said to Lord Wharton, "You would not swear at that rate, if you thought you were doing God honour."

A copy of verses kept in the cabinet, and only shewn to a few friends, is like a virgin much sought after and admired; but when printed and published, is like a common whore, whom anybody may purchase for half-a-crown.

Lewis the XIVth of France spent his life in turning a good name into a great.

Since the union of divinity and humanity is the great article of our religion, it is odd to see some clergymen, in their writings of divinity, wholly devoid of humanity.

The Epicureans began to spread at Rome in the empire of Augustus, as the Socinians, and even the

Epicureans too, did in England toward the end of King Charles the Second's reign; which is reckoned, though very absurdly, our Augustan age. They both seem to be corruptions occasioned by luxury and peace, and by politeness beginning to decline.

Sometimes I read a book with pleasure, and detest the author.

At a bookseller's shop some time ago I saw a book with this title; "Poems by the author of The Choice." * Not enduring to read a dozen lines, I asked the company with me, whether they had ever seen the book, or heard of the poem whence the author denominated himself; they were all as ignorant as I. But I find it common with these small dealers in wit and learning, to give themselves a title from their first adventure, as Don Quixote usually did from his last. This arises from that great importance which every man supposes himself to be of.

One Dennis, commonly called "the critic," who had writ a threepenny pamphlet against the power of France, being in the country, and hearing of a French privateer hovering about the coast, although he were twenty miles from the sea, fled to town, and told his friends, "they need not wonder at his haste; for the King of France, having got intelligence where he was, had sent a privateer on purpose to catch him."

Dr. Gee, prebendary of Westminster, who had writ a small paper against Popery, being obliged to travel for his health, affected to disguise his person, and change his name, as he passed through Portugal, Spain, and Italy; telling all the English he met, "that he was afraid of being murdered, or put into

---

* Swift will, perhaps, be thought here to have been rather too fastidious.

the Inquisition." He was acting the same farce at Paris, till Mr. Prior (who was then secretary to the embassy) quite disconcerted the doctor, by maliciously discovering the secret; and offering to engage body for body, that not a creature would hurt him, or had ever heard of him or his pamphlet.

A chambermaid to a lady of my acquaintance, thirty miles from London, had the very same turn of thought; when talking with one of her fellow-servants, she said, "I hear it is all over London already that I am going to leave my lady:" and so had a footman, who, being newly married, desired his comrade to tell him freely what the town said of it.

When somebody was telling a certain great minister that people were discontented, "Pho," said he, "half a dozen fools are prating in a coffeehouse, and presently think their own noise about their ears is made by the world."

The death of a private man is generally of so little importance to the world, that it cannot be a thing of great importance in itself; and yet I do not observe, from the practice of mankind, that either philosophy or nature have sufficiently armed us against the fears which attend it. Neither do I find anything able to reconcile us to it, but extreme pain, shame, or despair; for poverty, imprisonment, ill fortune, grief, sickness, and old age, do generally fail.

Whence comes the custom of bidding a woman look upon her apron-strings to find an excuse? Was it not from the apron of fig-leaves worn by Eve, when she covered herself, and was the first of her sex who made a bad excuse for eating the forbidden fruit.

I never wonder to see men wicked, but I often wonder to see them not ashamed.

Do not we see how easily we pardon our own actions and passions, and the very infirmities of our bodies; why should it be wonderful to find us pardon our own dulness?

There is no vice or folly that requires so much nicety and skill to manage, as vanity; nor any which, by ill management, makes so contemptible a figure.

Observation is an old man's memory.

Eloquence, smooth and cutting, is like a razor whetted with oil.

Imaginary evils soon become real ones by indulging our reflections on them; as he, who in a melancholy fancy sees something like a face on the wall or the wainscot, can, by two or three touches with a lead pencil, make it look visible, and agreeing with what he fancied.

Men of great parts are often unfortunate in the management of public business, because they are apt to go out of the common road by the quickness of their imagination. This I once said to my Lord Bolingbroke, and desired he would observe, that the clerks in his office used a sort of ivory knife with a blunt edge to divide a sheet of paper, which never failed to cut it even, only requiring a steady hand: whereas if they should make use of a sharp penknife, the sharpness would make it go often out of the crease and disfigure the paper.

"He who does not provide for his own house," St. Paul says, "is worse than an infidel." And I think, he who provides only for his own house, is just equal with an infidel.

Jealousy, like fire, may shrivel up horns, but it makes them stink.

A footman's hat should fly off to everybody: and therefore Mercury, who was Jupiter's footman, had wings fastened to his cap.

When a man pretends love, but courts for money, he is like a juggler, who conjures away your shilling, and conveys something very indecent under the hat.

All panegyrics are mingled with an infusion of poppy.

I have known men happy enough at ridicule, who upon grave subjects were perfectly stupid; of which Dr. Echard of Cambridge, who writ "The Contempt of the Clergy," was a great instance.

One top of Parnassus was sacred to Bacchus, the other to Apollo.

Matrimony has many children; Repentance, Discord, Poverty, Jealousy, Sickness, Spleen, Loathing, &c.

Vision is the art of seeing things invisible.

The two maxims of any great man at court are, always to keep his countenance, and never to keep his word.

I asked a poor man how he did? He said, he was like a washball, always in decay.

Hippocrates, Aph. 32, Sect. 6, observes, that stuttering people are always subject to a looseness. I wish physicians had power to remove the profusion of words in many people to the inferior parts.

A man dreamed he was a cuckold; a friend told him it was a bad sign, because, when a dream is true, Virgil says it passes through the horned gate.

Love is a flame, and therefore we say beauty is attractive; because physicians observe that fire is a great drawer.

Civis, the most honourable name among the Romans; a citizen, a word of contempt among us.

A lady who had gallantries and several children, told her husband he was like the austere man, who reaped where he did not sow.

We read that an ass's head was sold for eighty

pieces of silver; they have lately been sold ten thousand times dearer, and yet they were never more plentiful.

I must complain the cards are ill shuffled, till I have a good hand.

When I am reading a book, whether wise or silly, it seems to me to be alive and talking to me.

Whoever live at a different end of the town from me, I look upon as persons out of the world, and only myself and the scene about me to be in it.

When I was young, I thought all the world, as well as myself, was wholly taken up in discoursing upon the last new play.

My Lord Cromarty, after fourscore, went to his country house in Scotland, with a resolution to stay six years there and live thriftily, in order to save up money that he might spend in London.

It is said of the horses in the vision, that "their power was in their mouths and in their tails." What is said of horses in the vision, in reality may be said of women.

Elephants are always drawn smaller than life, but a flea always larger.

When old folks tell us of many passages in their youth between them and their company, we are apt to think how much happier those times were than the present.

Why does the elder sister dance barefoot, when the younger is married before her? Is it not that she may appear shorter, and consequently be thought younger than the bride?

No man will take counsel, but every man will take money: therefore money is better than counsel.

I never yet knew a wag, (as the term is,) who was not a dunce.

A person reading to me a dull poem of his own making, I prevailed on him to scratch out six lines together; in turning over the leaf, the ink being wet, it marked as many lines on the other side; whereof the poet complaining, I bid him be easy, "for it would be better if those were out too."

At Windsor I was observing to my Lord Bolingbroke, "that the tower where the maids of honour lodged (who at that time were very handsome) was much frequented with crows." My lord said, "it was because they smelt carrion."

A TREATISE

ON

GOOD MANNERS AND GOOD BREEDING.*

GOOD manners is the art of making those people easy with whom we converse.

Whoever makes the fewest persons uneasy is the best bred in the company.

As the best law is founded upon reason, so are the best manners. And as some lawyers have introduced unreasonable things into common law, so likewise many teachers have introduced absurd things into common good manners.

One principal point of this art is, to suit our behaviour to the three several degrees of men; our superiors, our equals, and those below us.

For instance, to press either of the two former to eat or drink is a breach of manners; but a tradesman or a farmer must be thus treated, or else it will be difficult to persuade them that they are welcome.

---

* Which Lord Chesterfield thus defines, "the result of much good sense, some good nature, and a little self-denial for the sake of others, and with a view to obtain the same indulgence from them."

Pride, ill nature, and want of sense, are the three great sources of ill manners; without some one of these defects, no man will behave himself ill for want of experience, or of what, in the language of fools, is called knowing the world.

I defy any one to assign an incident wherein reason will not direct us what to say or do in company, if we are not misled by pride or ill nature.

Therefore I insist that good sense is the principal foundation of good manners; but, because the former is a gift which very few among mankind are possessed of, therefore all the civilized nations of the world have agreed upon fixing some rules upon common behaviour, best suited to their general customs or fancies, as a kind of artificial good sense, to supply the defects of reason. Without which the gentlemanly part of dunces would be perpetually at cuffs, as they seldom fail when they happen to be drunk, or engaged in squabbles about women or play. And, God be thanked, there hardly happens a duel in a year, which may not be imputed to one of these three motives. Upon which account, I should be exceedingly sorry to find the legislature make any new laws against the practice of duelling; because the methods are easy, and many, for a wise man to avoid a quarrel with honour, or engage in it with innocence. And I can discover no political evil in suffering bullies, sharpers, and rakes, to rid the world of each other by a method of their own, where the law has not been able to find an expedient.

As the common forms of good manners were intended for regulating the conduct of those who have weak understandings; so they have been corrupted by the persons for whose use they were contrived. For these people have fallen into a needless and endless way of multiplying ceremonies, which have been extremely troublesome to those who practise them, and insupportable to everybody else: insomuch that wise men are often more uneasy at the over-civility of these refiners, than they could possibly be in the conversation of peasants or mechanics.

The impertinencies of this ceremonial behaviour are nowhere better seen than at those tables where the ladies preside, who value themselves upon account of their good breeding; where a man must reckon upon passing an hour without doing any one thing he has a mind to; unless he will be so hardy as to break through all the settled decorum of the family.* She determines what he loves best, and how much he shall eat; and if the master of the house happens to be of the same disposition, he proceeds in the same tyrannical manner, to prescribe in the drinking part: at the same time you are under the necessity of answering a thousand apologies for your entertainment. And although a good deal of this humour is pretty well worn off among many people of the best fashion, yet too much of it still remains, especially in the country; where an honest gentleman assured me, that having been kept four days against his will at a friend's house, with all the circumstances of hiding his boots, locking up the stable, and other contrivances of the like nature, he could not remember, from the moment he came into the house to the moment he left it, any one thing, wherein his inclination was not directly contradicted; as if the whole family had entered into a combination to torment him.

But, beside all this, it would be endless to recount the many foolish and ridiculous accidents I have

---

* In the Tatler, No. XX. p. 62 of this volume, these maxims are illustrated with some ludicrous examples.

observed among these unfortunate proselytes to ceremony. I have seen a duchess fairly knocked down, by the precipitancy of an officious coxcomb running to save her the trouble of opening a door. I remember, upon a birthday at court, a great lady was rendered utterly disconsolate by a dish of sauce let fall by a page directly upon her head-dress and brocade, while she gave a sudden turn to her elbow upon some point of ceremony with the person who sat next to her. Monsieur Buys, the Dutch envoy, whose politics and manners were much of a size, brought a son with him, about thirteen years old, to a great table at court. The boy and his father, whatever they put on their plates, they first offered round in order, to every person in company; so that we could not get a minute's quiet during the whole dinner. At last their two plates happened to encounter, and with so much violence, that, being china, they broke in twenty pieces, and stained half the company with wet sweetmeats and cream.

There is a pedantry in manners, as in all arts and sciences: and sometimes in trades. Pedantry is properly the over-rating of any kind of knowledge we pretend to. And if that kind of knowledge be a trifle in itself, the pedantry is the greater. For which reason I look upon fiddlers, dancing-masters, heralds, masters of the ceremony, &c., to be greater pedants than Lipsius, or the elder Scaliger. With this kind of pedants, the court, while I knew it, was always plentifully stocked; I mean from the gentleman usher (at least) inclusive, downward to the gentleman porter: who are, generally speaking, the most insignificant race of people that this island can afford, and with the smallest tincture of good manners; which is the only trade they profess. For, being wholly illiterate, and conversing chiefly with each other, they reduce the whole system of breeding within the forms and circles of their several offices: and, as they are below the notice of ministers, they live and die in court under all revolutions, with great obsequiousness to those who are in any degree of credit or favour, and with rudeness and insolence to everybody else. Whence I have long concluded, that good manners are not a plant of the court growth: for if they were, those people, who have understandings directly of a level for such acquirements, who have served such long apprenticeships to nothing else, would certainly have picked them up. For, as to the great officers, who attend the prince's person or councils, or preside in his family, they are a transient body, who have no better a title to good manners than their neighbours, nor will probably have recourse to gentlemen ushers for instruction. So that I know little to be learned at court upon this head, except in the material circumstance of dress; wherein the authority of the maids of honour must indeed be allowed to be almost equal to that of a favourite actress.

I remember a passage my Lord Bolingbroke told me; that going to receive Prince Eugene of Savoy at his landing, in order to conduct him immediately to the Queen, the prince said, he was much concerned that he could not see her Majesty that night; for Monsieur Hoffman (who was then by) had assured his Highness that he could not be admitted into her presence with a tied-up periwig; that his equipage was not arrived; and that he had endeavoured in vain to borrow a long one among all his valets and pages. My lord turned the matter into a jest, and brought the prince to her Majesty; for which he was highly censured by the whole tribe of gentlemen ushers; among whom Monsieur Hoffman, an old dull resident of the Emperor's, had picked up this material point of ceremony; and which, I believe, was the best lesson he had learned in five-and-twenty years' residence.*

I make a difference between good manners and good breeding; although, in order to vary my expression, I am sometimes forced to confound them. By the first, I only understand the art of remembering and applying certain settled forms of general behaviour. But good breeding is of a much larger extent; for, beside an uncommon degree of literature sufficient to qualify a gentleman for reading a play

---

* Swift's patron, Harley, would, however, have done wisely to have attended to this insignificant etiquette. Queen Anne, upon whom, in some case of emergency, he had waited in a tie-wig, said very resentfully, she supposed his lordship would next appear before her in his night-cap.

In the notes on my friend Mr. Southey's CID, he has quoted a passage which strongly illustrates that which we have in the text. "Sir John Finett, master of the ceremonies to James and Charles I., left behind him some choice observations touching the reception and precedence, the treatment and audience, the puntillios and contests of forren ambassadors in England, which Howell published under the title of *Finetti Philoxenis*. That any man should have lived about such a court in such times, and have left such memoirs of it, is truly surprising. A passage which shews that chairs and stools were as great objects of discussion in those days, as they were in the reign of King Don Alfonso, is a good specimen of the book. 'Sir John, who had a good genius for the worthy office which he held, had been sent in the King's name to invite the French ambassador to the marriage of Lady Jane Dromond, which was to be solemnized the next day, at Somerset House; and after many diplomatic difficulties the point seemed to be settled, that the ambassador, (postponing all other considerations,) be there both at dinner and supper. With this signification I returned to the Lord Lysle, (lord chamberlaine to the Queene,) who communicated it to the Earl of Worcester, master of her Majesty's horse, that he might convey it to her Majesty, as he should go with her in a coach, from Whitehall to Somerset-House. It hung yet in intention when the ambassador's secretary came to me from his lord, with a further exception, that howsoever the Queen were pleased that he should be present both dinner and supper, he would be bold to prefer this condition to her allowance, that he might not sit upon a stool, but on

or a political pamphlet, it takes in a great compass of knowledge; no less than that of dancing, fighting, gaming, making the circle of Italy, riding the great horse, and speaking French; not to mention some other secondary or subaltern accomplishments, which are more easily acquired. So that the difference between good breeding and good manners lies in this, that the former cannot be attained to by the best understandings without study and labour; whereas a tolerable degree of reason will instruct us in every part of good manners, without other assistance.

---

a chair, in the same manner as the bride should be seated. I answered, I thought that would be no great difficulty. But how (quoth I) if the prince were there, and have but a stool to sit on? If my lord ambassador were sure of that, replied the secretary, I presume he would make no further question, but in all bear his highness company. To be resolved of this, I went at his request to my Lord Lysle, my Lord Worcester, and my Lord Carew, vice chamberlain, whom I found all together; and having assurance from them of the prince, his presence with the bride at dinner, and requesting their lordships, (as the secretary desired me,) that they would not trouble the Queen any further concerning the ambassador till the secretary had been with him, and returned with his final satisfaction, he repaired that evening to my Lord Lysle, and propounding the same demand of a chair, as he had done to me in the afternoon, it was resolved he should have one with the prince; and so ended that difference. The next day he came, and the bride, (seated at the table's end, which was placed at the upper end of the hall,) had the prince at her left hand, as the better place nearest the wall, (his highness sitting with his right hand uppermost,) on her right hand the ambassador, both in chairs; and opposite to him, beneath the Prince, in a little distance, sat on a stool, a Duke of Saxony, here at that time to visit his Majesty.'—P. 17.

"For the *Puntillios* of an ambassador, Sir John had all possible respect. But when one of the king's gentlemen ushers objected to a guest's sitting on a stool, at the end of the table, in the council chamber, 'as being,' he said, 'irregular and unusual, that place being ever wont to be reserved empty for state;'—this, says Sir John, as a superstition of a gentleman usher's, was neglected."
—*Southey's* CID, p. 426.

I can think of nothing more useful upon this subject, than to point out some particulars, wherein the very essentials of good manners are concerned, the neglect or perverting of which does very much disturb the good commerce of the world, by introducing a traffic of mutual uneasiness in most companies.

First, a necessary part of good manners, is a punctual observance of time at our own dwellings, or those of others, or at third places; whether upon matter of civility, business, or diversion; which rule, though it be a plain dictate of common reason, yet the greatest minister I ever knew was the greatest trespasser against it; by which all his business doubled upon him, and placed him in a continual arrear. Upon which I often used to rally him, as deficient in point of good manners. I have known more than one ambassador, and secretary of state, with a very moderate portion of intellectuals, execute their offices with good success and applause, by the mere force of exactness and regularity. If you duly observe time for the service of another, it doubles the obligation; if upon your own account, it would be manifest folly, as well as ingratitude, to neglect it; if both are concerned, to make your equal or inferior attend on you to his own disadvantage, is pride and injustice.

Ignorance of forms cannot properly be styled ill manners; because forms are subject to frequent changes; and consequently, being not founded upon reason, are beneath a wise man's regard. Besides, they vary in every country; and after a short period of time, very frequently in the same; so that a man who travels, must needs be at first a stranger to them in every court through which he passes; and, perhaps, at his return, as much a stranger in his own; and after all, they are easier to be remembered or forgotten than faces or names.

Indeed, among the many impertinencies that superficial young men bring with them from abroad, this bigotry of forms is one of the principal, and more predominant than the rest; who look upon them not only as if they were matters capable of admitting of choice, but even as points of importance; and are therefore zealous on all occasions to introduce and propagate the new forms and fashions they have brought back with them; so that, usually speaking, the worst bred person in company is a young traveller just returned from abroad.

HINTS ON GOOD MANNERS.

GOOD Manners is the art of making every reasonable person in the company easy, and to be easy ourselves.

What passes for good manners in the world, generally produces quite contrary effects.

Many persons of both sexes, whom I have known, and who passed for well-bred in their own and the world's opinion, are the most troublesome in company to others and themselves.

Nothing is so great an instance of ill manners as flattery. If you flatter all the company, you please none: if you flatter only one or two, you affront the rest.

Flattery is the worst and falsest way of shewing our esteem.

Where the company meets, I am confident the few reasonable persons are every minute tempted to curse the man or woman among them, who endeavours to be most distinguished for their good manners.

A man of sense would rather fast till night, than dine at some tables, where the lady of the house is possessed with good manners; uneasiness, pressing to eat, teasing with civility; less practised in England than here.

HINTS ON GOOD MANNERS.

Courts are the worst of all schools to teach good manners.

A courtly bow, or gait, or dress, are no part of good manners; and therefore every man of good understanding is capable of being well-bred upon any occasion.

To speak in such a manner as may possibly offend any reasonable person in company, is the highest instance of ill manners. Good manners chiefly consist in action, not in words. Modesty and humility the chief ingredients.

I have known the Court of England under four reigns, the two last but for a short time; and whatever good manners or politeness I observed in any of them, was not of the Court growth, but imported; for a courtier by trade, as gentlemen ushers, bedchamber-women, maids of honour,   *   *

Of good Manners as to Conversation.

Men of wit and good understanding, as well as breeding, are sometimes deceived, and give offence, by conceiving a better opinion of those with whom they converse than they ought to do. Thus I have often known the most innocent raillery, and even of that kind which was meant for praise, to be mistaken for abuse and reflection.

Of gibing, and how gibers ought to suffer.

Of arguers, perpetual contradictors, long talkers, those who are absent in company, interrupters, not listeners, loud laughers.

Of those men and women whose face is ever in a smile, talk ever with a smile, condole with a smile, &c.

Argument, as usually managed, is the worst sort of conversation; as it is generally in books the worst sort of reading.

Good conversation is not to be expected in much company, because few listen, and there is continual interruption. But good or ill manners are discovered, let the company be ever so large.

Perpetual aiming at wit, a very bad part of conversation. It is done to support a character: it generally fails: it is a sort of insult on the company, and a constraint upon the speaker.

For a man to talk in his own trade, or business, or faculty, is a great breach of good manners. Divines, physicians, lawyers, soldiers, particularly poets, are frequently guilty of this weakness. A poet conceives that the whole kingdom   *   *   *   *

OF MEAN AND GREAT FIGURES,
MADE BY SEVERAL PERSONS.

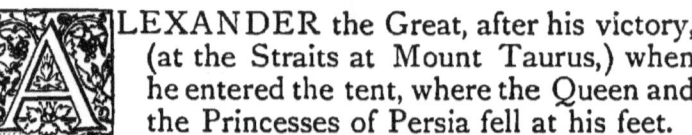

Of those who have made Great Figures in some particular Action or Circumstances of their Lives.

ALEXANDER the Great, after his victory, (at the Straits at Mount Taurus,) when he entered the tent, where the Queen and the Princesses of Persia fell at his feet.

Socrates, the whole last day of his life, and particularly from the time he took the poison until the moment he expired.

Cicero, when he was recalled from his banishment, the people, through every place he passed, meeting him with shouts of joy and congratulation, and all Rome coming out to receive him.

Regulus, when he went out of Rome attended by his friends to the gates, and returned to Carthage according to his word of honour, although he knew he must be put to a cruel death for advising the Romans to pursue their war with that commonwealth.

Scipio the elder, when he dismissed a beautiful captive lady presented to him after a great victory, turning his head aside to preserve his own virtue.

The same Scipio, when he and Hannibal met before the battle, if the fact be true.

Cincinnatus, when the messengers sent by the Senate to make him Dictator, found him at the plough.

Epaminondas, when the Persian ambassador came to his house, and found him in the midst of poverty.

The Earl of Stafford, the day that he made his own defence at his trial.*

King Charles the Martyr, during his whole trial, and at his death.

The Black Prince, when he waited at supper on the King of France, whom he had conquered and taken prisoner the same day.

Virgil, when, at Rome, the whole audience rose up, out of veneration, as he entered the theatre.

Mahomet the Great, when he cut off his beloved mistress's head, on a stage erected for that purpose, to convince his soldiers, who taxed him for preferring his love to his glory.

Cromwell, when he quelled a mutiny in Hyde Park.

Harry the Great of France, when he entered Paris, and sat at cards the same night with some great ladies, who were his mortal enemies.

Robert Harley, Earl of Oxford, at his trial.

Cato of Utica, when he provided for the safety of his friends, and had determined to die.

Sir Thomas More, during his imprisonment, and at his execution.

---

* Concerning which, Whitlocke, no friend to the Earl or his cause, has left the following testimony : " Certainly never any man acted such a part on such a theatre with more wisdome, constancy, and eloquence, with greater reason, judgment, and temper, and with a better grace in all his words and gestures, than this great and excellent person did ; and he moved the hearts of all his auditors, some few excepted, to remorse and pity."—WHITLOCKE's *Memorials*, p. 43.

Marius, when the soldier sent to kill him in the dungeon, was struck with so much awe and veneration that his sword fell from his hand.

Douglas, when the ship he commanded was on fire, and he lay down to die in it, because it should not be said that one of his family ever quitted their post.*

Of those who have made a Mean Contemptible Figure in some Action or Circumstance of their Lives.

Anthony, at Actium, when he fled after Cleopatra.

Pompey, when he was killed on the sea-shore, in Egypt.

Nero and Vitellius, when they were put to death.

Lepidus, when he was compelled to lay down his share of the triumvirate.

Cromwell, the day he refused the kingship out of fear.

Perseus, King of Macedon, when he was led in triumph.

Richard II., of England, after he was deposed.

The late King of Poland, when the King of Sweden forced him to give up his kingdom; and when he took it again, upon the King of Sweden's defeat by the Muscovites.

King James II., of England, when the Prince of Orange sent to him at midnight to leave London.

King William III., of England, when he sent to beg the House of Commons to continue his Dutch Guards, and was refused.

The late Queen Anne of England, when she sent

---

* This instance of stubborn desperation, rather than courage, happened when the Dutch burned some ships at Chatham in the reign of Charles II. Marvel celebrates the circumstance in his "Advice to a Painter."

Whitworth to Muscovy on an embassy of humiliation, for an insult committed here on that Prince's ambassador.*

The Lord Chancellor Bacon, when he was convicted of bribery.

The late Duke of Marlborough, when he was forced, after his own disgrace, to carry his Duchess's gold key to the Queen.†

The old Earl of Pembroke, when a Scotch lord gave him a lash with a whip at Newmarket, in presence of all the nobility, and he bore it with patience.‡

King Charles II., of England, when he entered into the second Dutch war; and in many other actions during his whole reign.

---

* He was arrested by a creditor, and carried, after some resistance and ill usage, to a common spunging house. The Czar Peter demanded that the offenders should be capitally punished; and as it was difficult to make him comprehend, that the English law did not permit such summary vengeance, he threatened to make our trade feel the effect of his resentment, and was appeased with great difficulty.

† It may be doubted, whether the Queen on this occasion might not make the lesser figure of the two.

‡ It was Philip Earl of Pembroke and Montgomery, who disgraced his ancient family, by submitting to this gross insult. He received the blow from Ramsay Earl of Holderness.

"It was at a horse-race, where many both Scotch and English met; the latter of which did upon this accident draw together, with a resolution to make it a national quarrel, so far as Mr. John Pinchback, though a maimed man, having but the perfect use of his two fingers, rode about with his dagger in his hand, crying, Let us break our fast with them here, and dine with the rest at London! But Herbert not offering to strike again, there was nothing spilt but the reputation of a gentleman; in lieu of which, if I am not mistaken, the King made him a Knight, a Baron, a Viscount, and an Earl, in one day; as he well deserved, having for his sake, or rather out of fear, transgressed all the gradations of honour."—OSBORNE'S *Traditional Memorials*, apud *Works*, Lond. 1673, 8vo, p. 505.

Philip II., of Spain, after the defeat of the Armada.

The Emperor Charles V., when he resigned his crown, and nobody would believe his reasons.

King Charles I., of England, when, in gallantry to his Queen, he thought to surprise her with a present of a diamond buckle, which he pushed down her breast, and tore her flesh with the tongue; upon which she drew it out, and flung it on the ground.

Fairfax, the Parliament general, at the time of King Charles's trial.*

Julius Cæsar, when Anthony offered to put a diadem on his head, and the people shouted for joy to see him decline it; which he never offered to do, until he saw their dislike in their countenances.

Coriolanus, when he withdrew his army from Rome at the entreaty of his mother.

Hannibal, at Antiochus's court.

Beau Fielding,† at fifty years old, when, in a

---

* When he was generally supposed to have determined on saving the King, but suffered himself to be outwitted by Cromwell.

† Robert Fielding of Fielding Hall, commonly called Beau Fielding. He was very handsome, and set up as a fortune-hunter; but, meeting with a female more able than himself, he was tricked into marriage, under the idea of her being possessed of a large fortune, while, in truth, she was as penniless as obscure. This incident, he conceived, ought not to suspend his career of fortune, and accordingly, sixteen days after it took place, Beau Fielding united himself to the most noble Barbara Duchess of Cleaveland. He was tried for felony at the Old Bailey, and his second marriage set aside. He himself had the benefit of clergy, and this odd adventure closed the long list of the Duchess of Cleaveland's gallantries, which, commencing with the Restoration, had ran through nearly four reigns, not a little distinguished by their promiscuous and motley complexion. Fielding is described by the Tatler, No. 50, under the name of Orlando, and is said to be "full, but not loaded with years." From the account there given of him, as well as the anecdote in the text, it would seem that conceit of his conquests, and vanity of his figure, had crazed his brain. He received the wound mentioned by Swift, at Mrs.

quarrel upon the stage, he was run into his breast, which he opened and shewed to the ladies, that he might move their love and pity; but they all fell a-laughing.

The Count de Bussy Rabutin, when he was recalled to court after twenty years' banishment into the country, and affected to make the same figure he did in his youth.

The Earl of Sunderland, when he turned Papist, in the time of King James II., and underwent all the forms of a heretic converted.

Pope Clement VII., when he was taken prisoner, at Rome, by the Emperor Charles the Fifth's forces.

Queen Mary of Scotland, when she suffered Bothwell to ravish her, and pleaded that as an excuse for marrying him.

King John of England, when he gave up his kingdom to the Pope, to be held as a fief to the see of Rome.

Oldfield's benefit. The combat took place betwixt him and Mr. Fullwood, a barrister, whose foot he had trodden upon, in pressing forward to display his person to most advantage. His antagonist was killed in a duel the very same night, having engaged in a second theatrical quarrel. The conduct of the hero might be sufficiently absurd; but a wound of several inches' depth was an odd subject of ridicule. Fielding died about 1712.

OF PUBLIC ABSURDITIES

IN

ENGLAND.

———o———

T is a common topic of satire, which you will hear not only from the mouths of ministers of state, but of every whiffler in office, that half a dozen obscure fellows, over a bottle of wine or a dish of coffee, shall presume to censure the actions of Parliaments and Councils, to form schemes of government, and new-model the commonwealth; and this is usually ridiculed as a pragmatical disposition to politics, in the very nature and genius of the people. It may possibly be true: and yet I am grossly deceived if any sober man, of very moderate talents, when he reflects upon the many ridiculous hurtful maxims, customs, and general rules of life, which prevail in this kingdom, would not with great reason be tempted, according to the present turn of his humour, either to laugh, lament, or be angry; or, if he were sanguine enough, perhaps to dream of a remedy. It is the mistake of wise and good men, that they expect more reason and virtue from human nature, than, taking it in the bulk, it is in any sort capable of. Whoever has been present at councils or assem-

blies of any sort, if he be a man of common prudence, cannot but have observed such results and opinions to have frequently passed a majority, as he would be ashamed to advance in private conversation. I say nothing of cruelty, oppression, injustice, and the like, because these are fairly to be accounted for in all assemblies, as best gratifying the passions and interest of leaders; which is a point of such high consideration, that all others must give place to it. But I would be understood here to speak only of opinions ridiculous, foolish, and absurd; with conclusions and actions suitable to them, at the same time when the most reasonable propositions are often unanimously rejected. And as all assemblies of men are liable to this accusation, so likewise there are natural absurdities from which the wisest states are not exempt; which proceed less from the nature of their climate, than that of their government; the Gauls, the Britons, the Spaniards, and Italians, having retained very little of the characters given them in ancient history.

By these and the like reflections, I have been often led to consider some public absurdities in our own country, most of which are, in my opinion, directly against the rules of right reason, and are attended with great inconveniencies to the state. I shall mention such of them as come into memory, without observing any method; and I shall give my reason why I take them to be absurd in their nature, and pernicious in their consequence.

It is absurd that any person, who professes a different form of worship from that which is national, should be trusted with a vote for electing members into the House of Commons: because every man is full of zeal for his own religion, although he regards not morality; and, therefore, will endeavour, to his utmost, to bring in a representative of his own principles, which, if they be popular, may endanger the religion established; and which, as it has formerly happened, may alter the whole frame of government.

A standing army in England, whether in time of peace or war, is a direct absurdity: for it is no part of our business to be a warlike nation, otherwise than by our fleets. In foreign wars we have no concern, farther than in conjunction with allies, whom we may either assist by sea, or by foreign troops paid with our money: but mercenary troops in England can be of no use, except to awe senates, and thereby promote arbitrary power, in a monarchy or oligarchy.

That the election of senators should be of any charge to the candidates, is an absurdity: but that it should be so to a ministry, is a manifest acknowledgment of the worst designs. If a ministry intended the service of their Prince and country, or well understood wherein their own security best consisted, (as it is impossible that a Parliament freely elected, according to the original institution, can do any hurt to a tolerable Prince or tolerable ministry,) they would use the strongest methods to leave the people to their own free choice; the members would then consist of persons who had the best estates in the neighbourhood or country, or, at least, never of strangers. And surely this is at least full as requisite a circumstance to a legislator, as to a juryman, who ought to be, if possible, *ex vicinio;* since such persons must be supposed the best judges of the wants and desires of their several boroughs and counties. To choose a representative for Berwick, whose estate is at Land's End, would have been thought in former times a very great solecism. How much more as it is at present, where so many persons are returned for boroughs, who do not possess a foot of land in the kingdom?

By the old constitution, whoever possessed a freehold in land, by which he was a gainer of forty shillings a-year, had the privilege to vote for a knight of the shire. The good effects of this law are wholly eluded, partly by the course of time, and partly by corruption. Forty shillings, in those ages, were equal to twenty pounds in ours; and, therefore, it was then a want of sagacity to fix that privilege to a determinate sum, rather than to a certain quantity of land, arable or pasture, able to produce a certain quantity of corn and hay. And, therefore, it is highly absurd, and against the intent of the law, that this defect is not regulated.

But the matter is still worse; for any gentleman can, upon occasion, make as many freeholders as his estate of settlement will allow, by making leases for life of land at a rack-rent of forty shillings; where a tenant, who is not worth one farthing a-year when his rent is paid, shall be held a legal voter for a person to represent his county. Neither do I enter into half the frauds that are practised upon this occasion.

It is likewise absurd, that boroughs decayed are not absolutely extinguished, because the returned members do in reality represent nobody at all; and that several large towns are not represented, though full of industrious townsmen, who must advance the trade of the kingdom.

The claim of senators, to have themselves and servants exempted from lawsuits and arrests, is manifestly absurd. The proceedings at law are already so scandalous a grievance, upon account of the delays, that they little need any addition. Whoever is either not able, or not willing, to pay his just debts, or, to keep other men out of their lands, would evade the decision of the law, is surely but ill qualified to be a legislator. A criminal with as good reason might sit on the bench, with a power of condemning men to be hanged for their honesty. By the annual sitting of Parliaments, and the days of privilege preceding and subsequent, a senator is one-half of the year beyond the reach of common justice.

That the sacred person of a senator's footman shall be free from arrest, although he undoes the poor ale-wife by running on score, is a circumstance of equal wisdom and justice, to avoid the great evil of his master's lady wanting her complement of liveries behind the coach.

OF THE EDUCATION OF LADIES.

THERE is a subject of controversy which I have frequently met with, in mixed and select companies of both sexes, and sometimes only of men:—"Whether it be prudent to choose a wife who has good natural sense, some taste of wit and humour, sufficiently versed in her own natural language, able to read and relish history, books of travels, moral or entertaining discourses, and be a tolerable judge of the beauties in poetry?" This question is generally determined in the negative by the women themselves, but almost universally by the men.

We must observe, that in this debate, those whom we call men and women of fashion are only to be understood, not merchants, tradesmen, or others of such occupations who are not supposed to have shared in a liberal education. I except, likewise, all ministers of state during their power, lawyers and physicians in great practice, persons in such employments as take up the greater part of the day, and perhaps some other conditions of life which I cannot call to mind. Neither must I forget to except all gentlemen of the army, from the general to the ensign; because those qualifications above-mentioned in a wife, are wholly out of their element and comprehension; together with all mathematicians, and gentlemen lovers of music, metaphysicians, virtuosi, and great talkers, who have all amusements enough of their own. All these put together, will amount to a great number of adversaries, whom I shall have no occasion to encounter, because I am already of their sentiments. Those persons whom I mean to include, are the bulk of lords, knights, and squires, throughout England, whether they reside between the town and country, or generally in either. I do also include those of the clergy, who have tolerably good preferments in London or any other parts of the kingdom.

The most material arguments that I have met with, on the negative side of this great question, are what I shall now impartially report, in as strong a light as I think they can bear.

It is argued, " That the great end of marriage is propagation: that, consequently, the principal business of a wife is to breed children, and to take care of them in their infancy: That the wife is to look to her family, watch over the servants, see that they do their work: That she be absent from her house as little as possible: That she is answerable for everything amiss in her family: That she is to obey all the lawful commands of her husband, and visit or be visited by no persons whom he disapproves: That her whole business, if well performed, will take up most hours of the day: That the greater she is, and the more servants she keeps, her inspection must increase accordingly; for, as a family represents a kingdom, so the wife, who is her husband's first minister, must, under him, direct all the officers of state, even to the lowest; and report their behaviour to her husband, as the first minister does to his prince: That such a station requires much time, and thought, and order; and, if well executed, leaves but little time for visits or diversions: That a humour of reading books, except those of devotion or housewifery, is apt to turn a woman's brain: That plays, romances, novels, and love-poems, are only proper to instruct them how to carry on an intrigue: That all affectation of knowledge, beyond what is merely domestic, renders them vain, conceited, and pretending: That the natural levity of woman wants ballast; and when she once begins to think she knows more than others of her sex, she will begin to despise her husband, and grow fond of every coxcomb who pretends to any knowledge in books: That she will learn scholastic words; make herself ridiculous by pronouncing them wrong, and applying them absurdly in all companies: That in the meantime, her household affairs, and the care of her children, will be wholly laid aside; her toilet will be crowded with all the under-wits, where the conversation will pass in criticising on the last play or poem that comes out, and she will be careful to remember all the remarks that were made, in order to retail them in the next visit, especially in company who know nothing of the matter: That she will have all the impertinence of a pedant, without the knowledge; and for every new acquirement, will become so much the worse."

To say the truth, that shameful and almost universal neglect of good education among our nobility, gentry, and indeed among all others who are born to good estates, will make this essay of little use to the present age; for, considering the modern way of training up both sexes in ignorance, idleness, and vice, it is of little consequence how they are coupled together. And therefore my speculations on this subject can be only of use to a small number; for, in the present situation of the world, none but wise and good men can fail of missing their match, whenever they are disposed to marry ; and consequently there is no reason for complaint on either side. The forms by which a husband and wife are to live, with regard to each other and to the world, are sufficiently known and fixed, in direct contradiction to every precept of morality, religion, or civil institution ; it would be therefore an idle attempt to aim at breaking so firm an establishment.

But, as it sometimes happens, that an elder brother dies late enough to leave the younger at the university, after he has made some progress in learning; if we suppose him to have a tolerable genius, and a desire to improve it, he may consequently learn to value and esteem wisdom and knowledge wherever he finds them, even after his father's death, when his title and estate come into his own possession. Of this kind, I reckon, by a favourable computation, there may possibly be found, by a strict search among the nobility and gentry throughout England, about five hundred. Among those of all other callings or trades, who are able to maintain a son at the university, about treble that number. The sons of clergymen, bred to learning with any success, must, by reason of their parents' poverty, be very inconsiderable, many of them being only admitted servitors in colleges, and consequently proving good for nothing : I shall therefore count them to be not above fourscore. But, to avoid fractions, I shall suppose there may possibly be a round number of two thousand male human creatures in England, including Wales, who have a tolerable share of reading and good sense. I include in this list all persons of superior abilities, or great genius, or true judgment and taste, or of profound literature, who, I am confident, we may reckon to be at least five-and-twenty.

I am very glad to have this opportunity of doing an honour to my country, by a computation which I am afraid foreigners may conceive to be partial; when, out of only fifteen thousand families of lords and estated gentlemen, which may probably be their number, I suppose one in thirty to be tolerably educated, with a sufficient share of good sense. Perhaps the censure may be just. And therefore, upon cooler thoughts, to avoid all cavils, I shall reduce them to one thousand, which, at least, will be a number sufficient to fill both Houses of Parliament.

The daughters of great and rich families, computed after the same manner, will hardly amount to above half the number of the male; because the care of their education is either entirely left to their mothers, or they are sent to boarding-schools, or put into the hands of English or French governesses, and generally the worst that can be gotten for money. So that, after the reduction I was compelled to, from two thousand to one, half the number of well-educated nobility and gentry must either continue in a single life, or be forced to couple themselves with women for whom they can possibly have no esteem; I mean fools, prudes, coquettes, gamesters, saunterers, endless talkers of nonsense, splenetic idlers, intriguers, given to scandal and censure, * * * * * *

CHARACTER OF ARISTOTLE.*

ARISTOTLE, the disciple of Plato, and tutor to Alexander the Great. His followers were called peripatetics, from a Greek word which signifies to walk, because he taught his disciples walking: we have not all his works, and some of those which are imputed to him are supposed not genuine. He writ upon logic, or the art of reasoning; upon moral and natural philosophy; upon oratory, poetry, &c., and seems to be a person of the most comprehensive genius that ever lived.

---

* This fragment is preserved in the Essay of Deane Swift, Esq., who tells us, "he transcribed it without any variation; and that he found it by accident in a little book of instructions, which Dr. Swift was pleased to draw up for the use of a lady, enjoining her to get it all by heart."

CHARACTER OF HERODOTUS.

HE underwritten is copied from Dr. Swift's hand-writing, in an edition of Herodotus, by Paul Stephens, the gift of the Earl of Clanricard to the library of Winchester College.

"Judicium de Herodoto post longum tempus relecto.

"Ctesias mendacissimus Herodotum mendaciorum arguit, exceptis paucissimis, (ut mea fert sententia,) omnimodo excusandum. Cæterum, diverticulis abundans, hic pater historicorum filum narrationis ad tædium abrumpit : unde oritur (ut par est) legentibus confusio, et exindè oblivio. Quin et forsan ipsæ narrationes circumstantiis nimium pro re scatent. Quod ad cætera, hunc scriptorem inter apprimè laudandos censeo, neque Græcis neque Barbaris plus æquo faventem aut iniquum : in orationibus ferè brevem, simplicem, nec nimis frequentem. Neque absunt dogmata e quibus eruditus lector prudentiam tam moralem quam civilem haurire poterit.

"J. SWIFT.*

"*Julii* 6, 1720."

---

* "I do hereby certify, that the above is the hand-writing of the late Dr. Jonathan Swift, D. S. P. D., from whom I have had many letters, and printed several pieces from his original MSS.

"GEORGE FAULKNER.

"*Dublin, August* 21, 1762."

CHARACTER OF PRIMATE MARSH.*

MARSH has the reputation of most profound and universal learning; this is the general opinion, neither can it be easily disproved. An old rusty iron chest in a banker's shop, strongly locked, and wonderfully heavy, is full of gold; this is the general

---

* Dr. Narcissus Marsh, successively Bishop of Ferns, Dublin, and Armagh. He was promoted to the last see in 1702, and died in 1713. He founded a public library in Dublin, and distinguished himself by other acts of munificence. But he was at variance with Archbishop King, to whom Swift at this time looked up as a patron. The following character is engraved on his tomb-stone. The truth probably lies somewhat between the epitaph and the satire.

> Now take the talents of his mind,
> Which were equal to, nay even greater
> Than all these employments.
> As Provost, Prelate, and Governor,
> He promoted, encreased, and established,
> In the university, the study of sound learning,
> In the church, piety and primitive discipline,
> In the republic, peace and reverence for the laws;
> By living always a pious and unblameable life,.
> By encouraging the learned,
> By defending his fellow-citizens.
> Among all these great duties,
> He dedicated his leisure hours
> To the study of mathematics and natural philosophy,

opinion, neither can it be disapproved, provided the key be lost, and what is in it be wedged so close that it will not by any motion discover the metal by the chinking. Doing good is his pleasure; and as no man consults another in his pleasures, neither does he in this; by his awkwardness and unadvisedness disappointing his own good designs. His high station has placed him in the way of great employments, which, without in the least polishing his native rusticity, have given him a tincture of pride and ambition. But these vices would have passed concealed under his natural simplicity, if he had not endeavoured to hide them by art. His disposition to study is the very same with that of a usurer to hoard up money, or of a vicious young fellow to a wench; nothing but avarice and evil concupiscence, to which his constitution has fortunately given a more innocent turn. He is sordid and suspicious in his domestics, without love or hatred; which is but reasonable, since he has neither friend nor enemy; without joy or grief; in short, without all passions but fear, to which of all others he has least temptation, having nothing to get or to lose; no posterity, relation, or friend, to be solicitous about; and placed by his station above the reach of fortune or envy. He has found out the secret of preferring men with-

---

And above all was highly skilled
In the knowledge of languages, especially the oriental:
Endowed with the highest knowledge
Of the Scriptures and Ecclesiastical History,
He transferred
The truth and beauty of the Christian Religion
Into his life, and the government of the church.
Thus he became
Dear, worthy, and useful to all,
— — — — — — —
A Man born
For his country, the church, and the world.

out deserving their thanks; and where he dispenses his favours to persons of merit, they are less obliged to him than to fortune. He is the first of human race, that with great advantages of learning, piety, and station, ever escaped being a great man. That which relishes best with him, is mixed liquor and mixed company; and he is seldom unprovided with very bad of both. He is so wise as to value his own health more than other men's noses, so that the most honourable place at his table is much the worst, especially in summer. It has been affirmed, that originally he was not altogether devoid of wit, till it was extruded from his head to make room for other men's thoughts. He will admit a governor, provided it be one who is very officious and diligent, outwardly pious, and one that knows how to manage and make the most of his fear. No man will be either glad or sorry at his death, except his successor.

CHARACTER OF MRS. HOWARD.*

WRITTEN IN THE YEAR 1727.

 SHALL say nothing of her wit or beauty, which are allowed by all persons who can judge of either, when they hear or see her. Besides, beauty being transient, and a trifle, cannot justly make part of a character. And I leave others to celebrate

---

* This character was written when Tory courtiers as well as Tory poets saw, or thought they saw, some dawning of future favour in the dispositions of the Prince and Princess of Wales, from their affecting to encourage those who were discontented with the ministry of Sir Robert Walpole. The Tories knew well the advantages they had formerly enjoyed, during the predominating influence of Lady Masham over Queen Anne; and therefore failed not to cultivate the intimacy of Mrs. Howard, whose post near the princess's person, and high state of favour with her mistress, promised the exhibition of a part scarcely less important. Whatever might be the views of the courtiers, those of the poetical and literary adulators seem to have been limited to working forth the preferment of Gay. The reconciliation between Queen Caroline and Walpole, broke all the measures of the expectants. The obnoxious minister retained his power and emoluments, and Mrs. Howard, deafer than the adder, resisted all the tuneful flattery, by which Swift and Pope vainly hoped to bribe her favour for poor Gay.

The panegyric here pronounced on Mrs. Howard is truly elegant. But whether from Swift's deep knowledge of human nature, or from his natural disposition to satire, or that he anticipated the change which actually took place, the Dean has mingled food for future satire, even with the honey of his praises.

her wit, because it will be of no use in that part of her character which I intend to draw. Neither shall I relate any part of her history; farther than that she went, in the prime of her youth, to the court of Hanover with her husband, and became of the bedchamber to the present Princess of Wales, living in expectation of the Queen's death: upon which event she came over with her mistress, and has ever since continued in her service; where, from the attendance daily paid her by the ministers, and all expectants, she is reckoned much the greatest favourite of the court at Leicester House; a situation which she has long affected to desire that it might not be believed.

There is no politician who more carefully watches the motions and dispositions of things and persons at St. James's, nor can form his language with a more imperceptible dexterity to the present posture of a court, or more early foresee what style may be proper upon any approaching juncture of affairs; whereof she can gather early intelligence without asking it, and often when even those from whom she has it are not sensible that they are giving it to her, but equally with others admire her sagacity. Sir Robert Walpole and she both think they understand each other, and are both equally mistaken.

With persons where she is to manage, she is very dexterous in that point of skill which the French call *tâter le pavé;* with others, she is a very great vindicator of all present proceedings, but in such a manner, as if she were under no concern farther than her own conviction, and wondering how anybody can think otherwise. And the danger is, that she may come in time to believe herself; which, under a change of princes, and a great addition of credit, might have bad consequences. She is a most unconscionable dealer; for, in return of a few good words, which she gives to her lords and gentlemen daily waiters before their faces, she gets ten thousand from them behind her back, which are of real service to her character. The credit she has is managed with the utmost thrift: and whenever she employs it, which is very rarely, it is only upon such occasions where she is sure to get much more than she spends. For instance, she would readily press Sir Robert Walpole to do some favour for Colonel Churchill, or Doddington; the prince, for a mark of grace to Mr. Shutz; and the princess, to be kind to Mrs. Clayton. She sometimes falls into the general mistake of all courtiers, which is that of not suiting her talents to the abilities of others, but thinking those she deals with to have less art than they really possess, so that she may possibly be deceived when she thinks she deceives.

In all offices of life, except those of a courtier, she acts with justice, generosity, and truth. She is ready to do good as a private person, and I would almost think in charity that she will not do harm as a courtier, unless to please those in chief power.

In religion she is at least a latitudinarian, being not an enemy to books written by the freethinkers; and herein she is the more blameable, because she has too much morality to stand in need of them, requiring only a due degree of faith for putting her in the road to salvation. I speak this of her as a private lady, not as a court favourite; for, in the latter capacity, she can shew neither faith nor works.

If she had never seen a court, it is not impossible that she might have been a friend.

She abounds in good words, and expressions of good wishes, and will concert a hundred schemes for the service of those whom she would be thought to favour: schemes, that sometimes arise from them, and sometimes from herself; although, at the same time, she very well knows them to be without the least probability of succeeding. But, to do her justice, she never feeds or deceives any person with promises, where she does not at the same time intend a degree of sincerity.

She is, upon the whole, an excellent companion for men of the best accomplishments, who have nothing to desire or expect.*

What part she may act hereafter in a larger sphere, as lady of the bed-chamber to a great Queen, (upon supposing the death of his present Majesty, and of the Earl of Suffolk, to whose title her husband succeeds,) and in high esteem with a King, neither she nor I can foretell. My own opinion is natural and obvious; that her talents as a courtier will spread, enlarge, and multiply to such a degree, that her private virtues, for want of room and time to operate, will be laid up clean, (like clothes in a chest,) to be used and put on, whenever satiety, or some reverse of fortune, or increase of ill health, (to which last she is subject,) shall dispose her to retire. In the meantime, it will be her wisdom to take care that they may not be tarnished or moth-eaten, for want of airing and turning at least once a-year.

---

* "I wish I could tell you any agreeable news of what your heart is concerned in; but I have a sort of quarrel with Mrs. Howard, for not loving herself so well as she does her friends; for those she makes happy, but not herself. There is a sort of sadness about her, which grieves me, and which I have learned, by experience, will increase upon an indolent (I will not say an affected) resignation to it. It will dose in men, and much more in women, who have a natural softness which sinks them even when reason does not."—POPE, *Letters to a Lady*, p. 76.

ON THE DEATH

OF

MRS. JOHNSON [STELLA].

HIS day, being Sunday, January 28, 1727-8, about eight o'clock at night, a servant brought me a note, with an account of the death of the truest, most virtuous, and valuable friend, that I, or perhaps any other person, was ever blessed with. She expired about six in the evening of this day; and as soon as I am left alone, which is about eleven at night, I resolve, for my own satisfaction, to say something of her life and character.

She was born at Richmond, in Surrey, on the 13th day of March, in the year 1681. Her father was a younger brother of a good family in Nottinghamshire, her mother of a lower degree; and indeed she had little to boast of her birth. I knew her from six years old, and had some share in her education, by directing what books she should read, and perpetually instructing her in the principles of honour and virtue; from which she never swerved in any one action or moment of her life. She was sickly from her childhood until about the age of fifteen; but then grew into perfect health, and was looked upon as one of the most beautiful, graceful, and agreeable young women in London, only a little too fat. Her hair was blacker than a raven, and every feature of her face in perfection. She lived generally in the country, with a family where she contracted an intimate friendship with another lady of more advanced years. I was then, to my mortification, settled in Ireland; and about a year after, going to visit my friends in England, I found she was a little uneasy upon the death of a person on whom she had some dependence. Her fortune, at that time, was in all not above fifteen hundred pounds, the interest of which was but a scanty maintenance. Under this consideration, and indeed very much for my own satisfaction, who had few friends or acquaintance in Ireland, I prevailed with her and her dear friend and companion, the other lady, to draw what money they had into Ireland, a great part of their fortune being in annuities upon funds. Money was then ten *per cent.* in Ireland, besides the advantage of returning it, and all necessaries of life at half the price. They complied with my advice, and soon after came over; but I happening to continue some time longer in England, they were much discouraged to live in Dublin, where they were wholly strangers. She was at that time about nineteen years old, and her person was soon distinguished. But the adventure looked so like a frolic, the censure held for some time, as if there were a secret history in such a removal; which, however, soon blew off by her excellent conduct. She came over with her friend on the ——— in the year 170–;* and they both lived together until this day, when death removed her from us. For some

---

* Probably 1700.

years past, she had been visited with continual ill health; and several times, within these last two years, her life was despaired of. But, for this twelvemonth past, she never had a day's health; and, properly speaking, she has been dying six months, but kept alive, almost against nature, by the generous kindness of two physicians, and the care of her friends. Thus far I writ the same night between eleven and twelve.

Never was any of her sex born with better gifts of the mind, or who more improved them by reading and conversation. Yet her memory was not of the best, and was impaired in the latter years of her life. But I cannot call to mind that I ever once heard her make a wrong judgment of persons, books, or affairs. Her advice was always the best, and with the greatest freedom, mixed with the greatest decency. She had a gracefulness, somewhat more than human, in every motion, word, and action. Never was so happy a conjunction of civility, freedom, easiness, and sincerity. There seemed to be a combination among all that knew her, to treat her with a dignity much beyond her rank; yet people of all sorts were never more easy than in her company. Mr. Addison, when he was in Ireland, being introduced to her, immediately found her out; and, if he had not soon after left the kingdom, assured me he would have used all endeavours to cultivate her friendship. A rude or conceited coxcomb passed his time very ill, upon the least breach of respect; for, in such a case, she had no mercy, but was sure to expose him to the contempt of the standers-by, yet in such a manner, as he was ashamed to complain, and durst not resent. All of us who had the happiness of her friendship agreed unanimously, that, in an afternoon or evening's conversation, she never failed, before we parted, of delivering the best thing that was said in the company. Some of us have written down several of her sayings, or what the French call *bons mots*, wherein she excelled beyond belief. She never mistook the understanding of others; nor ever said a severe word, but where a much severer was deserved.

Her servants loved, and almost adored her at the same time. She would, upon occasions, treat them with freedom; yet her demeanour was so awful, that they durst not fail in the least point of respect. She chid them seldom, but it was with severity, which had an effect upon them for a long time after.

January 29. My head aches, and I can write no more.

January 30. Tuesday.

This is the night of the funeral, which my sickness will not suffer me to attend. It is now nine at night; and I am removed into another apartment, that I may not see the light in the church, which is just over against the window of my bedchamber.

With all the softness of temper that became a lady, she had the personal courage of a hero. She and her friend having removed their lodgings to a new house, which stood solitary, a parcel of rogues, armed, attempted the house, where there was only one boy. She was then about four-and-twenty; and having been warned to apprehend some such attempt, she learned the management of a pistol; and the other women and servants being half dead with fear, she stole softly to her dining-room window, put on a black hood to prevent being seen, primed the pistol fresh, gently lifted up the sash, and taking her aim with the utmost presence of mind, discharged the pistol, loaden with bullets, into the body of one villain, who stood the fairest mark. The fellow, mortally wounded, was carried off by the rest, and died the next morning; but his companions could not be found. The Duke of Ormond had often drunk her health to me upon that account, and had always a high esteem for her. She was indeed under some apprehensions of going in a boat, after some danger she had narrowly escaped by water, but she was reasoned thoroughly out of it. She was never known to cry out, or discover any fear, in a coach or on horseback; or any uneasiness by those sudden accidents with which most of her sex, either by weakness or affectation, appear so much disordered.

She never had the least absence of mind in conversation, or given to interruption, or appeared eager to put in her word, by waiting impatiently until another had done. She spoke in a most agreeable voice, in the plainest words, never hesitating, except out of modesty before new faces, where she was somewhat reserved; nor, among her nearest friends, ever spoke much at a time. She was but little versed in the common topics of female chat; scandal, censure, and detraction, never came out of her mouth; yet, among a few friends, in private conversation, she made little ceremony in discovering her contempt of a coxcomb, and describing all his follies to the life; but the follies of her own sex she was rather inclined to extenuate or to pity.

When she was once convinced, by open facts, of any breach of truth or honour in a person of high station, especially in the church, she could not conceal her indignation, nor hear them named without shewing her displeasure in her countenance; particularly one or two of the latter sort, whom she had known and esteemed, but detested above all mankind, when it was manifest that they had sacrificed those two precious virtues to their ambition, and would much sooner have forgiven them the common immoralities of the laity.

Her frequent fits of sickness, in most parts of her life, had prevented her from making that progress in reading which she would otherwise have done. She was well versed in the Greek and Roman story, and was not unskilled in that of France and England. She spoke French perfectly, but forgot much of it by neglect and sickness. She had read carefully all the best books of travels, which serve to open and enlarge the mind. She understood the Platonic and Epicurean philosophy, and judged very well of the defects of the latter. She made very judicious abstracts of the best books she had read. She understood the nature of government, and could point out all the errors of Hobbes, both in that and religion. She had a good insight into physic, and knew somewhat of anatomy; in both which she was instructed in her younger days by an eminent physician, who had her long under his care, and bore the highest esteem for her person and understanding. She had a true taste of wit and good sense, both in poetry and prose, and was a perfect good critic of style; neither was it easy to find a more proper or impartial judge, whose advice an author might better rely on, if he intended to send a thing into the world, provided it was on a subject that came within the compass of her knowledge. Yet, perhaps, she was sometimes too severe, which is a safe and pardonable error. She preserved her wit, judgment, and vivacity, to the last, but often used to complain of her memory.

Her fortune, with some accession, could not, as I have heard say, amount to much more than two thousand pounds, whereof a great part fell with her life, having been placed upon annuities in England, and one in Ireland.

In a person so extraordinary, perhaps it may be pardonable to mention some particulars, although of little moment, farther than to set forth her character. Some presents of gold pieces being often made to her while she was a girl, by her mother and other friends, on promise to keep them, she grew into such a spirit of thrift, that, in about three years, they amounted to above two hundred pounds. She used to shew them with boasting; but her mother, apprehending she would be cheated of them, prevailed, in some months, and with great importunities, to have them put out to interest; when the girl, losing the pleasure of seeing and counting her gold, which she never failed of doing many times in a day, and despairing of heaping up such another treasure, her humour took quite the contrary turn; she grew careless and squandering of every new acquisition, and so continued till about two-and-twenty; when, by advice of some friends, and the fright of paying large bills of tradesmen who enticed her into their debt, she began to reflect upon her own folly, and was never at rest until she had discharged all her shop bills, and refunded herself a considerable sum she had run out. After which, by the addition of a few years, and a superior understanding, she became, and continued all her life, a most prudent economist; yet still with a stronger bent to the liberal side, wherein she gratified herself by avoiding all expense in clothes (which she ever despised) beyond what was merely decent. And, although her frequent returns of sickness were very chargeable, except fees to physicians, of which she met with several so generous, that she could force nothing on them, (and indeed she must otherwise have been undone,) yet she never was without a considerable sum of ready money. Insomuch, that, upon her death, when her nearest friends thought her very bare, her executors found in her strong box about one hundred and fifty pounds in gold. She lamented the narrowness of her fortune in nothing so much as that it did not enable her to entertain her friends so often, and in so hospitable a manner, as she desired. Yet they were always welcome; and while she was in health to direct, were treated with neatness and elegance, so that the revenues of her and her companion passed for much more considerable than they really were. They lived always in lodgings; their domestics consisted of two maids and one man. She kept an account of all the family expenses, from her arrival in Ireland to some months before her death; and she would often repine, when looking back upon the annals of her household bills, that everything necessary for life was double the price, while interest of money was sunk almost to one half; so that the addition made to her fortune was indeed grown absolutely necessary.

[I since writ as I found time.]

But her charity to the poor was a duty not to be diminished, and therefore became a tax upon those tradesmen who furnish the fopperies of other ladies. She bought clothes as seldom as possible, and those as plain and cheap as consisted with the situation she was in; and wore no lace for many years. Either her judgment or fortune was extraordinary in the choice of those on whom she bestowed her charity, for it went farther in doing good than double the sum from any other hand. And I have heard her say, "she always met with gratitude from the poor;" which must be owing to her skill in distinguishing proper objects, as well as her gracious manner in relieving them.

But she had another quality that much delighted her, although it might be thought a kind of check upon her bounty; however, it was a pleasure she could not resist: I mean that of making agreeable presents; wherein I never knew her equal, although it be an affair of as delicate a nature as most in the course of life. She used to define a present, " That it was a gift to a friend of something he wanted, or was fond of, and which could not be easily gotten for money." I am confident, during my acquaintance with her, she has, in these and some other kinds of liberality, disposed of to the value of several hundred pounds. As to presents made to herself, she received them with great unwillingness, but especially from those to whom she had ever given any; being, on all occasions, the most disinterested mortal I ever knew or heard of.

From her own disposition, at least as much as from the frequent want of health, she seldom made any visits; but her own lodgings, from before twenty years old, were frequented by many persons of the graver sort, who all respected her highly, upon her good sense, good manners, and conversation. Among these were the late Primate Lindsay, Bishop Lloyd, Bishop Ashe, Bishop Brown, Bishop Sterne, Bishop Pulleyn, with some others of later date; and indeed the greatest number of her acquaintance was among the clergy. Honour, truth, liberality, good nature, and modesty, were the virtues she chiefly possessed, and most valued in her acquaintance: and where she found them, would be ready to allow for some defects; nor valued them less, although they did not shine in learning or in wit: but would never give the least allowance for any failures in the former, even to those who made the greatest figure in either of the two latter. She had no use of any person's liberality, yet her detestation of covetous people made her uneasy if such a one was in her company; upon which occasion she would say many things very entertaining and humorous.

She never interrupted any person who spoke; she laughed at no mistakes they made, but helped them out with modesty; and if a good thing were spoken, but neglected, she would not let it fall, but set it in the best light to those who were present. She listened to all that was said, and had never the least distraction or absence of thought.

It was not safe, nor prudent, in her presence, to offend in the least word against modesty; for she then gave full employment to her wit, her contempt, and resentment, under which even stupidity and brutality were forced to sink into confusion; and the guilty person, by her future avoiding him like a bear or a satyr, was never in a way to transgress a second time.

It happened, one single coxcomb, of the pert kind, was in her company, among several other ladies; and in his flippant way, began to deliver some double meanings; the rest flapped their fans, and used the other common expedients practised in such cases, of appearing not to mind or comprehend what was said. Her behaviour was very different, and perhaps may be censured. She said thus to the man: "Sir, all these ladies and I understand your meaning very well, having, in spite of our care, too often met with those of your sex who wanted manners and good sense. But, believe me, neither virtuous nor even vicious women love such kind of conversation. However, I will leave you, and report your behaviour; and whatever visit I make, I shall first inquire at the door whether you are in the house, that I may be sure to avoid you." I know not whether a majority of ladies would approve of such a proceeding; but I believe the practice of it would soon put an end to that corrupt conversation, the worst effect of dulness, ignorance, impudence, and vulgarity; and the highest affront to the modesty and understanding of the female sex.

By returning very few visits, she had not much company of her own sex, except those whom she most loved for their easiness, or esteemed for their good sense: and those, not insisting on ceremony, came often to her. But she rather chose men for her companions, the usual topics of ladies' discourse being such as she had little knowledge of, and less relish. Yet no man was upon the rack to entertain her, for she easily descended to anything that was innocent and diverting. News, politics, censure, family management, or town-talk, she always diverted to something else; but these indeed seldom happened, for she chose her company better: and therefore many, who mistook her and themselves, having solicited her acquaintance, and finding themselves disappointed, after a few visits dropped off; and she was never known to inquire into the reason, nor ask what was become of them.

She was never positive in arguing; and she usually treated those who were so, in a manner which well enough gratified that unhappy disposition; yet in such a sort as made it very contemptible, and at the same time did some hurt to the owners. Whether this proceeded from her easiness in general, or from her indifference to persons, or from her despair of mending them, or from the same practice which she much liked in Mr. Addison, I cannot determine; but when she saw any of the company very warm in a wrong opinion, she was more inclined to confirm them in it than oppose them. The excuse she commonly gave, when her friends asked the reason, was, "That it prevented noise, and saved time." Yet I have known her very angry with some, whom she much esteemed, for sometimes falling into that infirmity.

She loved Ireland much better than the generality of those who owe both their birth and riches to it; and having brought over all the fortune she had in money, left the reversion of the best part of it, one thousand pounds, to Dr. Stephens's Hospital. She detested the tyranny and injustice of England, in their treatment of this kingdom. She had indeed reason to love a country, where she had the esteem and friendship of all who knew her, and the universal good report of all who ever heard of her, without one exception, if I am told the truth by those who keep general conversation. Which character is the more extraordinary, in falling to a person of so much knowledge, wit, and vivacity, qualities that are used to create envy, and consequently censure; and must be rather imputed to her great modesty, gentle behaviour, and inoffensiveness, than to her superior virtues.

Although her knowledge, from books and company, was much more extensive than usually falls to the share of her sex; yet she was so far from making a parade of it, that her female visitants, on their first acquaintance, who expected to discover it by what they call hard words and deep discourse, would be sometimes disappointed, and say, "They found she was like other women." But wise men, through all her modesty, whatever they discoursed on, could easily observe that she understood them very well, by the judgment shewn in her observations, as well as in her questions.

BONS MOTS DE STELLA.

 LADY of my intimate acquaintance, both in England and Ireland, in which last kingdom she lived from the eighteenth year of her age, twenty-six years, had the most and finest accomplishments of any person I ever knew of either sex. It was observed by all her acquaintance, that she never failed in company to say the best thing that was said, whoever was by; yet her companions were usually persons of the best understanding in the kingdom. Some of us, who were her nearest friends, lamented that we never wrote down her remarks, and what the French call bons mots. I will recollect as many as I can remember.

We were diverting ourselves at a play called "What is it like?" One person is to think, and the rest, without knowing the thing, to say what it is like. The thing thought on was the spleen; she had said it was like an oyster, and gave her reason immediately, because it is removed by taking steel inwardly.

Dr. Sheridan, who squandered more than he could afford, took out his purse as he sat by the fire, and found it was very hot; she said the reason was, that his money burned in his pocket.

She called to her servants to know what ill smell

was in the kitchen; they answered, they were making matches: Well, said she, I have heard matches were made in Heaven, but by the brimstone one would think they were made in Hell.

After she had been eating some sweet thing, a little of it happened to stick on her lips: a gentleman told her of it, and offered to lick it off: she said, No, sir, I thank you, I have a tongue of my own.

In the late King's time, a gentleman asked Jervas the painter, where he lived in London? He answered, next door to the King, for his house was near St. James's. The other wondering how that could be; she said, You mistake Mr. Jervas, for he only means next door to the sign of a king.

A gentleman who had been very silly and pert in her company, at last began to grieve at remembering the loss of a child lately dead. A bishop sitting by comforted him; that he should be easy because the child was gone to Heaven. No, my lord, said she, that is it which most grieves him, because he is sure never to see his child there.

Having seen some letters writ by a king in a very large hand, and some persons wondering at them, she said it confirmed the old saying, That kings had long hands.

Dr. Sheridan, famous for punning, intending to sell a bargain, said, he had made a very good pun. Somebody asked, what it was? He answered, My a—. The other taking offence, she insisted the doctor was in the right, for everybody knew that punning was his blind side.

When she was extremely ill, her physician said, Madam, you are near the bottom of the hill, but we will endeavour to get you up again. She answered, Doctor, I fear I shall be out of breath before I get up to the top.

A dull parson talking of a very smart thing, said to another parson, as he came out of the pulpit, he was hammering a long time, but could not remember the jest; she being impatient, said, I remember it very well, for I was there, and the words were these; Sir, you have been blundering at a story this half hour, and can neither make head nor tail of it.

A very dirty clergyman of her acquaintance, who affected smartness and repartees, was asked by some of the company how his nails came to be so dirty: He was at a loss; but she solved the difficulty, by saying, The doctor's nails grew dirty by scratching himself.

A quaker apothecary sent her a vial corked; it had a broad brim, and a label of paper about its neck. "What is that?" said she; "my apothecary's son?" The ridiculous resemblance, and the suddenness of the question, set us all a-laughing.*

---

* Of these *bon mots* the reader will probably think some flat and others coarse; but enough will remain to vindicate the praises of Stella's wit.

THREE PRAYERS

USED BY THE DEAN FOR MRS. JOHNSON,

IN HER LAST SICKNESS, 1727.

I.

ALMIGHTY and most gracious Lord God, extend, we beseech thee, thy pity and compassion toward this thy languishing servant; teach her to place her hope and confidence entirely in thee: give her a true sense of the emptiness and vanity of all earthly things: make her truly sensible of all the infirmities of her life past; and grant to her such a true sincere repentance as is not to be repented of. Preserve her, O Lord, in a sound mind and understanding, during this thy visitation; keep her from both the sad extremes of presumption and despair. If thou shalt please to restore her to her former health, give her grace, to be ever mindful of that mercy, and to keep those good resolutions she now makes in her sickness; so that no length of time nor prosperity may entice her to forget them. Let no thought of her misfortunes distract her mind, and prevent the means toward her recovery, or disturb her in her preparations for a better life. We beseech thee also, O Lord, of thy infinite goodness, to remember the good actions of this thy servant; that the naked she hath clothed, the hungry she hath fed, the sick and the fatherless whom she hath relieved, may be reckoned, according to thy gracious promise, as if they had been done unto thee.—Hearken, O Lord, to the prayers offered up by the friends of this thy servant in her behalf, and especially those now made by us unto thee. Give thy blessing to those endeavours used for her recovery; but take from her all violent desire either of life or death, farther than with resignation to thy holy will. And now, O Lord, we implore thy gracious favour toward us here met together. Grant that the sense of this thy servant's weakness may add strength to our faith; that we, considering the infirmities of our nature, and the uncertainty of life, may, by this example, be drawn to repentance, before it shall please thee to visit us in the like manner. Accept these prayers, we beseech thee, for the sake of thy dear Son Jesus Christ, our Lord; who, with Thee and the Holy Ghost, liveth and reigneth, ever one God, world without end. Amen.

---o---

II.

WRITTEN OCTOBER 17, 1727.

Most merciful Father, accept of our humblest prayers in behalf of this thy languishing servant: forgive the sins, the frailties, and infirmities of her life past. Accept the good deeds she hath done in such a manner, that at whatever time thou shalt please to call her, she may be received into everlasting habitations. Give her grace to continue sincerely thankful to thee for the many favours thou hast bestowed upon her, the ability and inclination and practice to do good, and those virtues, which have procured the esteem and love of her friends, and a most unspotted name in the world. O God, thou dispensest thy blessings and thy punishments as it becometh infinite justice and mercy: and since it was thy pleasure to afflict her with a long, constant, weakly state of health, make her truly sensible, that it was for very wise ends, and was largely made up to her in other blessings more valuable and less common. Continue to her, O Lord, that firmness and constancy of mind, wherewith thou hast most graciously endowed her, together with that contempt of worldly things and vanities, that she hath shewn in the whole conduct of her life. O all-powerful Being, the least motion of whose will can create or destroy a world; pity us, the mournful friends of thy distressed servant, who sink under the weight of her present condition, and the fear of losing the most valuable of our friends: restore her to us, O Lord, if it be thy gracious will, or inspire us with constancy and resignation, to support ourselves under so heavy an affliction. Restore her, O Lord, for the sake of those poor, who by losing her will be desolate; and those sick, who will not only want her bounty, but her care and tending; else, in thy mercy, raise up some other in her place, with equal disposition and better abilities. Lessen, O Lord, we beseech thee, her bodily pains, or give her a double strength of mind to support them. And if thou wilt soon take her to thyself, turn our thoughts rather upon that felicity, which, we hope, she shall enjoy, than upon that unspeakable loss we shall endure. Let her memory be ever dear unto us; and the example of her many virtues, as far as human infirmity will admit, our constant imitation.

Accept, O Lord, these prayers, poured from the very bottom of our hearts, in thy mercy, and for the merits of our blessed Saviour. Amen.

---o---

III.

WRITTEN NOV. 6, 1727.

O Merciful Father, who never afflictest thy children, but for their own good, and with justice, over which thy mercy always prevaileth, either to turn them to repentance, or to punish them in the present life, in order to reward them in a better; take pity, we beseech thee, upon this thy poor afflicted servant, languishing so long and so grievously under the weight of thy hand. Give her strength, O Lord, to support her weakness; and patience to endure her pains, without repining at thy correction. Forgive every rash and inconsiderate expression which her anguish may at any time force from her tongue, while her heart continueth in an entire submission to thy will. Suppress in her, O Lord, all eager desires of life, and lessen her fears of death, by inspiring into her an humble, yet assured hope of thy mercy. Give her a sincere repentance for all her transgressions and omissions, and a firm resolution to pass the remainder of her life in endeavouring to her utmost to observe all thy precepts. We beseech thee likewise to compose her thoughts; and preserve to her the use of her memory and reason, during the course of her sickness. Give her a true conception of the vanity, folly, and insignificancy of all human things; and strengthen her so as to beget in her a sincere love of thee in the midst of her sufferings. Accept and impute all her good deeds, and forgive her all those offences against thee which she hath sincerely repented of, or through the frailty of memory hath forgot. And now, O Lord, we turn unto thee, in behalf of ourselves, and the rest of her sorrowful friends. Let not our grief afflict her mind, and thereby have an ill effect on her present distemper. Forgive the sorrow and weakness of those among us, who sink under the grief and terror of losing so dear and useful a friend. Accept and pardon our most earnest prayers and wishes for her longer continuance in this evil world, to do what thou art pleased to call thy service, and is only her bounden duty; that she may be still a comfort to us, and to all others who will want the benefit of her conversation, her advice, her good offices, or her charity. And since thou hast promised, that where two or three are gathered together in thy name, thou wilt be in the midst of them, to grant their requests; O gracious Lord, grant to us who are here met in thy name, that those requests, which in the utmost sincerity and earnestness of our hearts we have now made in behalf of this thy distressed servant, and of ourselves, may effectually be answered through the merits of Jesus Christ our Lord. Amen.

AN EVENING PRAYER,

BY DEAN SWIFT.

FROM THE ORIGINAL MANUSCRIPT FOUND AMONGST DR. LYON'S PAPERS.

———o———

H! Almighty God, the searcher of all hearts, and from whom no secrets are hid, who hast declared that all such as shall draw nigh to thee with their lips, when their hearts are far from thee, are an abomination unto thee; cleanse, we beseech thee, the thoughts of our hearts, by the inspiration of thy Holy Spirit, that no wandering, vain, nor idle thoughts may put out of our minds that reverence and godly fear that becomes all those who come in thy presence.

We know, O Lord, that while we are in these bodies, we are absent from the Lord, for no man can see thy face and live. The only way that we can draw near unto thee in this life, is by prayer; but, O Lord, we know not how to pray, nor what to ask for as we ought. We cannot pretend by our supplications or prayers to turn or change thee, for thou art the same yesterday, to-day, and for ever; but the coming into thy presence, the drawing near unto thee, is the only means to be changed ourselves, to become like thee in holiness and purity, to be followers of thee as thy dear children. O, therefore, turn not away thy face from us, but let us see so much of the excellencies of thy divine nature, of thy goodness, and justice, and mercy, and forbearance, and holiness, and purity, as may make us hate everything in ourselves that is unlike to thee, that so we may abhor and repent of and forsake those sins that we so often fall into when we forget thee. Lord! we acknowledge and confess we have lived in a course of sin, and folly, and vanity, from our youth up, forgetting our latter end, and our great account that we must one day make, and turning a deaf ear to thy many calls to us, either by thy holy word, by our teachers, or by our own consciences; and even thy more severe messages by afflictions, sicknesses, crosses, and disappointments, have not been of force enough to turn us from the vanity and folly of our own ways. What then can we expect in justice, when thou shalt enter into judgment with us, but to have our portion with the hypocrites and unbelievers? to depart for ever from the presence of the Lord; to be turned into hell with those that forget God! But, O God, most holy! O God, most mighty! O holy and most merciful Saviour, deliver us not into the bitter pains of eternal death, but have mercy upon us, most merciful Father, and forgive us our sins for thy name's sake: for thou hast declared thyself to be a God slow to anger, full of goodness, forbearance, and long-suffering, and forgiving iniquity, transgression, and sin. O Lord, therefore, shew thy mercy upon us. O let it be in pardoning our sins past, and in changing our natures, in giving us a new heart, and a new spirit, that we may lead a new life, and walk before thee in newness of life, that so sin may not have dominion over us for the time to come. O let thy good Spirit, without which we can do nothing, O let that work in us both to will and do such things as may be well pleasing to thee. O let it change our thoughts and minds, and take them off the vain pleasures of this world, and place them there where only the true joys are to be found. O fill our minds every day more and more with the happiness of that blessed state of living for ever with thee, that we may make it our great work and business to work out our salvation,—to improve in the knowledge of thee, whom to know is life eternal. But, Lord, since we cannot know thee but by often drawing near unto thee, and coming into thy presence, which in this life, we can do only by prayer, O make us, therefore, ever sensible of these great benefits of prayer, that we may rejoice at all opportunities of coming into thy presence, and may ever find ourselves the better and more heavenly minded by it, and may never wilfully neglect any opportunity of thy worship and service. Awaken thoroughly in us a serious sense of these things, that so to-day, while it is called to-day, we may see and know the things that belong to our peace, before they be hid from our eyes, before that long night cometh when no man can work. O that every night may so effectually put us in mind of our last, that we may every day take care so to live, as we shall then wish we had lived when we come to die: that so when that night shall come, we may as willingly put off these bodies, as we now put off our clothes, and may rejoice to rest from our labours, and that our war with the world, the devil, and our own corrupt nature, is at an end. In the meanwhile, we beseech thee to take us, and ours, and all that belongs to us, into thy fatherly care this night. Let thy holy angels be our guard, while we are not in a condition to defend ourselves, that we may not be under the power of devils or wicked men; and preserve us also, O Lord, from every evil accident, that, after a comfortable and refreshing sleep, we may find ourselves, and all that belongs to us, in peace and safety. And now, O Lord, being ourselves still in the body, and compassed about with infirmities, we can neither be ignorant nor unmindful of the sufferings of our fellow-creatures. O Lord, we must acknowledge, that they are all but the effects of sin; and, therefore, we beseech thee so to sanctify their several chastisements to them, that at length they may bring forth the peaceable fruits of righteousness, and then be thou graciously pleased to remove thy heavy and afflicting hand from them. And O that the rest of mankind, who are not under such trials, may, by thy goodness, be led to repentance, that the consciences of hard-hearted sinners may be awakened, and the understandings of poor ignorant creatures enlightened, and that all that love and fear thee may ever find the joy and comfort of a good conscience, beyond all the satisfactions that this world can afford. And now, blessed Lord, from whom every good gift comes, it is meet, right, and our bounden duty, that we should offer up unto thee our thanks and praise for all thy goodness towards us, for preserving peace in our land, the light of thy gospel, and the true religion in our churches; for giving us the fruits of the earth in due season, and preserving us from the plague and sickness that rages in other lands. We bless thee for that support and maintenance, which thou art pleased to afford us, and that thou givest us a heart to be sensible of this thy goodness, and to return our thanks at this time for the same; and as to our persons, for that measure of health that any of us do enjoy, which is more than any of us do deserve. We bless

AN EVENING PRAYER.

thee, more particularly, for thy protection over us the day past; that thy good Spirit has kept us from falling into even the greatest sins, which, by our wicked and corrupt nature, we should greedily have been hurried into; and that, by the guard of thy holy angels, we have been kept safe from any of those evils that might have befallen us, and which many are now groaning under, who rose up in the morning in safety and peace as well as we. But above all, for that great mercy of contriving and effecting our redemption, by the death of our Saviour Jesus Christ, whom, of thy great love to mankind, thou didst send into this world, to take upon him our flesh, to teach us thy will, and to bear the guilt of our transgressions, to die for our sins, and to rise again for our justification; and for enabling us to lay hold of that salvation, by the gracious assistances of thy Holy Spirit. Lord, grant that the sense of this wonderful love of thine to us, may effectually encourage us to walk in thy fear, and live to thy glory, that so when we shall put off this mortal state, we may be made partakers of that glory that shall then be revealed, which we beg of thee, for the sake of thy Son Jesus Christ, who died to procure it for us, and in whose name and words we do offer up the desires of our souls unto thee, saying,

"Our Father," &c.

LETTER

TO

MR. —— ARCHI-RABBI SOPHI DIOTREPHES, &c.

———o———

THE following ludicrous letter, composed in ridicule of the practice of using hard words, which he detested, is ascribed to Swift, in a Dublin collection of his pieces, called "The Drapier's Miscellany:"

"A Letter, which was actually sent to a young country clergyman, (who used hard words in his sermon,) in behalf of his poor ignorant congregation, by a gentleman who accidentally heard him."

———o———

"To the most Deuteronomical Polydoxologist, Pantophilological Linguist, Mr. —— Archi-Rabbi Sophi Diotrephes, &c.

"SIR,—The unanimous and humillemous desiderations, as well of your parochian, ac hic-et-ubique semipaganian auditors, beg leave submissively to remonstrate, That although by your specious proems and spacious introductions, promising great perspicuity in predication, you endeavour to inveigle our affections, in order to indoctrinate our agricolated intellects; yet, through the caliginous imbecillity of internexed conundrums, tonitruating with obstreperous cadences, you rather obfusiate than illuminate our A-B-C-darian conceptions, so that we generally return not at all edified, but puzzled, confounded, and astonished: We, therefore, for our souls' good, (en bonne esperance that your urbanity will not be exasperated at the presentation of these our cordial desires,) do, from the nadir of our rusticity, almacantarize to the very zenith of your unparalleled sphere of activity, in beseeching your exuberant genius to nutriate our rational appetites with intelligible theology, suited to our plebeian apprehensions, and to recondite your acroamaticall locutions for more scholastic auscultators. For while our first, second, and third selves, together with our domestics, all of Ignoramus's offspring, hear you gigantize in Lycophonian and Pharigenous raptures, in words we never met with in holy writ, as corollaries, ephemeris, and such other heterogeneal language, without delucidation of their original signification, we lose the whole system of your doctrine in admiration of your agemious erudition. Being, therefore, under a panic timidity, lest we should see a restoration of the dialect of Babel, and that some sesquipedalian circumforaneous saltimbanco should mount the rostrum, and, after your example, should, in spagirical bombast, repuzzle the quintessential of our ingeniosities, with more amalgamations, cohabitations, and fexations; we beg you to call to mind St. Austin's saying, *Mallem ut reprehendant grammatici, quam non intelligant populi;* 'I had rather that the grammarians should blame, than that the people should not understand me.'

"And now, egregious Sir, we supplicate your clemency, not to look upon these lines as derogatory to your most excellent parts and profound science, for we rather admire such superlative acquisitions, which, however, we humbly opine are more proper to be displayed among learned academicians than mechanical and agrestical auditors. And we estimate ourselves abundantly justified, in this our humble application, in the authority of St. Paul, much greater than that of St. Austin, who says, interpreted in plain English, 'If I know not the meaning of the voice, I shall be unto him that speaketh a barbarian, and he that speaketh shall be a barbarian unto me.' 1 Cor. xiv. And thus having copulated our plebeian endeuvours, we exosculate the subumbrations of your subligacles; and sooner shall the surges of the sandiferous sea ignify and evaporate, than the cone of our duty towards you be in the least uncatenate or dissolved; always wishing you health and happiness.

"A, B, C, D, &c.

"P.S.—To render our petition in this epistle the more acceptable to you, we prevailed with the schoolmaster to draw it up in a style as near as he could to your own."

CHARACTER OF DR. SHERIDAN.

WRITTEN IN THE YEAR 1738.*

OCTOR THOMAS SHERIDAN died at Rathfarnham, the 10th of October, 1738, at three of the clock in the afternoon: his diseases were a dropsy and asthma. He was doubtless the best instructor of youth in these kingdoms, or, perhaps, in Europe; and as great a master of the Greek and Roman languages. He had a very fruitful invention, and a talent for poetry. His English verses were full of wit and humour, but neither his prose nor verse sufficiently correct: however, he would readily submit to any friend who had a true taste in prose or verse. He has left behind him a very great collection, in several volumes, of stories, humorous,

---

* As Swift advanced in years and infirmities, it became more difficult to please him, or even to soothe his habitual irritation. We have mentioned, in his Life, his unfortunate quarrel with Sheridan, the most sincere, as well as the most officious of his friends and admirers. The present character retains some traces of friendship become cold and broken. The defects of imprudence are more strongly insisted upon than is consistent with the respect due to the memory of a departed friend; nor has the praise that affectionate warmth which the long and revered attachment of the deceased so particularly deserved.

witty, wise, or some way useful, gathered from a vast number of Greek, Roman, Italian, Spanish, French, and English writers. I believe I may have seen about thirty, large enough to make as many moderate books in octavo. But among these extracts, there were many not worth regard; for five or six, at least, were of little use or entertainment. He was (as it is frequently the case in men of wit and learning) what the French call a *dupe*, and in a very high degree. The greatest dunce of a tradesman could impose upon him, for he was altogether ignorant in worldly management. His chief shining quality was that of a schoolmaster: here he shone in his proper element. He had so much skill and practice in the physiognomy of boys, that he rarely mistook at the first view. His scholars loved and feared him. He often rather chose to shame the stupid, but punish the idle, and expose them to all the lads, which was more severe than lashing. Among the gentlemen in this kingdom who have any share of education, the scholars of Dr. Sheridan infinitely excel, in number and knowledge, all their brethren sent from other schools.

To look on the doctor in some other lights, he was in many things very indiscreet, to say no worse. He acted like too many clergymen, who are in haste to get married when very young; and from hence proceeded all the miseries of his life. The portion he got proved to be just the reverse of £500, for he was poorer by a thousand: so many incumbrances of a mother-in-law, and poor relations, whom he was forced to support for many years. Instead of breeding up his daughters to housewifery and plain clothes, he got them at a great expense, to be clad like ladies who had plentiful fortunes; made them only learn to sing and dance, to draw and design, to give them rich silks and other fopperies; and his two eldest were married, without his consent, to young lads who had nothing to settle on them. However, he had one son, whom the doctor sent to Westminster school, although he could ill afford it. The boy was there immediately taken notice of, upon examination: although a mere stranger, he was, by pure merit, elected a king's scholar. It is true, their maintenance falls something short: the doctor was then so poor, that he could not add fourteen pounds to enable the boy to finish the year; which if he had done, he would have been removed to a higher class, and, in another year, would have been *sped off* (that is the phrase) to a fellowship in Oxford or Cambridge: but the doctor was forced to recall him to Dublin, and had friends in our university to send him there, where he has been chosen of the foundation; and, I think, has gotten an exhibition, and designs to stand for a fellowship.*

The doctor had a good church living, in the south parts of Ireland, given him by Lord Carteret; who, being very learned himself, encourages it in others. A friend of the doctor's prevailed on his excellency to grant it. The living was well worth £150 per annum. He changed it very soon for that of Dunboyn; which, by the knavery of the farmers, and power of the gentlemen, fell so very low, that he could never get £80. He then changed that living for the free school of Cavan, where he might have lived well in so cheap a country, on £80 salary

---

* This was Thomas Sheridan, an actor of considerable celebrity, and who afterwards distinguished himself by Lectures on Elocution, and an excellent Life of Swift. He was, however, still more remarkable, as the father of the celebrated and highly-gifted Richard Brinsley Sheridan, M.P., one of the most gifted men of a period when talents were the profuse attribute of those who dedicated themselves to the public service.

per annum, besides his scholars; but the air, he said, was too moist and unwholesome, and he could not bear the company of some persons in that neighbourhood. Upon this he sold the school for about £400, spent the money, grew into disease, and died.*

It would be very honourable, as well as just, in those many persons of quality and fortune, who had the advantage of being educated under Dr. Sheridan, if they would please to erect some decent monument over his body, in the church where it is deposited.

---

* "Dr. Sheridan's friend and physician, Dr. Helsham, foretold the manner, and almost the very time of his death. He said his disorder was a polypus in the heart, which was so far advanced, that it would probably put an end to his existence in a short time, and so suddenly as to give him no warning of it; and therefore recommended it to him to settle his affairs. The doctor, upon this, retired to a house of one of his scholars, Mr. O'Callaghan, at Rathfarnham, three miles from Dublin. In a few days he sent for his friend and namesake, Counsellor Sheridan, to draw his will; and when that was done he seemed cheerful and in good spirits. The counsellor, and a brother of Mr. O'Callaghan's, who lent him his house, upon being called away to another part of the kingdom, dined with him that day. Soon after dinner the conversation happened to turn on the weather, and one of them observed that the wind was easterly. The doctor upon this said, 'Let it blow, east, west, north, or south, the immortal soul will take its flight to the destined point.' These were the last words he ever spoke, for he immediately sunk back in his chair, and expired without a groan, or the smallest struggle. His friends thought he had fallen asleep, and in that belief retired to the garden, that they might not disturb his repose; but, on their return, after an hour's walk, to their great astonishment, they found he was dead. Upon opening the body, Dr. Helsham's sagacious prognostic proved to be true, as the polypus in the heart was discovered to be the immediate cause of his death. I know not whether it is worth mentioning, that the surgeon said he never saw so large a heart in a human body."—*Sheridan's Life of Swift.*

THE HISTORY

OF

THE SECOND SOLOMON.* 1729.

AMONG all the painful circumstances attendant upon the d
solution of a long and affectionate intercourse between friends
ancient standing, there is none more bitter than when, before
final rupture has taken place, one party avails himself of all t
freedom and familiarity of their former relation, to express hi
self concerning his friend's foibles, with more bitterness than
could pretend to treat those of an enemy. In these momen
every trivial circumstance of untimely raillery, and effusion
temporary resentment, is eagerly mustered and arraigned as
article of indictment against the offender; and former disput
which, when they happened, were only considered as matter
jest, are then arrayed as grounds of accusation. The followi
character of Dr. Sheridan, in which his foibles are treated
unmercifully, and where some slight instances of disrespe
occurring in the course of familiar and jocular intercourse, a
preferred as charges of ingratitude, argues that state of mind
the author, which could not long consist with intimacy. The
is, besides, an assumption of superiority through the whole, whi
seems to place the " Person distinguished for poetical and oth
writings," and occupying " an eminent station," in contrast, v
degrading to his more humble, and, one would almost suppo
his dependent friend. This is one of the pieces in which Sw
has indulged his irritable temperament, at the expense of his he
and heart.

---

* Dr. Sheridan.—D. S.

E became acquainted with a person distinguished for poetical and other writings, and in an eminent station, who treated him with great kindness on all occasions, and he became familiar in this person's house.* In three months' time, Solomon, without the least provocation, writ a long poem, describing that person's muse to be dead, and making a funeral solemnity with asses, owls, &c., and gave the copy among all his acquaintance.†

Solomon became acquainted with a most deserving lady, an intimate friend of the above person,‡ who entertained him also as she would a brother; and, upon giving him a little good advice in the most decent manner, with relation to his wife, he told her, "She was like other women, as bad as she was; and that they were all alike." §

Although his wife be, in every regard, (except gallantry, which no creature would attempt,) the most disagreeable beast in Europe, he lets his wife (whom he pretends to hate as she deserves) govern, insult, and ruin him, as she pleaseth. Her character is this: Her person is detestably disagreeable; a most filthy slut; lazy, and slothful, and luxurious, ill-natured, envious, suspicious; a scold, expensive on herself, covetous to others: She takes thieves

---

* Dean Swift.—D. S.

† "This does not seem to occur, even in the Whimsical Miscellany, the grand repository of the *jeux d'esprit* that passed between Swift and Sheridan. However seriously the Dean seems here to regard it, the verses were probably at the time considered as mere food for laughter.

‡ Stella.—D. S.

§ The Doctor's best defence may be, that it was hardly possible to give advice in a decent, at least delicate manner, upon such a subject.

and whores, for cheapness, to be her servants, and turns them off every week; positive, insolent, and ignorant, prating, overweening fool; a lover of the dirtiest, meanest company: an abominable tattler, affecting to be jealous of her husband, with ladies of the best rank and merit, and merely out of affectation, for perfect vanity.

Solomon has no ill design upon any person but himself, and he is the greatest deceiver of himself on all occasions.

His thoughts are sudden, and the most unreasonable always comes uppermost; and he constantly resolves and acts upon his first thoughts, and then asks advice, but never once before.

The person above mentioned, whom he lampooned in three months after their acquaintance, procured him a good preferment from the Lord-lieutenant:* upon going down to take possession, Solomon preached, at Corke, a sermon on King George's birthday, on this text, "Sufficient to the day is the evil thereof." Solomon having been famous for a High Tory, and suspected as a Jacobite, it was a most difficult thing to get anything for him: but that person, being an old friend of Lord Carteret, prevailed against all Solomon's enemies, and got him made likewise one of his excellency's chaplains. But, upon this sermon, he was struck out of the list, and forbid the castle, until that same person brought him again to the lieutenant, and made them friends.

A fancy sprung in Solomon's head, that a house near Dublin would be commodious for him and his boarders, to lodge in on Saturdays and Sundays; immediately, without consulting with any creature, he takes a lease of a rotten house at Rathfarnham, the worst air in Ireland, for nine hundred and ninety-

---

* Lord Carteret.—D. S.

nine years, at twelve pounds a-year; the land, which was only a strip of ground, not being worth twenty shillings a-year. When the same person whom he lampooned heard the thing, he begged Solomon to get a clause to surrender, and at last prevailed to have it done after twenty-one years; because it was a madness to pay eleven pounds a-year, for a thousand years, for a house that could not last twenty. But Solomon made an agreement with his landlady, that he should be at liberty to surrender his lease in seven years; and if he did not do it at that time, should be obliged to keep it for nine hundred and ninety-nine years. In the meantime, he expends about one hundred pounds on the house and garden-wall; and in less than three years, contracts such a hatred to the house, that he lets it run to ruin: so that, when the seven years were expired, he must either take it for the remainder of the nine hundred and ninety-nine years, or be sued for waste, and lose all the money he laid out: and now he pays twelve pounds a-year for a place he never sees.

Solomon has an estate of about thirty-five pounds *per annum*, in the county of Cavan; upon which, instead of ever receiving one penny rent, he hath expended above thirty pounds *per annum* in buildings and plantations, which are all gone to ruin.

Solomon is under-tenant to a bishop's lease;[*]

---

[*] It would be unjust to suppress the manner in which Sheridan became possessed of this valuable property. It had its rise in his memorable text on King George's birthday.

"But though, as Swift expresses it, the Doctor had thus, by mere chance-medley, shot his own fortune dead with a single text, yet it was the mean of his receiving a considerable addition to his fortune, of more intrinsic value than the largest benefice he might have reason to expect. As this proceeded from an act of uncommon generosity, it deserves well to be recorded. Archdeacon Russel, in whose pulpit the sermon was preached, considered himself as instrumental, however accidentally, to the ruin

he is bound by articles to his lordship to renew and pay a fine, whenever the bishop renews with his landlord, and to raise his rent as the landlord shall raise it to the bishop. Seven years expire: Solomon's landlord demands a fine, which he readily pays; then asks for a lease: the landlord says, "He may have it at any time." He never gets it. Another seven years elapse: Solomon's landlord demands another fine, and an additional rent: Solomon pays both, asks to have his lease renewed: the steward answers, "He will speak to his master." Seventeen years have elapsed; the landlord sends Solomon word, "That his lease is forfeited, because he hath not renewed and paid his fines according to articles;" and now they are at law, upon this admirable case.

It is Solomon's great happiness, that, when he acts in the common concerns of life against common sense and reason, he values himself thereupon, as if it were the mark of great genius, above little regards or arts, and that his thoughts are too exalted to

---

of the Doctor's expectations. He was for some time uneasy in his mind on this account, and at last determined to make him a noble compensation. He had a great friendship for the Doctor, whom he saw loaded with a numerous offspring, upon a precarious income, while he himself was possessed of a considerable property, and without any family. Urged on by those nice scruples in his mind before mentioned, he thought he could not make a better use of his fortune, than to apply the superfluity of it towards making the Doctor easy in his circumstances, and thus enabling him to make a provision for his children. With this view, he took a journey to Dublin, in order to make over to him, by an irrevocable deed of gift, the valuable manor of Drumlane, in the county of Cavan, a bishop's lease, which at that time produced a clear profit rent of two hundred and fifty pounds *per annum*. An act of such liberality, and seldom to be paralleled in this degenerate and selfish age, deserves well to be rescued from oblivion; nor could the author of these memoirs, without ingratitude, pass it over."—*Sheridan's Life of Swift.*

descend into the knowledge of vulgar management; and you cannot make him a greater compliment than by telling instances to the company, before his face, how careless he was in any affair that related to his interest and fortune.

He is extremely proud and captious, apt to resent as an affront and indignity what was never intended for either.*

He is allured as easily by every new acquaintance, especially among women, as a child is by a new plaything; and is led at will by them to suspect and quarrel with his best friends, of whom he hath lost the greatest part, for want of that indulgence which they ought to allow for his failings.

He is a generous, honest, good-natured man; but his perpetual want of judgment and discretion, makes him act as if he were neither generous, honest, nor good-natured.

The person above-mentioned, whom he lampooned, and to whom he owes preferment, being in the country and out of order, Solomon had appointed to come for him with a chaise, and bring him to town. Solomon sent him word that he was to set out on Monday, and did accordingly, but to another part of the kingdom, thirty miles wide of the place appointed, in compliment to a lady who was going that way; there staid, with her and her family, a month; then sent the chaise, in the midst of winter, to bring the said person where Solomon would meet him, declaring he could not venture himself for fear of the frost; and, upon the said person's refusing to go in the chaise alone, or to trust to Solomon's appointment, and being in ill health, Solomon fell

---

* Swift was as likely as most men to exercise a temper such as is here described. His long intimacy with Sheridan is a pretty good proof that his description was overcharged.

into a formal quarrel with that person, and foully misrepresented the whole affair, to justify himself.

Solomon had published a humorous ballad, called "Ballyspellin," whither he had gone to drink the waters, with a new favourite lady. The ballad was in the manner of Mr. Gay's on Molly Mogg, pretending to contain all the rhymes of Ballyspellin. His friend, the person so often mentioned, being at a gentleman's house in the neighbourhood, and merry over Solomon's ballad, they agreed to make another, in dispraise of Ballyspellin Wells, which Solomon had celebrated, and with all new rhymes not made use of in Solomon's. The thing was done, and all in a mere jest and innocent merriment. Yet Solomon was prevailed upon, by the lady he went with, to resent this as an affront on her and himself; which he did accordingly, against all the rules of reason, taste, good nature, judgment, gratitude, or common manners.*

He will invite six or more people of condition to dine with him on a certain day, some of them living five or six miles from town. On the day appointed, he will be absent, and know nothing of the matter, and they all go back disappointed : when he is told of this, he is pleased, because it shews him to be a genius and a man of learning.

Having lain many years under the obloquy of a High Tory and Jacobite, upon the present Queen's birthday he writ a song, to be performed before the government and those who attended them, in praise of the Queen and King, on the common topics of her beauty, wit, family, love of England, and all other virtues, wherein the King and the royal children were sharers. It was very hard to avoid

---

* Those who choose to compare the ballads, will admit that both Sheridan and the lady had cause of complaint.

the common topics. A young collegian, who had done the same job the year before, got some reputation on account of his wit. Solomon would needs vie with him, by which he lost all the esteem of his old friends the Tories, and got not the least interest with the Whigs; for they are now too strong to want advocates of that kind; and therefore one of the lords justices, reading the verses in some company, said, " Ah, Doctor! this shall not do." His name was at length in the title-page; and he did this without the knowledge or advice of one living soul, as he himself confesseth.

His full conviction of having acted wrong in an hundred instances, leaves him as positive in the next instance, as if he had never been mistaken in his life; and if you go to him the next day, and find him convinced in the last, he hath another instance ready, wherein he is as positive as he was the day before.

A SERIOUS AND USEFUL SCHEME

TO MAKE AN

HOSPITAL FOR INCURABLES,

Of universal Benefit to all his Majesty's Subjects. Humbly addressed to the Right Honourable Lord * * * *, the Right Honourable Sir * * * *, and to the Right Honourable * * * * * *, Esq.

Fœcunda culpæ secula.—HOR.

———o———

THE following Treatise is indisputably written by Swift, though not hitherto received among his works. The pamphlet from which it is taken, contains also "The Petition of the Footmen in and about Dublin," both printed by George Faulkner, 1733: and to the tracts there is subjoined the original advertisement concerning Faulkner's edition of the Dean's Works, which we subjoin as there given.* There can be no doubt that, under such cir-

---

* Dublin, Nov. 21, 1733.

The writings of the Reverend Dr. J. S. D. S. P. D. were published six years ago in London, in three volumes, mingled with those of some other gentlemen his friends. Neither is it easy to distinguish the authors of several pieces contained in them.

But, besides those three volumes, there are several treatises relating to Ireland, that were first published in this kingdom, many of which are not contained in the Drapier's Letters.

It hath been long wished, by several persons of quality and distinction, that a new complete edition of this author's works should be printed by itself.

But this can nowhere be done so conveniently as in Ireland, where book-

cumstances, the bookseller dared not have placed the initials of Swift before a work which was not genuine. It remains to account for the tract's having been afterwards suppressed, though possessing so much of the Dean's peculiar humour. Dr. Barrett believes the reason to have been, lest the *jeu d'esprit* might be interpreted as casting a slur on an hospital erected upon Lazors-Hill, now on the Donny-Brook road near Dublin, for the reception of persons afflicted with incurable maladies.

———o———

HERE is not anything which contributes more to the reputation of particular persons, or to the honour of a nation in general, than erecting and endowing proper edifices for the reception of those who labour under different kinds of distress. The

---

sellers cannot pretend to any property in what they publish, either by law or custom.

This is, therefore, to give notice, that the undertaker, George Faulkner, printer, in Essex Street, is now printing, by subscription, all the works that are generally allowed to have been written by the said Dr. S. in four volumes; which are now in the press, at 17s. and 4d. bound, beautifully printed on a fine paper, in octavo, and shall be delivered to the subscribers by the 25th of March next; eight English shillings to be paid at the time of subscribing, and the remainder at the delivery of a complete set. Whoever subscribes for six copies, shall have a seventh gratis.

The first volume shall contain the prose part of the author's Miscellanies, printed many years ago in London and Dublin; together with several other Treatises since published in small papers, or in the three volumes set out and signed Jonathan Swift, and Alexander Pope.

The second volume shall contain the author's Poetical Works, all joined together; with many Original Poems, that have hitherto only gone about in manuscript.

The third volume shall contain the Travels of Captain Lemuel Gulliver, in four parts, wherein many alterations made by the London printers will be set right, and several omissions inserted. Which alterations and omissions were without the author's knowledge, and much to his displeasure, as we have learned from an intimate friend of the author's, who, in his own copy, transcribed in blank paper the several paragraphs omitted, and settled the alterations and changes according to the original copy.

The last volume shall contain the author's Letters, written under the name of M. B. Drapier; with two additional ones never printed before; and likewise several papers relating to Ireland, acknowledged to be of the same author.

In this edition, the gross errors committed by the printers, both here and in London, shall be faithfully corrected; the true original, in the author's own hand, having been communicated to us by a friend in whom the author much confided, and who had leave to correct his own printed copies from the

diseased and unfortunate are thereby delivered from the misery of wanting assistance, and others are delivered from the misery of beholding them.

It is certain, that the genius of the people of England is strongly turned to public charities, and to so noble a degree, that almost in every part of this great and opulent city, and also in many of the adjacent villages, we meet with a great variety of hospitals, supported by the generous contributions of private families, as well as by the liberality of the public. Some for seamen worn out in the service of their country, and others for infirm disabled soldiers; some for the maintenance of tradesmen decayed, and others for their widows and orphans; some for the service of those who linger under tedious distempers, and others for such as are deprived of their reason.

But I find, upon nice inspection, that there is one kind of charity almost totally disregarded, which, nevertheless, appears to me of so excellent a nature, as to be at present more wanted, and better calculated for the ease, quietness, and felicity of this whole kingdom, than any other can possibly be. I mean an hospital for incurables.

I must indeed confess, that an endowment of this nature would prove a very large and perpetual expense. However, I have not the least diffidence, that I shall be able effectually to convince the world

---

author's most finished manuscript, where several changes were made, not only in the style, but in other material circumstances.

N.B.—A complete edition of the author's works can never be printed in England; because some of them were published without his knowledge or liking, and consequently belong to different proprietors; and likewise, because, as they now stand, they are mingled with those of other gentlemen his friends.

The author's Effigies, curiously engraven by Mr. Vertue, shall be prefixed to each volume. There will also be several other cuts, proper to the work.

Subscriptions will be taken till the latter end of December, and no longer.

N.B.—After the subscribers are served, no other persons shall have the works for less than a guinea.

that my present scheme for such an hospital is very practicable, and must be very desirable by every one who hath the interest of his country, or his fellow-creatures, really at heart.

It is observable, that, although the bodies of human creatures be affected with an infinite variety of disorders, which elude the power of medicine, and are often found to be incurable, yet their minds are also overrun with an equal variety, which no skill, no power, no medicine, can alter or amend. And I think, that, out of regard to the public peace and emolument, as well as the repose of many pious and valuable families, this latter species of incurables ought principally to engage our attention and beneficence.

I believe an hospital for such incurables will be universally allowed necessary, if we only consider what numbers of absolute incurables every profession, rank, and degree, would perpetually produce, which, at present, are only national grievances, and of which we can have no other effectual method to purge the kingdom.

For instance, let any man seriously consider what numbers there are of incurable fools, incurable knaves, incurable scolds, incurable scribblers, (besides myself,) incurable coxcombs, incurable infidels, incurable liars, incurable whores, in all places of public resort;—not to mention the incurably vain, incurably envious, incurably proud, incurably affected, incurably impertinent, and ten thousand other incurables, which I must of necessity pass over in silence, lest I should swell this essay into a volume. And, without doubt, every unprejudiced person will agree, that, out of mere Christian charity, the public ought to be eased as much as possible of this troublesome and intolerable variety of incurables.

And, first, Under the denomination of incurable

fools, we may reasonably expect, that such an hospital would be furnished with considerable numbers of the growth of our own universities, who, at present, appear in various professions in the world, under the venerable titles of physicians, barristers, and ecclesiastics.

And as those ancient seminaries have been, for some years past, accounted little better than nurseries of such sort of incurables, it should seem highly commendable to make some kind of provision for them, because it is more than probable, that, if they are to be supported by their own particular merit in their several callings, they must necessarily acquire but a very indifferent maintenance.

I would not, willingly, be here suspected to cast reflections on any order of men, as if I thought that small gains from the profession of any art or science were always an undoubted sign of an equally small degree of understanding; for I profess myself to be somewhat inclined to a very opposite opinion, having frequently observed, that at the bar, the pulse, and the pulpit, those who have the least learning or sense to plead, meet generally with the largest share of promotions and profit: of which many instances might be produced; but the public seems to want no conviction in this particular.

Under the same denominations we may further expect a large and ridiculous quantity of old rich widows, whose eager and impatient appetites inflame them with extravagant passions for fellows of a very different age and complexion from themselves, who purchase contempt and aversion with good jointures, and being loaded with years, infirmities, and probably ill-humour, are forced to bribe into their embraces such whose fortunes and characters are equally desperate.

Besides, our collection of incurable fools would

receive an incredible addition from every one of the following articles :—

From young extravagant heirs, who are just of a competent age to become the bubbles of jockeys, sportsmen, gamesters, bullies, sharpers, courtezans, and such sort of honourable pickpockets.

From misers, who half starve themselves to feed the prodigality of their heirs, and who proclaim to the world how unworthy they are of possessing estates, by the wretched and ridiculous methods they take to enjoy them.

From contentious people, of all conditions, who are content to waste the greatest part of their own fortunes at law, to be the instruments of impoverishing others.

From those who have any confidence in profession of friendship, before trial, or any dependence on the fidelity of a mistress.

From young illiterate squires, who travel abroad to import lewdness, conceit, arrogance, vanity, and foppery, of which commodities there seems to be so great an abundance at home.

From young clergymen, who contrive by matrimony, to acquire a family, before they have obtained the necessary means to maintain one.

From those who have considerable estates in different kingdoms, and yet are so incurably stupid as to spend their whole incomes in this.

These, and several other articles which might be mentioned, would afford us a perpetual opportunity of easing the public, by having an hospital for the accommodation of such incurables; who, at present, either by the overfondness of near relations, or the indolence of the magistrates, are permitted to walk abroad, and appear in the most crowded places of this city, as if they were indeed reasonable creatures.

I had almost forgot to hint, that under this article, there is a modest probability that many of the clergy would be found properly qualified for admittance into the hospital, who might serve in the capacity of chaplains, and save the unnecessary expense of salaries.

To these fools, in order succeed such as may justly be included under the extensive denomination of incurable knaves; of which our several Inns of Court would constantly afford us abundant supplies.

I think, indeed, that, of this species of incurables, there ought to be a certain limited number annually admitted, which number, neither any regard to the quiet or benefit of the nation, nor any other charitable or public-spirited reason, should tempt us to exceed; because, if all were to be admitted on such a foundation, who might be reputed incurable of this distemper; and if it were possible for the public to find any place large enough for their reception, I have not the least doubt that all our inns, which are at this day so crowded, would in a short time be emptied of their inhabitants, and the law, that beneficial craft, want hands to conduct it.

I tremble to think what herds of attorneys, solicitors, pettifoggers, scriveners, usurers, hackney-clerks, pickpockets, pawn-brokers, jailors, and justices of the peace, would hourly be driven to such an hospital; and what disturbance it might also create in several noble and wealthy families.

What unexpected distress might it prove to several men of fortune and quality, to be suddenly deprived of their rich stewards, in whom they had for many years reposed the utmost confidence, and to find them irrecoverably lodged among such a collection of incurables!

How many orphans might then expect to see

their guardians hurried away to the hospital; and how many greedy executors find reason to lament the want of opportunity to pillage!

Would not Exchange Alley have cause to mourn for the loss of its stock-jobbers and brokers; and the Charitable Corporation for the confinement of many of its directors?

Might not Westminster-Hall, as well as all the gaming houses in this great city, be entirely unpeopled; and the professors of art in each of those assemblies become useless in their vocations, by being deprived of all future opportunity to be dishonest?

In short, it might put the whole kingdom into confusion and disorder; and we should find that the entire revenues of this nation would be scarce able to support so great a number of incurables, in this way, as would appear qualified for admission into our hospital.

For if we only consider how this kingdom swarms with quadrille-tables, and gaming houses, both public and private, and also how each of those houses, as well as Westminster-Hall aforesaid, swarms with knaves who are anxious to win, or fools who have anything to lose, we may be soon convinced how necessary it will be to limit the number of incurables, comprehended under these titles, lest the foundation should prove insufficient to maintain any others besides them.

However, if, by this scheme of mine, the nation can be eased of twenty or thirty thousand such incurables, I think it ought to be esteemed somewhat beneficial, and worthy of the attention of the public.

The next sort for whom I would gladly provide, and who for several generations have proved in-

supportable plagues and grievances to
people of England, are those who may p
admitted under the character of incurable

I own this to be a temper of so desperat
that few females can be found willing to
selves anyway addicted to it; and yet, it
that there is scarce a single parson, 'pren
man, squire, or husband, who would not
avouch the very reverse.

I could wish, indeed, that the word scol
changed for some more gentle term, of e
fication; because I am convinced, that
name is as offensive to female ears, as the
that incurable distemper are to the ears of
which to be sure, is inexpressible.

And that it hath been always customary
the very same kind of actions with differe
tions, only to avoid giving offence, is
common observation.

For instance: How many lawyers,
solicitors, under-sheriffs, intriguing chan
and counter-officers, are continually guilt
tion, bribery, oppression, and many other
knaveries, to drain the purses of those w
they are anyway concerned! And yet,
different expedients to raise a fortune, pas
under the milder names of fees, perquisi
presents, gratuities, and such like; alt
strictness of speech, they should be calle
and consequently be rewarded with a gibb

Nay, how many honourable gentlemen
enumerated, who keep open shop to mal
of iniquity; who teach the law to wink
power or profit appears in her way; and c
grow rich by the vice, the contention, or
of mankind; and who, nevertheless, instea

branded with the harsh-sounding names of knaves, pilferers, or public oppressors, (as they justly merit,) are only distinguished by the title of justices of the peace; in which single term, all those several appellations are generally thought to be implied.

But to proceed. When first I determined to prepare this scheme for the use and inspection of the public, I intended to examine one whole ward in this city, that my computation of the number of incurable scolds might be more perfect and exact. But I found it impossible to finish my progress through more than one street.

I made my first application to a wealthy citizen in Cornhill, common council-man for his ward, to whom I hinted, that if he knew e'er an incurable scold in the neighbourhood, I had some hope to provide for her in such a manner, as to hinder her from being further troublesome. He referred me with great delight to his next-door friend; yet whispered me, that, with much greater ease and pleasure, he could furnish me out of his own family ———, and begged the preference.

His next-door friend owned readily that his wife's qualifications were not misrepresented, and that he would cheerfully contribute to promote so useful a scheme; but positively asserted, that it would be of small service to rid the neighbourhood of one woman, while such multitudes would remain all equally insupportable.

By which circumstance I conjectured, that the quantity of these incurables in London, Westminster, and Southwark, would be very considerable, and that a generous contribution might reasonably be expected for such an hospital as I am recommending.

Besides, the number of these female incurables would probably be very much increased by additional quantities of old maids, who, being wearied with concealing their ill-humour for one-half of their lives, are impatient to give it full vent in the other. For old maids, like old thin-bodied wines, instead of growing more agreeable by years, are observed, for the most part, to become intolerably sharp, sour, and useless.

Under this denomination also, we may expect to be furnished with as large a collection of old bachelors, especially those who have estates, and but a moderate degree of understanding. For, an old wealthy bachelor, being perpetually surrounded with a set of flatterers, cousins, poor dependants, and would-be heirs, who, for their own views, submit to his perverseness and caprice, becomes insensibly infected with this scolding malady, which generally proves incurable, and renders him disagreeable to his friends, and a fit subject for ridicule to his enemies.

As to the incurable scribblers, (of which society I have the honour to be a member,) they probably are innumerable; and, of consequence, it will be absolutely impossible to provide for one-tenth part of their fraternity. However, as this set of incurables are generally more plagued with poverty than any other, it will be a double charity to admit them on the foundation; a charity to the world, to whom they are a common pest and nuisance; and a charity to themselves, to relieve them from want, contempt, kicking, and several other accidents of that nature, to which they are continually liable.

Grub-street itself would then have reason to rejoice, to see so many of its half-starved manufacturers amply provided for, and the whole tribe of meagre incurables would probably shout for joy, at being delivered from the tyranny and garrets of printers, publishers, and booksellers.

What a mixed multitude of ballad-writers, ode-makers, translators, farce-compounders, opera-mongers, biographers, pamphleteers, and journalists, would appear crowding to the hospital; not unlike the brutes resorting to the ark before the deluge! And what an universal satisfaction would such a sight afford to all, except pastry-cooks, grocers, chandlers, and tobacco-retailers, to whom alone the writings of those incurables were anyway profitable!

I have often been amazed to observe, what a variety of incurable coxcombs are to be met with between St. James's and Limehouse, at every hour of the day; as numerous as Welsh parsons, and equably contemptible. How they swarm in all coffeehouses, theatres, public walks, and private assemblies; how they are incessantly employed in cultivating intrigues, and every kind of irrational pleasure; how industrious they seem to mimic the appearance of monkeys, as monkeys are emulous to imitate the gestures of men: And from such observations, I concluded, that to confine the greatest part of those incurables, who are so many living burlesques of human nature, would be of eminent service to this nation; and I am persuaded that I am far from being singular in that opinion.

As for the incurable infidels and liars, I shall range them under the same article, and would willingly appoint them the same apartment in the hospital; because there is a much nearer resemblance between them than is generally imagined.

Have they not an equal delight in imposing falsities on the public, and seem they not equally desirous to be thought of more sagacity and importance than others? Do they not both report what both know to be false; and both confidently assert what they are conscious is most liable to contradiction?

The parallel might easily be carried on much further, if the intended shortness of this essay would admit it. However, I cannot forbear taking notice, with what immense quantities of incurable liars his Majesty's kingdoms are overrun; what offence and prejudice they are to the public; what inconceivable injury to private persons; and what a necessity there is for an hospital, to relieve the nation from the curse of so many incurables.

This distemper appears almost in as many different shapes as there are persons afflicted with it; and, in every individual, is always beyond the power of medicine.

Some lie for their interest, such as fishmongers, flatterers, pimps, lawyers, fortune-hunters, and fortune-tellers; and others lie for their entertainment, as maids, wives, widows, and all other tea-table attendants.

Some lie out of vanity, as poets, painters, players, fops, military officers, and all those who frequent the levees of the great: and others lie out of ill-nature, as old maids, &c.

Some lie out of custom, as lovers, coxcombs, footmen, sailors, mechanics, merchants, and chambermaids; and others lie out of complaisance or necessity, as courtiers, chaplains, &c. In short, it were endless to enumerate them all, but this sketch may be sufficient to give us some small imperfect idea of their numbers.

As to the remaining incurables, we may reasonably conclude, that they bear at least an equal proportion to those already mentioned; but with regard to the incurable whores in this kingdom, I must particularly observe, that such of them as are public, and make it their profession, have proper hospitals for their reception already, if we could find magistrates with-

HOSPITAL FOR INCURABLES. 327

out passions, or officers without an incurable itch to a bribe. And such of them as are private, and make it their amusement, I should be unwilling to disturb, for two reasons:—

First, Because it might probably afflict many noble, wealthy, contented, and unsuspecting husbands, by convincing them of their own dishonour, and the unpardonable disloyalty of their wives: And, secondly, Because it will be for ever impossible to confine a woman from being guilty of any kind of misconduct, when once she is firmly resolved to attempt it.

From all which observations, every reasonable man must infallibly be convinced, that an hospital for the support of these different kinds of incurables would be extremely beneficial to these kingdoms. I think, therefore, that nothing further is wanting, but to demonstrate to the public, that such a scheme is very practicable; both by having an undoubted method to raise an annual income, at least sufficient to make the experiment, (which is the way of founding all hospitals,) and by having also a strong probability, that such an hospital would be supported by perpetual benefactions; which, in very few years, might enable us to increase the number of incurables to nine-tenths more than we can reasonably venture on at first.

A Computation of the Daily and Annual Expenses of an Hospital, to be erected for Incurables.

Per day

INCURABLE fools are almost infinite; however, at first, I would have only twenty thousand admitted; and, allowing to each person but one shilling per day for maintenance, which is as low as possible, the daily expense for this article will be £1000

Incurable knaves are, if possible, more numerous, including foreigners, especially Irishmen. Yet I would limit the number of these to about thirty thousand; which would amount to 1500

Incurable scolds would be plentifully supplied from almost every family in the kingdom. And indeed, to make this hospital of any real benefit, we cannot admit fewer, even at first, than thirty thousand, including the ladies of Billingsgate and Leaden-hall market, which is 1500

The incurable scribblers are undoubtedly a very considerable society, and of that denomination I would admit at least forty thousand; because it is to be supposed that such incurables will be found in greatest distress for a daily maintenance. And if we had not great encouragement to hope, that many of that class would properly be admitted among the incurable fools, I should strenuously intercede to have ten or twenty thousand more added. But their allowed number will amount to . 2000

Incurable coxcombs are very numerous; and, considering what numbers are annually imported from France and Italy, we cannot admit fewer than ten thousand, which will be 500

Incurable infidels (as they affect to be called) should be received into the hospital to the number of ten thousand. However, if it should accidentally happen to grow into a fashion to be believers, it is probable that the great part of them would, in a very short time, be dismissed from the hospital, as perfectly cured. Their expense would be . £500

Incurable liars are infinite in all parts of the kingdom; and, making allowance for citizens' wives, mercers, prentices, newswriters, old maids, and flatterers, we cannot possibly allow a smaller number than thirty thousand, which will amount to 1500

The incurable envious are in vast quantities throughout this whole nation. Nor can it reasonably be expected that their numbers should lessen, while fame and honours are heaped upon some particular persons, as the public reward of their superior accomplishments, while others, who are equally excellent, in their own opinions, are constrained to live unnoticed and contemned. And, as it would be impossible to provide for all those who are possessed with this distemper, I should consent to admit only twenty thousand at first, by way of experiment, amounting to . 1000

Of the incurable vain, affected, and impertinent, I should at least admit ten thousand; which number I am confident will appear very inconsiderable, if we include all degrees of females, from the duchess to the chambermaid; all poets, who have had a little success, especially in the dramatic way, and all players, who have met with a small degree of approbation. Amounting only to . 500

By which plain computation it is evident, that two hundred thousand persons will be daily provided for, and the allowance for maintaining this collection of incurables may be seen in the following account.

SCHEME TO MAKE AN

For the Incurable

		Per day.
Fools, being	20,000 at one shilling each	£1000
Knaves	30,000 ditto	1500
Scolds	30,000	1500
Scribblers	40,000	2000
Coxcombs	10,000	500
Infidels	10,000	500
Liars	30,000.	1500

For the Incurably

Envious	20,000	1000
Vain	10,000	500

Total maintained, 200,000   Total expense, £10,000

From whence it appears, that the daily expense will amount to such a sum, as in 365 days comes to £3,650,000

And I am fully satisfied that a sum, much greater than this, may easily be raised, with all possible satisfaction to the subject, and without interfering in the least with the revenues of the crown.

In the first place, a large proportion of this sum might be raised by the voluntary contribution of the inhabitants.

The computed number of people in Great Britain is very little less than eight millions, of which, upon a most moderate computation, we may account one half to be incurables. And as all those different incurables, whether acting in the capacity of friends, acquaintances, wives, husbands, daughters, counsellors, parents, old maids, or old bachelors, are inconceivable plagues to all those with whom they happen to be concerned; and, as there is no hope of being eased of such plagues, except by such an hospital, which, by degrees, might be enlarged to contain them all, I think it cannot be doubted, that at least three millions and a half of people, out of the remaining proportion, would be found both able and desirous to contribute so small a sum as twenty shillings per annum, for the quiet of the kingdom, the peace of private families, and the credit of the nation in general. And this contribution would amount to very near our requisite sum.

Nor can this by any means be esteemed a wild conjecture; for where is there a man of common sense, honesty, or good-nature, who would not gladly propose even a much greater sum to be freed from a scold, a knave, a fool, a liar, a coxcomb conceitedly repeating the compositions of others, or a vain impertinent poet repeating his own?

In the next place, it may justly be supposed, that many young noblemen, knights, squires, and extravagant heirs, with very large estates, would be confined in our hospital. And I would propose, that the annual income of every particular incurable's estate should be appropriated to the use of the house. But, besides these, there will undoubtedly be many old misers, aldermen, justices, directors of companies, templars, and merchants of all kinds, whose personal fortunes are immense, and who should proportionably pay to the hospital.

Yet, lest, by being here misunderstood, I should seem to propose an unjust or oppressive scheme, I shall further explain my design.

Suppose, for instance, a young nobleman, possessed of ten or twenty thousand pounds per annum, should accidentally be confined there as an incurable, I would have only such a proportion of his estate applied to the support of the hospital, as he himself would spend if he were at liberty. And, after his death, the profits of the estate should regularly devolve to the next lawful heir, whether male or female.

And my reason for this proposal is, because considerable estates, which probably would be squandered away among hounds, horses, whores, sharpers, surgeons, tailors, pimps, masquerades, or architects, if left to the management of such incurables, would, by this means, become of some real use, both to the public and themselves. And perhaps this may be the only method which can be found to make such young spendthrifts of any real benefit to their country.

And although the estates of deceased incurables might be permitted to descend to the next heirs, the hospital would probably sustain no great disadvantage; because it is very likely that most of these heirs would also gradually be admitted under some denomination or other, and consequently their estates would again devolve to the use of the hospital.

As to the wealthy misers, &c., I would have their private fortunes nicely examined and calculated; because, if they were old bachelors, (as it would frequently happen,) their whole fortunes should be appropriated to the endowment; but, if married, I would leave two-thirds of their fortunes for the support of their families; which families would cheerfully consent to give away the remaining third, if not more, to be freed from such peevish and disagreeable governors.

So that, deducting from the two hundred thousand incurables the forty thousand scribblers, who to be sure would be found in very bad circumstances, I believe, among the remaining hundred and sixty thousand fools, knaves, and coxcombs, so many would be found of large estates and easy fortunes, as would at least produce two hundred thousand pounds per annum.

As a further addition to our endowment, I would have a tax upon all inscriptions and tombstones, monuments and obelisks, erected to the honour of the dead, or on porticoes and trophies, to the honour of the living; because these will naturally and properly come under the article of lies, pride, vanity, &c.

And if all inscriptions throughout this kingdom were impartially examined, in order to tax those which should appear demonstrably false or flattering, I am convinced that not one-fifth part of the number would, after such a scrutiny, escape exempted.

Many an ambitious turbulent spirit would then be found, belied with the opposite title of lover of his country; and many a Middlesex justice, as improperly described, sleeping in hope of salvation.

Many an usurer, discredited by the appellations of honest and frugal; and many a lawyer, with the character of conscientious and equitable.

Many a British statesman and general, decaying with more honour than they lived, and their dusts distinguished with a better reputation than when they were animated.

Many dull parsons, improperly styled eloquent; and as many stupid physicians, improperly styled learned.

Yet, notwithstanding the extensiveness of a tax upon such monumental impositions, I will count only upon twenty thousand, at five pounds per annum each, which will amount to one hundred thousand pounds annually.

To these annuities I would also request the Parliament of this nation to allow the benefit of two lotteries yearly, by which the hospital would gain two hundred thousand pounds clear. Nor can such a request seem anyway extraordinary, since it would be appropriated to the benefit of fools and knaves, which is the sole cause of granting one for this present year.

In the last place, I would add the estate of Richard Norton, Esq.; and, to do his memory all possible honour, I would have his statue erected in the very first apartment of the hospital, or in any other which might seem more apt. And on his monument I would permit a long inscription, composed by his dearest friends, which should remain tax-free for ever.

From these several articles, therefore, would annually arise the following sums:—

	M. Th. H. P. Ann.
From the voluntary contribution,	£3,500,000
From the estates of the incurables,	200,000
By the tax upon tombstones, monuments, &c., (that of Richard Norton, Esq., always excepted,)	100,000
By two annual lotteries,	200,000
By the estate of Richard Norton, Esq.,	60,000
Total,	£4,600,000
And the necessary sum for the hospital being	£3,650,000
There will remain annually over and above,	£356,000

Which sum of £356,000 should be applied towards erecting the building, and answer accidental expenses, in such a manner as should seem most proper to promote the design of the hospital. But the whole management of it should be left to the skill and discretion of those who are to be constituted governors.

It may, indeed, prove a work of some small difficulty to fix upon a commodious place, large enough for a building of this nature. I should have thoughts of attempting to enclose all Yorkshire, if I were not apprehensive that it would be crowded with so many incurable knaves of its own growth, that there would not be the least room left for the reception of any others; by which accident our whole project might be retarded for some time.

Thus have I set this matter in the plainest light I could, that every one may judge of the necessity, usefulness, and practicableness of this scheme: and I shall only add a few scattered hints, which, to me, seem not altogether unprofitable.

I think the prime minister for the time being ought largely to contribute to such a foundation; because his high station and merits must of necessity infect a great number with envy, hatred, lying, and such sort of distempers; and, of consequence, furnish the hospital annually with many incurables.

I would desire that the governors appointed to direct this hospital should have (if such a thing were possible) some appearance of religion and belief in God; because those who are to be admitted as incurable infidels, atheists, deists, and freethinkers, most of which tribe are only so out of pride, conceit, and affectation, might perhaps grow gradually into believers, if they perceived it to be the custom of the place where they lived.

Although it be not customary for the natives of Ireland to meet with any manner of promotion in this kingdom, I would, in this respect, have that national prejudice entirely laid aside; and request, that, for the reputation of both kingdoms, a large apartment in the hospital may be fitted up for Irishmen particularly, who, either by knavery, lewdness, or fortune-hunting, should appear qualified for admittance; because their numbers would certainly be very considerable.

I would further request, that a father, who seems delighted at seeing his son metamorphosed into a fop, or a coxcomb, because he hath travelled from London to Paris, may be sent along with the young gentleman to the hospital, as an old fool, absolutely incurable.

If a poet hath luckily produced anything, especially in the dramatic way, which is tolerably well received by the public, he should be sent immediately to the hospital; because incurable vanity is always the consequence of a little success. And, if his compositions be ill received, let him be admitted as a scribbler.

And I hope, in regard to the great pains I have taken about this scheme, that I shall be admitted upon the foundation as one of the scribbling incurables. But, as an additional favour, I entreat, that I may not be placed in an apartment with a poet who hath employed his genius for the stage; because he will kill me with repeating his own compositions: and I need not acquaint the world, that it is extremely painful to bear any nonsense—except our own.

My private reason for soliciting so early to be admitted is, because it is observed that schemers and projectors are generally reduced to beggary; but, by my being provided for in the hospital, either as an incurable fool or a scribbler, that discouraging observation will for once be publicly disproved, and my brethren in that way will be secure of a public reward for their labours.

It gives me, I own, a great degree of happiness,

to reflect, that although in this short treatise the characters of many thousands are contained, among the vast variety of incurables, yet, not any one person is likely to be offended; because, it is natural to apply ridiculous characters to all the world, except ourselves. And I dare be bold to say, that the most incurable fool, knave, scold, coxcomb, scribbler, or liar, in this whole nation, will sooner enumerate the circle of their acquaintance as addicted to those distempers, than once imagine themselves anyway qualified for such an hospital.

I hope, indeed, that our wise legislature will take this project into their serious consideration, and promote an endowment, which will be of such eminent service to multitudes of his Majesty's unprofitable subjects, and may in time be of use to themselves and their posterity.

From my Garret in Moorfields, Aug. 20, 1733.

A COMPLETE

COLLECTION

OF GENTEEL AND INGENIOUS

CO'NVERSATION,

ACCORDING TO THE MOST

POLITE MODE AND METHOD,

NOW USED

AT COURT, AND IN THE BEST COMPANIES

OF ENGLAND.

IN THREE DIALOGUES.

By SIMON WAGSTAFF, Esq.

A COMPLETE COLLECTION, &c.

In the admirable ironical introduction to this lively *jeu d'esprit*, its purpose is sufficiently explained. It was the intention of Swift to turn into ridicule that sort of cant in conversation, which depends upon introducing and repeating, with an affectation of originality and vivacity, a set of quaint phrases, brought together by the mere exertion of memory; a particular string of which is, by the courtesy of the fashionable world, permitted to pass current as wit and lively repartee. The affected solemnity with which Lord Orrery treats this lively and curious satire as among the *minutissimæ* of Swift's performances, and one which he would scarcely have published but for the decay of his understanding, leads us to suspect that his lordship had either traced some resemblance to his own conversation in that of my Lord Smart or my Lord Sparkish, or at least that he considered the bon-ton society as sacred by their privileges from the lash of satire. Dr. Hawkesworth, with more justice, considers the Essay on Polite Conversation as a counterpart to the Tritical Essay on the Faculties of the Mind, intended to explode from society the absurd and indiscriminate use of cant phrases and catch-words, and to bring it back to the combination and expression of natural sentiment. It is impossible to peruse the treatise without being astonished at the marvellous command which it exhibits of the very tropes it is meant to ridicule; and it must, I fear, be admitted, that, if antiquated allusions were retrenched, Tom Neverout and Miss Notable would sustain their parts very respectably in the fashionable society of the present day.

The Dean himself, in his letters, describes it as a trial to reduce the whole politeness, wit, humour, and style of England into a short system, for the use of all persons of quality, and particularly the Maids of Honour.

INTRODUCTION.

AS my life has been chiefly spent in consulting the honour and welfare of my country for more than forty years past, not without answerable success, if the world and my friends have not flattered me; so there is no point wherein I have so much laboured, as that of improving and polishing all parts of conversation between persons of quality, whether they meet by accident or invitation, at meals, tea, or visits, mornings, noon, or evenings.

I have passed perhaps more time than any other man of my age and country in visits and assemblies, where the polite persons of both sexes distinguish themselves; and could not without much grief observe how frequently both gentlemen and ladies are at a loss for questions, answers, replies, and rejoinders. However, my concern was much abated when I found that these defects were not occasioned by any want of materials, but because those materials were not in every hand: for instance, one lady can give an answer better than ask a question: one gentleman is happy at a reply; another excels in a rejoinder: one can revive a languishing conversation by a sudden surprising sentence; another is more dexterous in seconding; a third can fill up the gap with laughing, or commending what has been said: thus fresh hints may be started, and the ball of the discourse kept up.

But, alas! this is too seldom the case, even in the most select companies. How often do we see at court, at public visiting days, at great men's levees, and other places of general meeting, that the conversation falls and drops to nothing, like a fire without supply of fuel! This is what we all ought to lament; and against this dangerous evil I take upon me to affirm, that I have in the following papers provided an infallible remedy.

It was in the year 1695, and the sixth of his late majesty King William the Third, of ever-glorious and immortal memory, who rescued three kingdoms from Popery and slavery,* when, being about the age of six-and-thirty, my judgment mature, of good reputation in the world, and well acquainted with the best families in town, I determined to spend five mornings, to dine four times, pass three afternoons, and six evenings, every week, in the houses of the most polite families, of which I would confine myself to fifty; only changing as the masters or ladies died, or left the town, or grew out of vogue, or sunk in their fortunes, or (which to me was of the highest moment) became disaffected to the government; which practice I have followed ever since to this very day; except when I happened to be sick, or in the spleen upon cloudy weather, and except when I entertained four of each sex at my own lodgings once in a month, by way of retaliation.

I always kept a large table-book in my pocket; and as soon as I left the company I immediately

---

* There seems to be a sneer intended. Swift had been so long a Tory, that he now perhaps approached in principle to a Jacobite.

entered the choicest expressions that passed during the visit: which, returning home, I transcribed in a fair hand, but somewhat enlarged; and had made the greatest part of my collection in twelve years, but not digested into any method, for this I found was a work of infinite labour, and what required the nicest judgment, and consequently could not be brought to any degree of perfection in less than sixteen years more.

Herein I resolved to exceed the advice of Horace, a Roman poet, which I have read in Mr. Creech's admirable translation, that an author should keep his works nine years in his closet, before he ventured to publish them: and, finding that I still received some additional flowers of wit and language, although in a very small number, I determined to defer the publication, to pursue my design, and exhaust (if possible) the whole subject, that I might present a complete system to the world: for I am convinced, by long experience, that the critics will be as severe as their old envy against me can make them: I foresee they will object, that I have inserted many answers and replies, which are neither witty, humorous, polite, nor authentic; and have omitted others that would have been highly useful, as well as entertaining. But let them come to particulars, and I will boldly engage to confute their malice.

For these last six or seven years I have not been able to add above nine valuable sentences to enrich my collection: from whence, I conclude that what remains will amount only to a trifle. However, if, after the publication of this work, any lady or gentleman, when they have read it, shall find the least thing of importance omitted, I desire they will please to supply my defects by communicating to me their discoveries; and their letters may be directed to

Simon Wagstaff, Esq., at his lodgings next door to the Gloucester-head in St. James's Street, paying the postage. In return of which favour, I shall make honourable mention of their names in a short preface to the second edition.

In the meantime, I cannot but with some pride, and much pleasure, congratulate with my dear country, which has outdone all the nations of Europe, in advancing the whole art of conversation to the greatest height it is capable of reaching; and therefore, being entirely convinced that the collection I now offer to the public is full and complete, I may at the same time boldly affirm, that the whole genius, humour, politeness, and eloquence of England, are summed up in it; nor is the treasure small, wherein are to be found at least a thousand shining questions, answers, repartees, replies, and rejoinders, fitted to adorn every kind of discourse that an assembly of English ladies and gentlemen, met together for their mutual entertainment, can possibly want: especially when the several flowers shall be set off and improved by the speakers, with every circumstance of preface and circumlocution, in proper terms; and attended with praise, laughter, or admiration.

There is a natural, involuntary distortion of the muscles, which is the anatomical cause of laughter: but there is another cause of laughter, which decency requires, and is the undoubted mark of a good taste, as well as of a polite obliging behaviour; neither is this to be acquired without much observation, long practice, and sound judgment; I did therefore once intend, for the ease of the learner, to set down, in all parts of the following dialogues, certain marks, asterisks, or *nota benes* (in English, mark-wells) after most questions, and every reply or answer; directing exactly the moment when one, two, or all the company are to laugh: but, having duly considered that this expedient would too much enlarge the bulk of the volume, and consequently the price; and likewise that something ought to be left for ingenious readers to find out, I have determined to leave that whole affair, although of great importance, to their own discretion.

The reader must learn by all means to distinguish between proverbs and those polite speeches which beautify conversation; for, as to the former, I utterly reject them out of all ingenious discourse.* I acknowledge, indeed, that there may possibly be found in this treatise a few sayings, among so great a number of smart turns of wit and humour as I have produced, which have a proverbial air; however, I hope it will be considered that even these were not originally proverbs, but the genuine productions of superior wits, to embellish and support conversation; whence, with great impropriety as well as plagiarism, (if you will forgive a hard word,) they have most injuriously been transferred into proverbial maxims; and therefore, in justice, ought to be resumed out of vulgar hands, to adorn the drawing-rooms of princes both male and female, the levees of great ministers, as well as the toilet and tea-table of the ladies.

I can faithfully assure the reader, that there is not one single witty phrase in this whole collection, which has not received the stamp and approbation of at least one hundred years, and how much longer, it is hard to determine; he may therefore be secure to find them all genuine, sterling, and authentic.

But, before this elaborate treatise can become of

---

* This is ironical, for almost all the repartees in the dialogue turn upon proverbial expressions.

universal use and ornament to my native country, two points, that will require much time and much application, are absolutely necessary.

For, first, whatever person would aspire to be completely witty, smart, humorous, and polite, must, by hard labour, be able to retain in his memory every single sentence contained in this work, so as never to be once at a loss in applying the right answers, questions, repartees, and the like, immediately, and without study or hesitation.

And, secondly, after a lady or gentleman has so well overcome this difficulty as never to be at a loss upon any emergency, the true management of every feature, and almost every limb, is equally necessary; without which an infinite number of absurdities will inevitably ensue. For instance, there is hardly a polite sentence in the following dialogues, which does not absolutely require some peculiar graceful motion in the eyes, or nose, or mouth, or forehead, or chin, or suitable toss of the head, with certain offices assigned to each hand; and in ladies, the whole exercise of the fan, fitted to the energy of every word they deliver; by no means omitting the various turns and cadence of the voice, the twistings, and movements, and different postures of the body, the several kinds and gradations of laughter, which the ladies must daily practise by the looking-glass, and consult upon them with their waiting-maids.

My readers will soon observe what a great compass of real and useful knowledge this science includes; wherein, although nature, assisted by genius, may be very instrumental, yet a strong memory and constant application, together with example and precept, will be highly necessary. For these reasons, I have often wished, that certain male and female instructors, perfectly versed in this science, would set up schools, for the instruction of young ladies and gentlemen therein.

I remember, about thirty years ago, there was a Bohemian woman, of that species commonly known by the name of gipsies, who came over thither from France, and generally attended Isaac the dancing-master, when he was teaching his art to misses of quality; and while the young ladies were thus employed, the Bohemian, standing at some distance, but full in their sight, acted before them all proper airs, and heavings of the head, and motion of the hand, and twistings of the body; whereof you may still observe the good effects in several of our elder ladies.

After the same manner, it were much to be desired that some expert gentlewomen gone to decay would set up public schools, wherein young girls of quality, or great fortunes, might first be taught to repeat this following system of conversation, which I have been at much pains to compile; and then to adapt every feature of their countenances, every turn of their hands, every screwing of their bodies, every exercise of their fans, to the humour of the sentences they hear or deliver in conversation. But above all, to instruct them in every species and degree of laughing in the proper seasons, at their own wit or that of the company. And if the sons of the nobility and gentry, instead of being sent to common schools, or put into the hands of tutors at home, to learn nothing but words, were consigned to able instructors, in the same art, I cannot find what use there could be of books, except in the hands of those who are to make learning their trade, which is below the dignity of persons born to titles or estates.

It would be another infinite advantage, that, by cultivating this science, we should wholly avoid the vexations and impertinence of pedants, who affect to talk in a language not to be understood; and whenever a polite person offers accidentally to use any of their jargon terms, have the presumption to laugh at us for pronouncing those words in a genteeler manner. Whereas I do here affirm, that, whenever any fine gentleman or lady condescends to let a hard word pass out of their mouths, every syllable is smoothed and polished in the passage; and it is a true mark of politeness, both in writing and reading, to vary the orthography as well as the sound; because we are infinitely better judges of what will please a distinguishing ear, than those who call themselves scholars can possibly be; who, consequently, ought to correct their books, and manner of pronouncing, by the authority of our example, from whose lips they proceed with infinitely more beauty and significancy.

But, in the meantime, until so great, so useful, and so necessary a design can be put in execution, (which, considering the good disposition of our country at present, I shall not despair of living to see,) let me recommend the following treatise to be carried about as a pocket companion, by all gentlemen and ladies, when they are going to visit, or dine, or drink tea; or where they happen to pass the evening without cards, as I have sometimes known it to be the case upon disappointments or accidents unforeseen; desiring they would read their several parts in their chairs or coaches, to prepare themselves for every kind of conversation that can possibly happen.

Although I have, in justice to my country, allowed the genius of our people to excel that of any other nation upon earth, and have confirmed this truth by an argument not to be controlled, I mean, by producing so great a number of witty sentences in the ensuing dialogues, all of undoubted authority, as well as of our own production, yet I must confess at the same time, that we are wholly indebted for them to our ancestors; for, as long as my memory reaches, I do not recollect one new phrase of importance to have been added; which defect in us moderns I take to have been occasioned by the introduction of cant words in the reign of King Charles the Second. And those have so often varied, that hardly one of them, of above a year's standing, is now intelligible; nor anywhere to be found, excepting a small number strewed here and there in the comedies, and other fantastic writings of that age.

The Honourable Colonel James Graham, my old friend and companion, did likewise, toward the end of the same reign, invent a set of words and phrases, which continued almost to the time of his death. But, as these terms of art were adapted only to courts and politicians, and extended little further than among his particular acquaintance, (of whom I had the honour to be one,) they are now almost forgotten.

Nor did the late D. of R—— and E. of E—— succeed much better, although they proceeded no further than single words; whereof, except bite, bamboozle, and one or two more, the whole vocabulary is antiquated.

The same fate has already attended those other town wits, who furnish us with a great variety of new terms, which are annually changed, and those of the late season sunk in oblivion. Of these I was once favoured with a complete list by the Right Honourable the Lord and Lady H——, with which I made a considerable figure one summer in the country; but, returning up to town in winter, and venturing to produce them again, I was partly hooted, and partly not understood.

The only invention of late years, which has anyway contributed towards politeness in discourse, is that of abbreviating or reducing words of many syllables into one, by lopping off the rest. This refinement having begun about the time of the Revolution, I had some share in the honour of promoting it; and I observe, to my great satisfaction, that it makes daily advancements, and I hope in time will raise our language to the utmost perfection; although I must confess, to avoid obscurity, I have been very sparing of this ornament in the following dialogues.

But, as for phrases invented to cultivate conversation, I defy all the clubs or coffeehouses in this town to invent a new one, equal in wit, humour, smartness, or politeness, to the very worst of my set, which clearly shews, either that we are much degenerated, or that the whole stock of materials has been already employed. I would willingly hope, as I do confidently believe, the latter; because, having myself for several months racked my invention to enrich this treasure (if possible) with some additions of my own, (which, however, should have been printed in a different character, that I might not be charged with imposing upon the public,) and having shewn them to some judicious friends, they dealt very sincerely with me, all unanimously agreeing that mine were infinitely below the true old helps to discourse drawn up in my present collection, and confirmed their opinion with reasons, by which I was perfectly convinced, as well as ashamed of my great presumption.

But I lately met a much stronger argument to confirm me in the same sentiments; for, as the great Bishop Burnet of Salisbury informs us, in the preface to his admirable History of his Own Times, that he intended to employ himself in polishing it every

POLITE CONVERSATION. 351

day of his life,* (and indeed in its kind it is almost equally polished with this work of mine,) so it has been my constant business, for some years past, to examine, with the utmost strictness, whether I could possibly find the smallest lapse in style or propriety through my whole collection, that, in emulation with the bishop, I might send it abroad as the most finished piece of the age.

It happened one day, as I was dining in good company of both sexes, and watching, according to my custom, for new materials wherewith to fill my pocket-book, I succeeded well enough till after dinner, when the ladies retired to their tea, and left us over a bottle of wine. But I found we were not able to furnish any more materials that were worth the pains of transcribing: for the discourse of the company was all degenerated into smart sayings of their own invention, and not of the true old standard; so that, in absolute despair, I withdrew, and went to attend the ladies at their tea; whence I did then conclude, and still continue to believe, either that wine does not inspire politeness, or that our sex is not able to support it without the company of women, who never fail to lead us into the right way, and there to keep us.

It much increases the value of these apophthegms, that unto them we owe the continuance of our language for at least a hundred years; neither is this to be wondered at, because indeed, beside the smartness of the wit, and fineness of the raillery, such is

---

* The passage hardly justifies this sarcasm. It runs thus:—
"I look on the perfecting of this work, and the carrying it on through the remaining part of my life, as the greatest service I can do to God, and to the world; and therefore I set about it with great care and caution." The proposed revision, therefore, does not apply to the style, as maliciously insinuated by Swift, but to the accuracy of the facts, and continuation of the history.

the propriety and energy of expression in them all, that they never can be changed, but to disadvantage, except in the circumstance of using abbreviations; which, however, I do not despair in due time to see introduced, having already met them at some of the choice companies in town.

Although this work be calculated for all persons of quality and fortune of both sexes, yet the reader may perceive, that my particular view was to the officers of the army, the gentlemen of the inns of court, and of both the universities; to all courtiers, male and female, but principally to the maids of honour; of whom I have been personally acquainted with two-and-twenty sets, all excelling in this noble endowment, till, for some years past, I know not how, they came to degenerate into selling of bargains* and free-thinking; not that I am against either of these entertainments, at proper seasons, in compliance with company who may want a taste for more exalted discourse, whose memories may be short, who are too young to be perfect in their lessons, or (although it be hard to conceive) who have no inclination to read and learn my instructions. And, besides, there is a strong temptation for court ladies to fall into the two amusements above mentioned, that they may avoid the censure of affecting singularity against the general current and fashion of all about them: but, however, no man will pretend to affirm that either bargains or blasphemy, which are the principal ornaments of free-thinking, are so good a fund of polite discourse, as what is to be met with in my collection. For, as to bargains, few of them seem to be excellent in their kind, and have not

---

* This ingenious piece of wit consisted in leading the purchaser of the bargain to ask some question; to which the answer given was the popular name of the most sedentary part of the seller's body.

much variety, because they all terminate in one single point; and to multiply them would require more invention than people have to spare. And as to blasphemy or freethinking, I have known some scrupulous persons of both sexes, who, by prejudiced education, are afraid of sprights. I must, however, except the maids of honour, who have been fully convinced, by a famous court chaplain that there is no such place as hell.*

I cannot, indeed, controvert the lawfulness of freethinking, because it has been universally allowed that thought is free. But, however, although it may afford a large field of matter, yet, in my poor opinion, it seems to contain very little of wit or humour; because it has not been ancient enough among us to furnish established authentic expressions, I mean such as must receive a sanction from the polite world, before their authority can be allowed; neither was the art of blasphemy or freethinking invented by the court, or by persons of great quality, who, properly speaking, were patrons rather than inventors of it; but first brought in by the fanatic faction toward the end of their power, and after the Restoration carried to Whitehall by the converted rumpers, with very good reason, because they knew that King Charles the Second, from a wrong education, occasioned by the troubles of his father, had time enough to observe, that fanatic enthusiasm directly led to atheism, which agreed with the dissolute inclinations of his youth; and perhaps these principles were further cultivated

---

* Though this reverend gentleman seems to have gone a step farther than Pope's dean,

"Who never mentions hell to ears polite,"

it seems probable that the same original was intended.

in him by the French Huguenots, who have been often charged with spreading them among us; however, I cannot see where the necessity lies of introducing new and foreign topics for conversation, while we have so plentiful a stock of our own growth.

I have likewise, for some reasons of equal weight, been very sparing in double *entendres;* because they often put ladies upon affected constraints and affected ignorance. In short, they break, or very much entangle, the thread of discourse; neither am I master of any rules to settle the disconcerted countenances of the females in such a juncture; I can therefore only allow innuendoes of this kind to be delivered in whispers, and only to young ladies under twenty, who being in honour obliged to blush, it may produce a new subject for discourse.

Perhaps the critics may accuse me of a defect in my following system of Polite Conversation; that there is one great ornament of discourse, whereof I have not produced a single example; which indeed I purposely omitted, for some reasons that I shall immediately offer; and, if those reasons will not satisfy the male part of my gentle readers, the defect may be applied in some manner by an appendix to the second edition; which appendix shall be printed by itself, and sold for sixpence, stitched, and with a marble cover, that my readers may have no occasion to complain of being defrauded.

The defect I mean is, my not having inserted into the body of my book all the oaths now most in fashion for embellishing discourse, especially since it could give no offence to the clergy, who are seldom or never admitted to these polite assemblies. And it must be allowed, that oaths well chosen are not only very useful expletives to matter, but great ornaments of style.

POLITE CONVERSATION. 355

What I shall here offer in my own defence upon this important article, will, I hope, be some extenuation of my fault.

First, I reasoned with myself, that a just collection of oaths, repeated as often as the fashion requires, must have enlarged this volume at least to double the bulk, whereby it would not only double the charge, but likewise make the volume less commodious for pocket carriage.

Secondly, I have been assured by some judicious friends, that themselves have known certain ladies to take offence (whether seriously or not) at too great a profusion of cursing and swearing, even when that kind of ornament was not improperly introduced, which, I confess, did startle me not a little, having never observed the like in the compass of my own several acquaintance, at least for twenty years past. However, I was forced to submit to wiser judgments than my own.

Thirdly, as this most useful treatise is calculated for all future times, I considered, in this maturity of my age, how great a variety of oaths I have heard since I began to study the world, and to know men and manners. And here I found it to be true, what I have read in an ancient poet:

> For, now-a-days, men change their oaths
> As often as they change their clothes.

In short, oaths are the children of fashion; they are in some sense almost annuals, like what I observed before of cant words; and I myself can remember about forty different sets. The old stock oaths, I am confident, do not amount to above forty-five, or fifty at most; but the way of mingling and compounding them is almost as various as that of the alphabet.

Sir JOHN PERROT was the first man of quality,

whom I find upon the record to have sworn by *God's wounds.** He lived in the reign of Queen Elizabeth, and was supposed to be a natural son of Henry the Eighth, who might also probably have been his instructor.† This oath indeed still con-

---

* Sir John Perrot was lord-deputy of Ireland, in the reign of Queen Elizabeth. On his return from that charge, he fell under the displeasure of the Queen, chiefly by the predominating influence of his enemy, Sir Christopher Hatton. Being a man of a violent and passionate temper, he had made use of some irreverent expressions towards the Queen, for which, an unconscientious jury found him guilty of high treason. The following are some of these explosions, garnished, as usual, by his favourite oath:

"Upon receiving her Majesty's letter to prefer Mr. Errington to the office of clerk of the Exchequer, Sir John Perrot used these undutiful speeches: 'This fiddling woman troubles me out of measure. God's wounds, he shall not have the office; I will give it to Sir Thomas Williams.' Further, he was accused, that, when his secretary was writing to the Queen, and used the dutiful expression, 'he would be sacrificed for her,' Sir John scratched it out, saying, 'he had little cause to be sacrificed for her.' Moreover, when, on the Spanish threat of invasion, his secretary said, 'he hoped God would bless them for her Majesty's sake,' he answered, 'God's wounds, and why for her sake?—never the more for her sake.' But the highest and most unpardonable of these irreverent expressions was used to one Garland, who brought to Perrot a letter from the Queen, at the terms of which this putative son of Henry VIII. conceived such displeasure as to exclaim, 'God's wounds, this it is to serve a base bastard, piss-kitchen woman; if I had served any prince in Christendom, I had not been so dealt withal.'"—SOMERS's *Tracts*, ed. 1809, vol. I. p. 269, note 1.

† Sir John Perrot's hasty and choleric temper confirms this tradition, which is mentioned by Naunton. "The Queen, on the news of his condemnation, swore by her wonted oath, that the jury were all knaves; and they delivered it with assurance, that, on his returne to the towne after his trial, he said, with oathes and with fury to the lieutenant, Sir Owen Hopton, 'What, will the Queene suffer her brother to be offered up a sacrifice to my skipping adversaries?' Which being made knowne to the Queene, and somewhat enforced, she refused to sign it, and swore he should not die, for he was an honest and faithfull man; and surely, though not altogether to set our rest and faith upon tradi-

tinues, and is a stock oath to this day; so do several others that have kept their natural simplicity; but infinitely the greater number has been so frequently changed and dislocated, that if the inventors were now alive, they could hardly understand them.

Upon these considerations, I began to apprehend, that if I should insert all the oaths that are now current, my book would be out of vogue with the first change of fashion, and grow as useless as an old dictionary; whereas the case is quite otherwise with my collection of polite discourse; which, as I before observed, has descended by tradition for at least a hundred years, without any change in the phraseology. I therefore determined with myself to leave out the whole system of swearing, because both the male and female oaths are all perfectly well known and distinguished; new ones are easily learned, and, with a moderate share of discretion, may be properly applied on every fit occasion. However, I must here, upon this article of swearing, most earnestly recommend to my male readers, that they would please a little to study variety. For it is the opinion of our most refined swearers, that the same oath or curse cannot, consistently with true politeness, be repeated above nine times in the same company, by the same person, and at one sitting.

I am far from desiring, or expecting, that all the polite and ingenious speeches contained in this work should, in the general conversation between ladies

---

tion and old reports, as that Sir Thomas Perrot, his father, was a gentleman of the privy chamber, and in the court married to a lady of great honour, which are presumptions in some implications; but, if we goe a little farther, and compare 'his pictures, his qualities, gesture and voyce, with that of the King, which memory retains yet amongst us, they will plead strongly that he was a surreptitious child of the blood royal."—NAUNTON's *Fragmenta Regalia*, apud SOMERS's *Tracts*, ed. 1809, vol. I. p. 269.

and gentlemen, come in so quick and so close as I have here delivered them. By no means: on the contrary, they ought to be husbanded better, and spread much thinner. Nor do I make the least question, but that, by a discreet and thrifty management, they may serve for the entertainment of a whole year to any person who does not make too long, or too frequent visits in the same family. The flowers of wit, fancy, wisdom, humour, and politeness, scattered in this volume, amount to one thousand seventy and four. Allowing then to every gentleman and lady thirty visiting families, (not insisting upon fractions,) there will want but a little of a hundred polite questions, answers, replies, rejoinders, repartees and remarks, to be daily delivered fresh in every company for twelve solar months; and even this is a higher pitch of delicacy than the world insists on, or has reason to expect. But I am altogether for exalting this science to its utmost perfection.

It may be objected, that the publication of my book may, in a long course of time, prostitute this noble art to mean and vulgar people; but I answer, that it is not so easy an acquirement as a few ignorant pretenders may imagine. A footman may swear, but he cannot swear like a lord. He can swear as often, but can he swear with equal delicacy, propriety, and judgment? No, certainly, unless he be a lad of superior parts, of good memory, a diligent observer, one who has a skilful ear, some knowledge in music, and an exact taste, which hardly fall to the share of one in a thousand among that fraternity, in as high favour as they now stand with their ladies. Neither has one footman in six so fine a genius as to relish and apply those exalted sentences comprised in this volume which I offer to the world. It is true, I cannot see that the same ill consequences would follow from the waiting-woman, who, if she had been bred to read romances, may have some small subaltern or second-hand politeness; and if she constantly attends the tea, and be a good listener, may, in some years, make a tolerable figure, which will serve, perhaps, to draw in the young chaplain or the old steward. But, alas! after all, how can she acquire those hundred graces, and motions, and airs, the whole military management of the fan, the contortions of every muscular motion in the face, the risings and fallings, the quickness and slowness of the voice, with the several turns and cadences; the proper juncture of smiling and frowning, how often and how loud to laugh, when to gibe and when to flout, with all the other branches of doctrine and discipline above recited?

I am, therefore, not under the least apprehension that this art will ever be in danger of falling into common hands, which requires so much time, study, practice, and genius, before it arrives at perfection; and, therefore, I must repeat my proposal for erecting public schools, provided with the best and ablest masters and mistresses, at the charge of the nation.

I have drawn this work into the form of a dialogue, after the pattern of other famous writers in history, law, politics, and most other arts and sciences; and I hope it will have the same success: for who can contest it to be of greater consequence to the happiness of these kingdoms, than all human knowledge put together? Dialogue is held the best method of inculcating any part of knowledge; and I am confident that public schools will soon be founded for teaching wit and politeness, after my scheme, to young people of quality and fortune. I have determined next sessions to deliver a petition to the House of Lords, for an Act of Parliament to establish my book as the standard grammar in all the principal cities of the kingdom, where this art is to be taught by able masters, who are to be approved and recommended by me ; which is no more than Lilly obtained only for teaching words in a language wholly useless. Neither shall I be so far wanting to myself, as not to desire a patent, granted, of course, to all useful projectors ; I mean, that I may have the sole profit of giving a licence to every school to read my grammar for fourteen years.

The reader cannot but observe what pains I have been at in polishing the style of my book to the greatest exactness; nor have I been less diligent in refining the orthography, by spelling the words in the very same manner as they are pronounced by the chief patterns of politeness at court, at levees, at assemblies, at playhouses, at the prime visiting-places, by young templars, and by gentlemen commoners of both universities, who have lived at least in town, and kept the best company. Of these spellings the public will meet with many examples in the following book. For instance, *can't, han't, shan't, didn't, cou'dn't, wou'dn't, isn't, en't*, with many more; besides several words which scholars pretend are derived from Greek and Latin, but now pared into a polite sound by ladies, officers of the army, courtiers and templars, such as *jommetry* for *geometry, vardi* for *verdict, lard* for *lord, learnen* for *learning*; together with some abbreviations exquisitely refined; as *pozz* for *positive; mob* for *mobile; phizz* for *physiognomy; rep* for *reputation; plenipo* for *plenipotentiary; incog* for *incognito; hypps,* or *hippo,* for *hypochondriacs; bam* for *bamboozle,* and *bamboozle* for *God knows what;* whereby much time is saved, and the high road to conversation cut short by many a mile.

I have, as it will be apparent, laboured very much, and, I hope, with felicity enough, to make every character in the dialogue agreeable with itself to a degree, that whenever any judicious person shall read my book aloud, for the entertainment and instruction of a select company, he need not so much as name the particular speakers, because all the persons, throughout the several subjects of conversation, strictly observe a different manner peculiar to their characters, which are of different kinds: but this I leave entirely to the prudent and impartial reader's discernment.*

Perhaps the very manner of introducing the several points of wit and humour may not be less entertaining and instructing than the matter itself. In the latter I can pretend to little merit; because it entirely depends upon memory, and the happiness of having kept polite company; but the art of contriving that those speeches should be introduced naturally, as the most proper sentiments to be delivered upon so great a variety of subjects, I take to be a talent somewhat uncommon, and a labour that few people could hope to succeed in, unless they had a genius, particularly turned that way, added to a sincere, disinterested love of the public.

Although every curious question, smart answer, and witty reply, be little known to many people, yet there is not one single sentence in the whole collection, for which I cannot bring most authentic vouchers, whenever I shall be called: and even for some ex-

---

* It is remarkable that this is the compliment paid by Pope to the characters of Shakespeare.

"Every single character in Shakespeare is as much an individual as those in life itself: it is as impossible to find any two alike; and such as, from their affinity in any respect, appear most to be twins, will, upon comparison, be found remarkably distinct. To this life and variety we must add the wonderful preservation of it, which is such throughout his plays, that, had all the speeches been printed without the very names of the persons, I believe one might have applied them with certainty to every speaker."—POPE's *Preface to Shakespeare.*

pressions, which, to a few nice ears, may, perhaps, appear somewhat gross, I can produce the stamp of authority from courts, chocolate-houses, theatres, assemblies, drawing-rooms, levees, card-meetings, balls, and masquerades, from persons of both sexes, and of the highest titles next to royal. However, to say the truth, I have been very sparing in my quotations of such sentiments as seem to be over free; because, when I began my collection, such kind of converse was almost in its infancy, till it was taken into the protection of my honoured patronesses at court, by whose countenance and sanction it has become a choice flower in the nosegay of wit and politeness.

Some will perhaps object, that, when I bring my company to dinner, I mention too great a variety of dishes, not always consistent with the art of cookery, or proper for the season of the year; and part of the first course mingled with the second; besides a failure in politeness, by introducing a black pudding to a lord's table, and at a great entertainment; but, if I had omitted the black pudding, I desire to know what would have become of that exquisite reason given by Miss Notable for not eating it? the world, perhaps, might have lost it for ever, and I should have been justly answerable for having left it out of my collection. I therefore cannot but hope, that such hypercritical readers will please to consider, my business was to make so full and complete a body of refined sayings as compact as I could, only taking care to produce them in the most natural and probable manner, in order to allure my readers into the very substance and marrow of this most admirable and necessary art.

I am heartily sorry, and was much disappointed to find, that so universal and polite an entertainment as cards, has hitherto contributed very little to the enlargement of my work. I have sat by many hundred times with the utmost vigilance, and my table-book ready, without being able, in eight hours, to gather matter for one single phrase in my book. But this, I think, may be easily accounted for, by the turbulence and justling of passions, upon the various and surprising turns, incidents, revolutions, and events of good and evil fortune, that arrive in the course of a long evening at play; the mind being wholly taken up, and the consequences of non-attention so fatal.

Play is supported upon the two great pillars of deliberation and action. The terms of art are few, prescribed by law and custom; no time allowed for digressions or trials of wit. Quadrille, in particular, bears some resemblance to a state of nature, which, we are told, is a state of war, wherein every woman is against every woman; the unions short, inconstant, and soon broke; the league made this minute without knowing the ally, and dissolved in the next. Thus, at the game of quadrille, female brains are always employed in stratagem, or their hands in action. Neither can I find that our art has gained much by the happy revival of masquerading among us; the whole dialogue in those meetings being summed up in one (sprightly, I confess, but) single question, and as sprightly an answer. "Do you know me?" "Yes, I do." And, "Do you know me?" "Yes, I do." For this reason I did not think it proper to give my readers the trouble of introducing a masquerade, merely for the sake of a single question and a single answer; especially when, to perform this in a proper manner, I must have brought in a hundred persons together of both sexes, dressed in fantastic habits, for one minute, and dismiss them the next.

Neither is it reasonable to conceive, that our science can be much improved by masquerades, where the wit of both sexes is altogether taken up in contriving singular and humorous disguises; and their thoughts entirely employed in bringing intrigues and assignations of gallantry to a happy conclusion.

The judicious reader will readily discover, that I make Miss Notable my heroine, and Mr. Thomas Neverout my hero. I have laboured both their characters with my utmost ability. It is into their mouths that I have put the liveliest questions, answers, repartees, and rejoinders, because my design was, to propose them both as patterns, for all young bachelors, and single ladies, to copy after. By which I hope very soon to see polite conversation flourish between both sexes, in a more consummate degree of perfection than these kingdoms have yet ever known.

I have drawn some lines of Sir John Linger's character, the Derbyshire knight, on purpose to place it in counterview or contrast with that of the other company, wherein I can assure the reader, that I intended not the least reflection upon Derbyshire, the place of my nativity. But my intention was only to shew the misfortune of those persons who have the disadvantage to be bred out of the circle of politeness, whereof I take the present limits to extend no farther than London, and ten miles round; although others are pleased to confine it within the bills of mortality. If you compare the discourses of my gentlemen and ladies, with those of Sir John, you will hardly conceive him to have been bred in the same climate, or under the same laws, language, religion, or government; and, accordingly, I have introduced him speaking in his own rude dialect, for no other reason than to teach my scholars how to avoid it.

The curious reader will observe, that, when conversation appears in danger to flag, which in some places I have artfully contrived, I took care to invent some sudden question, or turn of wit, to revive it; such as these that follow: "What! I think here's a silent meeting! Come, madam, a penny for your thought;" with several others of the like sort. I have rejected all provincial or country turns of wit and fancy, because I am acquainted with very few: but indeed chiefly, because I found them so much inferior to those at court, especially among the gentlemen-ushers, the ladies of the bed-chamber, and the maids of honour; I must also add the hither end of our noble metropolis.

When this happy art of polite conversing shall be thoroughly improved, good company will be no longer pestered with dull, dry, tedious story-tellers, nor brangling disputers: for a right scholar of either sex in our science, will perpetually interrupt them with some sudden surprising piece of wit, that shall engage all the company in a loud laugh; and if after a pause, the grave companion resumes his thread in the following manner: "Well, but to go on with my story," new interruptions come from the left and the right, till he is forced to give over.

I have likewise made some few essays toward the selling of bargains, as well for instructing those who delight in that accomplishment, as in compliance with my female friends at court. However, I have transgressed a little in this point, by doing it in a manner somewhat more reserved than is now practised at St. James's. At the same time, I can hardly allow this accomplishment to pass properly for a branch of that perfect polite conversation, which makes the constituent subject of my treatise; and for this I have already given my reasons. I have likewise, for further caution, left a blank in the critical point of each bargain, which the sagacious reader may fill up in his own mind.

As to myself, I am proud to own, that, except some smattering in the French, I am what the pedants and scholars call a man wholly illiterate, that is to say, unlearned. But as to my own language, I shall not readily yield to many persons. I have read most of the plays and all the miscellany poems that have been published for twenty years past. I have read Mr. Thomas Brown's* works entire, and had the honour to be his intimate friend, who was universally allowed to be the greatest genius of his age.

Upon what foot I stand with the present chief reigning wits, their verses recommendatory, which they have commanded me to prefix before my book, will be more than a thousand witnesses. I am, and have been, likewise particularly acquainted with Mr. Charles Gildon,† Mr. Ward,‡

---

* The facetious Tom Brown gave up, for the character of a London wag, the pretensions which he might really have set up to talent and learning. He led a dissolute and indigent life, in the course of which he often saw (as he expresses it) his last Carolus reduced from an *integer* to decimal fractions; and died about 1704.

† Gildon, a well-known hero of the Dunciad, was brought up at the Catholic seminary at Douay. It cost him, by his own account, seven years' close study to overcome the prejudices of this education; after which he emerged a wit, a dramatist, and a deist. He wrote three plays, which meeting with little attention, the corruption of a poet became in this, as in other cases, the generation of a critic. By Remarks upon Pope's Rape of the Lock, he drew down the vengeance of that irritable author. Posterity is, in some degree, obliged to Gildon for a continuation of Langbaine's Account of Dramatic Poets, in which, though not very accurate, he has preserved some literary anecdotes. He died 12th Jan. 1723.

‡ Edward Ward, a poetaster, who wrote doggrel verses upon the poetical occurrences of the day. He was a keen Tory, and, as he had some occasional glimmerings of humour, was not an altogether useless partizan. Jacob described him as keeping a public-house in the city, with which Ward was much affronted,

Mr. Dennis,* that admirable critic and poet, and several others. Each of these eminent persons (I mean those who are still alive) have done me the honour to read this production five times over, with the strictest eye of friendly severity, and proposed some, although very few amendments, which I gratefully accepted, and do here publicly return my acknowledgment for so singular a favour.

And I cannot conceal, without ingratitude, the great assistance I have received from those two illustrious writers, Mr. Ozell † and Captain Stevens.

---

and confuted him, by shewing that it was situated in Moorfields. He wrote, among other things, a blackguard work, called the London Spy, which contains some good pictures of low life, and of London manners, in the beginning of the eighteenth century.

* Poor Dennis ill deserved the unqualified severity with which he has been treated by Pope and Swift. "Let us remember," says Mr. Bowles, with just feeling, "what is due to disappointment. Dennis came into the world with ardent hopes as a man of literature, and with respectable connections. He found all his expectations crossed, though he was conscious of his acquirements; and after long and ineffectual struggles towards attaining what he considered his deserved rank of literary eminence, he sunk at last, poor and unfriended, into old age."—*Notes on* POPE's *Prologue to the Satires*, vol. IV. p. 28.

† John Ozell was educated for holy orders, but preferred a situation in a public office of accounts; a choice which, according to Cibber or Shiels, is sufficient to "denominate him a little tinctured with dulness." He was a good linguist, and made various translations, especially from the French, Italian, and Spanish, of which his Don Quixote is now alone remembered. Pope, in passing, galled him by a single allusion in the Dunciad, which produced the following extraordinary advertisement, published in the Weekly Medley, Sept. 1729: "As to my learning, this envious wretch knew, and everybody knows, that the whole bench of bishops, not long ago, were pleased to give me a purse of guineas for discovering the erroneous translations of the Common Prayer in Portuguese, Spanish, French, Italian, &c. As for my genius, let Mr. Cleland shew better verses in all Pope's works, than Ozell's Version of Boileau's Lutrin; which the late Lord Halifax was so pleased with, that he complimented him with leave

These, and some others of distinguished eminence, in whose company I have passed so many agreeable hours, as they have been the great refiners of our language, so it has been my chief ambition to imitate them. Let the Popes, the Gays, the Arbuthnots, the Youngs, and the rest of that snarling brood, burst with envy at the praises we receive from the court and kingdom.

But to return from this digression.

The reader will find that the following collection of polite expressions will easily incorporate with all subjects of genteel and fashionable life. Those which are proper for morning tea will be equally useful at the same entertainment in the afternoon, even in the same company, only by shifting the several questions, answers, and replies, into different hands; and such as are adapted to meals will indifferently serve for dinners, or suppers, only distinguishing between daylight and candle-light. By this method no diligent person of a tolerable memory can ever be at a loss.

It has been my constant opinion, that every man who is intrusted by nature with any useful talent of the mind, is bound by all the ties of honour, and that justice which we all owe our country, to propose to himself some one illustrious action to be

---

to dedicate it to him, &c. &c. Let him shew better and truer poetry in the Rape of the Lock than in Ozell's Rape of the Bucket, which because an ingenious author happened to mention in the same breath with Pope's, viz.,

'Let Ozell sing the Bucket, Pope the Lock,'

the little gentleman had like to have run mad: And Mr. Toland and Mr. Gildon publicly declared Ozell's Translation of Homer to be, as it was prior, so likewise superior, to Pope's.—Surely, surely, every man is free to deserve well of his country! JOHN OZELL."—CIBBER's *Lives of the Poets*, vol. IV. p. 355.

performed in his life, for the public emolument: and I freely confess, that so grand, so important an enterprise, as I have undertaken, and executed to the best of my power, well deserved a much abler hand, as well as a liberal encouragement from the crown. However, I am bound so far to acquit myself, as to declare, that I have often and most earnestly entreated several of my above-named friends, universally allowed to be of the first rank in wit and politeness, that they would undertake a work so honourable to themselves, and so beneficial to the kingdom; but so great was their modesty, that they all thought fit to excuse themselves, and impose the task on me; yet in so obliging a manner, and attended with such compliments on my poor qualifications, that I dare not repeat. And at last their entreaties, or rather their commands, added to that inviolable love I bear to the land of my nativity, prevailed upon me to engage in so bold an attempt.

I may venture to affirm, without the least violation of modesty, that there is no man now alive, who has, by many degrees, so just pretensions as myself to the highest encouragement from the crown, the parliament, and the ministry toward bringing this work to due perfection. I have been assured, that several great heroes of antiquity were worshipped as gods, upon the merit of having civilized a fierce and barbarous people. It is manifest I could have no other intentions; and I dare appeal to my very enemies, if such a treatise as mine had been published some years ago, and with as much success as I am confident this will meet, I mean, by turning the thoughts of the whole nobility and gentry to the study and practice of polite conversation, whether such mean stupid writers as the Craftsman, and his abettors, could have been able to corrupt the principles of so many hundred thousand subjects, as, to the shame and grief of every whiggish, loyal, and true protestant heart, it is too manifest they have done. For I desire the honest judicious reader to make one remark, that, after having exhausted the whole *in sickly pay-day** (if I may so call it) of politeness and refinement, and faithfully digested it into the following dialogues, there cannot be found one expression relating to politics; that the ministry is never mentioned, nor the word king, above twice or thrice, and then only to the honour of his majesty; so very cautious were our wiser ancestors in forming rules for conversation, as never to give offence to crowned heads, nor interfere with party-disputes in the state. And, indeed, although there seems to be a close resemblance between the two words politeness and politics, yet no ideas are more inconsistent in their natures. However, to avoid all appearance of disaffection, I have taken care to enforce loyalty by an invincible argument, drawn from the very fountain of this noble science, in the following short terms, that ought to be writ in gold,—" MUST is for the King:" which uncontrollable maxim I took particular care of introducing in the first page of my book, thereby to instil early the best Protestant loyal notions into the minds of my readers. Neither is it merely my own private opinion, that politeness is the firmest foundation upon which loyalty can be supported;† for thus happily sings the divine Mr.

---

* This word is spelt by Latinists *Encyclopædia;* but the judicious author wisely prefers the polite reading before the pedantic.
† The edition 1772 has this additional passage and note, levelled at Lord Harvey, the antagonist of Pope, and Stephen Duck, the favourite poet of Queen Caroline:—" For thus happily

Tibbalds,* or Theobalds, in one of his birth-day poems:

> I am no schollard, but I am polite;
> Therefore be sure I am no Jacobite.

Hear, likewise, to the same purpose, that great master of the whole poetic choir, our most illustrious laureat, Mr. Colley Cibber:

> Who in his talk can't speak a polite thing,
> Will never loyal be to George our King.

I could produce many more shining passages, out of our principal poets of both sexes, to confirm this momentous truth: Whence I think it may be fairly concluded, that whoever can most contribute towards propagating the science contained in the following sheets through the kingdoms of Great Britain and Ireland, may justly demand all the favour that the wisest court, and most judicious senate, are able to confer on the most deserving subject. I leave the application to my readers.

This is the work which I have been so hardy as to attempt, and without the least mercenary view. Neither do I doubt of succeeding to my full wish, except among the Tories and their abettors, who, being all Jacobites, and consequently Papists in their

---

sings the never-to-be-too-much-admired Lord H——,¹ in his truly sublime poem, called Loyalty Defined:

> Who's not polite, for the Pretender is;
> A Jacobite, I know him by his phiz."

* The well-known quarrel between Pope and Theobald, which began in their undertaking rival editions of Shakespeare, and ended in the latter being for a time exalted to the throne of the Dunciad, must be familiar to every reader.

¹ It is erroneously printed, in the London edition, Mr. Stephen Duck.

hearts, from a want of true taste, or by strong affectation, may perhaps resolve not to read my book, choosing rather to deny themselves the pleasure and honour of shining in polite company, among the principal geniuses of both sexes throughout the kingdom, than adorn their minds with this noble art; and probably apprehending, (as I confess nothing is more likely to happen,) that a true spirit of loyalty to the Protestant succession should steal in along with it.

If my favourable and gentle readers could possibly conceive the perpetual watchings, the numberless toils, the frequent risings in the night, to set down several ingenious sentences that I suddenly or accidentally recollected, and which, without my utmost vigilance, had been irrecoverably lost for ever; if they would consider with what incredible diligence I daily and nightly attended at those houses where persons of both sexes, and of the most distinguished merit, used to meet and display their talents; with what attention I listened to all their discourses, the better to retain them in my memory, and then, at proper seasons, withdrew, unobserved, to enter them in my table-book, while the company little suspected what a noble work I had then in embryo: I say, if all these were known to the world, I think it would be no great presumption in me to expect, at a proper juncture, the public thanks of both Houses of Parliament, for the service and honour I have done to the whole nation by my single pen.

Although I have never been once charged with the least tincture of vanity, the reader will, I hope, give me leave to put an easy question: What is become of all the King of Sweden's victories? where are the fruits of them at this day? or of what benefit will they be to posterity? Were not many of his greatest actions owing, at least in part, to fortune?

were not all of them owing to the valour of his troops, as much as to his own conduct? Could he have conquered the Polish King, or the Czar of Muscovy, with his single arm? Far be it from me to envy or lessen the fame he has acquired; but, at the same time, I will venture to say, without breach of modesty, that I, who have alone, with this right hand, subdued barbarism, rudeness, and rusticity, who have established and fixed for ever the whole system of all true politeness and refinement in conversation, should think myself most inhumanly treated by my countrymen, and would accordingly resent it as the highest indignity, to be put on a level, in point of fame, in after ages, with Charles the Twelfth, late King of Sweden.

And yet so incurable is the love of detraction, perhaps beyond what the charitable reader will easily believe, that I have been assured, by more than one credible person, how some of my enemies have industriously whispered about, that one Isaac Newton, an instrument-maker, formerly living near Leicester-Fields, and afterwards a workman in the Mint at the Tower, might possibly pretend to vie with me for fame in future times. The man, it seems, was knighted for making sun-dials better than others of his trade, and was thought to be a conjurer, because he knew how to draw lines and circles upon a slate, which nobody could understand. But adieu to all noble attempts for endless renown, if the ghost of an obscure mechanic shall be raised up to enter into competition with me, only for his skill in making pot-hooks and hangers with a pencil; which many thousand accomplished gentlemen and ladies can perform as well with pen and ink upon a piece of paper, and in a manner as little intelligible as those of Sir Isaac.

My most ingenious friend already mentioned, Mr,

Colley Cibber, who does so much honour to the laurel crown he deservedly wears, (as he has often done to many imperial diadems placed on his head,) was pleased to tell me, that, if my treatise was shaped into a comedy,* the representation, performed to advantage on our theatre, might very much contribute to the spreading of polite conversation among all persons of distinction through the whole kingdom.

I own the thought was ingenious, and my friend's intentions good: but I cannot agree to his proposal; for Mr. Cibber himself allowed that the subjects handled in my work being so numerous and extensive, it would be absolutely impossible for one, two, or even six comedies, to contain them: Whence it will follow, that many admirable and essential rules for polite conversation must be omitted.

And here let me do justice to my friend Mr. Tibbalds, who plainly confessed before Mr. Cibber himself, that such a project, as it would be a great diminution to my honour, so it would intolerably mangle my scheme, and thereby destroy the principal end at which I aimed, to form a complete body or system of this most useful science in all its parts: And therefore Mr. Tibbalds, whose judgment was never disputed, chose rather to fall in with my proposal, mentioned before, of erecting public schools and seminaries all over the kingdom, to instruct the young people of both sexes in this art, according to my rules, and in the method that I have laid down.

I shall conclude this long, but necessary introduction, with a request, or indeed, rather a just and

---

* The proposal here stated in jest actually took place; for Faulkner informs us, that the Treatise on Polite Conversation being universally admired at Dublin, was exhibited at the theatre in Angler-Street as a dramatic performance, and received great applause.

reasonable demand from all lords, ladies, and gentlemen, that while they are entertaining and improving each other with those polite questions, answers, repartees, replies, and rejoinders, which I have with infinite labour, and close application during the space of thirty-six years, been collecting for their service and inprovement, they shall, as an instance of gratitude, on every proper occasion, quote my name after this or the like manner: " Madam, as our Master Wagstaff says,"—" My lord, as our friend Wagstaff has it." I do likewise expect that all my pupils shall drink my health every day at dinner and supper during my life, and that they, or their posterity, shall continue the same ceremony to my not inglorious memory, after my decease, for ever.

A COMPLETE

COLLECTION

OF POLITE AND INGENIOUS

CONVERSATION.

IN SEVERAL DIALOGUES.

THE MEN.	THE LADIES.
Lord SPARKISH.	Lady SMART.
Lord SMART.	Miss NOTABLE.
Sir JOHN LINGER.	Lady ANSWERALL.
Mr. NEVEROUT.	
Colonel ATWIT.	

ARGUMENT.

LORD SPARKISH and Colonel ATWIT meet in the morning upon the Mall: Mr. NEVEROUT joins them: they all go to breakfast at Lady SMART'S. Their conversation over their tea: after which they part; but my lord and the two gentlemen are invited to dinner:—Sir JOHN LINGER invited likewise, and comes a little too late. The whole conversation at dinner: after which, the ladies retire to their tea. The conversation of the ladies without the men, who are supposed to stay and drink a bottle, but, in some time, go to the ladies, and drink tea with them. The conversation there. After which, a party at quadrille until three in the morning; but no conversation set down. They all take leave, and go home.

POLITE CONVERSATION, &c.

ST. JAMES'S PARK.

Lord SPARKISH *meeting Col.* ATWIT.

Col. Well met, my lord.
Ld. Sparkish. Thank ye, colonel. A parson would have said, I hope we shall meet in heaven. When did you see Tom Neverout?
Col. He's just coming toward us. Talk of the devil—

NEVEROUT *comes up.*

Col. How do you do, Tom?
Neverout. Never the better for you.
Col. I hope you are never the worse: but pray where's your manners? Don't you see my Lord Sparkish?
Neverout. My lord, I beg your lordship's pardon.
Ld. Sparkish. Tom, how is it that you can't see the wood for trees? What wind blew you hither?
Neverout. Why, my lord, it is an ill wind blows nobody good; for it gives me the honour of seeing your lordship.

Col. Tom, you must go with us to Lady Smart's to breakfast.

Neverout. Must! why, colonel, must's for the King.   [*Col. offering, in jest, to draw his sword.*

Col. Have you spoke with all your friends?

Neverout. Colonel, as you are stout be merciful.

Ld. Sparkish. Come, agree, agree; the law's costly.   [*Col. taking his hand from his hilt.*

Col. Well, Tom, you are never the worse man to be afraid of me. Come along.

Neverout. What! do you think I was born in a wood to be afraid of an owl?

I'll wait on you. I hope Miss Notable will be there; 'egad, she's very handsome, and has wit at will.

Col. Why, every one as they like, as the good woman said when she kiss'd her cow.

Lord SMART's *House: they knock at the door; the Porter comes out.*

Ld. Sparkish. Pray, are you the porter?

Porter. Yes, for want of a better.

Ld. Sparkish. Is your lady at home?

Porter. She was at home just now, but she's not gone out yet.

Neverout. I warrant this rogue's tongue is well hung.

Lady SMART's *Anti-chamber.*

Lady SMART *and Lady* ANSWERALL *at the Tea-table.*

Lady Smart. My lord, your lordship's most humble servant.

Ld. Sparkish. Madam, you spoke too late; I was your ladyship's before.

DIALOGUE I.

Lady Smart. O! colonel, are you here?

Col. As sure as you're there, madam.

Lady Smart. O, Mr. Neverout! What, such a man alive!

Neverout. Ay, madam, alive, and alive like to be, at your ladyship's service.

Lady Smart. Well, I'll get a knife, and nick it down, that Mr. Neverout came to our house. And pray, what news, Mr. Neverout?

Neverout. Why, madam, Queen Elizabeth's dead.

Lady Smart. Well, Mr. Neverout, I see you are no changeling.

Miss NOTABLE *comes in.*

Neverout. Miss, your slave: I hope your early rising will do you no harm. I find you are but just come out of the cloth market.

Miss. I always rise at eleven, whether it be day or not.

Col. Miss, I hope you are up for all day.

Miss. Yes, if I don't get a fall before night.

Col. Miss, I heard you were out of order; pray how are you now?

Miss. Pretty well, colonel, I thank you.

Col. Pretty and well, miss! that's two very good things.

Miss. I mean I am better than I was.

Neverout. Why, then, 'tis well you were sick.

Miss. What! Mr. Neverout, you take me up before I'm down.

Lady Smart. Come, let us leave off children's play; and go to push-pin.

Miss. [*To Lady Smart.*] Pray, madam, give me some more sugar to my tea.

Col. O! miss, you must needs be very good-humour'd, you love sweet things so well.

Neverout. Stir it up with the spoon, miss; for the deeper the sweeter.

Lady Smart. I assure you, miss, the colonel has made you a great compliment.

Miss. I am sorry for it; for I have heard say, complimenting is lying.

Lady Smart. [*To Lord Sparkish.*] My lord, methinks the sight of you is good for sore eyes; if we had known of your coming, we should have strewn rushes for you: How has your lordship done this long time?

Col. Faith, madam, he's better in health than in good conditions.

Ld. Sparkish. Well, I see there's no worse friend than one brings from home with one; and I am not the first man has carried a rod to whip himself.

Neverout. Here's poor miss has not a word to throw at a dog. Come, a penny for your thought.

Miss. It is not worth a farthing; for I was thinking of you.

Colonel rising up.

Lady Smart. Colonel, where are you going so soon? I hope you did not come to fetch fire.

Col. Madam, I must needs go home for half an hour.

Miss. Why, colonel, they say the devil's at home.

Lady Answ. Well, but sit while you stay, 'tis as cheap sitting as standing.

Col. No, madam, while I'm standing I'm going.

Miss. Nay, let him go; I promise him we won't tear his clothes to hold him.

Lady Smart. I suppose, colonel, we keep you from better company, I mean only as to myself.

Col. Madam, I am all obedience.

Colonel sits down.

Lady Smart. Lord, miss, how can you drink your tea so hot? sure your mouth's pav'd.

How do you like this tea, colonel?

Col. Well enough, madam; but methinks it is a little more-ish.

Lady Smart. O! colonel, I understand you.—Betty, bring the canister. I have but very little of this tea left; but I don't love to make two wants of one; want when I have it, and want when I have it not. He, he, he, he! [*Laughs.*

Lady Answ. [*To the maid.*] Why, sure, Betty, you are bewitched; the cream is burnt too.

Betty. Why, madam, the bishop has set his foot in it.

Lady Smart. Go, run, girl, and warm some fresh cream.

Betty. Indeed, madam, there's none left; for the cat has eaten it all.

Lady Smart. I doubt it was a cat with two legs.

Miss. Colonel, don't you love bread and butter with your tea?

Col. Yes, in a morning, miss; for they say, butter is gold in a morning, silver at noon, but it is lead at night.

Neverout. Miss, the weather is so hot, that my butter melts on my bread.

Lady Answ. Why, butter, I've heard 'em say, is mad twice a-year.

Ld. Sparkish. [*To the maid.*] Mrs. Betty, how does your body politic?

Col. Fie, my lord, you'll make Mrs. Betty blush.

Lady Smart. Blush! ay, blush like a blue dog.

Neverout. Pray, Mrs. Betty, are you not Tom Johnson's daughter?

Betty. So my mother tells me, sir.

Ld. Sparkish. But, Mrs. Betty, I hear you are in love.

Betty. My lord, I thank God, I hate nobody; I am in charity with all the world.

Lady Smart. Why, wench, I think thy tongue runs upon wheels this morning. How came you by that scratch upon your nose; have you been fighting with the cats?

Col. [*To Miss.*] Miss, when will you be married?

Miss. One of these odd-come-shortly's, colonel.

Neverout. Yes; they say the match is half made; the spark is willing, but miss is not.

Miss. I suppose the gentleman has got his own consent for it.

Lady Answ. Pray, my lord, did you walk through the Park in the rain?

Ld. Sparkish. Yes, madam, we were neither sugar nor salt; we were not afraid the rain would melt us. He, he, he! [*Laugh.*

Col. It rained, and the sun shone at the same time.

Neverout. Why, then the devil was beating his wife behind the door with a shoulder of mutton.
[*Laugh.*

Col. A blind man would be glad to see that.

Lady Smart. Mr. Neverout, methinks you stand in your own light.

Neverout. Ah! madam, I have done so all my life.

Ld. Sparkish. I'm sure he sits in mine. Pr'ythee, Tom, sit a little farther; I believe your father was no glazier.

Lady Smart. Miss, dear girl, fill me out a dish of tea, for I'm very lazy.

DIALOGUE I.

Miss fills a dish of tea, sweetens it, and then tastes it.

Lady Smart. What, miss, will you be my taster?

Miss. No, madam; but they say 'tis an ill cook that can't lick her own fingers.

Neverout. Pray, miss, fill me another.

Miss. Will you have it now, or stay till you get it?

Lady Answ. But, colonel, they say you went to court last night very drunk; nay, I'm told for certain, you had been among the Philistines: No wonder the cat wink'd, when both her eyes were out.

Col. Indeed, madam, that's a lie.

Lady Answ. 'Tis better I should lie than you should lose your good manners: besides, I don't lie; I sit.

Neverout. O! faith, colonel, you must own you had a drop in your eye; when I left you, you were half seas over.

Ld. Sparkish. Well, I fear Lady Answerall can't live long, she has so much wit.

Neverout. No; she can't live, that's certain; but she may linger thirty or forty years.

Miss. Live long! ay, longer than a cat or a dog, or a better thing.

Lady Answ. O! miss, you must give your vardi too!

Ld. Sparkish. Miss, shall I fill you another dish of tea?

Miss. Indeed, my lord, I have drank enough.

Ld. Sparkish. Come, it will do you more good than a month's fasting; here, take it.

Miss. No, I thank your lordship; enough's as good as a feast.

Ld. Sparkish. Well; but if you always say no, you'll never be married.

Lady Answ. Do, my lord, give her a dish; for, they say, maids will say no, and take it.

Ld. Sparkish. Well; and I dare say miss is a maid, in thought, word, and deed.

Neverout. I would not take my oath of that.

Miss. Pray, sir, speak for yourself.

Lady Smart. Fie, miss; they say maids should be seen and not heard.

Lady Answ. Good miss, stir the fire, that the tea-kettle may boil.—You have done it very well: now it burns purely. Well, miss, you'll have a cheerful husband.

Miss. Indeed, your ladyship could have stirred it much better.

Lady Answ. I know that very well, hussy; but I won't keep a dog and bark myself.

Neverout. What! you are stuck,[*] miss.

Miss. Not at all; for her ladyship meant you.

Neverout. O! faith, miss, you are in Lob's pound; get out as you can.

Miss. I won't quarrel with my bread and butter for all that; I know when I'm well.

Lady Answ. Well; but, miss—

Neverout. Ah! dear madam, let the matter fall; take pity on poor miss; don't throw water on a drowned rat.

Miss. Indeed, Mr. Neverout, you should be cut for the simples this morning; say a word more and you had as good eat your nails.

Ld. Sparkish. Pray, miss, will you be so good as to favour us with a song?

Miss. Indeed, my lord, I can't; for I have a great cold.

---

[*] Later editions—*sick*.

Col. O! miss, they say all good singers have colds.

Ld. Sparkish. Pray, madam, does not miss sing very well?

Lady Answ. She sings, as one may say, my lord.

Miss. I hear Mr. Neverout has a very good voice.

Col. Yes, Tom sings well, but his luck's nought.

Neverout. Faith, colonel, you hit yourself a devilish box on the ear.

Col. Miss, will you take a pinch of snuff?

Miss. No, colonel, you must know that I never take snuff but when I am angry.

Lady Answ. Yes, yes, she can take snuff, but she has never a box to put it in.

Miss. Pray, colonel, let me see that box.

Col. Madam, there's never a C upon it.

Miss. Maybe there is, colonel.

Col. Ay, but May bees don't fly now, miss.

Neverout. Colonel, why so hard upon poor miss? Don't set your wit against a child. Miss, give me a blow, and I'll beat him.

Miss. So she prayed me to tell you.

Ld. Sparkish. Pray, my Lady Smart, what kin are you to Lord Pozz?

Lady Smart. Why, his grandmother and mine had four elbows.

Lady Answ. Well, methinks here's a silent meeting. Come, miss, hold up your head, girl; there's money bid for you.   [*Miss starts.*

Miss. Lord, madam, you frighten me out of my seven senses!

Ld. Sparkish. Well, I must be going.

Lady Answ. I have seen hastier people than you stay all night.

Col. [*To Lady Smart.*] Tom Neverout and I are to leap to-morrow for a guinea.

Miss. I believe, Colonel, Mr. Neverout can leap at a crust better than you.

Neverout. Miss, your tongue runs before your wit: nothing can tame you but a husband.

Miss. Peace! I think I hear the church-clock.

Neverout. Why, you know, as the fool thinks—

Lady Smart. Mr. Neverout, your handkerchief's fallen.

Miss. Let him set his foot on it, that it mayn't fly in his face.

Neverout. Well, miss—

Miss. Ay, ay; many a one says well that thinks ill.

Neverout. Well, miss, I'll think on this.

Miss. That's rhyme, if you take it in time.

Neverout. What! I see you are a poet.

Miss. Yes, if I had but the wit to shew it.

Neverout. Miss, will you be so kind as to fill me a dish of tea?

Miss. Pray let your betters be served before you; I'm just going to fill one for myself; and, you know, the parson always christens his own child first.

Neverout. But I saw you fill one just now for the Colonel: Well, I find kissing goes by favour.

Miss. But pray, Mr. Neverout, what lady was that you were talking with in the side-box last Tuesday?

Neverout. Miss, can you keep a secret?

Miss. Yes, I can.

Neverout. Well, miss, and so can I.

Col. Odd-so! I have cut my thumb with this cursed knife!

Lady Answ. Ay; that was your mother's fault, because she only warned you not to cut your fingers.

Lady Smart. No, no; 'tis only fools cut their fingers, but wise folks cut their thumbs.

Miss. I'm sorry for it, but I can't cry.

Col. Don't you think miss is grown?

Lady Answ. Ay, ill weeds grow apace.

A puff of smoke comes down the chimney.

Lady Answ. Lord, madam, does your ladyship's chimney smoke?

Col. No, madam; but they say smoke always pursues the fair, and your ladyship sat nearest.*

Lady Smart. Madam, do you love bohea tea?

Lady Answ. Why, madam, I must confess I do love it, but it does not love me.

Miss. [*To Lady Smart.*] Indeed, madam, your ladyship is very sparing of your tea; I protest, the last I took was no more than water bewitch'd.

Col. Pray, miss, if I may be so bold, what lover gave you that fine etuy?

Miss. Don't you know?—then keep counsel.

Lady Answ. I'll tell you, Colonel, who gave it her: it was the best lover she will ever have while she lives—her own dear papa.

Neverout. Methinks, miss, I don't much like the colour of that riband.

Miss. Why, then, Mr. Neverout, do you see, if you don't much like it, you may look off it.

Ld. Sparkish. I don't doubt, madam, but your ladyship has heard that Sir John Brisk has got an employment at court.

---

* "That smoke doth follow the fairest, is an usual saying with us, and in many parts of Europe, whereof, although there seem no natural ground, yet is it the continuation of a very ancient opinion, as Petras Victorius and Casaubon have observed, from a passage in Athenæus, wherein a parasite thus describeth himself:—

> 'To every table first I come,
> Whence Porridge I am call'd by some:
> A Capaneus at stares I am,
> To enter any roome a ramme;
> Like whipps and thongs, to all I ply;
> Like smoke, unto the fair I fly.'"
>   BROWNE's *Vulgar Errours*, Lond. p. 226.

Lady Smart. Yes, yes; and I warrant he thinks himself no small fool now.

Neverout. Yes, madam; I have heard some people take him for a wise man.

Lady Smart. Ay, ay; some are wise, and some are otherwise.

Lady Answ. Do you know him, Mr. Neverout?

Neverout. Know him! ay, as well as the beggar knows his dish.

Col. Well, I can only say that he has better luck than honester folks. But, pray, how came he to get this employment?

Ld. Sparkish. Why, by chance, as the man killed the devil.

Neverout. Why, miss, you are in a brown study: what's the matter? Methinks you look like Mumchance, that was hanged for saying nothing.

Miss. I'd have you to know, I scorn your words.

Neverout. Well, but scornful dogs will eat dirty puddings.

Miss. Well, my comfort is, your tongue is no slander. What! you would not have one be always on the high grin?

Neverout. Cry mapsticks, madam; no offence, I

Lady SMART *breaks a tea-cup.*

Lady Answ. Lord, madam, how came you to break your cup?

Lady Smart. I can't help it, if I would cry my eyes out.

Miss. Why, sell it, madam, and buy a new one with some of the money.

Col. 'Tis a folly to cry for spilt milk.

Lady Smart. Why, if things did not break, or wear out, how would tradesmen live?

Miss. Well, I am very sick, if anybody cared for

it. [*She spits.*] I believe I shall die, for I can't spit from me.

Neverout. Come, then, miss, e'en make a die of it, and then we shall have a burying of our own.

Miss. The devil take you, Neverout! besides all | oath, small curses.

Lady Answ. Marry come up! What, plain Neverout! methinks you might have an M under your girdle, miss.

Lady Smart. Well, well, nought's never in danger. I warrant miss will spit in her hand, and hold fast. —Colonel, do you like this biscuit?

Col. I'm like all fools; I love everything that's good.

Lady Smart. Well, and isn't it pure good?

Col. 'Tis better than a worse.

Footman brings the Colonel a letter.

Lady Answ. I suppose, Colonel, that's a billet-doux from your mistress.

Col. 'Egad, I don't know whence it comes; but, whoe'er writ it, writes a hand like a foot.

Miss. Well, you may make a secret of it, but we can spell, and put together.

Neverout. Miss, what spells b double uzzard?

Miss. Buzzard, in your teeth, Mr. Neverout.

Lady Smart. Now you are up, Mr. Neverout, will you do me the favour to do me the kindness to take off the tea-kettle?

Ld. Sparkish. I wonder what makes these bells ring.

Lady Answ. Why, my lord, I suppose, because they pull the ropes. [*Here all laugh.*

NEVEROUT *plays with a tea-cup.*

Miss. Now, a child would have cried half an

hour, before it would have found out such a pretty plaything.

Lady Smart. Well said, miss! I vow, Mr. Neverout, the girl is too hard for you.

Neverout. Ay; miss will say anything but her prayers, and those she whistles.

Miss. Pray, Colonel, make me a present of that pretty pen-knife.

Ld. Sparkish. Ay, miss, catch him at that, and hang him.

Col. Not for the world, dear miss; it will cut love.

Ld. Sparkish. Colonel, you shall be married first; I was going to say that.

Lady Smart. Well, but, for all that, I can tell who is a great admirer of miss. Pray, miss, how do you like Mr. Spruce? I swear I have often seen him cast a sheep's eye out of a calf's head at you: deny it if you can.

Miss. O, madam, all the world knows that Mr. Spruce is a general lover.

Col. Come, miss, 'tis too true to make a jest on.

[*Miss blushes.*

Lady Answ. Well, however, blushing is some sign of grace.

Neverout. Miss says nothing; but I warrant she pays it off with thinking.

Miss. Well, ladies and gentlemen, you are pleased to divert yourselves; but, as I hope to be saved, there's nothing in it.

Lady Smart. Touch a gall'd horse, and he'll wince. Love will creep where it dare not go. I'd hold a hundred pound, Mr. Neverout was the inventor of that story; and, colonel, I doubt you had a finger in the pie.

Lady Answ. But, colonel, you forgot to salute miss when you came in; she said you had not been here a long time.

DIALOGUE I.

Miss. Fie, madam!—I vow, colonel, I said no such thing.—I wonder at your ladyship!

Col. Miss, I beg your pardon—

Goes to salute her; she struggles a little.

Miss. Well, I'd rather give a knave a kiss for once, than be troubled with him; but, upon my word, you are more bold than welcome.

Lady Smart. Fie, fie, miss! for shame of the world, and speech of good people.

NEVEROUT *to Miss, who is cooking her tea and bread and butter.*

Neverout. Come, come, miss, make much of naught; good folks are scarce.

Miss. What! and you must come in with your two eggs a penny, and three of them rotten.*

Col. [*To Ld. Sparkish.*] But, my lord, I forgot to ask you, how you like my new clothes?

Ld. Sparkish. Why, very well, colonel; only, to deal plainly with you, methinks the worst piece is in the middle. [*Here a loud laugh, often repeated.*

Col. My lord, you are too severe on your friends.

Miss. Mr. Neverout, I'm hot, are you a sot?

Neverout. Miss, I'm cold, are you a scold? Take you that.

Lady Smart. I confess that was home. I find, Mr. Neverout, you won't give your head for the washing, as they say.

Miss. O! he's a sore man where the skin's off. I see Mr. Neverout has a mind to sharpen the edge of his wit on the whetstone of my ignorance.

---

* This is a favourite proverb of Swift's, and occurs often in the Journal.

Ld. Sparkish. Faith, Tom, you are struck! I never heard a better thing.

Neverout. Pray, Miss, give me leave to scratch you for that fine speech.

Miss. Pox on your picture! it cost me a groat the drawing.

Neverout. [*To Lady Smart.*] 'Sbuds, madam, I have burnt my hand with your plaguy tea-kettle.

Lady Smart. Why, then, Mr. Neverout, you must say, God save the King.

Neverout. Did you ever see the like?

Miss. Never, but once at a wedding.

Col. Pray, Miss, how old are you?

Miss. Why I am as old as my tongue, and a little older than my teeth.

Ld. Sparkish. [*To Lady Answ.*] Pray, madam, is Miss Buxom married? I hear 'tis all over the town.

Lady Answ. My lord, she's either married, or worse.

Col. If she ben't married, at least she's lustily promised. But, is it certain that Sir John Blunderbuss is dead at last?

Ld. Sparkish. Yes, or else he's sadly wronged, for they have buried him.

Miss. Why, if he be dead, he'll eat no more bread.

Col. But, is he really dead?

Lady Answ. Yes, colonel, as sure as you're alive.

Col. They say he was an honest man.

Lady Answ. Yes, with good looking to.

Miss feels a pimple on her face.

Miss. Lord! I think my goodness is coming out. Madam, will your ladyship please to lend me a patch?

Neverout. Miss, if you are a maid, put your hand upon your spot.

Miss. There—
           [*Covering her face with both her hands.*
Lady Smart. Well, thou art a mad girl.
                              [*Gives her a tap.*
Miss. Lord, madam, is that a blow to give a child?

Lady SMART *lets fall her handkerchief, and the Colonel stoops for it.*

Lady Smart. Colonel, you shall have a better office.

Col. O, madam, I can't have a better than to serve your ladyship. Madam, has your ladyship read the new play, written by a lord? It is called Love in a Hollow Tree.*

Lady Smart. No, colonel.

Col. Why, then your ladyship has one pleasure to come.

Miss sighs.

Neverout. Pray, miss, why do you sigh?
Miss. To make a fool ask, and you are the first.

---

* Sir William Grimston, created Viscount Grimston in the year 1719, wrote, when a boy, the Lawyer's Fortune, or Love in a Hollow Tree, a comedy, to be acted by his school-fellows. It was printed in 1705; but, at a more mature age, his lordship, conscious of its want of merit, wished to suppress it, and would have succeeded, had not the Duchess of Marlborough, with whom he had a dispute relative to the borough of St. Albans, caused a new edition to be printed, with an elephant dancing on a rope as a vignette on the title-page. His lordship bought up this edition also; but her grace caused the play to be re-printed in Holland, and distributed the impression among the electors of St. Albans. He was chosen representative for this borough in 1713, 1714, and 1727, and died Oct. 15, 1756.

Neverout. Why, miss, I find there is nothing but a bit and a blow with you.

Lady Answ. Why, you must know, miss is in love.

Miss. I wish my head may never ache till that day.

Ld. Sparkish. Come, miss, never sigh, but send for him.

[*Lady* SMART *and Lady* ANSWERALL *speaking together.*

If he be hanged he'll come hopping; and if he be drowned he'll come dropping.*

Miss. Well, I swear you will make one die with laughing.

Miss plays with a tea-cup, and NEVEROUT *plays with another.*

Neverout. Well, I see one fool makes many.

Miss. And you are the greatest fool of any.

Neverout. Pray, miss, will you be so kind to tie this string for me, with your fair hands? it will go all in your day's work.

Miss. Marry, come up, indeed! tie it yourself, you have as many hands as I; your man's man will have a fine office truly: come, pray stand out of my spitting-place.

Neverout. Well, but, miss, don't be angry.

Miss. No; I was never angry in my life but once, and then nobody cared for it; so I resolved never to be angry again.

---

* The allusion is to the popular spell by which country girls attempted to conjure up the figure of their sweetheart, by sowing hemp-seed. The phantom appeared with the badges of his trade, and often with circumstances which indicated what death he should die.

Neverout. Well; but if you'll tie it, you shall never know what I'll do for you.

Miss. So I suppose, truly.

Neverout. Well; but I'll make you a fine present one of these days.

Miss. Ay; when the devil's blind, and his eyes are not sore yet.

Neverout. No, miss, I'll send it you to-morrow.

Miss. Well, well; to-morrow's a new day; but, I suppose, you mean to-morrow come never.

Neverout. O: 'tis the prettiest thing: I assure you, there came but two of them over in three ships.

Miss. Would I could see it, quoth blind Hugh. But why did you not bring me a present of snuff this morning?

Neverout. Because, miss, you never asked me: and 'tis an ill dog that's not worth whistling for.

Ld. Sparkish. [*To Lady Answ.*] Pray, madam, how came your ladyship, last Thursday, to go to that odious puppet-show?

Col. Why, to be sure, her ladyship went to see and to be seen.

Lady Answ. You have made a fine speech, colonel: pray, what will you take for your mouthpiece?

Ld. Sparkish. Take that, colonel: but, pray, madam, was my Lady Snuff* there? They say she's extremely handsome.

Lady Smart. They must not see with my eyes that think so.

Neverout. She may pass muster well enough.

Lady Answ. Pray, how old do you take her to be?

Col. Why, about five or six-and-twenty.

---

* Lady Dimple.—Ed. 1772.

Miss. I swear she's no chicken; she's on the wrong side of thirty, if she be a day.

Lady Answ. Depend upon it, she'll never see five-and-thirty, and a bit to spare.

Col. Why, they say she's one of the chief toasts in town.

Lady Smart. Ay, when all the rest are out of it.

Miss. Well; I wou'dn't be as sick as she's proud for all the world.

Lady Answ. She looks as if butter wou'dn't melt in her mouth; but, I warrant, cheese won't choke her.

Neverout. I here my lord What-d'ye-call-him is courting her.

Ld. Sparkish. What lord d'ye mean, Tom?

Miss. Why, my lord, I suppose Mr. Neverout means the lord of the Lord knows what.

Col. They saw she dances very fine.

Lady Answ. She did; but I doubt her dancing days are over.

Col. I can't pardon her for her rudeness to me.

Lady Smart. Well; but you must forget and forgive.

Footman comes in.

Lady Smart. Did you call Betty?
Footman. She's coming, madam.
Lady Smart. Coming! ay, so is Christmas.

BETTY *comes in.*

Lady Smart. Come, get ready my things. Where has the wench been these three hours?

Betty. Madam, I can't go faster than my legs will carry me.

Lady Smart. Ay, thou hast a head, and so has a pin. But, my lord, all the town has it that Miss

Caper is to be married to Sir Peter Gibeall; one thing is certain, that she has promised to have him.

Ld. Sparkish. Why, madam, you know promises are either broken or kept.

Lady Answ. I beg your pardon, my lord; promises and pie-crust are made to be broken.

Lady Smart. Nay, I had it from my Lady. Carrylie's own mouth. I tell you my tale and my tale's author; if it be a lie, you had it as cheap as I.

Lady Answ. She and I had some words last Sunday at church; but I think I gave her her own.

Lady Smart. Her tongue runs like the clapper of a mill; she talks enough for herself and all the company.

Neverout. And yet she simpers like a firmity kettle.

Miss looking in a glass.

Miss. Lord, how my head is drest to-day!
Col. O madam! a good face needs no band.
Miss. No; and a bad one deserves none.
Col. Pray, miss, where is your old acquaintance, Mrs. Wayward?
Miss. Why, where should she be? you must needs know, she's in her skin.
Col. I can answer that; what if you were as far out as she's in.
Miss. Well, I promised to go this evening to Hyde Park on the water: but I protest I'm half afraid.
Neverout. Never fear, miss; you have the old proverb on your side, Naught's ne'er in danger.
Col. Why, miss, let Tom Neverout wait on you, and then, I warrant, you'll be as safe as a thief in a mill; for you know, He that's born to be hang'd, will never be drown'd.

Neverout. Thank you, colonel, for your good word; but faith, if ever I hang, it shall be about a fair lady's neck.

Lady Smart. Who's there? Bid the children be quiet, and not laugh so loud.

Lady Answ. O! madam, let'm laugh, they'll ne'er laugh younger.

Neverout. Miss, I'll tell you a secret, if you'll promise never to tell it again.

Miss. No, to be sure: I'll tell it to nobody but friends and strangers.

Neverout. Why then, there's some dirt in my teacup.

Miss. Come, come, the more there's in't the more there's on't.

Lady Answ. Poh! you must eat a peck of dirt before you die.

Col. Ay, ay; it goes all one way.

Neverout. Pray, miss, what's a clock?

Miss. Why, you must know, 'tis a thing like a bell, and you a fool that can't tell.

Neverout. [*To Lady Answ.*] Pray, madam, do you tell me; for I have let my watch run down.

Lady Answ. Why, 'tis half an hour past hanging time.

Col. Well; I'm like the butcher that was looking for his knife, and had it in his mouth: I have been searching my pockets for my snuff-box, and, egad, here it is in my hand.

Miss. If it had been a bear, it would have bit you, colonel: well, I wish I had such a snuff-box.

Neverout. You'll be long enough before you wish your skin full of eyelet holes.

Col. Wish in one hand—

Miss. Out upon you: Lord, what can the man mean?

Ld. Sparkish. This tea is very hot.

Lady Answ. Why, it came from a hot place, my lord.

Colonel spills his tea.

Lady Smart. That's as well done as if I had done it myself.

Col. Madam, I find you live by ill neighbours, when you are forced to praise yourself.

Lady Smart. So they pray'd me to tell you.

Neverout. Well, I won't drink a drop more; if I do 'twill go down like chopt hay.

Miss. Pray, don't say no, till you are asked.

Neverout. Well, what you please, and the rest again.

Miss stooping for a pin.

Miss. I have heard 'em say, that a pin a day is a groat a-year. Well, as I hope to be married, forgive me for swearing, I vow 'tis a needle.

Col. O! the wonderful works of nature, that a black hen should lay a white egg!

Neverout. What! you have found a mare's nest, and laugh at the eggs?

Miss. Pray keep you breath to cool your porridge.

Neverout. Miss, there was a very pleasant accident last night at St. James's Park.

Miss. [*To Lady Smart.*] What was it your ladyship was going to say just now?

Neverout. Well, miss; tell a mare a tale—

Miss. I find you love to hear yourself talk.

Neverout. Why, if you won't hear my tale, kiss my, &c.

Miss. Out upon you, for a filthy creature!

Neverout. What, miss! must I tell you a story and find you ears?

Ld. Sparkish. [*To Lady Smart.*] Pray, madam, don't you think Mrs. Spendall very genteel?

Lady Smart. Why, my lord, I think she was cut

out for a gentlewoman, but she was spoil'd in the making: she wears her clothes as if they were thrown on her with a pitchfork; and, for the fashion, I believe they were made in the reign of Queen Bess.

Neverout. Well, that's neither here nor there; for, you know, the more careless the more modish.

Col. Well, I'd hold a wager there will be a match between her and Dick Dolt: and I believe I can see as far into a millstone as another man.

Miss. Colonel, I must beg your pardon a thousand times; but they say an old ape has an old eye.

Neverout. Miss, what do you mean? you'll spoil the colonel's marriage, if you call him old.

Col. Not so old nor yet so cold—You know the rest, miss.

Miss. Manners is a fine thing, truly.

Col. Faith, miss, depend upon't, I'll give you as good as you bring: what! if you give a jest you must take a jest.

Lady Smart. Well, Mr. Neverout, you'll ne'er have done till you break that knife, and then the man won't take it again.

Miss. Why, madam, fools will be meddling; I wish he may cut his fingers. I hope you can see your own blood without fainting.

Neverout. Why, miss, you shine this morning like a sh—n barn door: you'll never hold out at this rate; pray save a little wit for to-morrow.

Miss. Well, you have said your say; if people will be rude, I have done; my comfort is, 'twill be all one a thousand years hence.

Neverout. Miss, you have shot your bolt: I find you must have the last word—Well, I'll go to the opera to-night.—No, I can't, neither, for I have some business,—and yet I think I must, for I promised to squire the countess to her box.

Miss. The Countess of Puddledock, I suppose.

Neverout. Peace or war, miss?

Lady Smart. Well, Mr. Neverout, you'll never be mad, you are of so many minds.

As Miss rises, the chair falls behind her.

Miss. Well; I shan't be lady mayoress this year.

Neverout. No, miss, 'tis worse than that; you won't be married this year.

Miss. Lord! you make me laugh, though I an't well.

NEVEROUT, *as Miss is standing, pulls her suddenly on his lap.*

Neverout. Now, colonel, come sit down on my lap; more sacks upon the mill.

Miss. Let me go; ar'n't you sorry for my heaviness?

Neverout. No, miss; you are very light; but I don't say you are a light hussy. Pray take up the chair for your pains.

Miss. 'Tis but one body's labour, you may do it yourself; I wish you would be quiet, you have more tricks than a dancing bear.

NEVEROUT *rises to take up the chair, and Miss sits in his.*

Neverout. You wou'dn't be so soon in my grave, madam.

Miss. Lord! I have torn my petticoat with your odious romping; my rents are coming in; I'm afraid I shall fall into the ragman's hands.

Neverout. I'll mend it, miss.

Miss. You mend it! go, teach your grannam to suck eggs.

Neverout. Why, miss, you are so cross, I could find in my heart to hate you.

Miss. With all my heart; there will be no love lost between us.

Neverout. But pray, my Lady Smart, does not miss look as if she could eat me without salt?

Miss. I'll make you one day sup sorrow for this.

Neverout. Well, follow your own way, you'll live the longer.

Miss. See, madam, how well I have mended it.

Lady Smart. 'Tis indifferent, as Doll danced.

Neverout. 'Twill last as many nights as days.

Miss. Well, I knew it should never have your good word.

Lady Smart. My lord, my Lady Answerall and I was walking in the Park last night till near eleven; 'twas a very fine night.

Neverout. Egad, so was I; and I'll tell you a comical accident; egad, I lost my understanding.

Miss. I'm glad you had any to lose.

Lady Smart. Well, but what do you mean?

Neverout. Egad, I kick'd my foot against a stone, and tore off the heel of my shoe, and was forced to limp to a cobbler in the Pall-mall to have it put on. He, he, he, he. [*All laugh.*

Col. O! 'twas a delicate night to run away with another man's wife.

NEVEROUT *sneezes.*

Miss. God bless you! if you han't taken snuff.

Neverout. Why, what if I have, miss?

Miss. Why then, the deuce take you!

Neverout. Miss, I want that diamond ring of yours.

Miss. Why then, want's like to be your master.

NEVEROUT *looking at the ring.*

Neverout. Ay, marry, this is not only, but also; where did you get it?

Miss. Why, where 'twas to be had; where the devil got the friar.

Neverout. Well; if I had such a fine diamond ring, I wou'dn't stay a day in England: but you know, far fetch'd and dear bought is fit for ladies. I warrant, this cost your father two-pence halfpenny.

Miss sitting between NEVEROUT *and the Colonel.*

Miss. Well, here's a rose between two nettles.

Neverout. No, madam, with submission, there's a nettle between two roses.*

Colonel stretching himself.

Lady Smart. Why, colonel, you break the king's laws; you stretch without a halter.

Lady Answ. Colonel, some ladies of your acquaintance have promised to breakfast with you, and I am to wait on them; what will you give us?

Col. Why, faith, madam, bachelors' fare; bread and cheese and kisses.

Lady Answ. Poh! what have you bachelors to do with your money, but to treat the ladies? you have nothing to keep but your own four quarters.

Lady Smart. My lord, has Captain Brag the honour to be related to your lordship?

Ld. Sparkish. Very nearly, madam; he's my cousin-german, quite removed.

Lady Answ. Pray, is he not rich?

---

* These two speeches are restored from the first edition.

Ld. Sparkish. Ay, a rich rogue, two shirts and a rag.

Col. Well, however, they say he has a great estate, but only the right owner keeps him out of it.

Lady Smart. What religion is he of?

Ld. Sparkish. Why, he is an Anythingarian.

Lady Answ. I believe he has his religion to choose, my lord.

NEVEROUT *scratches his head.*

Miss. Fie, Mr. Neverout, ar'n't you ashamed! I beg pardon for the expression, but I'm afraid your bosom friends are become your backbiters.

Neverout. Well, miss, I saw a flea once in your pinner, and a louse is a man's companion, but a flea is a dog's companion :* however, I wish you would scratch my neck with your pretty white hand.

Miss. And who would be fool, then? I wou'dn't touch a man's flesh for the universe. You have the wrong sow by the ear, I assure you; that's meat for your master.

Neverout. Miss Notable, all quarrels laid aside, pray step hither for a moment.

Miss. I'll wash my hands, and wait on you, sir; but pray come hither, and try to open this lock.

Neverout. We'll try what we can do.

Miss. We!——what, have you pigs in your belly?

Neverout. Miss, I assure you, I am very handy at all things.

---

* This was a speech of Louis XI. An attendant had detected, on the royal robe, one of the "beasts familiar to man," and the King ordered him a reward. A courtier, in hopes to be a like gainer, affected the next day to find a flea in the same place. The King, aware of his roguery, made the distinction in the text, and ordered him a drubbing for his officiousness. Erasmus tells the anecdote in his *Convivium Fabulosum.*

Miss. Marry, hang them that can't give themselves a good word: I believe you may have an even hand to throw a louse in the fire.

Col. Well, I must be plain; here's a very bad smell.

Miss. Perhaps, colonel, the fox is the finder.

Neverout. No, colonel; 'tis only your teeth against rain: but——

Miss. Colonel, I find you would make a very bad poor man's sow.

Colonel coughing.

Col. I have got a sad cold.

Lady Answ. Ay; 'tis well if one can get anything these hard times.

Miss. [*To Col.*] Choke, chicken, there's more a-hatching.

Lady Smart. Pray, colonel, how did you get that cold?

Ld. Sparkish. Why, madam, I suppose the colonel got it by lying abed barefoot.

Lady Answ. Why then, colonel, you must take it for better for worse, as a man takes his wife.

Col. Well, ladies, I apprehend you without a constable.

Miss. Mr. Neverout! Mr. Neverout! come hither this moment.

Lady Smart. [*Imitating her.*] Mr. Neverout! Mr. Neverout! I wish he were tied to your girdle.

Neverout. What's the matter? whose mare's dead now?

Miss. Take your labour for your pains; you may go back again, like a fool, as you came.

Neverout. Well, miss, if you deceive me a second time, 'tis my fault.

Lady Smart. Colonel, methinks your coat is too short.

Col. It will be long enough before I get another, madam.

Miss. Come, come; the coat's a good coat, and come of good friends.

Neverout. Ladies, you are mistaken in the stuff; 'tis half silk.

Col. Tom Neverout, you are a fool, and that's your fault.

A great noise below.

Lady Smart. Hey, what a clattering is here! one would think hell was broke loose.

Miss. Indeed, madam, I must take my leave, for I a'n't well.

Lady Smart. What! you are sick of the mulligrubs with eating chopt hay?

Miss. No, indeed, madam; I'm sick and hungry, more need of a cook than a doctor.

Lady Answ. Poor miss! she's sick as a cushion; she wants nothing but stuffing.

Col. If you are sick, you shall have a caudle of calf's eggs.

Neverout. I can't find my gloves.

Miss. I saw the dog running away with some dirty thing a while ago.

Col. Miss, you have got my handkerchief; pray, let me have it.

Lady Smart. No; keep it, miss; for they say, possession is eleven points of the law.

Miss. Madam, he shall never have it again; 'tis in hucksters' hands.

Lady Answ. What! I see 'tis raining again.

Ld. Sparkish. Why, then, madam, we must do as they do in Spain.

Miss. Pray, my lord, how is that?

Ld. Sparkish. Why, madam, we must let it rain.

Miss whispers Lady SMART.

Neverout. There's no whispering, but there's lying.

Miss. Lord! Mr. Neverout, you are as pert as a pearmonger this morning.

Neverout. Indeed, miss, you are very handsome.

Miss. Poh! I know that already; tell me news.

Somebody knocks at the door.

Footman comes in.

Footman. [*To Col.*] An please your honour, there's a man below wants to speak to you.

Col. Ladies, your pardon for a minute. [*Goes out.*

Lady Smart. Miss, I sent yesterday to know how you did, but you were gone abroad early.

Miss. Why, indeed, madam, I was hunch'd up in a hackney-coach with three country acquaintance, who called upon me to take the air as far as Highgate.

Lady Smart. And had you a pleasant airing?

Miss. No, madam; it rained all the time; I was jolted to death; and the road was so bad, that I scream'd every moment, and called to the coachman, Pray, friend, don't spill us.

Neverout. So, miss, you were afraid that pride would have a fall.

Miss. Mr. Neverout, when I want a fool, I'll send for you.

Ld. Sparkish. Miss, didn't your left ear burn last night?*

---

* "When our cheek burneth, or ear tingleth, we usually say that somebody is talking of us; which is an ancient conceit, and ranked among superstitious opinions by Pliny. *Absentes tinnitu*

Miss. Pray why, my lord?

Ld. Sparkish. Because I was then in some company where you were extoll'd to the skies, I assure you.

Miss. My lord, that was more their goodness than my desert.

Ld. Sparkish. They said, that you were a complete beauty.

Miss. My lord, I am as God made me.

Lady Smart. The girl's well enough, if she had but another nose.

Miss. O! madam, I know I shall always have your good word; you love to help a lame dog over the stile.

One knocks.

Lady Smart. Who's there? you're on the wrong side of the door; come in, if you be fat.

Colonel comes in again.

Ld. Sparkish. Why, colonel, you are a man of great business.

Col. Ay, ay, my lord, I'm like my lord mayor's fool, full of business, and nothing to do.

Lady Smart. My lord, don't you think the colonel's mightily fall'n away of late?

---

aurium præsentire sermones de se, receptum est, according to that distich noted by Dalecampius:

> *Garrula quid totis resonas mihi noctibus auris?*
> *Nescio quem dicis nunc meminisse mei.*

Which is a conceit hardly to be made out without the concession of a signifying genius or universal Mercury; conducting sounds unto their distant subjects, and teaching us to hear by touch."— BROWNE'S *Vulgar Errours,* p. 225.

Ld. Sparkish. Ay, fall'n from a horseload to a cartload.

Col. Why, my lord, egad I am like a rabbit, fat and lean in four and twenty hours.

Lady Smart. I assure you, the colonel walks as straight as a pin.

Miss. Yes; he's a handsome-bodied man in the face.

Neverout. A handsome foot and leg; god-a-mercy shoe and stocking!

Col. What! three upon one! that's foul play: this would make a parson swear.

Neverout. Why, miss, what's the matter? you look as if you had neither won nor lost.

Col. Why, you must know, miss lives upon love.

Miss. Yes, upon love and lumps of the cupboard.

Lady Answ. Ay; they say love and pease porridge are two dangerous things; one breaks the heart; and the other the belly.

Miss. [*Imitating Lady Answerall's tone.*] Very pretty! one breaks the heart, and the other the belly.

Lady Answ. Have a care; they say, mocking is catching.

Miss. I never heard that.

Neverout. Why, then, miss, you have a wrinkle ——more than ever you had before.

Miss. Well; live and learn.

Neverout. Ay; and be hang'd and forget all.

Miss. Well, Mr. Neverout, take it as you please; but, I swear, you are a saucy Jack, to use such expressions.

Neverout. Why, then, miss, if you go to that, I must tell you there's ne'er a Jack but there's a Gill.

Miss. O! Mr. Neverout, everybody knows that you are the pink of courtesy.

Neverout. And, miss, all the world allows that you are the flower of civility.

Lady Smart. Miss, I hear there was a great deal of company where you visited last night: pray, who were they?

Miss. Why, there was old Lady Forward, Miss To-and-again, Sir John Ogle, my Lady Clapper, and I, quoth the dog.

Col. Was your visit long, miss?

Miss. Why, truly, they went all to the opera; and so poor pilgarlic came home alone.

Neverout. Alackaday, poor miss! methinks it grieves me to pity you.

Miss. What! you think you said a fine thing now; well, if I had a dog with no more wit, I would hang him.

Ld. Sparkish. Miss, if it is manners, may I ask which is oldest, you or Lady Scuttle?

Miss. Why, my lord, when I die for age, she may quake for fear.

Lady Smart. She's a very great gadder abroad.

Lady Answ. Lord! she made me follow her last week through all the shops like a Tantiny pig.*

Lady Smart. I remember, you told me, you had been with her from Dan to Beersheba.

Colonel spits.

Col. Lord! I shall die; I cannot spit from me.

Miss. O! Mr. Neverout, my little Countess has just litter'd; speak me fair, and I'll set you down for a puppy.

---

* St. Anthony, having been originally a swineherd, was always painted with a pig following him. Hence, as St. Anthony was never seen without his pig, "To follow like a Tantiny pig," became a common saying, to express a person constantly attending at the heels of another.—H.

Neverout. Why, miss, if I speak you fair, perhaps I mayn't tell truth.

Ld. Sparkish. Ay, but, Tom, smoke that, she calls you puppy by craft.

Neverout. Well, miss, you ride the fore-horse to-day.

Miss. Ay, many a one says well, that thinks ill.

Neverout. Fie, miss; you said that once before; and, you know, too much of one thing is good for nothing.

Miss. Why, sure we can't say a good thing too often.

Ld. Sparkish. Well, so much for that, and butter for fish; let us call another cause. Pray, madam, does your ladyship know Mrs. Nice?

Lady Smart. Perfectly well, my lord; she's nice by name, and nice by nature.

Ld. Sparkish. Is it possible she could take that booby, Tom Blunder, for love?

Miss. She had good skill in horse flesh, that could choose a goose to ride on.

Lady Answ. Why, my lord, 'twas her fate; they say, marriage and hanging go by destiny.

Col. I believe she'll ne'er be burnt for a witch.

Ld. Sparkish. They say, marriages are made in Heaven; but I doubt, when she was married, she had no friend there.

Neverout. Well, she's got out of God's blessing into the warm sun.

Col. The fellow's well enough, if he had any guts in his brains.

Lady Smart. They say thereby hangs a tale.

Ld. Sparkish. Why, he is a mere hobbledehoy, neither a man nor a boy.

Miss. Well, if I were to choose a husband, I would never be married to a little man.

Neverout. Pray, why so, miss? for they say, of all evils we ought to choose the least.

Miss. Because folks would say, when they saw us together, There goes the woman and her husband.

Col. [*To Lady Smart.*] Will your ladyship be on the Mall to-morrow night?

Lady Smart. No, that won't be proper; you know to-morrow's Sunday.

Ld. Sparkish. What then, madam! they say, the better day, the better deed.

Lady Answ. Pray, Mr. Neverout, how do you like Lady Fruzz?

Neverout. Pox on her! She is as old as Poles.*

Miss. So will you be, if you ben't hanged when you're young.

Neverout. Come, miss, let us be friends: will you go to the Park this evening?

Miss. With all my heart, and a piece of my liver; but not with you.

Lady Smart. I'll tell you one thing, and that's not two; I am afraid I shall get a fit of the headach to-day.

Col. O! madam, don't be afraid; it comes with a fright.

Miss. [*To Lady Answerall.*] Madam, one of your ladyship's lappets is longer than t'other.

Lady Answ. Well, no matter; they that ride on a trotting horse, will ne'er perceive it.

Neverout. Indeed, miss, your lappets hang worse.

Miss. Well, I love a liar in my heart, and you fit me to a hair.

Miss rises up.

Neverout. Deuce take you, miss: you trod on my foot: I hope you don't intend to come to my bed-side.

---

* For St. Paul's Church.—H.

Miss. In troth, you are afraid of your friends, and none of them near you.

Ld. Sparkish. Well said, girl! [*Giving her a chuck.*] Take that: they say a chuck under the chin is worth two kisses.

Lady Answ. But, Mr. Neverout, I wonder why such a handsome, straight, young gentleman as you, don't get some rich widow.

Ld. Sparkish. Straight! ay, straight as my leg, and that's crooked at knee.

Neverout. Faith, madam, if it rained such widows, none of them would fall upon me. Egad, I was born under a three-penny planet, never to be worth a groat.

Lady Answ. No, Mr. Neverout; I believe you were born with a caul on your head, you are such a favourite among the ladies: but what think you of widow Prim? she's immensely rich.

Neverout. Hang her! they say her father was a baker.

Lady Smart. Ay; but it is not, What is she? but, What has she? now-a-days.

Col. Tom, faith, put on a bold face for once, and have at the widow. I'll speak a good word for you to her.

Lady Answ. Ay; I warrant you'll speak one word for him, and two for yourself.

Miss. Well, I had that at my tongue's end.

Lady Answ. Why, miss, they say good wits jump.

Neverout. Faith, madam, I had rather marry a woman I loved in her smock, than widow Prim, if she had her weight in gold.

Lady Smart. Come, come, Mr. Neverout, marriage is honourable, but housekeeping is a shrew.

Lady Answ. Consider, Mr. Neverout, four bare legs in a bed; and you are a younger brother.

Col. Well, madam, the younger brother is the

better gentleman : however, Tom, I would advise you to look before you leap.

Ld. Sparkish. The colonel says true ; besides, you can't expect to wive and thrive in the same year.

Miss. [*Shuddering.*] Lord ! there's somebody walking over my grave.

Col. Pray, Lady Answerall, where was you last Wednesday, when I did myself the honour to wait on you ? I think your ladyship is one of the tribe of Gad.

Lady Answ. Why, colonel, I was at church.

Col. Nay, then, I will be hang'd, and my horse too.

Neverout. I believe her ladyship was at a church with a chimney in it.

Miss. Lord, my petticoat! how it hangs by jommetry !

Neverout. Perhaps the fault may be in your shape.

Miss. [*Looking gravely.*] Come, Mr. Neverout, there's no jest like the true jest ; but I suppose you think my back is broad enough to bear everything.

Neverout. Madam, I humbly beg your pardon.

Miss. Well, sir, your pardon's granted.

Neverout. Well, all things have an end, and a pudding has two, up-up-on me-my-my word.

[*Stutters.*

Miss. What! Mr. Neverout, can't you speak without a spoon ?

Ld. Sparkish. [*To Lady Smart.*] Has your ladyship seen the duchess since your falling out ?

Lady Smart. Never, my lord, but once at a visit, and she looked at me as the devil looked over Lincoln.[*]

---

[*] "Some refer this to Lincoln-minster, over which, when first finished, the devil is supposed to have looked with a fierce and terrific countenance, as incensed and alarmed at this costly in-

Neverout. Pray, miss, take a pinch of my snuff.

Miss. What! you break my head, and give me a plaster; well, with all my heart; once, and not use it.

Neverout. Well, miss, if you wanted me and your victuals, you'd want your two best friends.

Col. [*To Neverout.*] Tom, miss and you must kiss and be friends.

Neverout salutes Miss.

Miss. Anything for a quiet life: my nose itch'd, and I knew I should drink wine, or kiss a fool.

Col. Well, Tom, if that ben't fair, hang fair.

Neverout. I never said a rude thing to a lady in my life.

Miss. Here's a pin for that lie; I'm sure liars had need of good memories. Pray, colonel, was not he very uncivil to me but just now?

Lady Answ. Mr. Neverout, if miss will be angry for nothing, take my counsel, and bid her turn the buckle of her girdle behind her.

Neverout. Come, Lady Answerall, I know better things: miss and I are good friends; don't put tricks upon travellers.

Col. Tom, not a word of the pudding, I beg you.

Lady Smart. Ah, colonel! you'll never be good, nor then neither.

Ld. Sparkish. Which of the goods d'ye mean? good for something, or good for nothing?

Miss. I have a blister on my tongue, yet I don't remember I told a lie.

---

stance of devotion. Ray thinks it more probable that it took its rise from a small image of the devil, placed on the top of Lincoln College, Oxford, over which he looks, seemingly with much fury."
—GROSE'S *Provincial Glossary, with a Collection of Local Proverbs*, Lond. 1787–8.

Lady Answ. I thought you did just now.

Ld. Sparkish. Pray, madam, what did thought do?

Lady Smart. Well, for my life, I cannot conceive what your lordship means.

Ld. Sparkish. Indeed, madam, I meant no harm.

Lady Smart. No, to be sure, my lord! you are as innocent as a devil of two years old.

Neverout. Madam, they say ill-doers are ill-deemers; but I don't apply it to your ladyship.

Miss, mending a hole in her lace.

Miss. Well, you see I'm mending; I hope I shall be good in time. Look, Lady Answerall, is it not well mended?

Lady Answ. Ay, this is something like a tansy.

Neverout. Faith, miss, you have mended as a tinker mends a kettle; stop one hole and make two.

Lady Smart. Pray, colonel, are you not very much tann'd?

Col. Yes, madam; but a cup of Christmas ale will soon wash it off.

Ld. Sparkish. Lady Smart, does not your ladyship think Mrs. Fade is greatly altered since her marriage?

Lady Answ. Why, my lord, she was handsome in her time; but she cannot eat her cake and have her cake; I hear she's grown a mere otomy.

Lady Smart. Poor creature! the black ox has set his foot upon her already.

Miss. Ay; she has quite lost the blue on the plum.

Lady Smart. And yet, they say, her husband is very fond of her still.

Lady Answ. O, madam, if she would eat gold, he would give it her.

Neverout. [*To Lady Smart.*] * Madam, have you heard that Lady Queasy was lately at the play-house incog.?

Lady Smart. What! Lady Queasy of all women in the world! do you say it upon rep.?

Neverout. Poz, I saw her with my own eyes; she sat among the mob in the gallery; her own ugly phiz: and she saw me look at her.

Col. Her ladyship was plaguily bamb'd; I warrant it put her into the hips.

Neverout. I smoked her huge nose, and, egad, she put me in mind of the woodcock, that strives to hide his long bill, and then thinks nobody sees him.

Col. Tom, I advise you, hold your tongue; for you'll never say so good a thing again.

Lady Smart. Miss, what are you looking for?

Miss. O, madam, I have lost the finest needle—

Lady Answ. Why, seek till you find it, and then you won't lose your labour.

Neverout. The loop of my hat is broke, how shall I mend it? [*He fastens it with a pin.*] Well, hang him, say I, that has no shift.

Miss. Ay, and hang him that has one too many. —Well, but I don't like such jesting.†

Neverout. O, miss, I have heard a sad story of you.

Miss. I defy you, Mr. Neverout; nobody can say black's my eye.

Neverout. I believe you wish they could.

Miss. Well, but who was your author? Come, tell truth and shame the devil.

Neverout. Come then, miss; guess who it was that told me? come, put on your considering cap.

---

* Here the author, for variety, runs into some cant words.— *Orig. Note.*

† From the first edition.

Miss. Well, who was it?

Neverout. Why, one that lives within a mile of an oak.

Miss. Well, go hang yourself in your own garters, for I'm sure the gallows groans for you.

Neverout. Bite, miss!* I was but in jest.

Miss. Well, but don't let that stick in your gizzard.

Col. My lord, does your lordship know Mrs. Talkall?

Ld. Sparkish. Only by sight; but I hear she has a great deal of wit; and, egad, as the saying is, mettle to the back.

Lady Smart. So I hear.

Col. Why, Dick Lubber said to her t'other day, Madam, you can't cry bo to a goose: Yes, but I can, said she; and, egad, cry'd bo full in his face. We all thought we should break our hearts with laughing.

Ld. Sparkish. That was cutting with a vengeance: And, prithee, how did the fool look?

Col. Look! egad, he look'd for all the world like an owl in an ivy-bush.

A Child comes in screaming.

Miss. Well, if that child was mine, I'd whip it till the blood came; peace, you little vixen! if I were near you, I would not be far from you.

Lady Smart. Ay, ay! bachelors' wives and maids' children are finely tutor'd.

Lady Answ. Come to me, master; and I'll give you a sugar-plum. Why, miss, you forget that ever you was a child yourself. [*She gives the child a lump of sugar.*] I have heard 'em say, boys will long.

---

* A cant phrase of the time. Later editions read, Pretty, miss.

Col. My lord, I suppose you know that Mr. Buzzard has married again.

Lady Smart. This is his fourth wife; then he has been shod·round.

Col. Why, you must know she had a month's mind to Dick Frontless, and thought to run away with him; but her parents forced her to take the old fellow for a good settlement.

Ld. Sparkish. So the man got his mare again.

Lady Smart. I'm told he said a very good thing to Dick; said he, You *think* us old fellows are fools; but we old fellows *know* young fellows are fools.

Col. I know nothing of that; but I know he's devilish old, and she's very young.

Lady Answ. Why, they call that a match of the world's making.

Miss. What if he had been young and she old?

Neverout. Why, miss, that would have been a match of the devil's making; but when both are young, that's a match of God's making.*

Miss, searching her pocket for a thimble, brings out a nutmeg.

Neverout. O, miss, have a care; for if you carry a nutmeg in your pocket, you'll certainly be married to an old man.

---

* Such was the distinction of Elizabeth's courtiers, when they were passing criticism upon the marriage of Dr. Goodwin, Bishop of Bath and Wells. All united in censuring the poor bishop for various reasons, and one "told of three sorts of marriage; of God's making, of man's making, and of the devil's making: of God's making, as when Adam and Eve, two younge folke, were coupled; of man's making, when one is old and the other younge, as Joseph's marriage; and of the devil's making, when two old folks marry, not for comfort, but for covetousness."—*Nugæ Antiquæ*, Lond. 1804, 8, ii. 152.

Miss. Well, if I ever be married, it shall be to an old man; they always make the best husbands; and it is better to be an old man's darling, than a young man's warling.

Neverout. Faith, miss, if you speak as you think, I'll give you my mother for a maid.

Lady Smart rings the bell.

Footman comes in.

Lady Smart. Harkee, you fellow; run to my Lady Match, and desire she will remember to be here at six to play at quadrille: d'ye hear, if you fall by the way, don't stay to get up again.

Footman. Madam, I don't know the house.

Lady Smart. That's not for want of ignorance; follow your nose; go, inquire among the servants.

Footman goes out, and leaves the door open.

Lady Smart. Here, come back you fellow; why did you leave the door open? Remember, that a good servant must always come when he's called, do what he's bid, and shut the door after him.

The Footman goes out again, and falls down stairs.

Lady Answ. Neck or nothing; come down, or I'll fetch you down: well, but I hope the poor fellow has not saved the hangman a labour.

Neverout. Pray, madam, smoke miss yonder, biting her lips, and playing with her fan.

Miss. Who's that takes my name in vain?

She runs up to them, and falls down.

Lady Smart. What, more falling! do you intend the frolic should go round?

Lady Answ. Why, miss, I wish you may not have broke her ladyship's floor.

Neverout. Miss, come to me, and I'll take you up.

Ld. Sparkish. Well, but, without a jest, I hope, miss, you are not hurt.

Col. Nay, she must be hurt for certain; for you see her head is all of a lump.

Miss. Well, remember this, colonel, when I have money, and you have none.

Lady Smart. But, colonel, when do you design to get a house, and a wife, and a fire to put her in?

Miss. Lord! who would be married to a soldier, and carry his knapsack?

Neverout. O, madam: Mars and Venus, you know.

Col. Egad, madam, I'd marry to-morrow, if I thought I could bury my wife just when the honey-moon is over; but, they say, a woman has as many lives as a cat.

Lady Answ. I find, the colonel thinks a dead wife under the table is the best goods in a man's house.

Lady Smart. O but, colonel, if you had a good wife, it would break your heart to part with her.

Col. Yes, madam; for, they say, he that has lost his wife and sixpence, has lost a tester.

Lady Smart. But, colonel, they say, that every married man should believe there's but one good wife in the world, and that's his own.

Col. For all that, I doubt, a good wife must be bespoke; for there's none ready made.

Miss. I suppose the gentleman's a woman-hater; but, sir, I think you ought to remember, that you had a mother: and, pray, if it had not been for a woman, where would you have been, colonel?

Col. Nay, miss, you cried whore first, when you talked of the knapsack.

Lady Answ. But I hope you won't blame the whole sex, because some are bad.

Neverout. And they say, he that hates woman, sucked a sow.

Col. O, madam; there's no general rule without an exception.

Lady Smart. Then, why don't you marry, and settle?

Col. Egad, madam, there's nothing will settle me but a bullet.

Ld. Sparkish. Well, colonel, there's one comfort, that you need not fear a cannon-bullet.

Col. Why so, my lord?

Ld. Sparkish. Because they say, he was cursed in his mother's belly that was kill'd by a cannon-bullet.

Miss. I suppose, the colonel was crossed in his first love, which makes him so severe on all the sex.

Lady Answ. Yes; and I'll hold a hundred to one, that the colonel has been over head and ears in love with some lady that has made his heart ache.

Col. O, madam, we soldiers are admirers of all the fair sex.

Miss. I wish I could see the colonel in love till he was ready to die.

Lady Smart. Ay, but, I doubt, few people die for love in these days.

Neverout. Well, I confess, I differ from the colonel; for I hope to have a rich and a handsome wife yet before I die.

Col. Ay, Tom; live, horse, and thou shalt have grass.

Miss. Well, colonel; but, whatever you say against women, they are better creatures than men;

for men were made of clay, but woman was made of man.

Col. Miss, you may say what you please; but faith you'll never lead apes in hell.

Neverout. No, no; I'll be sworn miss has not an inch of nun's flesh about her.

Miss. I understumble you, gentlemen. — *p. understanding*

Neverout. Madam, your humblecumdumble.

Ld. Sparkish. Pray, miss, when did you see your old acquaintance, Mrs. Cloudy? you and she are two, I hear.

Miss. See her! marry, I don't care whether I ever see her again! God bless my eye-sight!

Lady Answ. Lord! why she and you were as great as two inkle-weavers. I've seen her hug you as the devil hugged the witch.

Miss. That's true; but I'm told for certain, she's no better than she should be.

Lady Smart. Well, God mend us all; but you must allow, the world is very censorious; I never heard that she was a naughty pack.

Col. [*To Neverout.*] Come, Sir Thomas, when the king pleases, when do you intend to march?

Ld. Sparkish. Have patience. Tom, is your friend Ned Rattle married?

Neverout. Yes, faith, my lord; he has tied a knot with his tongue, that he can never untie with his teeth.

Lady Smart. Ah! marry in haste, and repent at leisure.

Lady Answ. Has he got a good fortune with his lady? for they say, something has some savour, but nothing has no flavour.

Neverout. Faith, madam, all he gets by her he may put into his eye, and see never the worse.

Miss. Then, I believe he heartily wishes her in Abraham's bosom.

Col. Pray, my lord, how does Charles Limber and his fine wife agree?

Ld. Sparkish. Why, they say, he's the greatest cuckold in town.

Neverout. O, but, my lord, you should always except my lord mayor.

Miss. Mr. Neverout!

Neverout. Hay, madam, did you call me?

Miss. Hay! why, hay is for horses.

Neverout. Why, miss, then you may kiss—

Col. Pray, my lord, what's o'clock by your oracle?

Ld. Sparkish. Faith, I can't tell; I think my watch runs upon wheels.

Neverout. Miss, pray be so kind to call a servant to bring me a glass of small beer: I know you are at home here.

Miss. Every fool can do as they're bid: make a page of your own age, and do it yourself.

Neverout. Choose, proud fool; I did but ask you.

Miss puts her hand upon her knee.

Neverout. What, miss, are you thinking of your sweetheart? is your garter slipping down?

Miss. Pray, Mr. Neverout, keep your breath to cool your porridge; you measure my corn by your bushel.

Neverout. Indeed, miss, you lie—

Miss. Did you ever hear anything so rude?

Neverout. I mean, you lie—under a mistake.

Miss. If a thousand lies could choke you, you would have been choked many a day ago.

Miss strives to snatch Mr. Neverout's snuff-box.

Neverout. Madam, you missed that, as you missed your mother's blessing.

She tries again, and misses.

Neverout. Snap short makes you look so lean, miss.

Miss. Poh! you are so robustious, you had like to put out my eye; I assure you, if you blind me, you must lead me.

Lady Smart. Dear miss, be quiet; and bring me a pin-cushion out of that closet.

Miss opens the closet-door, and squalls.

Lady Smart. Lord bless the girl! what's the matter now?

Miss. I vow, madam, I saw something in black; I thought it was a spirit.

Col. Why, miss, did you ever see a spirit?

Miss. No, sir; I thank God I never saw anything worse than myself.

Neverout. Well, I did a very foolish thing yesterday, and was a great puppy for my pains.

Miss. Very likely; for they say, many a true word's spoken in jest.

Footman returns.

Lady Smart. Well, did you deliver your message? you are fit to be sent for sorrow, you stay so long by the way.

Footman. Madam, my lady was not at home, so I did not leave the message.

Lady Smart. This it is to send a fool of an errand.

Ld. Sparkish. [*Looking at his watch.*] 'Tis past twelve o'clock.

Lady Smart. Well, what is that among all us?

Ld. Sparkish. Madam, I must take my leave: come, gentlemen, are you for a march?

Lady Smart. Well, but your lordship and the colonel will dine with us to-day; and, Mr. Neverout, I hope we shall have your good company; there will be no soul else, beside my own lord and these ladies; for everybody knows I hate a crowd; I would rather want vittles than elbow-room; we dine punctually at three.

Ld. Sparkish. Madam, we'll be sure to attend your ladyship.

Col. Madam, my stomach serves me instead of a clock.

Another Footman comes back.

Lady Smart. O! you are the t'other fellow I sent; well, have you been with my Lady Club? you are good to send of a dead man's errand.

Footman. Madam, my Lady Club begs your ladyship's pardon; but she is engaged to-night.

Miss. Well, Mr. Neverout, here's the back of my hand to you.

Neverout. Miss, I find you will have the last word. Ladies, I am more yours than my own.

DIALOGUE II.

Lord Smart and the former company at three o'clock coming to dine.

After salutations.

Ld. Smart. I'm sorry I was not at home this morning, when you all did us the honour to call here; but I went to the levee to-day.

Ld. Sparkish. O! my lord; I'm sure the loss was ours.

Lady Smart. Gentlemen and ladies, you are come to a sad dirty house; I am sorry for it, but we have had our hands in mortar.

Ld. Sparkish. O! madam; your ladyship is pleased to say so; but I never saw anything so clean and so fine; I profess it is a perfect paradise.

Lady Smart. My lord, your lordship is always very obliging.

Ld. Sparkish. Pray, madam, whose picture is that?

Lady Smart. Why, my lord, it was drawn for me.

Ld. Sparkish. I'll swear the painter did not flatter your ladyship.

Col. My lord, the day is finely cleared up.

Ld. Smart. Ay, colonel; 'tis a pity that fair weather should ever do any harm. [*To Neverout.*] Why, Tom, you are high in the mode.

Neverout. My lord, it is better to be out of the world than out of the fashion.

Ld. Smart. But, Tom, I hear you and miss are always quarrelling: I fear it is your fault; for I can assure you she is very good humour'd.

Neverout. Ay, my lord; so is the devil when he's pleased.

Ld. Smart. Miss, what do you think of my friend Tom?

Miss. My lord, I think he's not the wisest man in the world; and truly he's sometimes very rude.

Ld. Sparkish. That may be true; but yet, he that hangs Tom for a fool, may find a knave in the halter.

Miss. Well, however, I wish he were hanged, if it were only to try.

Neverout. Well, miss, if I must be hanged, I

won't go far to choose my gallows; it shall be about your fair neck.

Miss. I'll see your nose cheese first, and the dogs eating it; but, my lord, Mr. Neverout's wit begins to run low; for, I vow, he said this before; pray, colonel, give him a pinch, and I'll do as much for you.

Ld. Sparkish. My Lady Smart, your ladyship has a very fine scarf.

Lady Smart. Yes, my lord; it will make a flaming figure in a country church.

Footman comes in.

Footman. Madam, dinner's upon the table.

Col. Faith, I am glad of it; my belly began to cry cupboard.

Neverout. I wish I may never hear worse news.

Miss. What! Mr. Neverout, you are in great haste; I believe your belly thinks your throat is cut.

Neverout. No, faith, miss; three meals a-day, and a good supper at night, will serve my turn.

Miss. To say the truth, I'm hungry.

Neverout. And I'm angry; so let us both go fight.

They go in to dinner, and, after the usual compliments, take their seats.

Lady Smart. Ladies and gentlemen, will you eat any oysters before dinner?

Col. With all my heart. [*Takes an oyster.*] He was a bold man that first eat an oyster.

Lady Smart. They say oysters are a cruel meat, because we eat them alive: then they are uncharitable meat, for we leave nothing to the poor; and they are an ungodly meat, because we never say grace.

Neverout. Faith, that's as well said as if I had said it myself.

Lady Smart. Well, we are well set if we be but as well served: come, colonel, handle your arms; shall I help you to some beef?

Col. If your ladyship please; and pray, don't cut like a mother-in-law, but send me a large slice: for I love to lay a good foundation. I vow, 'tis a noble sirloin.

Neverout. Ay; here's cut and come again.

Miss. But pray, why is it call'd a sirloin?

Ld. Smart. Why, you must know, that our King James the First, who loved good eating, being invited to dinner by one of his nobles, and seeing a large loin of beef at his table, he drew out his sword, and in a frolic knighted it. Few people know the secret of this.

Ld. Sparkish. Beef is man's meat, my lord.

Ld. Smart. But, my lord, I say beef is the king of meat.

Miss. Pray, what have I done, that I must not have a plate?

Lady Smart. [*To Lady Answ.*] What will your ladyship please to eat?

Lady Answ. Pray, madam, help yourself.

Col. They say, eating and scratching wants but a beginning: if you'll give me leave, I'll help myself to a slice of this shoulder of veal.

Lady Smart. Colonel, you can't do a kinder thing; well, you are all heartily welcome, as I may say.

Col. They say there are thirty and two good bits in a shoulder of veal.

Lady Smart. Ay, colonel, thirty bad bits and two good ones; you see I understand you; but I hope you have got one of the two good ones.

Neverout. Colonel, I'll be of your mess.

Col. Then pray, Tom, carve for yourself; they say, two hands in a dish, and one in a purse: Hah! said I well, Tom?

Neverout. Colonel, you spoke like an oracle.

Miss. [*To Lady Answ.*] Madam, will your ladyship help me to some fish?

Ld. Smart. [*To Neverout.*] Tom, they say fish should swim thrice.

Neverout. How is that, my lord?

Ld. Smart. Why, Tom, first it should swim in the sea, (do you mind me?) then it should swim in butter; and at last, sirrah, it should swim in good claret. I think I have made it out.

Footman. [*To Ld. Smart.*] My lord, Sir John Linger is coming up.

Ld. Smart. God so! I invited him to dine with me to-day, and forgot it: well, desire him to walk in.

Sir John Linger comes in.

Sir John. What! you are at it! why, then, I'll be gone.

Lady Smart. Sir John, I beg you will sit down; come, the more the merrier.

Sir John. Ay; but the fewer the better cheer.

Lady Smart. Well, I am the worst in the world at making apologies; it was my lord's fault: I doubt you must kiss the hare's foot.

Sir John. I see you are fast by the teeth.

Col. Faith, Sir John, we are killing that that would kill us.

Ld. Sparkish. You see, Sir John, we are upon a business of life and death; come, will you do as we do? you are come in pudding-time.

Sir John. Ay; this would be doing if I were dead. What! you keep court hours, I see: I'll be going, and get a bit of meat at my inn.

Lady Smart. Why, we won't eat you, Sir John.

Sir John. It is my own fault; but I was kept by a fellow, who bought some Derbyshire oxen of me.

Neverout. You see, Sir John, we staid for you as one horse does for another.

Lady Smart. My lord, will you help Sir John to some beef? Lady Answerall, pray eat, you see your dinner; I am sure, if we had known we should have such good company, we should have been better provided; but you must take the will for the deed. I'm afraid you are invited to your loss.

Col. And pray, Sir John, how do you like the town? you have been absent a long time.

Sir John. Why, I find little London stands just where it did when I left it last.

Neverout. What do you think of Hanover-square? Why, Sir John, London is gone out of town since you saw it.

Lady Smart. Sir John, I can only say, you are heartily welcome; and I wish I had something better for you.

Col. Here's no salt; cuckolds will run away with the meat.

Lady Smart. Pray edge a little, to make more room for Sir John: Sir John, fall to: you know, half an hour is soon lost at dinner.

Sir John. I protest, I can't eat a bit, for I took share of a beefsteak and two mugs of ale with my chapman, besides a tankard of March beer, as soon as I got out of my bed.

Lady Answ. Not fresh and fasting, I hope?

Sir John. Yes, faith, madam; I always wash my kettle before I put the meat in it.

Lady Smart. Poh! Sir John, you have seen nine houses since you eat last: come, you have kept a corner in your stomach for a piece of venison pasty.

Sir John. Well, I'll try what I can do when it comes up.

Lady Answ. Come, Sir John, you may go farther and fare worse.

Miss. [*To Neverout.*] Pray, Mr. Neverout, will you please to send me a piece of tongue?

Neverout. By no means, madam; one tongue is enough for a woman.

Col. Miss, here's a tongue that never told a lie.

Miss. That was, because it could not speak. Why, colonel, I never told a lie in my life.

Neverout. I appeal to all the company, whether that be not the greatest lie that ever was told?

Col. [*To Neverout.*] Prithee, Tom, send me the two legs, and rump, and liver of that pigeon; for, you must know, I love what nobody else loves.

Neverout. But what if any of the ladies should long? Well, here take it, and the d—l do you good with it.

Lady Answ. Well; this eating and drinking takes away a body's stomach.

Neverout. I am sure I have lost mine.

Miss. What! the bottom of it, I suppose?

Neverout. No, really, miss; I have quite lost it.

Miss. I should be very sorry a poor body had found it.

Lady Smart. But, Sir John, we hear you are married since we saw you last: what! you have stolen a wedding, it seems?

Sir John. Well; one can't do a foolish thing once in one's life, but one must hear of it a hundred times.

Col. And, pray, Sir John, how does your lady unknown?

Sir John. My wife's well, colonel, and at your service in a civil way. Ha! ha! [*He laughs.*

Miss. Pray, Sir John, is your lady tall or short?

Sir John. Why, miss, I thank God, she is a little evil.

Ld. Sparkish. Come, give me a glass of claret.

Footman fills him a bumper.

Ld. Sparkish. Why do you fill so much?

Neverout. My lord, he fills as he loves you.

Lady Smart. Miss, shall I send you some cucumber?

Miss. Madam, I dare not touch it: for they say cucumbers are cold in the third degree.

Lady Smart. Mr. Neverout, do you love pudding?

Neverout. Madam, I'm like all fools, I love everything that is good; but the proof of the pudding is in the eating.   — repet

Col. Sir John, I hear you are a great walker when you are at home.

Sir John. No, faith, colonel; I always love to walk with a horse in my hand: but I have had devilish bad luck in horse flesh of late.

Ld. Smart. Why, then, Sir John, you must kiss a parson's wife.

Lady Smart. They say, Sir John, that your lady has a great deal of wit.

Sir John. Madam, she can make a pudding, and has just wit enough to know her husband's breeches from another man's.

Ld. Smart. My Lord Sparkish, I have some excellent cider; will you please to taste it?

Ld. Sparkish. My lord, I should like it well enough, if it were not treacherous.

Ld. Smart. Pray, my lord, how is it treacherous?

Ld. Sparkish. Because it smiles in my face, and cuts my throat.   [*Here a loud laugh.*]

Miss. Odd so! madam; your knives are very sharp, for I have cut my finger.   — repet

Lady Smart. I am sorry for it : pray which finger ? (God bless the mark!)

Miss. Why, this finger : no, 'tis this : I vow I can't find which it is.

Neverout. Ay ; the fox had a wound, and he could not tell where, &c. Bring some water to throw in her face.

Miss. Pray, Mr. Neverout, did you ever draw a sword in anger ? I warrant, you would faint at the sight of your own blood.

Lady Smart. Mr. Neverout, shall I send you some veal ?

Neverout. No, madam ; I don't love it.

Miss. Then pray for them that do. I desire your ladyship will send me a bit.

Ld. Smart. Tom, my service to you.

Neverout. My lord, this moment I did myself the honour to drink to your lordship.

Ld. Smart. Why, then, that's Hertfordshire kindness.*

Neverout. Faith, my lord, I pledged myself; for I drank twice together without thinking.

Ld. Sparkish. Why then, colonel, my humble service to you.

Neverout. Pray, my lord, don't make a bridge of my nose.

Ld. Sparkish. Well, a glass of this wine is as comfortable as matrimony to an old woman.

---

* "That is, any one drinking back to his right-hand man ; *i.e.*, the person who immediately before drank to him ; perhaps a method practised by some persons of this county. Fuller says, this adage is meant to express a return for a favour or benefit conferred. It rather seems to mean returning a favour at the expense of others, as, by this inversion in the circulation of the glass, some of the company are deprived of their turn."—GROSE *ut supra*, sign. N. 4.

Col. Sir John, I design, one of these days, to come and beat up your quarters in Derbyshire.

Sir John. Faith, colonel, come, and welcome: and stay away, and heartily welcome: but you were born within the sound of Bow-bell, and don't care to stir so far from London.

Miss. Pray, colonel, send me some fritters.

Colonel takes them out with his hand.

Col. Here, miss; they say fingers were made before forks, and hands before knives.

Lady Smart. Methinks this pudding is too much boil'd.

Lady Answ. O! madam, they say a pudding is poison when it is too much boil'd.

Neverout. Miss, shall I help you to a pigeon? here's a pigeon so finely roasted, it cries, Come eat me.

Miss. No, sir; I thank you.

Neverout. Why, then you may choose.

Miss. I have chosen already.

Neverout. Well you may be the worse offer'd before you are twice married.

The Colonel fills a large plate of soup.

Ld. Smart. Why, colonel, you don't mean to eat all that soup?

Col. O! my lord, this is my sick dish; when I'm well I'll have a bigger.

Miss. [*To Col.*] Sup, Simon; very good broth.

Neverout. This seems to be a good pullet.

Miss. I warrant, Mr. Neverout knows what's good for himself.

Ld. Sparkish. Tom, I shan't take your word for it; help me to a wing.

NEVEROUT *tries to cut off a wing.*

Neverout. Egad, I can't hit the joint.

Ld. Sparkish. Why then, think of a cuckold.

Neverout. O! now I have nick'd it.

[*Gives it to Ld. Sparkish.*

Ld. Sparkish. Why, a man may eat this though his wife lay a-dying.

Col. Pray, friend, give me a glass of small beer, if it be good.

Ld. Smart. Why, colonel, they say, there is no such thing as good small beer, good brown bread, or a good old woman.

Lady Smart. [*To Lady Answ.*] Madam, I beg your ladyship's pardon; I did not see you when I was cutting that bit.

Lady Answ. O! madam; after you is good manners.

Lady Smart. Lord! here's a hair in the sauce.

Ld. Sparkish. Then, madam, set the hounds after it.

Neverout. Pray, colonel, help me, however, to some of that same sauce.

Col. Come, I think you are more sauce than pig.

Ld. Smart. Sir John, cheer up: my service to you: well, what do you think of the world to come?

Sir John. Truly, my lord, I think of it as little as I can.

Lady Smart. [*Putting a skewer on a plate.*] Here, take this skewer, and carry it down to the cook, to dress it for her own dinner.

Neverout. I beg your ladyship's pardon; but this small beer is dead.

Lady Smart. Why, then, let it be buried.

Col. This is admirable black-pudding: miss, shall I carve you some? I can just carve pudding, and that's all; I am the worst carver in the world; I should never make a good chaplain.

Miss. No, thank ye, colonel; for they say those that eat black-pudding will dream of the devil.

Ld. Smart. O, here comes the venison pasty: here, take the soup away.

Ld. Smart. [*He cuts it up and tastes the venison.*] 'Sbuds! this venison is musty.

NEVEROUT *eats a piece and it burns his mouth.*

Ld. Smart. What's the matter, Tom? you have tears in your eyes, I think: what dost cry for, man?

Neverout. My lord, I was just thinking of my poor grandmother! she died just this very day seven years.

Miss takes a bit and burns her mouth.

Neverout. And pray, miss, why do you cry too?

Miss. Because you were not hang'd the day your grandmother died.

Ld. Smart. I'd have given forty pounds, miss, to have said that.

Col. Egad, I think the more I eat the hungrier I am.

Ld. Sparkish. Why, colonel, they say, one shoulder of mutton drives down another.

Neverout. Egad, if I were to fast for my life, I would take a good breakfast in the morning, a good dinner at noon, and a good supper at night.

Ld. Sparkish. My lord, this venison is plaguily pepper'd; your cook has a heavy hand.

Ld. Smart. My lord, I hope you are pepper-proof: come, here's a health to the founders.

Lady Smart. Ay; and to the confounders too.

Ld. Smart. Lady Answerall, does your ladyship love venison?

Lady Answ. No, my lord, I can't endure it in my sight: therefore please to send me a good piece of meat and crust.

Ld. Sparkish. [*Drinks to Neverout.*] Come, Tom; not always to my friends, but once to you.

Neverout. [*Drinks to Lady Smart.*] Come, madam; here's a health to our friends, and hang the rest of our kin.

Lady Smart. [*To Lady Answ.*] Madam, will your ladyship have any of this hare?

Lady Answ. No, madam, they say 'tis melancholy meat.

Lady Smart. Then, madam, shall I send you the brains? I beg your ladyship's pardon; for they say, 'tis not good manners to offer brains.

Lady Answ. No, madam; for perhaps it will make me harebrain'd.

Neverout. Miss, I must tell you one thing.

Miss. [*With a glass in her hand.*] Hold your tongue, Mr. Neverout; don't speak in my tip.

Col. Well, he was an ingenious man that first found out eating and drinking.

Ld. Sparkish. Of all vittles drink digests the quickest: give me a glass of wine.

Neverout. My lord, your wine is too strong.

Ld. Smart. Ay, Tom, as much as you're too good.

Miss. This almond-pudding was pure good; but it is grown quite cold.

Neverout. So much the better, miss, cold pudding will settle your love.

Miss. Pray, Mr. Neverout, are you going to take a voyage?

Neverout. Why do you ask, miss?

Miss. Because you have laid in so much beef.

Sir John. You two have ate up the whole pudding between you.

Miss. Sir John, here's a little bit left; will you please to have it?

Sir John. No, thankee; I don't love to make a fool of my mouth.

Col. [*Calling to the butler.*] John, is your small beer good?

Butler. An please your honour, my lord and lady like it: I think it is good.

Col. Why then, John, d'ye see, if you are sure your small beer is good, d'ye mark? then, give me a glass of wine. [*All laugh.*

Colonel tasting the wine.

Ld. Smart. Sir John, how does your neighbour Gatherall of the Peak? I hear he has lately made a purchase.

Sir John. O! Dick Gatherall knows how to butter his bread as well as any man in Derbyshire.

Ld. Smart. Why he used to go very fine, when he was here in town.

Sir John. Ay; and it became him, as a saddle becomes a sow.

Col. I know his lady, and I think she is a very good woman.

Sir John. Faith, she has more goodness in her little finger than he has in his whole body.

Ld. Smart. Well, colonel, how do you like that wine?

Col. This wine should be eaten, it is too good to be drunk.

Ld. Smart. I'm very glad you like it; and pray don't spare it.

Col. No, my lord; I'll never starve in a cook's shop.

Ld. Smart. And pray, Sir John, what do you say to my wine?

Sir John. I'll take another glass first: second thoughts are best.

Ld. Sparkish. Pray, Lady Smart, you sit near that ham; will you please to send me a bit?

Lady Smart. With all my heart. [*She sends him a piece.*] Pray, my lord, how do you like it?

Ld. Sparkish. I think it is a limb of Lot's wife. [*He eats it with mustard.*] Egad, my lord, your mustard is very uncivil.

Lady Smart. Why uncivil, my lord?

Ld. Sparkish. Because it takes me by the nose, egad.

Lady Smart. Mr. Neverout, I find you are a very good carver.

Col. O madam, that is no wonder; for you must know, Tom Neverout carves o' Sundays.

NEVEROUT *overturns the saltcellar.*

Lady Smart. Mr. Neverout, you have overturned the salt, and that's a sign of anger: I'm afraid miss and you will fall out.

Lady Answ. No, no; throw a little of it into the fire, and all will be well.

Neverout. O, madam, the falling out of lovers, you know.

Miss. Lovers! very fine! fall *out* with him! I wonder when we were *in*.

Sir John. For my part, I believe the young gentlewoman is his sweetheart, there is so much fooling and fiddling betwixt them: I'm sure, they say in our country, that shiddle-come-sh—'s the beginning of love.

Miss. I own, I love Mr. Neverout as the devil loves holy water: I love him like pie, I'd rather the devil had him than I.

Neverout. Miss, I'll tell you one thing.

Miss. Come, here's t'ye, to stop your mouth.

Neverout. I'd rather you would stop it with a kiss.

Miss. A kiss! marry come up, my dirty cousin; are you no sicker? Lord! I wonder what fool it was that first invented kissing!

Neverout. Well, I'm very dry.

Miss. Then you're the better to burn and the worse to fry.

Lady Answ. God bless you, colonel, you have a good stroke with you.

Col. O, madam, formerly I could eat all, but now I leave nothing; I eat but one meal a-day.

Miss. What! I suppose, colonel, that is from morning till night?

Neverout. Faith, miss; and well was his wont.

Ld. Smart. Pray, Lady Answerall, taste this bit of venison.

Lady Answ. I hope your lordship will set me a good example.

Ld. Smart. Here's a glass of cider fill'd: miss, you must drink it.

Miss. Indeed, my lord, I can't.

Neverout. Come, miss; better belly burst than good liquor be lost.

Miss. Pish! well, in life there was never anything so teazing; I had rather shed it in my shoes: I wish it were in your guts for my share.

Ld. Smart. Mr. Neverout, you ha'n't tasted my cider yet.

Neverout. No, my lord; I have been just eating soup; and they say, if one drinks with one's porridge, one will cough in one's grave.

Ld. Smart. Come, take miss's glass, she wish'd it was in your guts; let her have her wish for once: ladies can't abide to have their inclinations cross'd.

Lady Smart. [*To Sir John.*] I think, Sir John, you have not tasted the venison yet.

Sir John. I seldom eat it, madam; however, please to send me a little of the crust.

Ld. Sparkish. Why, Sir John, you had as good eat the devil as the broth he is boil'd in.

Col. Well, this eating and drinking takes away a body's stomach, as Lady Answerall says.

Neverout. I have dined as well as my lord mayor.

Miss. I thought I could have eaten this wing of a chicken; but my eye's bigger than my belly.

Ld. Smart. Indeed, Lady Answerall, you have eaten nothing.

Lady Answ. Pray, my lord, see all the bones on my plate; they say a carpenter's known by his chips.

Neverout. Miss, will you reach me that glass of jelly?

Miss. [*Giving it to him.*] You see, 'tis but ask and have.

Neverout. Miss, I would have a bigger glass.

Miss. What! you don't know your own mind; you are neither well, full nor fasting; I think that is enough.

Neverout. Ay, one of the enoughs; I am sure it is little enough.

Miss. Yes; but you know, sweet things are bad for the teeth.

Neverout. [*To Lady Answ.*] Madam, I don't like that part of the veal you sent me.

Lady Answ. Well, Mr. Neverout, I find you are a true Englishman; you never know when you are well.

Col. Well, I have made my whole dinner of beef.

Lady Answ. Why, colonel, a bellyful's a bellyful, if it be but of wheat-straw.

Col. Well, after all, kitchen physic is the best physic.

Lady Smart. And the best doctors in the world are Doctor Diet, Doctor Quiet, and Doctor Merryman.

Ld. Sparkish. What do you think of a little house well fill'd?

Sir John. And a little land well till'd?

Col. Ay; and a little wife well will'd?

Neverout. My Lady Smart, pray help me to some of the breast of that goose.

Ld. Smart. Tom, I have heard that goose upon goose is false heraldry.

Miss. What! will you never have done stuffing?

Ld. Smart. This goose is quite raw: well, God sends meat, but the devil sends cooks.

Neverout. Miss, can you tell which is the gander, the white goose or the grey goose?

Miss. They say, a fool will ask more questions than the wisest body can answer.

Col. Indeed, miss, Tom Neverout has posed you.

Miss. Why, colonel, every dog has his day; but I believe I shall never see a goose again without thinking of Mr. Neverout.

Ld. Smart. Well said, miss; faith, girl, thou hast brought thyself off cleverly. Tom, what say you to that?

Col. Faith, Tom is nonpluss'd; he looks plaguily down in the mouth.

Miss. Why, my lord, you see he is the provokingest creature in life; I believe there is not such another in the varsal world.

Lady Answ. O, miss, the world's a wide place.

Neverout. Well, miss, I'll give you leave to call me anything, if you don't call me spade.

Ld. Smart. Well, but, after all, Tom, can you tell me what's Latin for a goose?

Neverout. O, my lord, I know that: why, brandy is Latin for a goose, and *tace* is Latin for a candle.

Miss. Is that manners, to shew your learning

before ladies? Methinks you are grown very brisk of a sudden; I think the man's glad he's alive.

Sir John. The devil take your wit, if this be wit; for it spoils company: pray, Mr. Butler, bring me a dram after my goose; 'tis very good for the wholesomes.

Ld. Smart. Come, bring me the loaf; I sometimes love to cut my own bread.

Miss. I suppose, my lord, you lay longest abed to-day?

Ld. Smart. Miss, if I had said so, I should have told a fib; I warrant you lay abed till the cows came home: but, miss, shall I cut you a little crust, now my hand is in?

Miss. If you please, my lord, a bit of undercrust.

Neverout. [*Whispering miss.*] I find you love to lie under.

Miss. [*Aloud, pushing him from her.*] What does the man mean! Sir, I don't understand you at all.

Neverout. Come, all quarrels laid aside: here, miss, may you live a thousand years. [*He drinks to her.*]

Miss. Pray, sir, don't stint me.

Ld. Smart. Sir John, will you taste my October? I think it is very good; but I believe not equal to yours in Derbyshire.

Sir John. My lord, I beg your pardon; but they say, the devil made askers.

Ld. Smart. [*To the butler.*] Here, bring up the great tankard, full of October, for Sir John.

Col. [*Drinking to miss.*] Miss, your health; may you live all the days of your life.

Lady Answ. Well, miss, you'll certainly be soon married; here's two bachelors drinking to you at once.

Lady Smart. Indeed, miss, I believe you were wrapt in your mother's smock, you are so well beloved.

Miss. Where's my knife? sure I ha'n't eaten it: O, here it is.

Sir John. No, miss; but your maidenhead hangs in your light.

Miss. Pray, Sir John, is that a Derbyshire compliment? Here, Mr. Neverout, will you take this piece of rabbit that you bid me carve for you?

Neverout. I don't know.

Miss. Why, take it, or let it alone.

Neverout. I will.

Miss. What will you?

Neverout. Why, I'll take it, or let it alone.

Miss. Well, you are a provoking creature.

Sir John. [*Talking with a glass of wine in his hand.*] I remember a farmer in our country—

Ld. Smart. [*Interrupting him.*] Pray, Sir John, did you ever hear of parson Palmer?

Sir John. No, my lord; what of him?

Ld. Smart. Why, he used to preach over his liquor.

Sir John. I beg your lordship's pardon; here's your lordship's health; I'd drink it up, if it were a mile to the bottom.

Lady Smart. Mr. Neverout, have you been at the new play?

Neverout. Yes, madam, I went the first night.

Lady Smart. Well, and how did it take?

Neverout. Why, madam, the poet is damn'd.

Sir John. God forgive you! that's very uncharitable: you ought not to judge so rashly of any Christian.

Neverout. [*Whispers Lady Smart.*] Was ever such a dunce! How well he knows the town! See how he stares like a stuck pig! Well, but, Sir John, are you acquainted with any one of our fine ladies yet? Any of our famous toasts?

Sir John. No; damn your fire-ships, I have a wife of my own.

Lady Smart. Pray, my Lady Answerall, how do you like these preserved oranges?

Lady Answ. Indeed, madam, the only fault I find is, that they are too good.

Lady Smart. O madam, I have heard 'em say, that too good is stark naught.

Miss drinking part of a glass of wine.

Neverout. Pray, let me drink your snuff.

Miss. No, indeed, you shan't drink after me; for you'll know my thoughts.

Neverout. I know them already; you are thinking of a good husband. Besides, I can tell your meaning by your mumping.

Lady Smart. Pray, my lord, did not you order the butler to bring up a tankard of our October to Sir John? I believe they stay to brew it.

The butler brings up the tankard to Sir John.

Sir John. Won't your ladyship please to drink first?

Lady Smart. No, Sir John; 'tis in a very good hand; I'll pledge you.

Col. [*To Ld. Smart.*] My lord, I love October as well as Sir John; and I hope you won't make fish of one and flesh of another.

Ld. Smart. Colonel, you're heartily welcome. Come, Sir John, take it by word of mouth, and then give it to the colonel.

Sir John drinks.

Ld. Smart. Well, Sir John, how do you like it?

Sir John. Not as well as my own in Derbyshire; 'tis plaguy small.

Lady Smart. I never taste malt liquor; but they say it is well hopp'd.

Sir John. Hopp'd! why, if it had hopp'd a little farther, it would have hopp'd into the river. O, my lord, my ale is meat, drink, and cloth; it will make a cat speak, and a wise man dumb.

Lady Smart. I was told ours was very strong.

Sir John. Ay, madam, strong of the water; I believe the brewer forgot the malt, or the river was too near him. Faith, it is mere whip-belly-vengeance; he that drinks most has the worst share.

Col. I believe, Sir John, ale is as plenty as water at your house.

Sir John. Why, faith, at Christmas, we have many comers and goers; and they must not be sent away without a cup of Christmas ale, for fear they should p—s behind the door.

Lady Smart. I hear Sir John has the nicest garden in England; they say, 'tis kept so clean, that you can't find a place where to spit.

Sir John. O, madam; you are pleased to say so.

Lady Smart. But, Sir John, your ale is terrible strong and heady in Derbyshire, and will soon make one drunk and sick; what do you then?

Sir John. Why, indeed, it is apt to fox one; but our way is, to take a hair of the same dog next morning. I take a new-laid egg for breakfast; and faith one should drink as much after an egg as after an ox.

Ld. Smart, Tom Neverout, will you taste a glass of October?

Neverout. No, faith, my lord; I like your wine, and won't put a churl upon a gentleman; your honour's claret is good enough for me.

Lady Smart. What! is this pigeon left for manners? Colonel, shall I send you the legs and rump.

Col. Madam, I could not eat a bit more, if the house was full.

Ld. Smart. [*Carving a partridge.*] Well, one may ride to Rumford upon this knife, it is so blunt.

Lady Answ. My lord, I beg your pardon; but they say an ill workman never had good tools.

Ld. Smart. Will your lordship have a wing of it?

Ld. Sparkish. No, my lord; I love the wing of an ox a great deal better.

Ld. Smart. I'm always cold after eating.

Col. My lord, they say, that's a sign of long life.

Ld. Smart. Ay; I believe I shall live till my friends are weary of me.

Col. Pray, does anybody here hate cheese? I would be glad of a bit.

Ld. Smart. An odd kind of fellow dined with me t'other day; and when the cheese came upon the table, he pretended to faint; so somebody said, Pray, take away the cheese: No, said I; pray take away the fool: said I well?

Here a loud and large laugh.

Col. Faith, my lord, you served the coxcomb right enough; and therefore I wish we had a bit of your lordship's Oxfordshire cheese.

Ld. Smart. Come, hang saving; bring us up a half-p'orth of cheese.

Lady Answ. They say, cheese digests everything but itself.

A Footman brings a great whole cheese.

Ld. Sparkish. Ay; this would look handsome if anybody should come in.

Sir John. Well: I'm weily brosten, as they say in Lancashire.

Ld. Smart. O! Sir John; I would I had something to brost you withal.

Lady Smart. Come, they say, 'tis merry in the hall when beards wag all.

Ld. Smart. Miss, shall I help you to some cheese, or will you carve for yourself?

Neverout. I'll hold fifty pounds, miss won't cut the cheese.

Miss. Pray, why so, Mr. Neverout?

Neverout. O, there is a reason, and you know it well enough.

Miss. I can't for my life understand what the gentleman means.

Ld. Smart. Pray, Tom, change the discourse: in troth you are too bad.

Col. [*Whispers Neverout.*] Smoke miss; faith, you have made her fret like gum taffeta.

Lady Smart. Well, but, miss, (hold your tongue, Mr. Neverout,) shall I cut you a piece of cheese?

Miss. No, really, madam; I have dined this half hour.

Lady Smart. What! quick at meat, quick at work, they say.

Sir John nods.

Ld. Smart. What! are you sleepy, Sir John? do you sleep after dinner?

Sir John. Yes, faith; I sometimes take a nap after my pipe; for when the belly is full, the bones would be at rest.

Lady Smart. Come, colonel; help yourself, and your friends will love you the better. [*To Lady Answ.*] Madam, your ladyship eats nothing.

Lady Answ. Lord, madam, I have fed like a farmer: I shall grow as fat as a porpoise; I swear, my jaws are weary of chewing.

Col. I have a mind to eat a piece of that sturgeon, but fear it will make me sick.

Neverout. A rare soldier indeed! let it alone, and I warrant it won't hurt you.

Col. Well, it would vex a dog to see a pudding creep.

Sir John rises.

Ld. Smart. Sir John, what are you doing?

Sir John. Swolks, I must be going, by'r lady; I have earnest business; I must do as the beggars do, go away when I have got enough.

Ld. Smart. Well, but stay till this bottle's out; you know, the man was hang'd that left his liquor behind him: and besides, a cup in the pate is a mile in the gate; and a spur in the head is worth two in the heel.

Sir John. Come then; one brimmer to all your healths. [*The footman gives him a glass half full.*] Pray, friend, what was the rest of this glass made for? an inch at the top, friend, is worth two at the bottom. [*He gets a brimmer and drinks it off.*] Well, there's no deceit in a brimmer, and there's no false Latin in this; your wine is excellent good, so I thank you for the next, for I am sure of this: madam, has your ladyship any commands in Derbyshire? I must go fifteen miles to-night.

Lady Smart. None, Sir John, but to take care of yourself; and my most humble service to your lady unknown.

Sir John. Well, madam, I can but love and thank you.

Lady Smart. Here, bring water to wash; though really, you have all eaten so little, that you have not need to wash your mouths.

Ld. Smart. But, prithee, Sir John, stay a while longer.

Sir John. No, my lord; I am to smoke a pipe with a friend before I leave the town.

Col. Why, Sir John, had not you better set out to-morrow?

Sir John. Colonel, you forget to-morrow is Sunday.

Col. Now I alway love to begin a journey on Sundays, because I shall have the prayers of the church, to preserve all that travel by land or by water.

Sir John. Well, colonel, thou art a mad fellow to make a priest of.

Neverout. Fie, Sir John! do you take tobacco? How can you make a chimney of your mouth?

Sir John. [*To Neverout.*] What! you don't smoke, I warrant you, but you smock. (Ladies, I beg your pardon.) Colonel, do you never smoke?

Col. No, Sir John; but I take a pipe sometimes.

Sir John. I'faith, one of your finical London blades dined with me last year in Derbyshire: so, after dinner, I took a pipe: so my gentleman turn'd away his head: so, said I, What, sir, do you never smoke? so he answered, as you do, colonel, No, but I sometimes take a pipe: so he took a pipe in his hand, and fiddled with it till he broke it: so, said I, Pray, sir, can you make a pipe? so he said, No: so, said I, Why then, sir, if you can't make a pipe, you should not break a pipe: so we all laugh'd.

Ld. Smart. Well; but, Sir John, they say, that the corruption of pipes is the generation of stoppers.*

---

* A burlesque upon an expression of Dryden's, that the corruption of a poet was the generation of a critic. The parody seems to have been proverbial.

Sir John. Colonel, I hear you go sometimes to Derbyshire; I wish you would come and foul a plate with me.

Col. I hope you will give me a soldier's bottle.

Sir John. Come and try. Mr. Neverout, you are a town wit; can you tell me what kind of herb is tobacco?

Neverout. Why, an Indian herb, Sir John.

Sir John. No; 'tis a pot herb; and so here's t'ye in a pot of my lord's October.

Lady Smart. I hear, Sir John, since you are married, you have foreswore the town.

Sir John. No, madam; I never foreswore anything but the building of churches.

Lady Smart. Well; but, Sir John, when may we hope to see you again in London?

Sir John. Why, madam, not till the ducks have eat up the dirt, as the children say.

Neverout. Come, Sir John: I foresee it will rain terribly.

Ld. Smart. Come, Sir John, do nothing rashly; let us drink first.

Ld. Sparkish. I know Sir John will go, though he was sure it would rain cats and dogs; but pray stay, Sir John; you'll be time enough to go to bed by candlelight.

Ld. Smart. Why, Sir John, if you must needs go, while you stay, make use of your time; here's my service to you, a health to our friends in Derbyshire: come, sit down; let us put off the evil hour as long as we can.

Sir John. Faith, I could not drink a drop more, if the house was full.

Col. Why, Sir John, you used to love a glass of good wine in former times.

Sir John. Why, so I do still, colonel; but a man may love his house very well, without riding on the ridge: besides, I must be with my wife on Tuesday, or there will be the devil and all to pay.

Col. Well, if you go to-day, I wish you may be wet to the skin.

Sir John. Ay; but they say the prayers of the wicked won't prevail.

Sir John *takes his leave and goes away.*

Ld. Smart. Well, miss, how do you like Sir John?

Miss. Why, I think he's a little upon the silly, or so: I believe he has not all the wit in the world: but I don't pretend to be a judge.

Neverout. Faith, I believe he was bred at Hog's Norton, where the pigs play upon the organs.*

Ld. Sparkish. Why, Tom, I thought you and he were hand in glove.

Neverout. Faith, he shall have a clean threshold for me; I never darkened his door in my life, neither in town or country; but he's a queer old duke, by my conscience; and yet, after all, I take him to be more knave than fool.

Lady Smart. Well, come; a man's a man, if he has but a nose on his face.

Col. I was once with him and some other company over a bottle, and, egad, he fell asleep, and snored so hard, that we thought he was driving his hogs to market.

Neverout. Why, what! you can have no more of a cat than her skin; you can't make a silk purse out of a sow's ear.

Ld. Sparkish. Well, since he's gone, the devil go

---

* The true name of this Leicestershire village is said to be Hock-Norton, vulgarly pronounced Hoggs-Norton. The organist there happened at one time to be named Piggs, which gave rise to the proverb.

with him and sixpence ; and there's money and company too.

Neverout. Faith, he's a country put. Pray, miss, let me ask you a question.

Miss. Well ; but don't ask questions with a dirty face : I warrant, what you have to say will keep cold.

Col. Come, my lord, against you are disposed : here's to all that love and honour you.

Ld. Sparkish. Ay, that was always Dick Nimble's health. I'm sure you know he's dead.

Col. Dead ! well, my lord, you love to be a messenger of ill news : I'm heartily sorry ; but, my lord, we must all die.

Neverout. I knew him very well : but, pray, how came he to die ?

Miss. There's a question ! you talk like a poticary : why, because he could live no longer.

Neverout. Well ; rest his soul : we must live by the living, and not by the dead.

Ld. Sparkish. You know, his house was burnt down to the ground.

Col. Yes ; it was in the news. Why, fire and water are good servants, but they are very bad masters.

Ld. Smart. Here, take away, and set down a bottle of Burgundy. Ladies, you'll stay and drink a glass of wine before you go to your tea.

All taken away, and the wine set down, &c.

Miss gives NEVEROUT *a smart pinch.*

Neverout. Lord, miss, what d'ye mean ? d'ye think I have no feeling ?

Miss. I'm forced to pinch, for the times are hard.

Neverout. [*Giving Miss a pinch.*] Take that, miss; what's sauce for a goose, is sauce for a gander.

Miss. [*Screaming.*] Well, Mr. Neverout, that shall neither go to heaven nor hell with you.

Neverout. [*Takes Miss by the hand.*] Come, miss, let us lay all quarrels aside, and be friends.

Miss. Don't be so teazing; you plague a body so! can't you keep your filthy hands to yourself?

Neverout. Pray, miss, where did you get that pick-tooth case?

Miss. I came honestly by it.

Neverout. I'm sure it was mine, for I lost just such a one; nay, I don't tell you a lie.

Miss. No; if you lie, it is much.

Neverout. Well; I'm sure 'tis mine.

Miss. What! you think everything is yours, but a little the king has.

Neverout. Colonel, you have seen my fine pick-tooth case; don't you think this is the very same?

Col. Indeed, miss, it is very like it.

Miss. Ay; what he says, you'll swear.

Neverout. Well; but I'll prove it to be mine.

Miss. Ay; do, if you can.

Neverout. Why, what's yours is mine, and what's mine is my own.

Miss. Well, run on till you're weary; nobody holds you.

NEVEROUT *gapes.*

Col. What! Mr. Neverout, do you gape for preferment?

Neverout. Faith, I may gape long enough, before it falls into my mouth.

Lady Smart. Mr. Neverout, my lord and I intend to beat up your quarters one of these days: I hear you live high.

Neverout. Yes, faith, madam; I live high, and lodge in a garret.

Col. But, miss, I forgot to tell you, that Mr.

Neverout got the devilishest fall in the Park to-day.

Miss. I hope he did not hurt the ground: but how was it, Mr. Neverout? I wish I had been there to laugh.

Neverout. Why, madam, it was a place where a cuckold had been buried, and one of his horns sticking out, I happened to stumble against it; that was all.

Lady Smart. Ladies, let us leave the gentlemen to themselves; I think it is time to go to our tea.

Lady Answ. and Miss. My lords and gentlemen, your most humble servant.

Ld. Smart. Well, ladies, we'll wait on you an hour hence.

The Gentlemen alone.

Ld. Smart. Come, John, bring us a fresh bottle.

Col. Ay, my lord; and pray, let him carry off the dead men, as we say in the army.

[*Meaning the empty bottles.*

Ld. Sparkish. Mr. Neverout, pray, is not that bottle full?

Neverout. Yes, my lord, full of emptiness.

Ld. Smart. And, d'ye hear, John, bring clean glasses.

Col. I'll keep mine; for I think wine is the best liquor to wash glasses in.

DIALOGUE III.

The Ladies at their tea.

Lady Smart. Well, ladies; now let us have a cup of discourse to ourselves.

Lady Answ. What do you think of your friend Sir John Spendall?

Lady Smart. Why, madam, 'tis happy for him that his father was born before him.

Miss. They say he makes a very ill husband to my lady.

Lady Answ. But he must be allowed to be the fondest father in the world.

Lady Smart. Ay, madam, that's true; for they say, the devil is kind to his own.

Miss. I am told my lady manages him to admiration.

Lady Smart. That I believe; for she's as cunning as a dead pig, but not half so honest.

Lady Answ. They say she's quite a stranger to all his gallantries.

Lady Smart. Not at all; but, you know, there's none so blind as they that won't see.

Miss. O, madam, I am told she watches him as a cat would watch a mouse.

Lady Answ. Well, if she ben't foully belied, she pays him in his own coin.

Lady Smart. Madam, I fancy I know your thoughts, as well as if I were within you.

Lady Answ. Madam, I was t'other day in company with Mrs. Clatter; I find she gives herself airs of being acquainted with your ladyship.

Miss. O the hideous creature! did you observe

her nails? they were long enough to scratch her grannum out of her grave.

Lady Smart. Well, she and Tom Gosling were banging compliments backward and forward: it looked like two asses scrubbing one another.

Miss. Ay, claw me, and I'll claw you: but, pray, madam, who were the company?

Lady Smart. Why, there was all the world and his wife; there was Mrs. Clatter, Lady Singular, the Countess of Talkham, (I should have named her first,) Tom Gosling, and some others, whom I have forgot.

Lady Answ. I think the countess is very sickly.

Lady Smart. Yes, madam; she'll never scratch a gray head, I promise her.

Miss. And pray, what was your conversation?

Lady Smart. Why, Mrs. Clatter had all the talk to herself, and was perpetually complaining of her misfortunes.

Lady Answ. She brought her husband ten thousand pounds: she has a town-house and country-house: would the woman have her a— hung with points?

Lady Smart. She would fain be at the top of the house before the stairs are built.

Miss. Well, comparisons are odious; but she's as like her husband as if she were spit out of his mouth; as like as one egg is to another: pray how was she drest?

Lady Smart. Why, she was as fine as fi'pence; but, truly, I thought there was more cost than worship.

Lady Answ. I don't know her husband: pray what is he?

Lady Smart. Why, he's a counsellor of the law; you must know he came to us as drunk as David's sow.

Miss. What kind of creature is he?

Lady Smart. You must know, the man and his wife are coupled like rabbits, a fat and a lean; he's as fat as a porpus, and she's one of Pharaoh's lean kine: the ladies and Tom Gosling were proposing a party at quadrille, but he refused to make one: Damn your cards, said he, they are the devil's books.

Lady Answ. A dull unmannerly brute! well, God send him more wit, and me more money.

Miss. Lord! madam, I would not keep such company for the world.

Lady Smart. O, miss, 'tis nothing when you are used to it: besides, you know, for want of company, welcome trumpery.

Miss. Did your ladyship play?

Lady Smart. Yes, and won; so I came off with fiddler's fare, meat, drink, and money.

Lady Answ. Ay; what says Pluck?

Miss. Well, my elbow itches; I shall change bedfellows.

Lady Smart. And my right hand itches; I shall receive money.

Lady Answ. And my right eye itches; I shall cry.

Lady Smart. Miss, I hear your friend Mistress Giddy has discarded Dick Shuttle: pray, has she got another lover?

Miss. I hear of none.

Lady Smart. Why, the fellow's rich, and I think she was a fool to throw out her dirty water before she got clean.

Lady Answ. Miss, that's a handsome gown of yours, and finely made; very genteel.

Miss. I am glad your ladyship likes it.

Lady Answ. Your lover will be in raptures; it becomes you admirably.

Miss. Ay; I assure you I won't take it as I have done; if this won't fetch him, the devil fetch him, say I.

Lady Smart. [*To Lady Answ.*] Pray, madam, when did you see Sir Peter Muckworm?

Lady Answ. Not this fortnight; I hear he's laid up with the gout.

Lady Smart. What does he do for it?

Lady Answ. I hear he's weary of doctoring it, and now makes use of nothing but patience and flannel.

Miss. Pray, how does he and my lady agree?

Lady Answ. You know he loves her as the devil loves holy water.

Miss. They say, she plays deep with sharpers, that cheat her of her money.

Lady Answ. Upon my word, they must rise early that would cheat her of her money; sharp's the word with her; diamonds cut diamonds.

Miss. Well, but I was assured from a good hand, that she lost at one sitting to the tune of a hundred guineas; make money of that!

Lady Smart. Well, but do you hear that Mrs. Plump is brought to bed at last?

Miss. And pray, what has God sent her?

Lady Smart. Why, guess if you can.

Miss. A boy, I suppose.

Lady Smart. No, you are out; guess again.

Miss. A girl, then.

Lady Smart. You have hit it; I believe you are a witch.

Miss. O, madam, the gentlemen say, all fine ladies are witches; but I pretend to no such thing.

Lady Answ. Well, she had good luck to draw Tom Plump into wedlock; she ris'd with her a—upwards.

Miss. Fie, madam; what do you mean?

Lady Smart. O, miss, 'tis nothing what we say among ourselves.

Miss. Ay, madam; but they say hedges have eyes, and walls have ears.

Lady Answ. Well, miss, I can't help it; you know, I'm old Telltruth; I love to call a spade a spade.

Lady Smart. [*Mistakes the tea-tongs for the spoon.*] What! I think my wits are a wool-gathering to-day.

Miss. Why, madam, there was but a right and a wrong.

Lady Smart. Miss, I hear that you and Lady Coupler are as great as cup and can.

Lady Answ. Ay, miss, as great as the devil and the Earl of Kent.*

Lady Smart. Nay, I am told you meet together with as much love as there is between the old cow and the haystack.

Miss. I own I love her very well; but there's difference between staring and stark mad.

Lady Smart. They say, she begins to grow fat.

Miss. Fat! ay, fat as a hen in the forehead.

Lady Smart. Indeed, Lady Answerall, (pray forgive me,) I think your ladyship looks thinner than when I saw you last.

Miss. Indeed, madam, I think not; but your ladyship is one of Job's comforters.

Lady Answ. Well, no matter how I look; I am bought and sold: but really, miss, you are so very obliging, that I wish I were a handsome young lord for your sake.

Miss. O, madam, your love's a million.

Lady Smart. [*To Lady Answ.*] Madam, will

---

* The villainous character, given by history to the celebrated Goodwin Earl of Kent, in the time of Edward the Confessor, occasioned this proverb.

your ladyship let me wait on you to the play to-morrow?

Lady Answ. Madam, it becomes me to wait on your ladyship.

Miss. What, then, I'm turned out for a wrangler?

The Gentlemen come in to the Ladies to drink tea.

Miss. Mr. Neverout, we wanted you sadly; you are always out of the way when you should be hang'd.

Neverout. You wanted me! pray, miss, how do you look when you lie?

Miss. Better than you when you cry. Manners, indeed! I find you mend like sour ale in summer.

Neverout. I beg your pardon, miss; I only meant, when you lie alone.

Miss. That's well turn'd; one turn more would have turn'd you down stairs.

Neverout. Come, miss, be kind for once, and order me a dish of coffee.

Miss. Pray, go yourself; let us wear out the oldest; besides, I can't go, for I have a bone in my leg.

Col. They say, a woman need but look on her apron-string to find an excuse.

Neverout. Why, miss, you are grown so peevish,- a dog would not live with you.

Miss. Mr. Neverout, I beg your diversion: no offence, I hope; but truly in a little time you intend to make the colonel as bad as yourself; and that's as bad as can be.

Neverout. My lord, don't you think miss improves wonderfully of late? Why, miss, if I spoil the colonel, I hope you will use him as you do me; for you know, love me, love my dog.

Col. How's that, Tom? Say that again: why, if I am a dog, shake hands, brother.

DIALOGUE III.

Here a great, loud, long laugh.

Ld. Smart. But pray, gentlemen, why always so severe upon poor miss? On my conscience, colonel ...¹ Tom Neverout, one of you two are both knaves.

Col. My Lady Answerall, I intend to do myself the honour of dining with your ladyship to-morrow.

Lady Answ. Ay, colonel, do if you can.

Miss. I'm sure you'll be glad to be welcome.

Col. Miss, I thank you; and, to reward you, I'll come and drink tea with you in the morning.

Miss. Colonel, there's two words to that bargain.

Col. [*To Lady Smart.*] Your ladyship has a very fine watch; well may you wear it.

Lady Smart. It is none of mine, colonel.

Col. Pray, whose is it then?

Lady Smart. Why, 'tis my lord's; for they say a married woman has nothing of her own but her wedding-ring and her hair-lace; but if women had been the law-makers, it would have been better.

Col. This watch seems to be quite new.

Lady Smart. No, sir; it has been twenty years in my lord's family; but *Quare* put a new case and dialplate to it.

Neverout. Why, that's for all the world like the man, who swore he kept the same knife forty years, only he sometimes changed the haft, and sometimes the blade.

Ld. Smart. Well, Tom, to give the devil his due, thou art a right woman's man.

Col. Odd so! I have broke the hinge of my snuffbox; I'm undone, besides the loss.

Miss. Alack-a-day, colonel! I vow I had rather have found forty shillings.

Neverout. Why, colonel, all that I can say to comfort you, is, that you must mend it with a new one.

Miss laughs.

Col. What, miss! you can't laugh, but you must shew your teeth.

Miss. I'm sure you shew your teeth when you can't bite: well, thus it must be, if we sell ale.

Neverout. Miss, you smell very sweet; I hope you don't carry perfumes?

Miss. Perfumes! No, sir; I'd have you to know, it is nothing but the grain of my skin.

Col. Tom, you have a good nose to make a poor man's sow.

Ld. Sparkish. So, ladies and gentlemen, methinks you are very witty upon one another: come, box it about; 'twill come to my father at last.

Col. Why, my lord, you see miss has no mercy; I wish she were married; but I doubt the gray mare would prove the better horse.

Miss. Well, God forgive you for that wish.

Ld. Sparkish. Never fear him, miss.

Miss. What, my lord, do you think I was born in a wood, to be afraid of an owl?

Ld. Smart. What have you to say to that, colonel?

Neverout. O, my lord, my friend, the colonel, scorns to set his wit against a child.

Miss. Scornful dogs will eat dirty puddings.

Col. Well miss, they say a woman's tongue is the last thing about her that dies; therefore, let's kiss and be friends.

Miss. Hands off! that's meat for your master.

Ld. Sparkish. Faith, colonel, you are for ale and cakes: but, after all, miss, you are too severe; you would not meddle with your match.

Miss. All they can say goes in at one ear and out at t'other for me, I can assure you: only

I wish they would be quiet, and let me drink my tea.

Neverout. What! I warrant you think all is lost that goes beside your own mouth.

Miss. Pray, Mr. Neverout, hold your tongue for once, if it be possible: one would think you were a woman in man's clothes, by your prating.

Neverout. No, miss, it is not handsome to see one hold one's tongue: besides, I should slobber my fingers.

Col. Miss, did you never hear, that three women and a goose are enough to make a market?

Miss. I'm sure, if Mr. Neverout or you were among them, it would make a fair.

Footman comes in.

Lady Smart. Here, take away the tea-table, and bring up candles.

Lady Answ. O, madam, no candles yet, I beseech you; don't let us burn day-light.

Neverout. I dare swear, miss, for her part, will never burn day-light, if she can help it.

Miss. Lord! Mr. Neverout, one cannot hear one's own ears for you.

Lady Smart. Indeed, madam, it is blindman's holiday; we shall soon be all of a colour.

Neverout. Why, then, miss, we may kiss where we like best.

Miss. Fogh! these men talk of nothing but kissing. [*She spits.*

Neverout. What miss, does it make your mouth water?

Lady Smart. It is as good to be in the dark as without light; therefore pray bring in candles: they say women and linen shew best by candlelight: come, gentlemen, are you for a party at quadrille?

Col. I'll make one with you three ladies.

← *Lady Answ.* I'll sit down and be a stander by.

Lady Smart. [*To Lady Answ.*] Madam, does your ladyship never play?

Col. Yes; I suppose her ladyship plays sometimes for an egg at Easter.

Neverout. Ay; and a kiss at Christmas.

Lady Answ. Come, Mr. Neverout, hold your tongue, and mind your knitting.

Neverout. With all my heart; kiss my wife, and welcome.

The Colonel, Mr. NEVEROUT, *Lady* SMART, *and Miss, go to quadrille, and sit there till three in the morning.*

They rise from cards.

Lady Smart. Well, miss, you'll have a sad husband, you have such good luck at cards.

Neverout. Indeed, miss, you dealt me sad cards; if you deal so ill by your friends, what will you do with your enemies?

Lady Answ. I'm sure 'tis time for honest folks to be a-bed.

Miss. Indeed my eyes draw straws.

She's almost asleep.

Neverout. Why, miss, if you fall asleep, somebody may get a pair of gloves.

Col. I'm going to the land of Nod.

Neverout. Faith, I'm for Bedfordshire.

Lady Smart. I'm sure I shall sleep without rocking.

Neverout. Miss, I hope you'll dream of your sweetheart.

Miss. O, no doubt of it. I believe I shan't be able to sleep for dreaming of him.

Col. [*To Miss.*] Madam, shall I have the honour to escort you?

Miss. No, colonel, I thank you; my mamma has sent her chair and footmen. Well, my Lady Smart, I'll give you revenge whenever you please.

Footman comes in.

Footman. Madam, the chairs are waiting.

They all take their chairs and go off.

END OF VOL. IX.

www.ingramcontent.com/pod-product-compliance
Lightning Source LLC
Chambersburg PA
CBHW051859300426
44117CB00006B/453